AF333493

*The Stained Glass Art of
William Jay Bolton*

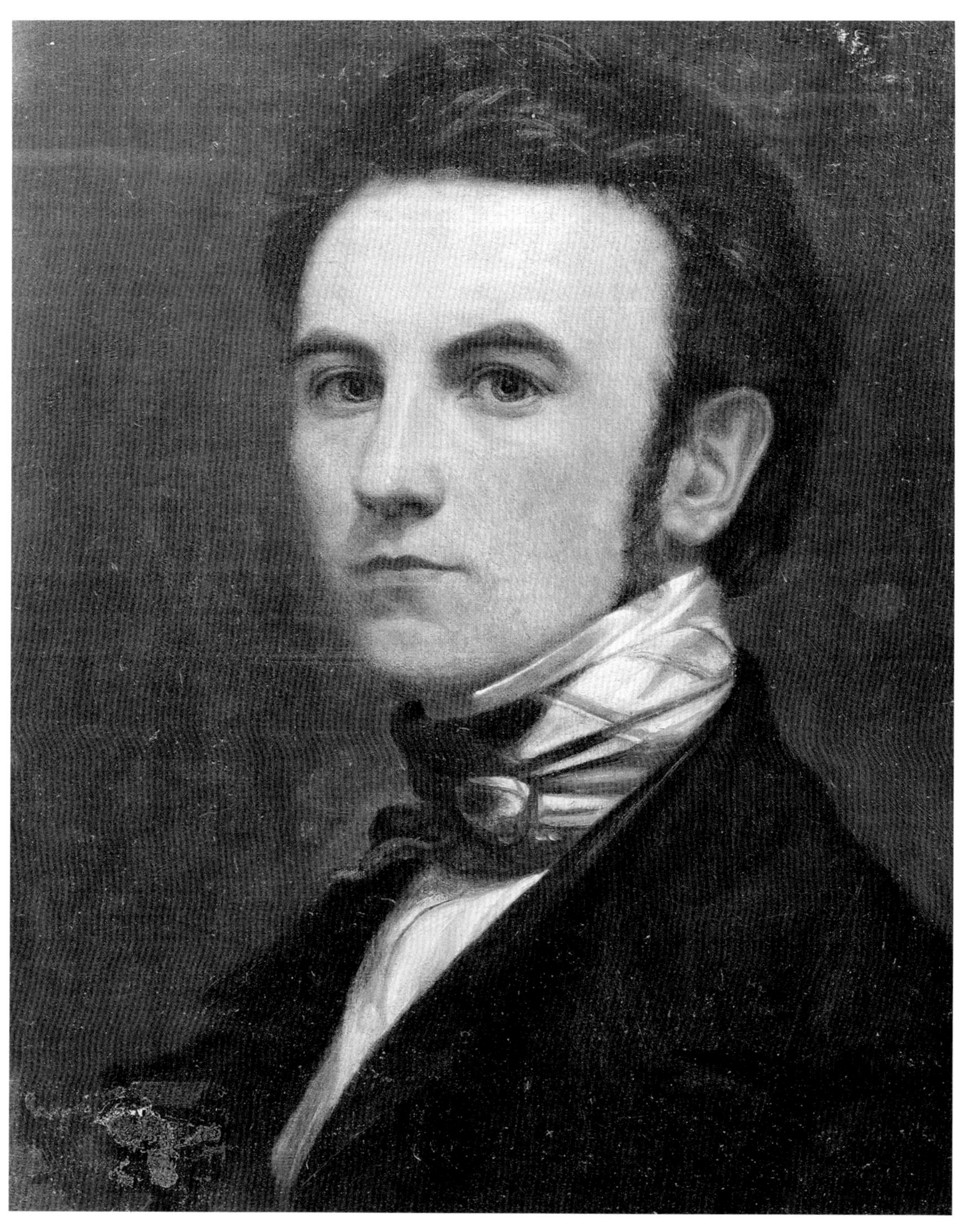

William Jay Bolton, self-portrait, 1845–46
(National Academy of Art, New York, N.Y.; photo: Frick Art Reference Library)

The Stained Glass Art of William Jay Bolton

Willene B. Clark

Photographs by Leland A. Cook

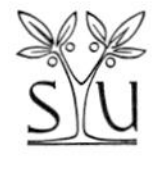

Syracuse University Press

First Edition 1992
92 93 94 95 96 97 98 99   6 5 4 3 2 1

This book is published with the assistance of a
grant from the Samuel H. Kress Foundation.

This book has been supported by a grant from
the National Endowment for the Humanities,
an independent federal agency.

The paper used in this publication meets the
minimum requirements of American National
Standard for Information Sciences—Permanence
of Paper for Printed Library Materials,
ANSI Z39.48-1984. ∞™

Library of Congress
Cataloging-in-Publication Data

Clark, Willene B.
The stained glass art of William Jay Bolton
/ Willene B. Clark ; photographs by
Leland A. Cook.—1st ed.
p.   cm.
Includes bibliographical references
and index.
ISBN 0-8156-2553-7
1. Bolton, William Jay, 1816?–1884
—Criticism and interpretation.
2. Glass painting and staining—
United States—History—19th century.
I. Title. NK5398.B65C53   1992
748.5913—dc20   91–18456
CIP

Manufactured in the United States of America

For Kerstin and Nevy

Biographical Sketches

Willene B. Clark received her doctorate from Yale University, and is professor of art history at Marlboro College. In 1978 she was a founder of the Census of Stained Glass Windows in America and became its first director; she remains on the board of governors. Her research in stained glass has been supported in part by the Ingram Merrill Foundation. In addition to articles on the Boltons, she has also published articles and books on medieval manuscript painting.

Leland A. Cook was for many years the advertising photographer for Tiffany & Company, pursuing at the same time his interest in the Boltons. For his work in stained glass photography he received the Freedoms Foundation George Washington Medal four times. He is the photographic consultant to the Stained Glass Association of America and the Census of Stained Glass Windows in America. He has published photographic studies on several subjects, including St. Patrick's Cathedral in New York City.

Contents

Contents

Preface

Some years ago I noticed a variety of handsome nineteenth-century stained glass windows, whole and in individual panels, for sale in antique shops. On inquiring of their new use, I learned that those that were purely decorative or secular in subject were purchased for installation in homes, shops, and restaurants, but that church windows with sacred subjects often went to craftspeople, both amateur and professional, who dismantled them to use the glass in lampshades and other household objects. That woeful discovery, and the precarious physical condition of many fine windows, initiated my interest in nineteenth-century stained glass and was the catalyst for me and several colleagues to establish the Census of Stained Glass Windows in America. The Census is a large project in which both professional and amateur researchers are cataloging stained glass of the nineteenth and early twentieth centuries in the United States, and developing approaches for its preservation. My own historical researches led quickly to the stained glass of William Jay Bolton and his brother John.

William Jay Bolton is the principal subject of this book because, of the two brothers, he is the more important as an artist and as a pioneer of the nineteenth-century stained glass revival. He was also by far the more prolific, and is noteworthy for his writings on both art and religion. The Boltons' lives and accomplishments are of interest to art historians and those who study Victorian culture and thought, as well as to stained glass artists and students of stained glass history. In order to address this varied audience, I have provided as complete documentation as possible and made every effort to place the Boltons in the cultural, intellectual, and spiritual context of their period and place. Technical features of the Boltons' art are summarized, and for those unfamiliar with the terminology of stained glass, there is a Glossary. Particulars of each project, including the iconography and a history of the building, are given in the Catalog; and the illustrations and the Catalog are cross-referenced.

At the outset of the Bolton project I benefited from the counsel of Jane Hayward in art history, and of Orin E. Skinner in researches on the Boltons. Kenneth W. Miller and his staff at the Archives of the Episcopal Diocese of Long Island kindly provided access to and information from the extensive Bolton materials there. I am extremely grateful to the rectors and staffs of the churches with Bolton glass, and to the present owner of the Bolton

Preface

home in Pelham, New York, all of whom graciously permitted me to study and photograph the windows and documents in their care. Special thanks are due the Reverend Franklin E. Vilas, Jr., and the Reverend William Persell, rectors of St. Ann and Holy Trinity, Brooklyn, and to the church Vestry, which initiated a restoration of the Bolton windows there. Felicia Furman Dryden and Laurie Beckelman of the New York Landmarks Conservancy were helpful on many occasions. Melville Greenland, chief restorer at St. Ann and Holy Trinity, and John Nussbaum and Richard Millard have been founts of technical information. Mary C. Higgins of the Greenland Studio, conservator Constance Silver, and former students Tracy Martin and Linda Dowdell checked details in the St. Ann and Holy Trinity windows for me at various times. Michael Cothren helped to record windows in the first phase of this research, and he and Mary Higgins provided a number of photographs for study. Hilary Wayment told me of the West Lynn windows and took me there to photograph them; he also provided information on the King's Chapel windows and several photographs. Mrs. J. Lewis Bolton gave me access to family documents and anecdotes, and a direct link to the subject of my study. Others who have provided helpful information and documents are Arthur L. Bolton, Guy Bolton, Richard M. Judd, the Reverend William Howard Melish, Linda Papanicolaou, Caroline H. Rubicam, James Sturm, Helene H. Weis, Virginia Wright of the Corning Museum, and still others who are acknowledged in the Notes. Without the help of so many people, this study of the Boltons' art would never have come to fruition. Finally, Regina Blaszczyk, William P. Davisson, and Helen Zakin were kind enough to read parts or all of this book at various stages, and to offer many excellent suggestions for its improvement. Early phases of this study were aided by generous grants from the Ingram Merrill Foundation.

My collaborator Leland Cook, for many years the photographer for Tiffany and Company, has photographed Bolton stained glass since 1957. He not only contributed most of the photographs to this volume, but he also shared his knowledge of several Bolton windows unknown to me and choice tidbits of Bolton lore. It has been a joy to work with him.

If I may be permitted a personal note, it was with considerable pleasure that I learned, several months into my Bolton researches, that the two stained glass artists belonged to the same Philadelphia-Savannah Bolton family from which I myself descend collaterally. Despite the rational attitude I try to maintain as a professional scholar, I sometimes wonder if the imperative to pursue this particular study was entirely my own.

Building Plans

(Drawn by Adrian Segar. For legend, see Catalog.)

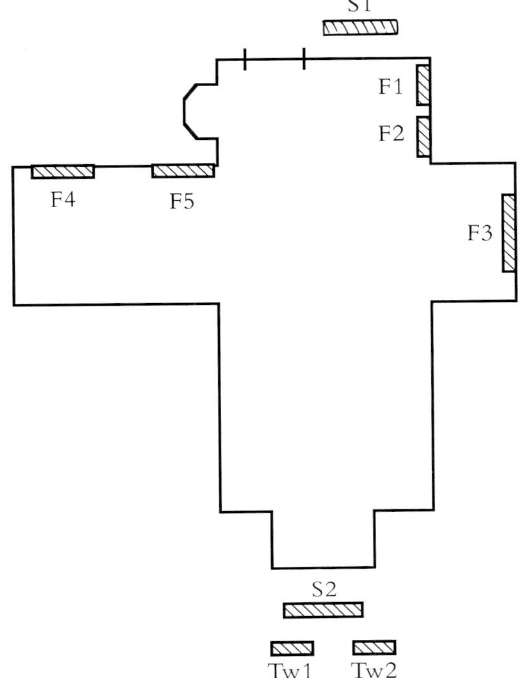

The Priory, Pelham, N.Y.

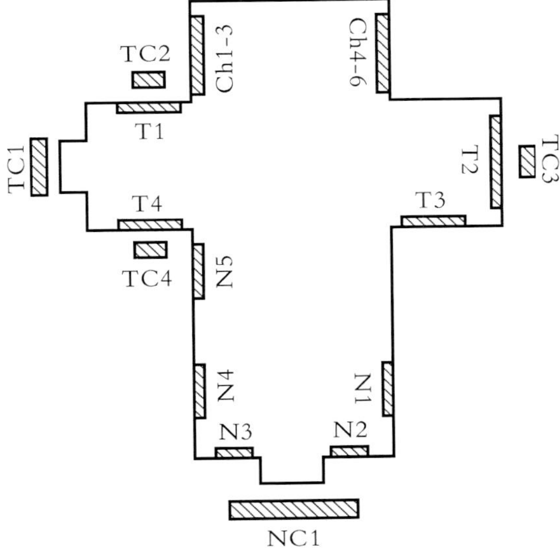

Christ Church, Pelham, N.Y.

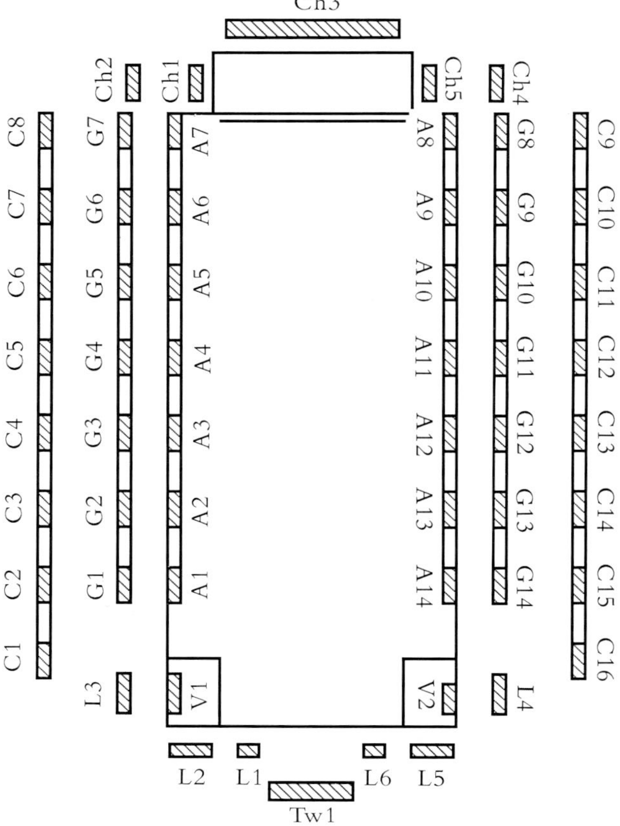

(St. Ann and) Holy Trinity, Brooklyn, N.Y.

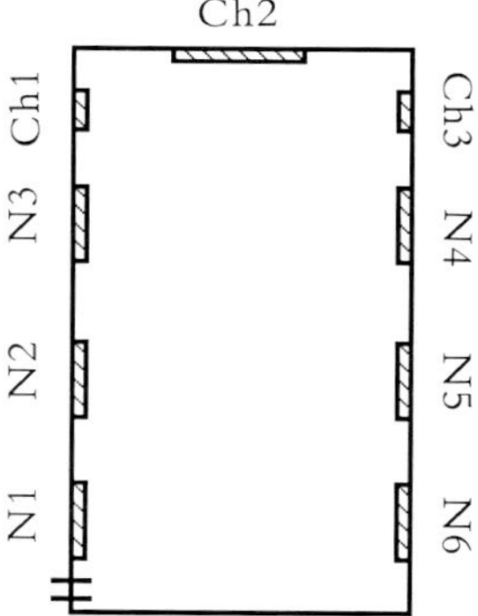

St. Peter's, West Lynn

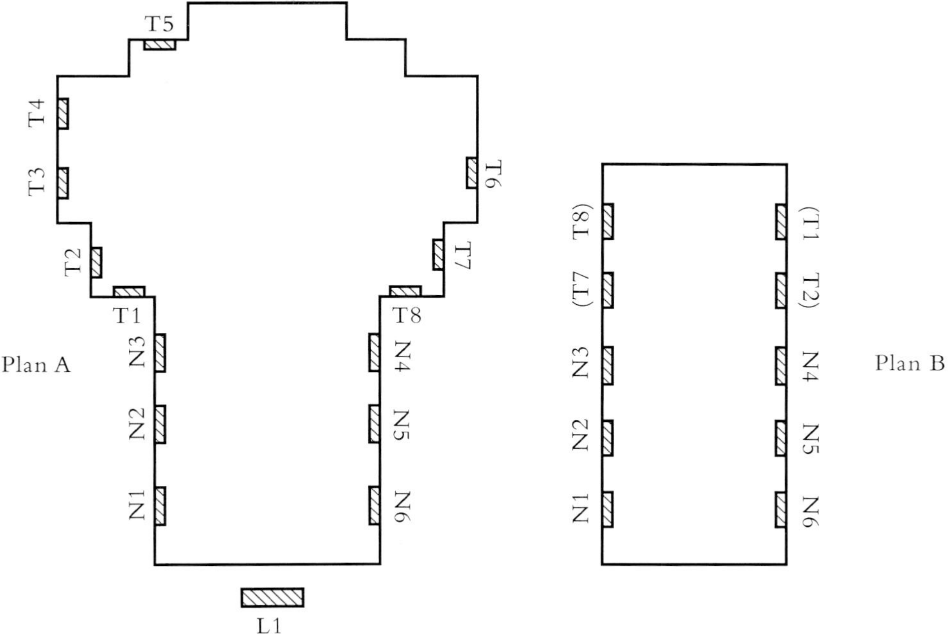

Holy Apostles, New York, N.Y.

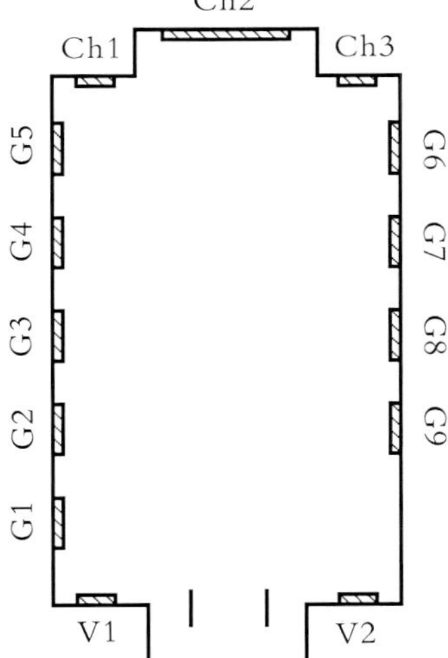

St. Andrew the Great, Cambridge

Colorplates

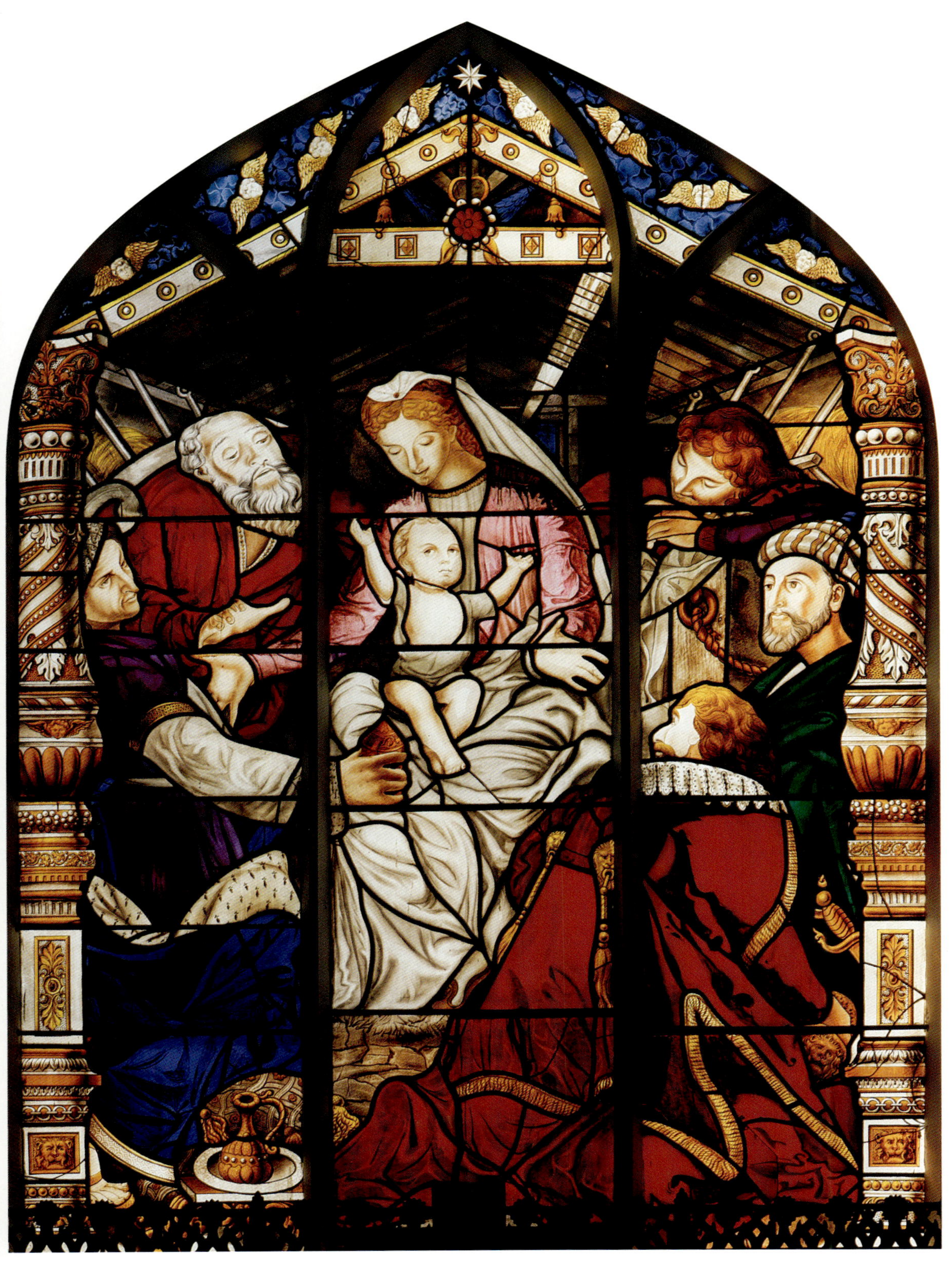

I. Christ Church, Pelham: *Adoration of the Magi*   Cat. II:T2

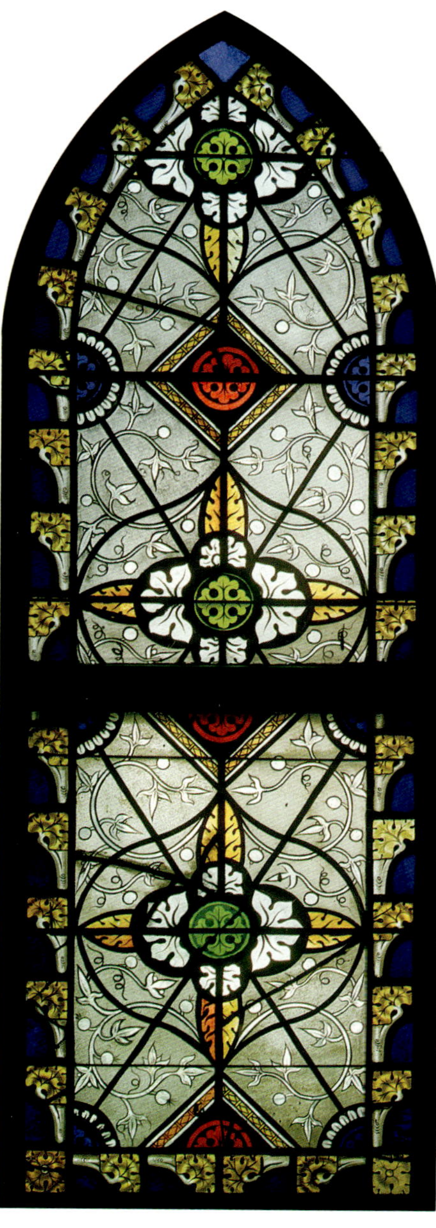

II. Christ Church, Pelham: Grisaille
window by William Jay Bolton
Cat. II:T4

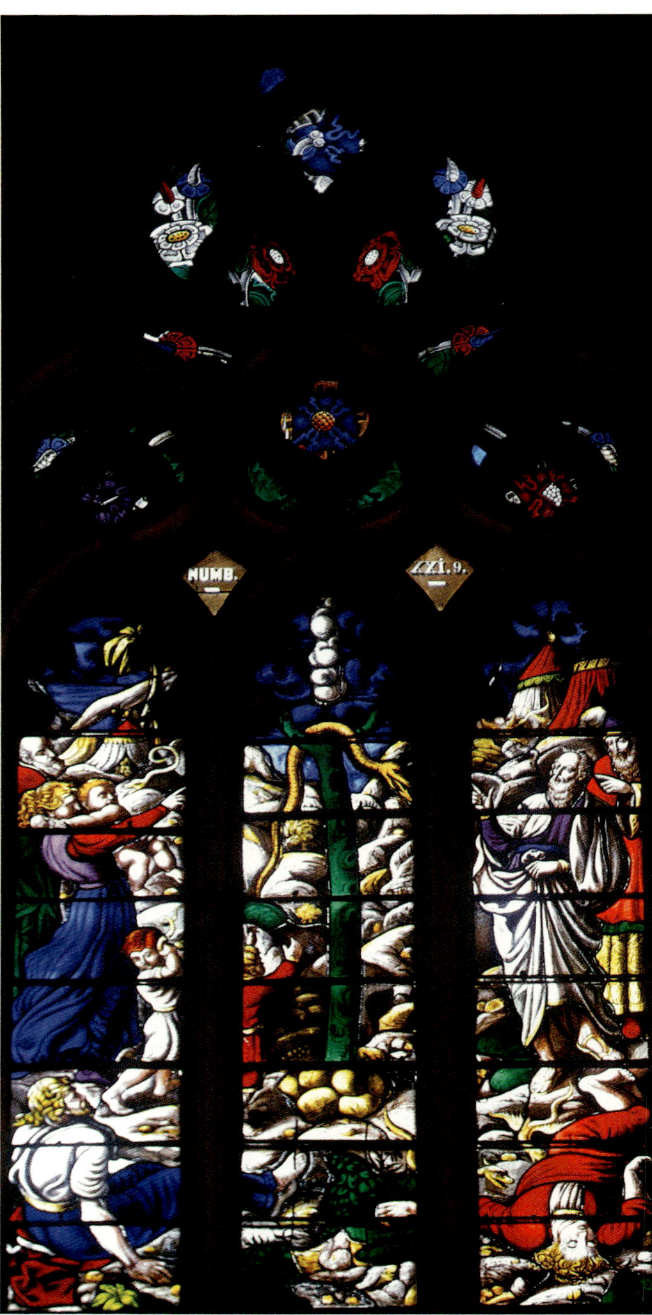

III. (St. Ann and) Holy Trinity, Brooklyn:
The Brazen Serpent   Cat. III:C3

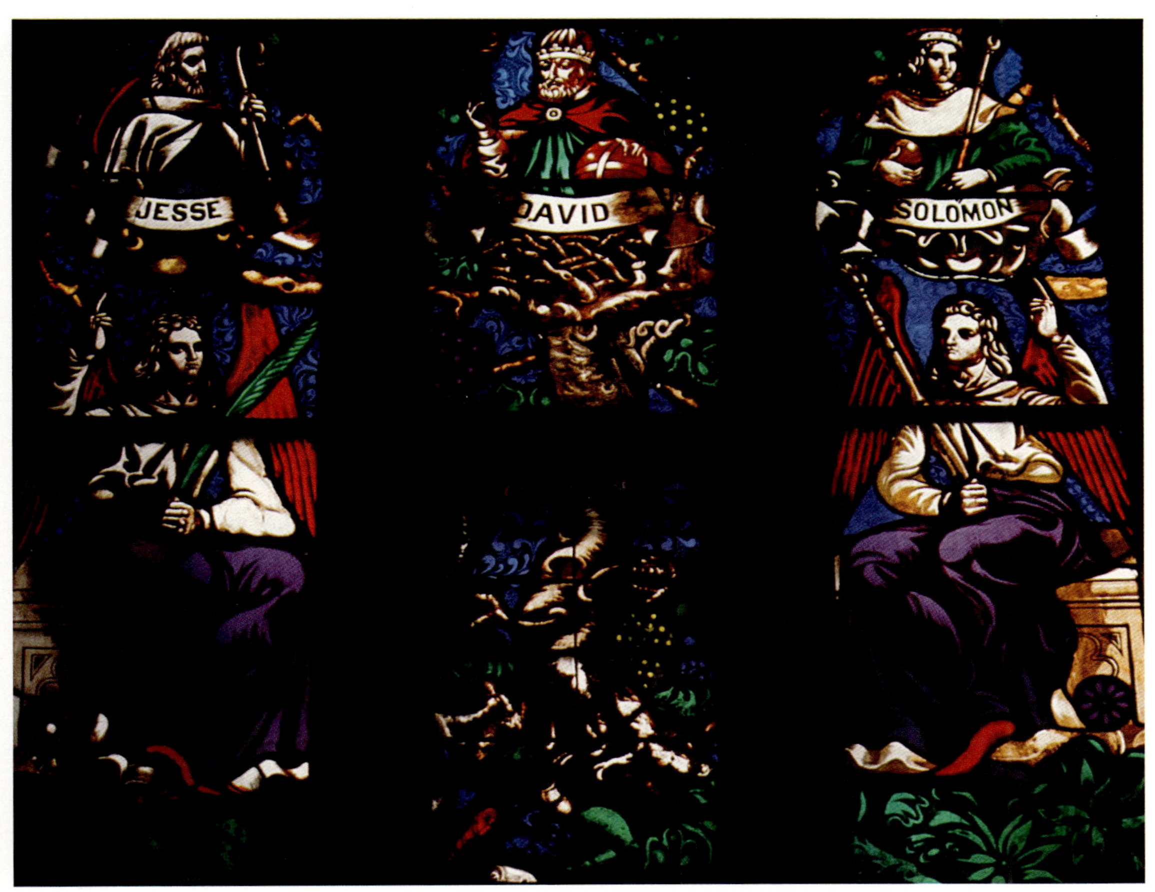

IV. (St. Ann and) Holy Trinity, Brooklyn: Tree of Jesse,
Jesse-David-Solomon (Photo: W. B. Clark)   Cat. III:A5

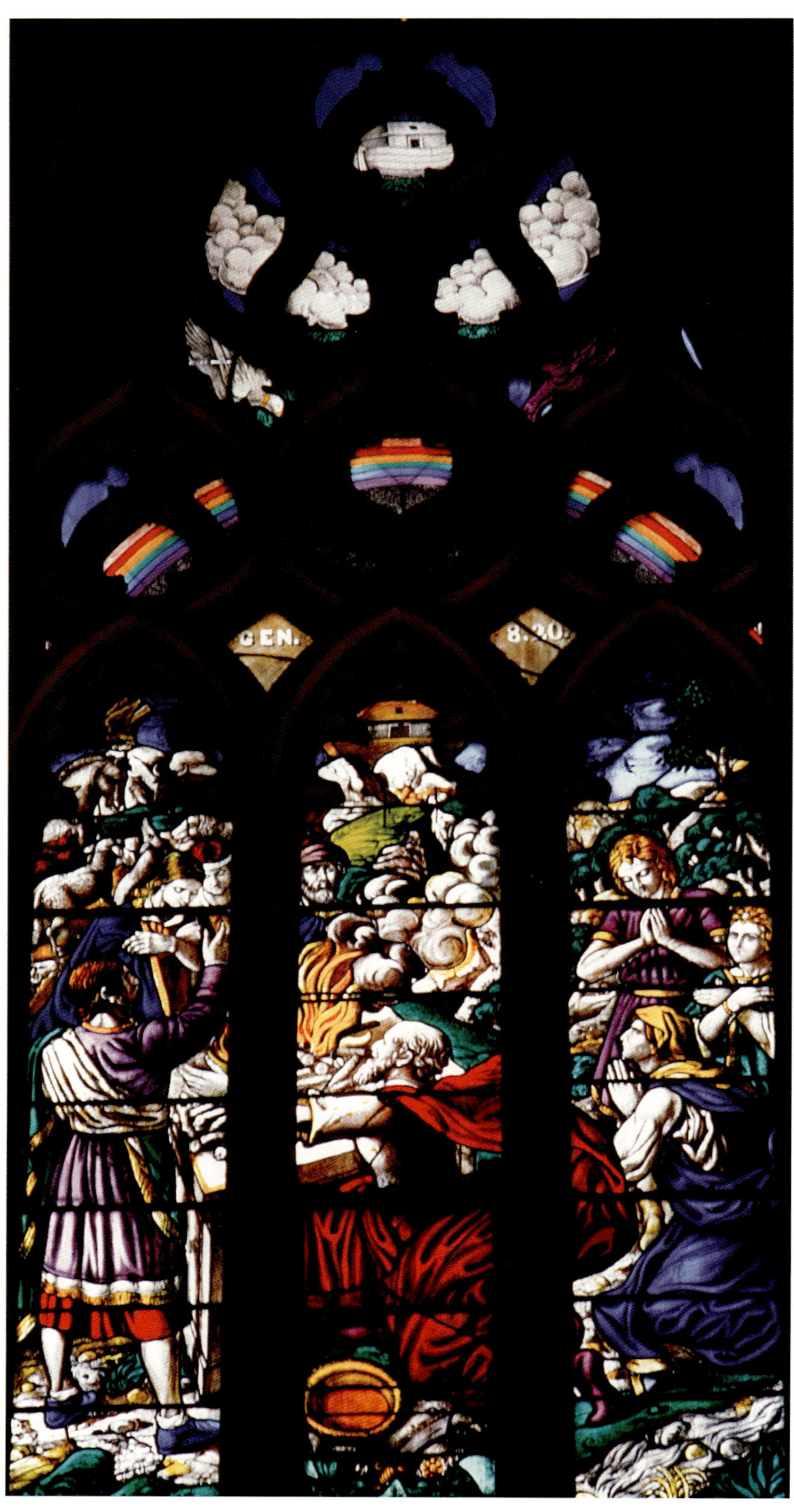

V. (St. Ann and) Holy Trinity, Brooklyn: *Noah's Sacrifice*   Cat. III:C12

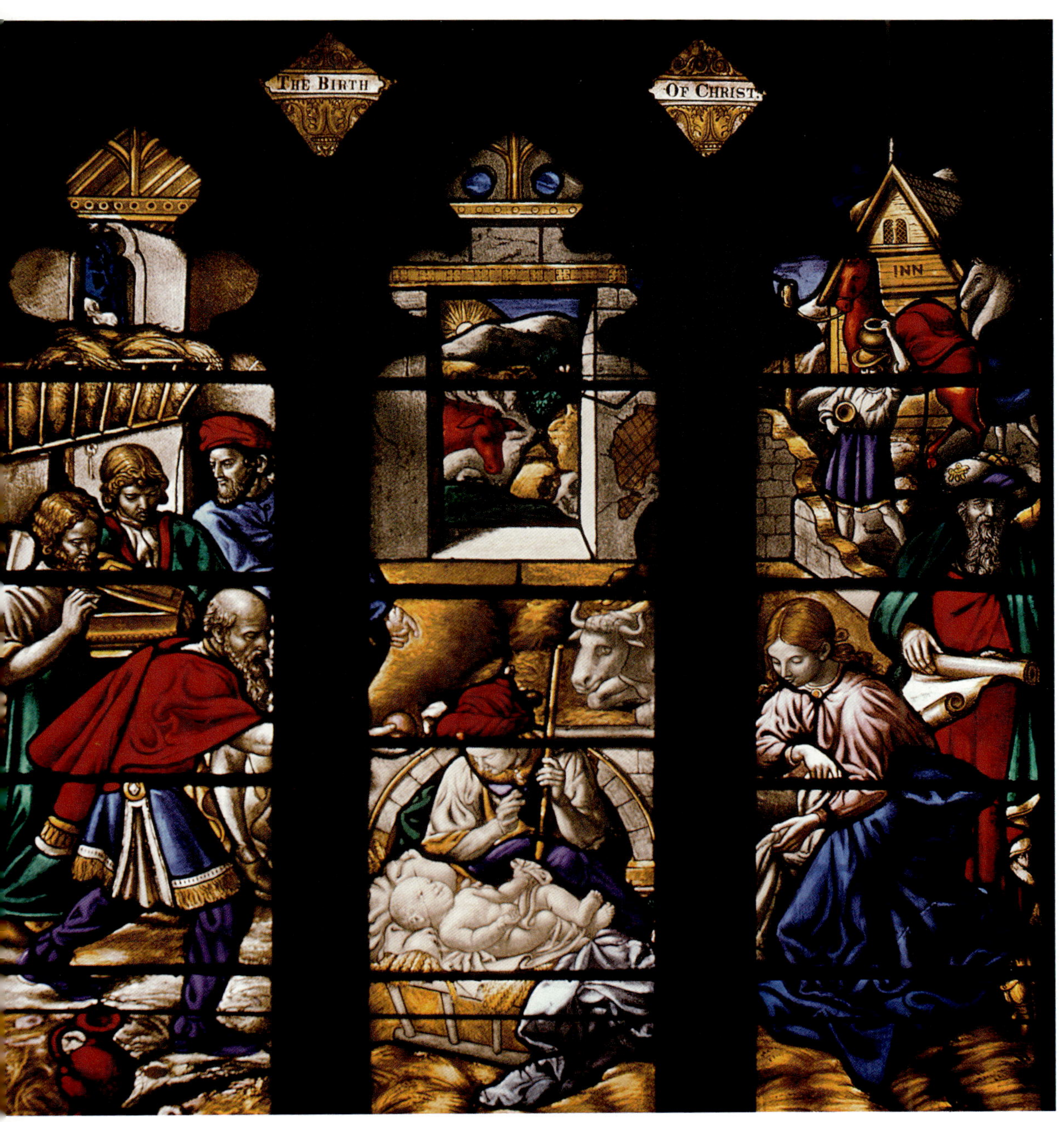

VI. (St. Ann and) Holy Trinity, Brooklyn: *The Birth of Christ*   (Photo: W. B. Clark)   Cat. III:G8

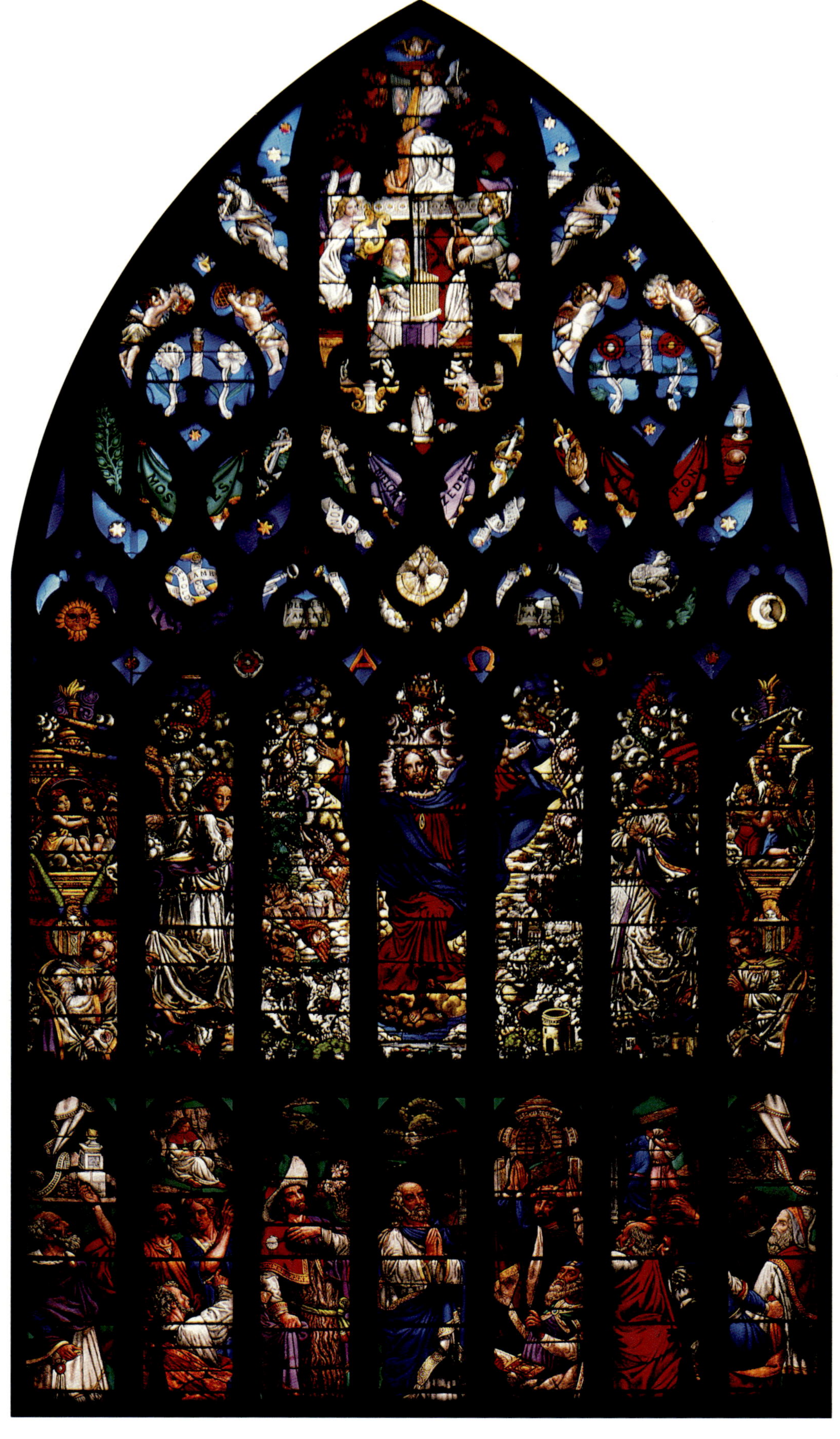

VII. (St. Ann and) Holy Trinity, Brooklyn: *Ascension of Christ*   Cat. III:Ch3

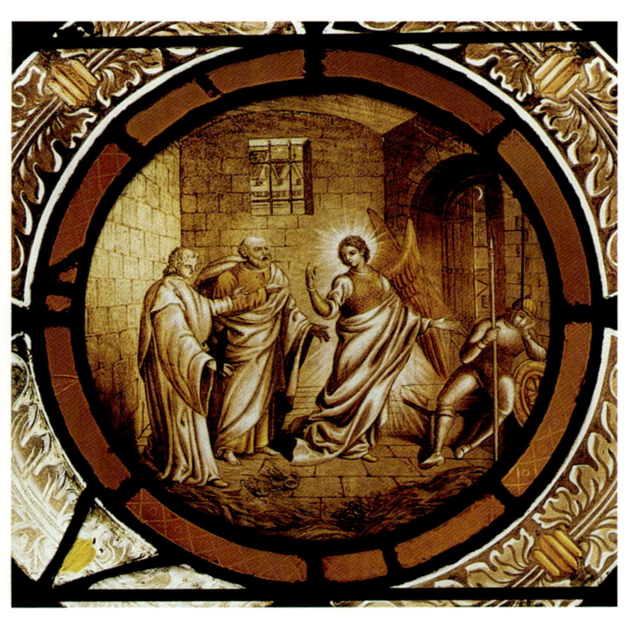

VIII. Holy Apostles, Manhattan:
The Deliverance of St. Peter & St. John   Cat. IV:N5

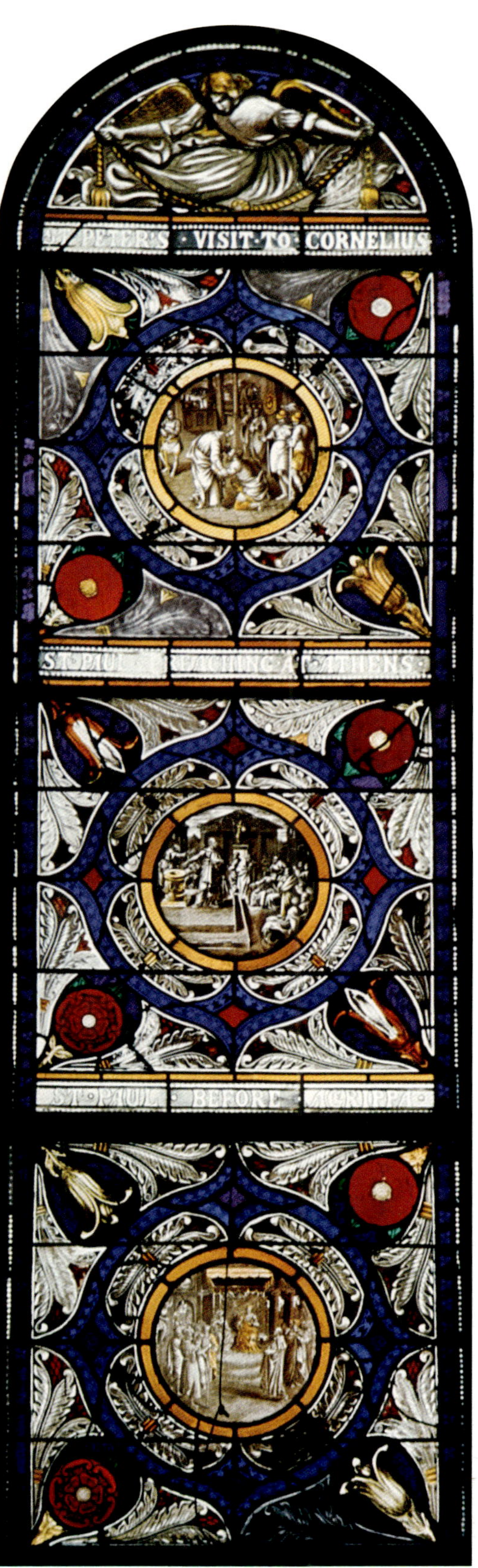

IX. Holy Apostles, Manhattan: *St. Peter's Visit to Cornelius, St. Paul Preaching at Athens, St. Paul before Agrippa* (Photo: W. B. Clark)   Cat. IV:N6

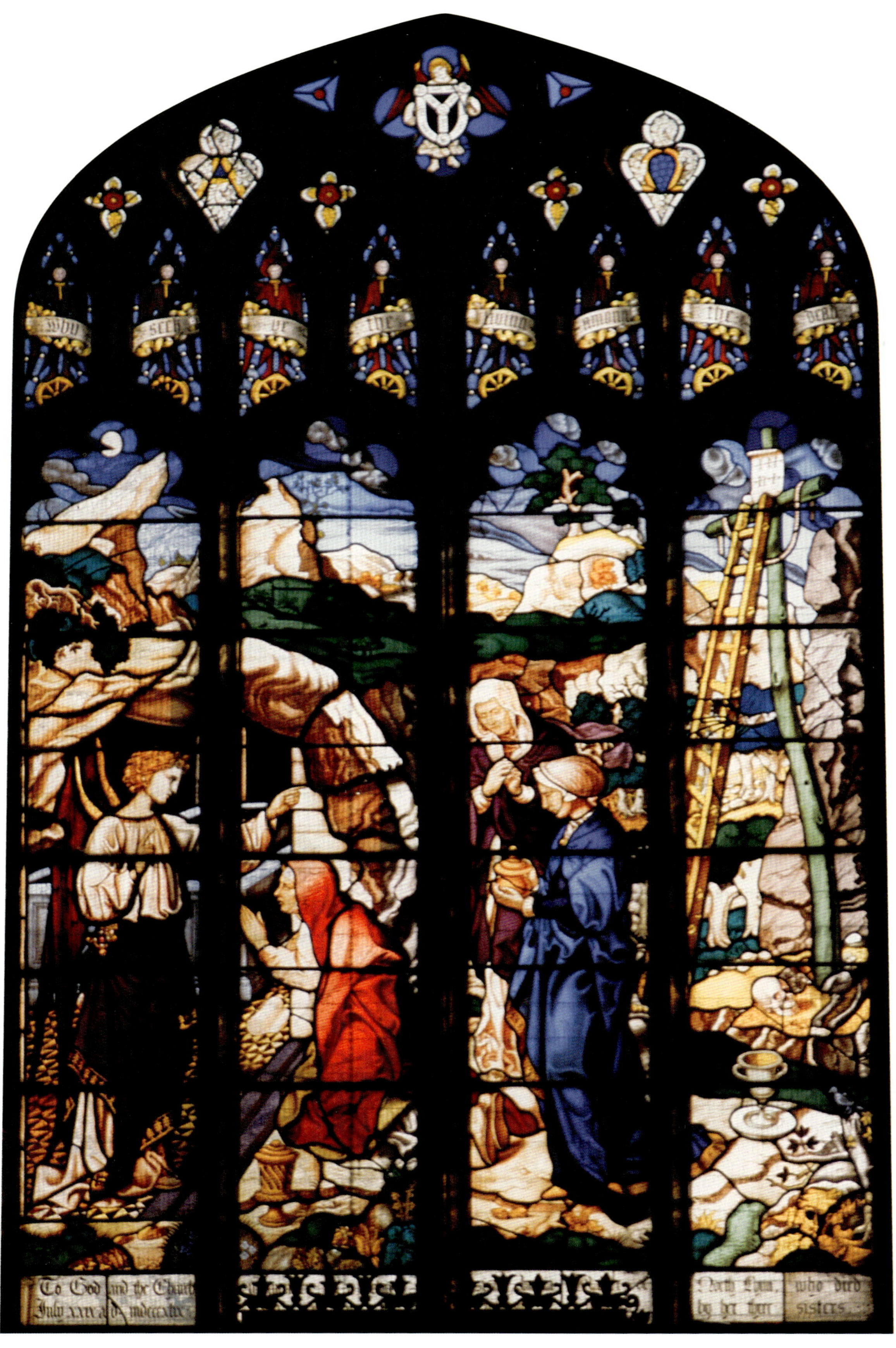

X. St. Peter's Church, West Lynn (Norfolk): *The Angel at the Tomb* (Photo: W. B. Clark)   Cat. V:Ch2

*The Stained Glass Art of
William Jay Bolton*

1

The Life of
William Jay Bolton

One of the last Victorian arts to be rediscovered in the twentieth century is stained glass. Long considered merely decoration for the architecture, which has received much public and scholarly attention, Victorian stained glass is now being recognized as a beautiful art form that can command considerable interest on its own. Its distinct character is marked by the context in which it was produced: the revival of medieval styles in architecture and the decorative arts. Some of the most important arbiters of taste in Victorian England, including John Ruskin, Augustus Welby Northmore Pugin, the Ecclesiologists, and their followers in the United States, favored Gothic as the building style proper to a renewal of both religion and the national moral fiber. Gothic was perceived as the style of a period of piety and devotion to high-minded ideals. For a while, except among the purists like Pugin, glazing the new churches with white-glass quarries was thought sufficient, but by the 1850s most revivalist architects were eager to fill their pointed windows with glass that looked medieval. In the early stages of the Gothic Revival, only the poorest reflections of the great age of stained glass were produced. In European stained glass shops medieval designs had long since been supplanted by the scenic illusionism and full-bodied figures of the Renaissance and beyond, and the methods of glazing in the medieval manner were all but lost.[1] Glaziers of the Gothic Revival therefore began to study extant medieval windows, and gradually discovered how to design and work according to medieval principles. The art flourished, and large quantities of stained glass windows were made in the second half of the century, some of them of superb quality. The Gothic Revival in stained glass survived into the first decade or so of the twentieth century, when it was rejected, along with other fantasies of Romanticism, by modernist taste that saw nineteenth-century glass merely as a weak and sentimental imitation of its model. While Gothic Revival architecture, with its prefiguration of modern theories of functionalism, attracted scholarly attention as early as 1928,[2] it is only since the late 1970s that nineteenth-century stained glass has been studied seriously. Today it is recognized as an art with its own interesting character, and an important representative of a period of taste in both the United States and Europe.

1

Stained Glass Art
of William Jay Bolton

The medieval revival in stained glass began in England, in the third decade of the century, principally in the work of Thomas Willement (1786–1871). It received considerable impetus through the efforts of the ardent Gothicist architect Pugin (1812–1852) and of Charles Winston (1814–1864), a lawyer who experimented in the production of medieval-type colored glass and who wrote the first modern treatise on medieval stained glass.[3] For Pugin, the proper window design was composed of figures that resemble those of the early fourteenth century in their decorative, non-realistic proportions and their patterned drapery. Winston, on the other hand, preferred the stained glass of sixteenth-century northern Europe, a style in some respects still medieval but imbued with Renaissance naturalism; he called it the "Cinque Cento" style.[4] The revivalists tended to gravitate to one or the other of these two points of view. One of the best early exponents of "Cinque Cento" eclecticism was William Jay Bolton, whose name must now be added to the list of pioneers in the revival.

By 1843, only fourteen years or so after Willement's first hesitant essays in Gothic Revival stained glass, Bolton completed a large and remarkably assured figural window in the medieval technique for his family's church in Pelham, New York (colorplate I). This is the first figural window of the revival known to have been made in the United States, and by a glazier who appears to have learned the methods on his own. Shortly thereafter, he designed and made at least forty-nine equally large windows for a church in Brooklyn, New York, the first extensive American-made figural program, and perhaps the largest ensemble of figural windows anywhere in his day by a single artist (e.g. colorplate VI). A smaller program in Manhattan (colorplate IX), and several even smaller in England, round out a career in glass that lasted only six or seven years, but that was brilliant and prolific. Despite Bolton's lack of previous experience in stained glass work before he embarked on the first projects, the quality of both the designs and the artistic manipulation of colored glass is extremely high. His genius for the medium is undeniable, and the art of stained glass suffered a severe loss when, in 1848, Bolton returned to his native England, made only a few windows there, and then entered the Anglican ministry. While John Bolton (fig. 2e), who had assisted his older brother in United States, continued work in stained glass, he exhibited neither the artistic talent nor the imagination of William Jay. In fact, there are no comparable American glaziers until Louis Comfort Tiffany and John La Farge near the end of the century. After 1848, Bolton's name, his achievements, and indeed the art of stained glass in the United States languished until the 1870s; nor was he remembered in England. Bolton's windows were known only to a few admiring glaziers, and would not receive full recognition until the 1970s, when scholarship and public interest, which had turned first to the works of Tiffany and La Farge, discovered the early phase of the Gothic Revival in stained glass.[5] A major restoration effort was begun on the Brooklyn windows in 1977, the first scholarly study of William Jay Bolton appeared in 1979, and one of his Brooklyn windows was installed in the American Wing of the Metropolitan Museum of Art in November 1985, proclaiming at last his important place in American art.[6]

William Jay Bolton—he was known in the family as Jay[7]—was born in Bath, England, in 1816, the son of an American father and an English mother. Little was done to preserve the documents of Bolton's life until well into this century, by which time many had been lost.[8] Those that remain show him to have been a genial man of great charm and wit, a devoted family man, and a devout Christian. Bolton's life, unlike that of many artists, provided him considerable satisfaction, although it was not always an easy one. His childhood and youth were happy times in a family that was loving and supportive. The Boltons were Evangelical, Low Church Anglicans, members of that branch of the English church that sought renewal not in the theological discourses and ceremonials of the Tractarians, but in a simpler practice that stressed humility and faith as the main requisites for salvation.[9] Daily devotions, exercised willingly and lovingly by all family members, were a part of Bolton life. The Reverend William Jay (1769–1853), Jay Bolton's grandfather, wrote that he was "blessed with children, who will not neglect a practice, to which, in the order of a happy family, they were so early accustomed, and which was never rendered irksome by tediousness; and they will—he knows they will—train up their children in the same holy and lovely usage."[10] And this, of course, they did. One measure of the family's commitment to religion is that Jay and his four brothers all became Anglican or Protestant Episcopal clergymen, following in the footsteps of their father; and the daughters, like their mother, gave tirelessly for the betterment of others.

The Boltons also had many and worthy secular interests, especially in literature, resulting eventually in a number of publications by each Bolton son; Robert, Jr. is still recognized as the principal historian of colonial and early nineteenth-century Westchester County, New York.[11] Family concern with handicrafts and the fine arts is represented by a variety of adornments for their homes, and of course by William Jay Bolton's painting and work in stained glass. The family home seems to have been the scene of ceaseless activity, including home-decorating and gardening projects, planning and fund-raising for church missions and Sunday schools, and even a family-run school. Piety was combined with openly expressed love, and intellectual pursuits with creative energy, producing an environment in which children could grow contentedly and talent of all kinds could flourish.

The family had both English and American forebears, and its piety was rooted in generations of clergy. The first ancestor of whom anything certain is known is Robert Bolton (1572–1632), a Puritan divine best known for his theological treatise, *The Last Four Things; Death, Judgement, Hell, Heaven.*[12] The earliest American ancestor was Robert Bolton of Brookhouse, Lancashire, a great-nephew of the Puritan Robert, who settled in Philadelphia in 1718 or 1720. Until recent years, all first sons of this line were named Robert, which provides a challenge to anyone trying to define the various generations.[13] The second American Robert moved to Savannah, Georgia, about 1741; in 1764 he became the first postmaster of the region. Two succeeding generations of Boltons prospered there, their wealth deriving from land-holdings, dry-goods trade, and later the export of cotton. They married into prominent southern families, and distinguished themselves on the American side in the Revolution. Accounts of family members show them to have been both pious and practical. Jay's grandfather Robert (1757–1802) bequeathed his portrait to "whichever of my sons may be inclined to much company and drinking," stating that he must "give [the portrait] the most conspicuous place in his dining room, that, when he views it, he may recollect that it represents a father who never was intoxicated, and whose detestation of that vice should restrain his sons from the practice of it." The recipient is not recorded, but moderation remained a hallmark of Bolton life.[14] In a deathbed letter to his children the same Robert outlined a moral code to guide them, the spirit of which was passed on to Jay's generation:

> Avoid bad company . . . the drunkard, the lascivious person, and those intoxicated with earthly pleasures. . . . Be you contented with enjoying a little good company, such as is calculated to improve you in your religious and moral life.
>
> Study the Holy Scriptures . . . they will furnish you with a fund of wholesome knowledge; other good books you can read to improve your understanding. . . .
>
> Never suffer the poor and distressed to depart from your doors with a frown. . . . Be kind to your servants, know that they are not your slaves by right, but by custom. God made all free; but man in his depraved state enslaves man.[15]

The next Robert, father of Jay Bolton, was born in Savannah in 1788. The family cotton business continued to prosper, and in 1807 Robert sailed

The Life of
William Jay Bolton

to England on a company ship to take a position in the Liverpool office. As a result of his sister's accounts of the Reverend William Jay, and at the urging of a business friend, he went to hear that well-known preacher at the Argyle Chapel, Bath.[16] The Reverend Jay taught "the new birth, justification by faith and 'the obediance of faith.' "[17] The chapel was frequented by people famous in many walks of life, but especially in Evangelical circles. No one can know whether it was the power of the Reverend Jay's sermons that touched Robert's spirit, or the beauty of Jay's daughter Ann (1793–1859) that touched the young man's heart, but soon after Robert determined to study for the ministry. He enrolled at Hoxton, a "dissenting academy," to prepare for his new vocation, and also studied for a time in Edinburgh. Evangelicalism itself was nothing new to Robert, as several generations of Boltons had espoused Nonconformist doctrines, beginning with the first Savannah Robert, a friend and follower of the Wesleyite missionary George Whitefield.[18] After promising Ann's father that he would settle in England, Robert received permission to marry her. The ceremony took place in Walcot Chapel, Bath, in May 1810, and the couple went to live in Liverpool, where Robert was to continue for a time in the cotton business.[19] He remained in close contact with Dissenting clergy and missionaries, however, and served as a lay preacher.

The War of 1812 initiated the decline of the Bolton cotton export business, and by 1820, when strikes at the English cotton mills added to the woes of the American growers and exporters by reducing the need for raw cotton, the Bolton company was in ruins. Meanwhile five babies, including Jay, had been born to Ann and Robert, and in 1821 his ever-decreasing financial assets forced Robert to take his growing family to the United States in the hope of recovering part of his interests in the firm and other Savannah holdings, leaving Ann and the children with relatives on Long Island while he went south. His efforts were in vain, and the Boltons returned to England in 1823.[20] At that point Robert took the step that he had long desired, according to his son Jay, and entered the ministry on a full-time basis. He was ordained at Henley-on-Thames in 1824 and served a parish there for twelve years, preaching occasionally at other places, including the Tabernacle Chapel and Tottenham Court Road Chapel in London. The Reverend Jay visited often at Henley, and among family friends were two other important Evangelicals, Hannah More and William Wilberforce.[21]

In the family tradition, Robert Bolton was a cultured man who accumulated a large library of works in literature as well as theology;[22] he was also fond of art, architecture, and gardening. The Boltons' circle of acquaintances included both writers and artists. Among the writers they met while

still living at Liverpool was Washington Irving, perhaps on an introduction
from a Bolton relative who lived not far from Irving in Westchester County,
New York. The warm friendship that developed between the Bolton and
Irving families is recorded in several letters and suggests that Irving may
have been a factor in the Boltons' later move to Pelham, in Westchester
County. The Boltons' circle in Liverpool also included the successful academic painter William Etty (1787–1849), a friend of the Reverend Jay, who
was a guest in the Bolton home at various times and made portraits and
portrait sketches of Robert, Ann, and their children (figs. 2a,b).[23] The
Reverend Jay, who was also fond of art, remarked sententiously that Etty
"with all his great talent, [is] no judge of beauty in the female countenance."[24] Nevertheless, the portraits Etty painted of Jay's daughters, including Ann Jay Bolton, are beautiful indeed.[25] Elsewhere the Reverend Jay
showed a more favorable attitude toward the artist when he wrote of Etty,
"Thy mind all taste, and ardor all thy heart."[26]

In 1814, Ann Jay Bolton had given birth to the first of her children, of
course named Robert, who would become the family historian. Thereafter
followed thirteen more, almost yearly (see Appendix C). The future glaziers, William Jay (1816–1884) and John Jay (1818–1898), were the third and
fourth born. William Jay, named for his maternal grandfather, was born on
31 August 1816 at the Jay home, 43 Pulteney Street in Bath.[27] The tenderness
and piety of the family into which he was born are reflected in the diary
entry for 11 May 1817 by his young mother, thinking of her husband and her
new baby: "another year has the Lord spared us to one another, and given us
another pledge of our love. May the dear child be spared." Although the
diary is now lost, passages recorded by Jay are filled with her love of her
family and her fellow creatures, and with repeated testimony to her abiding
faith (fig. 2a).[28]

It must have been difficult for such a devoted mother as Ann in 1823 to
send nine-year-old Robert, seven-year-old Jay, and the even younger Winter
off to boarding school at Mill Hill, near London, a well-known Nonconformist institution.[29] This was the beginning of Jay's life in art, however,
for it was apparently at Mill Hill that he learned to draw. At this time also he
began his frequent visits to his grandfather at Bath and his aunt Arabella Jay
Ashton at Cambridge. He was an eager traveling companion on the Reverend Jay's preaching tours of Devonshire and the south coast, and made
"charming & careful pencil drawings of Exeter, Sidmouth, Torquay, Paign-
ton, Teignmouth and many other places"; in fact, "wherever he went he
drew."[30] Such trips probably included pointers from the older man about
the works of art they saw, and about the medieval buildings encountered

---

along the way, for the Reverend Jay had firsthand experience with building in the Gothic style. At age fourteen he had worked as an apprentice alongside his stonemason father in the building of Fonthill Abbey, one of the monuments of the early Gothic Revival.[31] Jay must have loved his grandfather's company, for the old man was a charismatic preacher, and must have been a wonderful conversationalist. The owner of Fonthill Abbey, William Beckford, a wealthy importer and art collector, later compared the Reverend Jay's mind to "a clear transparent spring, flowing so freely as to impress us with the idea of its being inexhaustible."[32] When Jay Bolton was in Cambridge with Aunt Arabella, he had many opportunities to admire and learn from the great stained glass windows of King's College Chapel, which were to exercise such an important influence on his own work in that medium.

At the age of about sixteen, Jay left Mill Hill to join the engineering firm of Stoddart and Pitt at Bath.[33] His earliest known work of art is the large bird's-eye view he drew of that city in 1834, a work now in the Victoria Art Gallery and Municipal Libraries in Bath (fig. 60). According to his daughter Grace, he would rise at four in the morning, before the view could be obscured by smoking chimneys, and climb to Beechen Cliff overlooking the city to make parts of the drawing of the panorama.[34] During this period he painted portraits of family members, including his grandparents, parents, brothers, and sisters, as well as of friends. Grace says that he told her of how he painted "Miss Stoddart, the daughter of the head of the engineering firm, & how he kept her so long at the sitting that she fainted away, to his great consternation and embarrassment."[35] The only one of these family portraits known today is a later one, probably painted in the United States, of his sister Abby, and it survives only in an engraving (fig. 62).

The year 1837 brought a major change in the life of William Jay Bolton. In the previous year, funds to provide for the large Bolton family had reached a new and dangerous low, and Robert Bolton decided to move back to the United States in the hope of regaining some of his inheritance. In April 1836 he resigned the pulpit at Henley, and the family sailed on the *Toronto* bound for New York, leaving Jay and John to follow the next year.[36] Thinking to settle in the West, the Boltons took a journey along the Erie Canal to Skaneateles, but decided to return to the East Coast.[37] They visited relatives in Newport, Rhode Island, where there was a group of summer residents from Savannah, and then bought Pondfield Farm, on the Bronx River in Westchester County, renaming it Brook Farm. The Reverend Robert, somewhat to his discomfort, had to be re-ordained, this time in the Protestant Episcopal Church, in which he had been baptized as a baby.

Stained Glass Art
of William Jay Bolton

On 25 July 1837 he took the pulpit at St. Paul's, Eastchester, not far from the farm, having heard of the opening from a Savannah woman who lived in Eastchester.[38] This was a happy time for the family, with old friends close by, and plenty of healthy activity for the children, who loved the farm life, helped with the haying, and roamed the outlying forests. In his biography of his parents, Jay describes the beauties of Brook Farm, with its orchards, firs, myrtles, azaleas, oaks, spruce, and other trees, marshes with salvia, and rocks dotted with columbine.[39] There was abundant wildlife, and the family kept a small pack of foxhounds. The youngest son, James, later published a colorful account of this period in the family's history.[40] He describes a "Gothic villa" of wood built near the farm by a southern relative, Mrs. Evans of Savannah,[41] in which the hallway walls were "tastefully decorated with paintings by my brothers," the first mention of what would become extensive family projects in furnishing and ornamenting a home.[42]

There were several memorable events in the lives of the Boltons during the Brook Farm period. James relates that the Evans house burned a year after it was built. During the excitement rescuers threw from the windows such Victorian treasures as shell collections, Crusader swords, Norman helmets, dried butterflies and ostrich eggs, and an assemblage of autographs and letters of the famous that Robert Bolton kept at his cousin's home.[43] On another occasion, the Fourth of July 1837, the family paid a visit to Sunnyside, home of Washington Irving. There the jovial host showed off his treasures, and went for a carriage drive with his guests. Far less pleasant was the time the boys witnessed the death by stroke of a woman gathering grapes in the woods. They had the maturity and good sense not to run away in fear, but to carry the woman's corpse back to her house.[44] Because the date of Jay's arrival in the United States is unknown, it is not certain in which, if any, of these activities he participated; in James's accounts of them, he refers only to "the boys."

Summertime at Brook Farm was a period of family enterprises, fun, and learning; the winter spent there was another matter. The weather was extremely cold, forcing the Boltons to endure a number of hardships. Robert therefore decided to move to a more protected environment, and chose land in Pelham not too distant from his friends the Irvings. Thus, in 1838, with money from sales of Savannah property finally recovered, he bought thirty-three acres on the Pelham–New Rochelle town line from Elbert Roosevelt, and had a stone cottage built thereon to house the family while a larger residence was under construction.[45] As Jay Bolton remembers, the large house "was to be as English as possible - something of 'the

The Life of
William Jay Bolton

olden time.' "[46] Such language marks the Bolton architectural taste as an early expression of the Gothic Revival movement known as Old English, which was just getting under way in England.[47] The name chosen for the family home was the Priory, recalling the famous Bolton Priory, a medieval Augustinian monastery in Yorkshire. The large, three-story design of the Pelham Priory combines simple masses, asymmetry, unadorned exterior walls, gables, and clustered chimney pots of the English manor style with the towers, hood moldings, and crenellations of castle architecture (fig. 1a). Begun in 1838, the Priory is an early example of the castle style in the United States.[48] The house is built of local stone, except for the southern tower, which is of brick and may have been an afterthought. One twentieth-century writer supposed that the style was suggested by Washington Irving,[49] but very likely it was a Bolton product. John, the third son, is known to have designed several buildings at a later time, and may have been the architect for the family's new home (see Appendix B). The date 1838 is inscribed in yellow bricks over the main entrance, bricks reportedly given by Washington Irving from an old church tower in Sleepy Hollow. It is also said that Irving planted ivy at the Priory that he had brought from Kenilworth Castle in Warwickshire, one of the romantic late Gothic ruins popularized by Sir Walter Scott.[50] Set on a hill overlooking Long Island Sound, the Priory is still an imposing structure, although it is now hidden by trees and shrubbery, and the land just beyond has been developed for other residences.

The medieval exterior of the Priory is complemented on the interior by ogee-arched doorways, carved chimneypieces, and oak paneling. The ensemble, according to Robert Bolton, Jr., "accords well with its romantic situation."[51] Two important American architects of the day showed interest in the Priory. In the Day Book of Alexander Jackson Davis (1803–1892) is the following entry for 1 October 1841: "Rode to New Rochelle with Philip P. and Ogden Irving, dined at the Neptune House and visited Mr. Bolton. Sketched his places." And for 10 April 1844, "Drawing Bolton's Pelham Priory on Wood for [A. J.] Downing $10.00."[52]

As they had done for Mrs. Evans's house on Long Island, the Boltons put their many talents to work in furnishing and decorating the Priory. The construction was about half done when the contractor quit, at which point Robert took on that task himself. It was also then that several of the children, Jay probably among them, began sleeping in the house, guarded at night by a large dog tied to the door handle.[53] Bolton children report that each one was encouraged to produce useful things, during this enterprise and thereafter. The "whole family were now giving themselves in all manner of amateur arts & crafts for beautifying the new home."[54] The sons made furniture and carved mantles in a northern Renaissance manner, the style that became a major characteristic of Jay's stained glass. They also made stained glass armorials to decorate rooms on the first and second floors (figs. 1c,d). The material of the Priory furniture is often oak, and the heavy decorative carvings of flowers and animals accord well with the late medieval design of the house (fig. 1b). The model for several chairs was a carved oak chair that Robert Bolton, Sr. had bought from a washerwoman in England, brought to the United States, and given to St. Paul's Church, Eastchester.[55] Robert, Sr., who was an avid gardener, laid out the grounds "in the French and landscape styles," that is, formal and informal, with paths through the surrounding woods, a rustic bridge, a hermit's cave, arbors, and seats from which one might admire a particular view.[56] Sometime before 1848, a large greenhouse (later removed) was added on the southwest (fig. 1a).[57] Designs for the grounds of the Priory reflect a mainly European and, by the late 1830s, well-established taste for the picturesque, but the home and its furnishings display the historicism that was only recently fashionable in England and was making its first appearance in the United States. It is no wonder that the Priory aroused the admiration of architects Davis and Downing.[58]

The Boltons also shared with their age a preoccupation with literature, and after they had settled into the new home, Jay organized a family literary society, the products of which were informally published as the "Pelham Chronicle" and distributed about every two weeks to family and neighbors. Some of this poetry was in a medieval vein, and it is easy to imagine the family sitting before an open fire while Jay recited one of the several "medieval" romances he composed (see Chapter 2). Arabella Jay Bolton, a granddaughter of the Reverend Robert, described a Christmas Day's festivities in which one of the Bolton sons dressed as a troubadour and sat on a mantel, playing his guitar.[59] Jay later published selections of poetry from the "Chronicle" under the title *The Harp of Pelham*.[60] According to Jay's preface in the *Harp*, the "Chronicle" usually began with real or humorous advertisements, included reports of events of interest, "tales, essays, conundrums, &c," and poems. It was read by "a wide circle of friends." The proceeds from sales of the *Harp* went toward the building of a school. "We state this," wrote Jay in the introduction, "to console some who may not find their dollar's worth in our Book . . . and it will be no vain deed to have placed a stone in a school-house, which may stand when the harp of Pelham is silent, and the long grass of ages waves over us all." He himself frequently contributed to the "Chronicle," both poetry and prose. His love of writing poetry in these early Pelham years is revealed in a letter of 7 February 1845 to his brother James: "Touching Poetry I have not much time now & perhaps less ambition. Still she is like the 'voice of one that playeth well on an instrument' and I shall never forget her kindness to me in my youth."[61] Yet the voice of poetry stayed with him, and he is reported to have written verse all his life.[62]

Jay Bolton records that for Bolton children study was encouraged in many disciplines: history, science, languages, literature, and art.[63] At some time in these first Priory years, some Savannah friends learned of the interesting intellectual and practical education being given to the children. With little warning, the friends' daughter arrived in Pelham to join the merry crowd, initiating still another Bolton endeavor, a school for young ladies. Classes were held in the Armory, a large, paneled room containing several suits of medieval armor (fig. 1b), and were taught by Bolton daughters, with Nanette presiding. The school was attended not only by local girls but also by boarders from distinguished families of Boston, Providence, New York, and the South and West.[64] The library at the Priory is said to have been extensive, containing among other items original editions of Piranesi's prints in forty-two volumes that had belonged to Napoleon.[65] Thus involved with education, the family decided to finance a building for a public school nearby, the first such school in the area, which opened in May 1845.[66] The funds realized from *The Harp of Pelham* went toward the construction of this school. The building is in a Norman Romanesque style, and survives as the parish house of Christ Church, the latter also built by the Boltons, which is, however, getting ahead of the story. In addition to their teaching duties at the Priory, daughters Nanette and Adele started missions in Pelhamville and on City Island, which became, respectively, the Church of the Redeemer and Grace Church, both still active parishes.[67]

By this time William Jay Bolton was in his early twenties, a slim youth with dark hair and blue eyes, and the good looks that adorned all the Bolton children, a trait that persists in the family today (frontispiece). Jay's daughter Grace reports that he was of moderate height, and had a "very fine head. His countenance was very open, & very serene & cheerful & benevolent: people used to say it did them good to meet Mr. Bolton in the street & to receive one of his lovely smiles."[68] He must have had a nice sense of humor, to judge by comments in *The Harp of Pelham* and in letters, and by amusing visual details he occasionally slipped into his stained glass designs. His early successes can probably be ascribed in part to the personal charm that complemented his artistic talent, and that would have endeared him to patrons.

Stained Glass Art
of William Jay Bolton

In 1838 or 1839, Jay enrolled in classes at the National Academy of Design in New York, perhaps at the instigation of the family's friend, Washington Irving, who was an honorary member of the Academy. He became the pupil of Samuel F. B. Morse, President of the Academy and Professor of Sculpture and Painting and of the Literature of the Arts of Design at New York University. Jay was registered between 1839 and 1841 in the Antique School, where he was instructed in academic methods of drawing and painting.[69] His living quarters were in the university, where Morse also lived.[70] A student enrolled with Bolton in 1841 provides this interesting view of their teacher: "I engaged to become Morse's pupil, and subsequently went to New York and found him in a room in University Place. He had three other pupils, and I soon found that our professor had very little patronage. . . . Morse was a faithful teacher, and took much interest in our progress. . . . But he was very poor."[71] A fellow artist wrote of Morse that instead of devoting his time to art, Morse wasted it on "some silly invention, a machine by which he expects to send messages from one place to another."[72]

In true Bolton fashion, Jay apparently worked hard and earned the respect of the Academy faculty, for on 18 March 1840 he received the following letter from John L. Morton, Secretary of the Academy: "I have the honor to present to you in the name of the Academy the first premium in the third class for the best full length drawing of the Venus de Medicis, awarded to you at a meeting of the Council on the 10th Int."[73] The subject for the competition reflects the classicism fundamental to the Academy's curriculum, and typical for the period. Jay seems to have felt comfortable studying art in this tradition, despite his family's involvement with the Gothic Revival. In fact, it will be seen that even when his aesthetic goal is medieval, as it is in much of his stained glass, the underlying forms are classical.

It was probably during this period at the National Academy that Bolton painted a fresco, *The Defeat and Capture of Caractacus by the Romans,* over the library mantel at the Priory.[74] It is interesting that he would attempt a fresco, for even in England the art of fresco painting was a recent revival.[75] Only a few fragments of this painting remain after what must have been a chimney fire, sometime after 1933, because the mantelpiece below, carved by one of the Boltons, remains intact. The fragments show faint traces of several figures and parts of a horse in a lively battle scene. Jay began exhibiting at the National Academy in 1840, with what his nephew Reginald Pelham Bolton described as "a rather painful painting of 'The Massacre of the Innocents.'"[76] Whether this assessment of the work is

The Life of
William Jay Bolton

justified cannot be determined, as the painting is lost, along with most other Bolton works listed in the Academy's exhibition records.[77] In 1841, however, his *Canonicus and the Governor of Plymouth* was awarded a second prize.[78] Morse wrote to him on 22 April 1843, noting the upcoming "varnishing day" for the exhibition, and concluded by saying, "I like your pictures much, especially the family of Bethany, which is painted in the spirit and feeling of the Venetian school of color."[79] The painting is listed in National Academy records as *Christ with the Family of Bethany - a Sketch;* its present location is unknown. By 1844, Jay was exhibiting stained glass designs, beginning with one listed by the Academy as *Adoration,* which may be the little watercolor in the Long Island Diocese Archives, probably an early idea for the *Birth of Christ* window at Holy Trinity (fig. 27, colorplate VII). Other W. J. Bolton paintings exhibited in these years are, with exhibition dates: *Portrait of a Gentleman* (1841); *Head of an Old Lady* (1843); *A Sketch of Bath, England* (1843); *Descent from the Cross* (1844); *Head of a Fox Hound* (1845); *Long Island Sound, Morning* (1845); *Head of a Greyhound* (1845); *Christ Stilling the Tempest* (1847; ?fig. 33b); and his self-portrait (1847; frontispiece). All but the last or the last two have disappeared, unless the *Sketch of Bath, England* is the youthful drawing now in the Victoria Gallery in that city. There is nevertheless hope that other drawings and paintings are extant and may yet come to light. Grace Bolton mentions in a letter of 8 February 1907 to the National Academy, "We have a good many of his pictures - chiefly in oil, & nearly all painted in America."[80]

The Priory library fresco may not have been Jay's only venture in that medium. Although no others are known, Grace Bolton says that her father painted a number of frescoes, and "must have earned a good deal of money at this time," for in 1841 he could afford a trip to Europe. He sailed that spring on the transport *South America,* to study art and "to buy treasures for the adornment of the new home."[81] He was especially eager, she reports, to study stained glass. He spent most of the time in Italy, some eighteen months, including a number of weeks in Rome. There is evidence from his pictorial sources for stained glass made after the trip that he probably visited England, as well as the Low Countries, specifically Liège, where a window at the Church of St. Martin may have furnished the design for his first major window. During the trip he made numerous sketches in churches and museums, "& came back with his mind stored with all he had seen, & his imagination both chastened & fired, & with portfolios full of his drawings in pencil, chalk, watercolour & oils."[82] Some of the most interesting surviving drawings, made probably on this trip, are his tracings of two sixteenth-century Flemish roundels in Holy Trinity Church, Bradford-on-

Avon, near Bath. During his stay in Rome he seems to have been enchanted by the art of Raphael, and probably went more than once to see the Vatican Stanze and Logge frescoes, and the *Transfiguration* at the Vatican Gallery. The roundels and the Raphaels would soon appear in various forms in his own work; these drawings are discussed in Chapter 3 and the Catalog.

By a great misfortune most of the sketches Bolton made on this and other journeys, along with numerous of his designs and cartoons for stained glass windows, burned in a fire at the studio he founded in Cambridge, later W. H. Constable & Co. Ltd. of Cambridge.[83] The only travel drawing to survive is a pencil sketch on the back of a letter fragment, to an unknown addressee, showing the so-called Castor and Pollux, a Roman equestrian monument admired by Goethe, Flaxman, Canova, and other Romantics.[84] A tendency to stiffness of form in this sketch is present in most of Bolton's known drawings, and might even have been an advantage when he turned to the inflexible medium of stained glass. In the few oil paintings that survive he was able to overcome the rigidity of his draughtsmanship through the forgiving quality of that medium. On his return to Pelham in November 1842, Jay also brought home "2 complete suits of armour . . . pictures & prints, inlaid cabinets, bronzes, jars from Pompeii, cameos & wood carvings & many other things, including part of a very ancient Byzantine Triptich."[85] As part of the Priory adornment, the armor is what gave the mansion's schoolroom its name (fig. 1b). His purchases are typical of the bric-a-brac that the Victorian traveler favored.

Apparently it was not long after his return that Bolton began to work seriously in stained glass. His interest in this most medieval of arts began almost surely before the 1841 journey, with experiments in executing armorial windows for the Priory (figs. 1c,d; see Catalog I). The heraldic designs may well be the work of his older brother Robert, who had been interested in heraldry since childhood,[86] but the grisaille patterns into which the armorials are set are most likely by Jay and John, for they relate to the brothers' later designs for the family church. Jay may have visited stained glass studios during his travels, and received some instruction, but a letter, to be discussed later, suggests that that was not the case. Very likely the study of stained glass that Grace mentions consisted in merely looking at windows.

In making stained glass armorials for the Priory the Boltons were in the vanguard of the Gothic Revival. Revivalists in both England and the United States recognized that the Gothic-style buildings they championed must be complemented with correct appointments. Only a few years before, John Henry Hopkins, Protestant Episcopal Bishop of Vermont, on the subject of

The Life of
William Jay Bolton

Gothic Revival churches and their adornment, had written: "The custom of staining the glass of Church windows was admirably adapted not only to moderate the glare of light, but also to give it a rich, mellow effect."[87] He lamented the fact that in the United States it was "not yet practicable to apply this expedient extensively." Bishop Hopkins's book was undoubtedly known in the church circles in which the Boltons moved, and Jay had probably read the work.

Jay Bolton's first opportunity to produce a major stained glass window came in 1843. Pelham was without a church, and since 1840 the Reverend Robert Bolton had held Sunday services in the entry hall of the Priory. Attendance by friends and neighbors showed the need for a church, and Robert decided to solve the problem by building one himself. Ann Bolton wrote in her diary, "We are anxious to erect a little church here, but how it is to be done, I know not, only I know that the silver and gold are the Lord's and he can do it, whenever he pleases to use us as instruments."[88]

Over the next two years, while funds were being raised, there must have been excited planning for the building. Although the Boltons were Evangelicals in their churchmanship, their tastes in ecclesiastical architecture and adornment were consonant with, and perhaps even a little influenced by, the medievalism of the Tractarians, the Anglican ritualist reformers of Oxford, as well as of those self-styled arbiters of reformed architectural design, the Cambridge Camden Society (later, the Ecclesiological Society), formed in 1839. As Jay Bolton noted later, at the time in the United States, "Tractarianism had scarcely begun its career," starting at the Theological Seminary of New York, but it had already gained episcopal sanction.[89] Yet to an Evangelical, the forms of ritual and priestly intercession are hollow artifice, and dangerously similar to the ceremonials of "popery"; a church with an elaborate chancel and overly ornate appointments was equally "popish." The new church, although in the Gothic style, would have to be simple in its design, modest in its adornment. In a sermon preached at the laying of the foundation stone, the Reverend Bolton stated that the Pelham church would "not show too much attention to form," but rather would be suited to the Evangelical doctrines to be taught there:

> [T]he total fall and corruption of our nature, our complete redemption through the atoning death of our Lord Jesus Christ, and the renovation of our hearts and lives by the Holy Spirit. . . . [We shall] maintain, therefore, supreme and inviolable, the perfect word of God, and the right of private judgement, according to the Divine Command, "Search the Scriptures," and shall claim for our Church no higher distinction . . .

than that of a part of the blessed company of all Godly people—a "congregation of the faithful men" in which the pure word of God is preached, and the Sacraments—Baptism and the Lord's Supper—are rightly and duly administered.[90]

For 28 April 1843, Ann Bolton's diary recorded the laying of the foundation stone for the church.[91] Neighbors had raised $1,000 toward the construction, and the Boltons contributed another $2,000; these were large sums in the mid-nineteenth century. Built of native stone on a north-south axis, the church is small in size, and its heavy proportions, large front gable with bell tower, sturdy buttresses, and timbered ceiling all mark it as a type belonging to what Phoebe Stanton called the "parish church revival" (fig. 3a).[92] The original building had only a nave with aisles, and measured 65 × 22 feet. A small sanctuary without choir stalls was located at the south end (figs. 3b,c). There is no indication of who designed the building, but again it may have been John. Like the family home, the church has simple lines well suited to the rough-textured, grey local stone. The congenial relationship of design and material would have pleased even Pugin, the great purist of the Gothic Revival.[93] As Christ Church, the new building was consecrated on 15 October 1843, although the act of incorporation is dated 25 September with Isaac Roosevelt and four Bolton sons, Robert, Jr., Jay, John, and Winter, listed among the vestrymen.[94] The Reverend Robert Bolton became the first rector.

To decorate the interior of Christ Church the artistic talents of the Bolton family were once again called forth. One or more of the sons carved the delightful corbel figures, most of which depict angels holding heraldic shields or musical instruments (fig. 3c); one corbel is carved to represent Bishop Samuel Seabury, first bishop of the Protestant Episcopal Church, and former rector of the parish of Westchester. The angels bear a striking resemblance to the late medieval corbel figures at the Holy Sepulchre Church in Cambridge, near the home of Aunt Arabella Jay Ashton, where Jay and probably other Bolton children had often visited. The pulpit canopy (seen in fig. 3b) is likewise from late medieval models, and the original altar rail can also be attributed to the Boltons, as can two large Gothic-style chairs, a frame with cherubs and symbols of the Passion for a fifteenth-century crucifix, and wrought-iron lanterns.[95]

The glory of Christ Church, however, is the stained glass, which, according to the fourth Bolton son, Winter, was designed and made by Jay and John Bolton.[96] Jay was the principal artist and activating force in the enterprise. He seems to have been the first family member to learn to make stained glass, and it is he who designed the only large, figural window for the Pelham church, the marvelous *Adoration of the Magi* (1843), which can be considered the first extant figural window in the medieval manner made in the United States (colorplate I; see Catalog II). Evidence exists of even earlier windows produced by New York and Boston firms, but it is not known if these were figural, or if they were done in the medieval manner.[97]

It is reported that Jay Bolton used the Priory attic for making the cartoons for his windows, and did his glazing in a little workshop nearby.[98] The attic is actually a long, narrow room at the east end of the third floor, with a large skylight, and must have been ideal for Jay's purposes. The shop where he assembled the windows was at the back of an eighteenth-century cottage overlooking Long Island Sound (fig. 2f); his small muffle kiln, in which the painted glass was fired, was installed at the base of a chimney.[99] How much John Bolton aided his brother in making the Christ Church windows is uncertain, but it must have been more than a little, for John became an accomplished worker in the art, took part in the large Brooklyn project, and produced several programs of windows on his own (see Appendix B). Jay's hand is clearly recognizable in most figures, however, of the *Adoration of the Magi.* Altogether there are ten Bolton windows at Christ Church: the *Magi* and a small oculus above it by Jay, and eight grisaille windows by Jay and John (figs. 5, 6, 7; colorplate II).[100] While other family members may have helped in the stained glass project, only one assistant besides John is known for certain, Thomas Denton. Sometime after 1884, Denton gave a large window in the Nanette Bolton Memorial building (1884–85) near the church, and it is recorded that "in early youth" he assisted in the making of the Christ Church windows.[101] When the church was enlarged in 1910, a new east-west nave was built, making the old chancel with the *Magi* window into the south transept, and relocating several grisaille windows.

No particular reason has been found for the choice of the Adoration of the Magi (Matt. 2:11) as a subject for the principal window at Christ Church. The date of its installation is unknown, but if the window was in place for the consecration, and there is no evidence to the contrary, it would date from late 1843. The design models for the Christ Church windows demonstrate once again the Boltons' interest in both medieval and northern Renaissance styles, and their reconciliation of the two under a Gothic banner. The *Magi* window is in what the period called the "Cinque Cento" style, with large figures flanked by elaborate Mannerist columns (colorplate I). The figural group resembles the figures in a sixteenth-century panel of the same subject at the Church of St. Martin, Liège, where the windows are

---

filled with Mannerist architectural ornament much like that in the Pelham window (fig. 4). Jay Bolton may thus have visited Liège on his 1841 journey, and have made drawings of the St. Martin windows. It is certain that by 1854 he knew the Liège glass, for he mentioned it that year in a lecture at Cambridge.[102]

In the Christ Church windows the viewer is impressed by the amount and brilliance of color. A recently discovered letter written by Jay, and to be referred to frequently, provides valuable data on the materials and costs of the *Magi* window. It was made for a total of $50 to $60, plus $15 for the furnace:

The white glass for limbs, heads & white parts	$2
German glass for draperies from	$30 to 40
Leads at 12 $ per cwt.	12
Enamel colors &c	$6[103]

It is interesting to compare these costs, for a modest three-light window, with those for a large, six-light, traceried window he made about 1849 for the Church of St. Mary the Less, Cambridge, England, for which he asked £233, or about $1,128.[104] This fee must have included labor costs, which of course were not listed in Bolton's accounting of the window for the family church. In the letter just mentioned he quotes a figure of $1,000 as a fee that could be charged for a large window, but says it is too high. The conclusion is that stained glass production was somewhat better paid in England than in the United States. For modern specialists the most interesting fact learned from this letter is that Bolton obtained his potmetal glass from Germany.[105] He goes on to say that he cut the glass, leaded it up, and did the firing himself.

In the same letter Bolton reveals more about his beginnings in the art of stained glass:

> Glass stainers or [=are] often men of natural genius, it is true, but they as often want a <u>refined</u> & <u>general</u> <u>education</u> & so suppose it a wiser plan to mistify themselves & others. I was told that it was impossible without years of practise, I could attain the art, & should have believed it till now, but that for our little Church window's sake I obtained what information I could, built a furnace, procured leads & German glass & set to work myself. The result enables me to say that the whole matter is quite easy. . . . The only true difficulty . . . is to be able to design & draw well enough!

The letter reveals that Jay has apparently been in contact with other stained glass artists, for he feels secure in commenting on the fact that most

The Life of
William Jay Bolton

are poorly educated outside their art. There were at least two, possibly three, makers of stained glass windows in New York City at the time, although nothing of their work is known to survive. One was William Gibson, whose shop had opened by 1833, and the other Carse & Wert, in business by 1840 in what appears to have been the production of stained glass for nonchurch use. Gibson is reported to have made ecclesiastical glass, but his business failed probably "because his product lacked high merit," and people were not able to pay enough to keep him going.[106] A third glazier, George Edwards, made church windows, but is not recorded in the New York City Directory until 1845–46. In the contacts Bolton had with glaziers, he must have run into protective secrecy when he inquired about the techniques of stained glass making, as suggested by his statement that the glaziers tried to "mistify themselves." A mid-nineteenth-century writer on the art noted that one of the principal reasons it had declined was that "its rules being based so entirely upon empirical principles, those who practiced it were accustomed to consider the knowledge they had acquired in the thorny path of tedious and long-continued experiment, as their most valuable personal property," which they carried with them to their graves.[107] As for what Bolton could have learned on his 1841 journey, the glaziers willing, medieval techniques were still practiced in a few workshops, especially in England, and perhaps also in the Low Countries, but the majority of glaziers he would have encountered in Italy were turning out enamel painted windows.[108]

Undaunted, Bolton set about to learn the medieval form of the art for himself, probably from published instruction books. In 1843 there were a few technical manuals for making stained glass the medieval way, although none approach the step-by-step instructions of today's "how to" books, and Jay's achievement in teaching himself the traditional techniques of the art is in no way diminished by the availability of any of the existing manuals.[109] As he states, he bought leads, ordered glass, built a kiln, and found the procedures entirely within his capabilities. In 1841, about the time his interest in making stained glass must have begun, he was a progressive in seeking to learn the medieval technique, as well as in deciding that the Gothic style of the proposed Pelham church required appropriate stained glass. His beginnings as a glazier are coeval with the early achievements of Charles Winston and A. W. N. Pugin, who are usually singled out as leaders in the Gothic Revival in stained glass. Indeed, Bolton's first windows predate Winston's pioneering book on the subject.[110] From Jay's own comments on the *Magi* window, it is clear that the need to fill the Christ Church windows with stained glass was the impetus for his first serious efforts in the medium, and thus "but . . . for our little Church window's sake," the world might not have known the stained glass art of William Jay Bolton.

Meanwhile, Bolton continued to participate in National Academy exhibitions until his final year in the United States. He found himself in something of a flap with the Academy in 1844 or 1845 over his status as an Associate. Apparently he had heard of his election, but had not received official notice, or any information about the appropriate response, which was to submit his self-portrait within a year. In a letter written to the Academy sometime before May 1845, he states that he is "vex'd" that his name had been cut from the list of Associates, and hastens "to disabuse your minds of any <u>slight</u> on my part. . . . Being a little modest I have never taken any notice of it [i.e., the election as Associate] myself, & living altogether in the country & seeing so few artists, I suppose, it has never been notic'd to [*sic*] me. As to the <u>condition</u>, I never <u>saw</u> it." He presumes that he must wait to be reelected in May 1845, and send the self-portrait before [May] 1846, all of which took place.[111] The Academy is still in possession of the self-portrait (frontispiece), for which a preparatory sketch is also known (fig. 61).

When he was about twenty-eight years old, William Jay Bolton received his first professional commission for stained glass. It would be the most important of his career. He was called upon to make three ranks of large windows, forty-nine or fifty in all, for the Church of the Holy Trinity, now St. Ann and Holy Trinity, on the northwest corner of Montague and Clinton streets in Brooklyn Heights (fig. 9; colorplates III–VII).[112] Miraculously, all or all but one of the windows are extant. The church was privately built by Edgar John Bartow (1809–1864), a Huguenot and wealthy paper manufacturer married to one of the Pierreponts of Brooklyn. Bartow intended that Holy Trinity should be the most imposing edifice in New York.[113] The architect was Minard Lafever (1798–1854), likewise a Huguenot, and already well known for buildings in both the classical and the medieval styles; Holy Trinity has been called Lafever's "outstanding . . . most splendid achievement."[114] According to one account, Bartow was a member of the Reverend Robert Bolton's small congregation at St. Paul's, Eastchester, and upon learning of Jay's experiments in stained glass, he engaged him for Holy Trinity.[115] The date of the commission is not known, but it could have been in early 1844, as excavation for the foundation began in August of that year.[116] Jay's decision to accept such a commission appears either heroic or foolhardy in the face of his inexperience, but he seems to have been filled with great enthusiasm for making stained glass, and was probably carried along by the energy and optimism of youth.

The Life of
William Jay Bolton

There is no information on the negotiations and procedures for the building of Holy Trinity, probably because Bartow did the hiring and supervised the project himself; there was no building committee, and parish records mention only the official opening.[117] Even if more records existed, little might be said of Bolton or the glass, for anyone who has looked into nineteenth- or even twentieth-century American church archives knows all too well the dearth of information there on the stained glass windows, except perhaps for the names of the donors.[118] Other sources, however, provide interesting sidelights on the designing of the church. Bartow had brought a number of architectural drawings from England, including some of King's College Chapel, "which were carefully studied, and furnished many suggestive thoughts and tasteful adornments."[119] Lafever referred to the style of Holy Trinity as "Decorated Gothic [with] tracery of flamboyant character," that is to say, a fourteenth-century English style with windows of a fifteenth-century French type (fig.8).[120] Jacob Landy has traced some of Lafever's architectural details to the Perpendicular Gothic (the last phase of English Gothic) of King's Chapel, features that must have made the project a particular delight for Jay, with his fond childhood memories of the great chapel in Cambridge.[121] Indeed, Jay's recollections of the large figures and pictorial landscapes in the King's windows must be seen as an important foundation for his own designs at Holy Trinity. Although he did not base any Holy Trinity compositions directly on King's models, there are many reminiscences of the sixteenth-century Anglo-Flemish art at King's in Bolton's figures, in his figure groupings, in the architectural ornament, and in the landscapes.[122]

With their broad, mullioned openings and elaborate tracery, the Holy Trinity windows are in the late medieval tradition, but the large figures and illusionistic scenes are based on sixteenth-century design. Once again Bolton's art corresponds to Winston's "Cinque Cento" manner. The subjects together form a series spanning biblical history, from the Expulsion to Christ's Ascension, with particular significance for Evangelical Christians (see Catalog III).

By February 1845, in Jay's letter to his brother James, he comments that "I have now finished three quarters of my windows, and am satisfied that I shall be able to do something in the 'Ars Vitraria.'" This can refer only to the Holy Trinity project, as the Pelham series was by this date almost surely complete; but this means the sketches or the cartoons, not the finished windows. All the windows were still not installed when the church opened, 25 April 1847, and the *Brooklyn Daily Eagle* for 26 April remarked upon "the wind whistling through the boards that answer for glasses in the gallery windows." A completion date of 1848, probably early in the year, may be inferred from that date inscribed in silver stain on the *Resurrection* and *Christ at Emmaus* windows, which come near the end of the gallery series.[123]

Little is known of Jay's life during the time when he was working on the Holy Trinity windows, mentioned for the first time in the letter to James. Another statement in the same letter may also refer to the designs for Holy Trinity, but because Jay paragraphs very casually, it could refer as well to the easel paintings he must have been doing at the same time, to judge from his National Academy exhibition entries:

> I was wrecked once on the beautiful coast of <u>color</u>. <u>Design</u> now is all I sail
> for. And if I can only by the bribes of industry & perseverance induce
> some of the dignified figures who walk to & fro in my chambers of
> imagery to let me take their portraits, I will astonish the natives yet.

The "natives" are the people of his new land, which he makes clear elsewhere. If his earlier fascination with color refers to his glass, then the windows in question would undoubtedly be those of the Jesse Tree in the aisles of Holy Trinity, the first windows to be installed. They are rich in deep blues and purples (colorplate IV), and are probably the windows about which Bartow wrote to Bolton in August 1845:

> Having just returned to the City I find you have proceeded far enough to
> get in four of the lights. I am pleased with them and the few that have
> seen them appear also pleased. . . . Is there not rather too much of the
> plain blue glass, would they not look better with more variety of filling
> up, and would you not rather vary them more as to general appearance—
> but you must act your judgement and taste. I will be satisfied.[124]

Bartow's suggestion that there might be more variety in the designs must reflect the production method of the Jesse Tree windows, for which a few cartoons were reused in various ways in the fourteen windows. In the basic design, two angels in outer lights flank a large tree in the center, with the bust of an ancestor of Christ in the head of each light. The same tree appears throughout, in each window the angels are mirror images, and each pair of angels is repeated in another window (figs. 10a,b). All together, one cartoon tree made fourteen, and seven cartoon angels made twenty-eight, a procedure that eased and accelerated production.[125] The color schemes are changed in the repeat versions, and as if to atone for the repeated images, the ancestor busts are all different. It is clear from a later commission application that Bolton had a head for business, and the design shortcuts

The Life of
William Jay Bolton

seen in the Jesse Tree, and in some other windows, may have been taken to help him stay within his estimate of costs.

Although Jay probably made all the designs for the Holy Trinity windows, he was aided in their execution by another painter, undoubtedly his brother John, who is known to have made some of the windows at Christ Church, Pelham. It is not difficult to recognize the idiosyncrasies of John's facial and drapery styles, seen in several of his own later windows, and a number of figures are attributed to him in subsequent chapters and in the Catalog. However, efforts to confirm his participation, and perhaps that of one or two others, in the ornamental grounds and background landscapes at Holy Trinity have not been very successful. That John did not work regularly on the Holy Trinity project may be inferred from a remark in Jay's 1845 letter to James that John's "store is doing well, to others & himself too." Nothing more is said of the store except that it was located "opposite Irving Flandereau's."[126] However much assistance Jay had at Holy Trinity, the achievement of the whole program was his, and legend at the church has it that he put his own portrait on the young man holding a cloak before the donkey in the *Christ Enters Jerusalem* window, as though to present himself and his work as a humble offering (fig. 31b). A comparison of the face of the young man with the earlier self-portrait gives support to the legend (frontispiece).

Despite the small number of assistants in his stained glass shop, at the same time that Jay was designing the Brooklyn windows he applied for the job of making the altar window for Trinity Church, Manhattan, an important new building designed by Richard Upjohn, dedicated 21 May 1846. The details of Jay's application are known from his letter commenting on the production of the *Magi* window. It was written to William H. Harison of the Trinity Church building committee, and can be dated with some confidence to 19 October 1844; and from the letter to his brother James of February 1845 (both transcribed in Appendix A). To James, he notes that "Dr. Wainwright and Mr. Harris [*sic*] have promised to wait about Trinity Window til they have seen mine. This is something, but I have not much hope of the job."[127] It would have been a significant commission for the young glazier, and he would certainly have produced a window of greater interest and beauty than the one that was made. In any case, the episode provides facts about Bolton's career in glass, and about his ideas. In the letter to Mr. Harison he reflects a fundamental view of the Gothic Revivalist when he says that the window should be fully leaded "to suit outlines, folds &c. . . . . [E]very line of lead will <u>melt</u> <u>away</u> at a proper distance, or only serve to <u>distinguish</u> & <u>strengthen</u> the design as well as the colors." He advocates a "natural series of Scripture stories" instead of what he terms "grotesque" figures, by which he may mean copies of medieval figures; the latter he describes elsewhere as being ugly. For the altar window of the Manhattan church he suggests a series of designs based on Acts 1:22, beginning with the Baptism of Christ "in the <u>Easternmost</u> <u>lower</u> <u>side</u> window, & by a procession of subjects, <u>alternating</u> from left to right, & including how many glorious matters! you would be brought <u>gradually</u> & <u>happily</u> to the 'Ascension.'" The program is almost a summary in one window of his Holy Trinity, Brooklyn, series. He states that a Crucifixion might be an alternative to the Ascension, for either subject "carries you on from Earth to Heaven." A similar spiritual journey is also the goal of his altar window at Holy Trinity, which, despite conflicting recent interpretations, can best be identified as an Ascension. The didactic tone of the letter may be in response to a request from Harison for Jay to comment on another glazier's views of what the Trinity window should be. Bolton is diplomatic in his reply, but pleads with Harison and the committee not to choose "emblems & effigies" in order to reduce costs, for he says he can make figural windows as cheaply as he can nonfigural ones, "paint a head as soon as I could a cup."[128] Windows designed with a variety of Christian symbols were popular with Gothic Revival purists, and they were generally cheaper than figural windows, but could not accomplish the task that Bolton believed essential in ancient glass, "that of teaching Scripture History," for which figural windows were required. As to the "effigies," Bolton states, and the window eventually placed over the altar at Trinity Church bears him out, that "Apostles & saints in niches . . . may be made sublime & solemn doubtless, but they will not <u>interest</u> the people."[129] These comments suggest that Bolton had already seen the design that was finally chosen. It is uncertain who actually designed the window; one name mentioned as participating in its production is the "Mr. Hoppin" (Thomas F. Hoppin) whose views on the best design underlie Jay's concern throughout the letter.[130]

Bolton concludes the letter to Harison by saying that he wishes to present a more finished design before the final decision is made. This must be the drawing mentioned in the letter of February 1845 to James, and therefore the Harison letter, which bears the dateline "Pelham Priory, Oct. 19," must have been written the previous fall, that is, in 1844. These letters make clear that the only figural window at Trinity was not even commissioned until after February 1845. It is thus almost certain that Bolton's first figural windows installed in Brooklyn by August of that year precede the figural altar window at Trinity, Manhattan.[131]

Jay Bolton pursued the Trinity commission vigorously, even to the point of mentioning the name of Morse, then president of the National Academy and receiving the first accolades for his invention of the telegraph.[132] Yet he was also diplomatic, stating that although he feels "free from any mercenary desire of getting a job, yet I am young & cannot expect to have much weight with my elders." He notes that "Professor Morse . . . gave me so much encouragement to proceed" and that he, Bolton, would welcome further advice from his mentor, as well as from "such a tasteful gentleman" as Mr. Hoppin. Furthermore, he advises that the final design should not be chosen "without the united counsel of artists with architects," undoubtedly hoping that Upjohn would be as appreciative of his designs as Lafever had been.

As he anticipated, the commission was not to be his. Nor does he appear to have been successful, if indeed he even participated, in the competition mentioned in the beginning of his letter to his brother James. The subject he was considering, "an attack of British Chariots on a Roman legion," would have been suited to fresco, but it is too late a date for the famous Houses of Parliament fresco competition, completed in 1843.[133]

Nevertheless, before completing the windows at Holy Trinity, Jay managed after all to garner a second substantial commission, although for a less significant church: the ten windows for the Church of the Holy Apostles in the Chelsea district of Manhattan, another building designed by Minard Lafever.[134] Jay's sensitivity to style and his inventiveness are once again evident in his glass designs for this small building in what was termed "Tuscan Style," a version of Renaissance Revival. As was the case at Holy Trinity the commission for the glazing is undocumented, but it might be supposed that Lafever himself had a part in the arrangements, having observed Jay's accomplishments at Holy Trinity. The fact that Holy Apostles was "High Church" reinforces the idea that Bolton obtained the commission through his artistic rather than his ecclesiastical connections.[135] The cornerstone was laid 31 March 1846,[136] and it is likely that Bolton was assigned the glazing job shortly before. There is no way of knowing when he began work on the windows, but it had to have been while he was hard at work on those for Holy Trinity. Holy Apostles was used for public worship for the first time on 21 February and completed by 4 April 1848.[137]

In keeping with the church's design, the stained glass at Holy Apostles is Renaissance in spirit. The unusual design for the ten simple, round-headed openings consists of roundels painted in a thoroughly illusionistic sixteenth-century manner and containing scenes from the Life of Christ and the Acts of the Apostles. They are set three to a window, among grisaille acanthus leaves and colored flowers (colorplate IX). The colored and uncolored glass is beautifully balanced, and the windows command attention without overwhelming the simple lines of the architecture. There seems to be only one hand at work on the relatively small, refined figures of the roundels, although in some instances the paint has deteriorated too much to allow a conclusive judgment. A recent fire at Holy Apostles, described in the Catalog, further damaged the windows, making attribution even more difficult. Jay could have had help in carrying out the designs of the framing foliage and borders, for evidence of the use of stencils shows that at Holy Apostles, as at Holy Trinity, production was facilitated by certain shortcut methods.

Despite his growing patronage, and without any known warning or reason, William Jay Bolton left the United States in 1848, perhaps in the summer, to return permanently to England. He was now thirty-two years old, and had been in the United States for eleven years. Comments here and there in his writings imply that he never felt at home in the United States and always considered himself an Englishman. In the 1845 letter to James he speaks of Americans as "the natives" and England as "our country," and in his later published works he uses "us," "we," and "our" in referring to English people and things. In a poem to his sister Nanette in 1883, he wrote of the Priory as

> Our foreign home, the home of years
> Adorned by nature and by art.
> Creation of our father's taste,
> Nor less adorned with Christian grace
> By her who bore us all.[138]

At an unknown date, his brother James had returned to England and enrolled at Cambridge University. Jay now followed, and settled in Cambridge, where he established a stained glass studio. It is still in business under the name W. H. Constable & Co. Ltd.; Constable was one of Bolton's shop assistants.[139]

The year 1849 was a pivotal one in the life of the Boltons of Pelham, and of William Jay Bolton. On 16 June Jay's younger sister Abby died of consumption in Pelham, and was buried in a vault in the family church. Her sister Rhoda published a reminiscence of her, noting among her many accomplishments a conspicuous talent for painting. In quotations from her letters during a final visit to England the previous year, Abby tells of going to services at King's College Chapel, where she admired "those mysterious windows . . . one of man's noblest works."[140] Perhaps she too had helped Jay in his stained glass projects. He wrote the preface to her biography, extolling her many virtues; an engraving of his charming, informal portrait of her provides the frontispiece for the book (fig. 62). Her father was grief stricken, and wrote to Jay and James in England, "How I shall feel when I come to conduct the service on Sunday, with her precious body beneath, I can not think."[141] A highly Romantic poem that the elder Bolton wrote several years earlier, entitled "The Pains of Memory," anticipates his agony of 1849. In it he describes a hut built on a flowering hill,

> For even while I said,
> "I shall be happy here,"
> The memory of the dead,
> Would everywhere appear.[142]

The hut could as well be the Priory, the dead his beloved Abby, whom everyone in the family seems to have adored. Robert Bolton was finally unable to reconcile himself to his daughter's death and to serving a church that was her tomb. Thus, in the autumn of 1850, leaving the Priory to the care of daughters Nanette and Adele, he and Ann returned to England, where he died in 1857 and she in 1859, with Jay in attendance at each sad event.[143] In 1860, Jay published the loving and informative biography of his parents entitled *Footsteps of the Flock,* which has often served as a source of information for the present study.

Later in 1849, life took a more cheerful turn for Jay Bolton when, on 26 September he married Susannah Welch of King's Lynn, who was the sister of William Welch, a school friend of James Bolton.[144] It was almost certainly through the Welches that Jay was engaged to make the large altar window for St. Peter's Church, a late medieval structure in nearby West Lynn. The window was completed between late summer 1849 and July 1850 (colorplate X). It includes an inscription that, with two newspaper accounts of the installation, furnishes the dating *termini.*[145] Depicting the angel and three women at Christ's tomb, the window was given by the Misses Walker, daughters of Giles Walker of North Lynn, in memory of their sister Amelia, who died 29 July 1849 at the age of sixteen. It is an early example of the memorial-window genre, and one of the region's earliest examples of Gothic Revival stained glass without colored enamels. Not surprisingly, Bolton now draws directly on one of the windows of King's Chapel, and the resulting design may be counted among his finest achievements.[146] Moreover, Bolton glass in the tracery of a single nave window at St. Peter's suggests that a full program of glazing was planned, but halted by even more important events in Bolton's life. The small angels in oriels in this single tracery, here painted by an assistant, may have been a stock motif in the Cambridge shop (fig. 57). This same tracery design and the cherubim motif of the West Lynn chancel were executed by Jay himself for the tracery of two windows of the Church of St. Andrew the Great, Cambridge, perhaps in 1849. The cherubim motif appears a third time in the tracery of an Ascension window drawing Bolton must have made during this Cambridge period, for he reproduced two of the King's Chapel Messengers in the outer lights of the lower register (fig. 69). It was also at this time that he made an eastern window, of unknown subject, for the Church of St. Mary the Less, Cambridge, a window that was removed without trace about 1890.[147]

In that same busy year of 1849, Bolton was engaged as an assistant to architect John Pike Hedgeland in the restoration and cleaning of the King's Chapel windows.[148] He would later entertain his children with tales of how he worked from a basket slung from the timbering above the vaults.[149] The holes through which the basket ropes passed are still visible. During these operations Hedgeland removed many pieces of original glass, for which he was widely criticized. Jay saved some of the pieces, and his daughter Grace later returned them to King's.[150] Bolton approached his task at King's with great care, making copies, tracings, and studies of the windows, and diagrams of the armature and mountings.[151] His copies of several Tudor-period stained glass armorials in King's College can probably also be assigned to this period; these too were given to King's College by Grace Bolton.[152] The armorials, along with their sixteenth-century models, were subsequently installed in a chantry of King's College Chapel.[153] At an uncertain date, but probably during 1849, Jay made smaller copies of the same ancient armorials, apparently for the house in Christchurch, Hampshire, from which they were acquired in December 1927 by Dr. Eric Milner-White, Dean of King's College Chapel.[154] If so, they indicate that Bolton had private as well as ecclesiastical commissions.

Five years after his work at King's, Jay presented to the Section of Antiquities at Cambridge a paper on the chapel windows, which is the first historical study of the King's glass.[155] A note to the published version of the paper reveals that he was in communication with stained glass theorist Charles Winston.[156] How close the relationship was between the two pioneers in the revival is not known, but since there is no further mention of Winston in Bolton materials, it is likely that the two were only slightly acquainted. Jay's paper shows that his interest in the great complex of sixteenth-century windows in King's Chapel did not end with the cessation of his work in stained glass—which came all too soon—but remained fresh in his thoughts, perhaps even to the end of his days.

It seems almost impossible that Bolton could have added still more to

The Life of
William Jay Bolton

---

the activities and events of 1849, but on 8 June he matriculated at Cambridge University, with the academic title of fellow-commoner, to study theology at Gonville and Caius College.[157] As the West Lynn window could not have been started until after July 1849, it must have been a herculean task for him to complete the window, continue his work for Hedgeland, and begin his studies, all at the same time; no wonder he had to abandon any more glazing planned for West Lynn. By 1850, however, there are no further indications that he was working in stained glass. And once again tragedy entered Bolton's life: his young wife died giving birth to a daughter, Susannah. His grief was so great that a cousin, probably one of the Jays, sent him to the Continent for a few months to recover.[158]

Despite his artistic activities of 1849 and the events of 1850, Bolton's studies appear to have proceeded at a normal pace, and he received his B.A. in 1853, his M.A. in 1856.[159] In 1852 he entered and won the Hulsean Prize competition at Cambridge, which required a lengthy essay on a specified theological subject. His essay was published as *The Evidences of Christianity as Exhibited in the Writings of its Apologists Down to Augustine*.[160] Meanwhile, the Cambridge stained glass studio continued to function under Constable, and it is likely that Bolton at least visited there from time to time, perhaps even joining in the work. His only reference to his years at the university is an interesting comment in an article of 1872 on architecture, in which he notes that he had attended one or more lectures by "High Churchmen" of the Cambridge Camden Society. In the course of their investigations of medieval art, says Bolton, "they came upon Romish frescoes and piscinas [for washing liturgical vessels], and the like; and then they naturally asked what these things meant, and so began to connect Romanism with antiquarianism and conservatism, until at length their lectures—as I can testify—turned upon the history of Romish Saints."[161] The years spent in the center of artistic ecclesiology had not changed Bolton's Evangelical views.

William Jay Bolton then took up a new career and was ordained deacon in the Anglican Church on 13 November 1853, becoming curate of Barnwell; on 12 November 1854, in Ely Cathedral, he was ordained priest, the second Bolton son to take holy orders (James was the first).[162] Personal happiness again filled his life in 1855, for on 14 August he married Margaretta Elizabeth Jones Wilkinson (1827–1903), daughter of the Reverend Henry Watts Wilkinson, vicar of Sudbury, Suffolk. Their life together was blessed with five children, all born in the space of six years: William Henry (1859–1902), Arabella Sarah (1860–1861), Margaretta Grace (1861–after 1933),[163] James Edward (1863–1928), and Robert Wilkinson (1865–1896).[164]

In 1855 the Reverend and new Mrs. Bolton, and Jay's daughter Susannah, moved to Cheltenham, in Gloucestershire, where his parents had their last home, and where he served as curate of Holy Trinity until 1858. The effort he put into the care of souls and his intense feeling for the poor and afflicted are apparent in a small volume he published in 1856, a Christian's guide to "house to house visitation," as he put it.[165] The goal of such visits was to convert people, the rich and the poor, to a truly religious life in which they might find spiritual comfort in regular communion with God. In the often sentimental anecdotes he relates of the visits he himself had made, the reader sees him as a man of great tenderness and of sympathy for the individual, regardless of his or her condition. One chapter, entitled "The Artist," describes visits with a painter dying of tuberculosis, for whom Jay, remembering his sister Abby, must have had considerable sympathy. His lack of concern for his own safety in visiting the sick is exemplified in his activities during the cholera epidemic of 1866, when he was serving a parish just north of London. After sending his family away from the area, he stayed and visited hundreds of the sick and dying, helping with the nursing, and burying the dead by night. Grace believed that he was the only priest in the neighborhood who stayed to serve his flock during this crisis. "He was extraordinarily fearless, & a very good nurse," she noted. He had nursed his brother James through smallpox in 1856.[166]

After Cheltenham, his next parish was St. James, Brighton, from 1858 to 1864; thereafter Islington, as curate at the Chapel of Ease (later, St. Mary's Church) for a year. In 1865 he became rector of St. John's Church, Stratford Broadway, near London, which he was to serve for sixteen years. Grace Bolton reports that her father made drawings and sketches throughout his life, but that St. John's was a large and poor parish, "& there was no more time for pencil or brush, except in his yearly summer holiday, when he used to do a little sketching, as much as the demands of his five children, & his own need of rest, allowed him."[167] So far as is known, none of these drawings survives. He did, however, publish an interesting article on architecture and religion in 1872, which provides important insights into his thought as both artist and clergyman.[168] Among his other accomplishments at Stratford Broadway, Bolton initiated restoration of the church, built schools, and had a memorial erected to the thirteen Protestants of Stratford martyred during Queen Mary's reign.[169] It was from Stratford that he made one last trip to the United States, in 1879, to spend Christmas at the Priory.[170] Curiously enough, during all these years, he had never mentioned to his children the work he had done in stained glass in the United States, as though it might have been a time when he gave himself too much to thoughts of a secular career as an artist.[171]

The Life of
William Jay Bolton

Jay was a devoted family man and a loving father. His daughter Grace describes the family's life with him: "In his home he was like a rock of strength & comfort. His even temper & perfect balance of mind & nerves, were just what make a home perfectly happy. It was the rarest thing to see him ruffled, & his courage & resource were unfailing. . . . His humour also was so very charming & helped us through many difficult times."[172]

At the age of sixty-five, Bolton left Stratford Broadway, tired from many years of hard work, to accept the living at the Church of St. James at Bath, his place of birth. He settled with his family into a house at Pelham, Oldfield Park, Bath. His hair had turned grey at an early age, and by now he was bald and had become stout (fig. 2d).[173] He no longer had the energy he once had, and he hoped that St. James's would provide a more restful situation, but that was not to be.

Bolton found that all too near his small parish "was a hotbed of vice & that a court within a stone's throw of his Church was the sink of the city."[174] This was St. James's Court, an area of twenty brothels inhabited by sixty prostitutes, who solicited even near the church. After failing to persuade the town corporation to buy the properties and replace them with artisans' houses, Jay went to the brothel owners and "remonstrated with them myself. I showed them from Holy Scripture how they became partakers of the sin by encouraging it." Needless to say, the owners were not moved; one of them even sent his lawyer to request an apology of the Reverend Mr. Bolton. Invoking local moral codes, Jay, undaunted, then had a number of the women brought to trial. When they were convicted, he would ask that they be pardoned if they swore to reform their lives. He reports the salvation of some, and the marriage of one of them. He also brought suit against the property owners, accusing them of transgressing public-house laws. The result was that the public-house licenses were cancelled when they next came up for renewal. Jay was ridiculed by the brothel owners and his life was threatened, but after three years of "indescribably hard & unpleasant work," he succeeded in ameliorating the dreadful conditions. His success, however, was at the price of his health.[175] Perhaps feeling his time drawing near, Bolton went in the late spring of 1883 to see his ailing sister Nanette, who was visiting relatives in Switzerland; brother and sister would both be dead within a year.[176]

Grace describes the events of her father's last day, which had begun as most of his days began.[177] He awoke at an early hour on 28 May 1884 and went downstairs as usual to read his Greek New Testament. He then wrote some letters and a sermon for the Wednesday evening service. "After breakfast he walked in his garden, & brought a sweet & dewy rose to a sick daughter. Then he went to his study to begin his morning work but was taken with giddiness & fell & became unconscious. He lived almost an hour & then his spirit departed to God, very peacefully & his busy earthly life was finished." The doctor attributed his death to overwork, a view reflected in Grace's conclusion: "Like the Good Shepherd, he had given his life for his sheep." He was buried in the cemetery of St. James's Church, Bath, with the following inscription on his tombstone:

> The Law of Truth was in his mouth,
> And iniquity was not found in his life:
> He walked with God in peace and equity,
> And did turn many away from iniquity.

There is an interesting postscript to the story of William Jay Bolton in the discovery of his sketches now at the Archives of the Episcopal Diocese of Long Island, and the armorial windows installed at King's College Chapel. In 1906, Dr. Robert C. Dickinson, a physician, member of the Holy Trinity, Brooklyn, congregation, and admirer of Bolton art, traveled to England in search of Jay's descendants, guided by Pelham cousins. On Endless Street in Salisbury he found Margaretta Grace Bolton and her older half-sister Susannah, the two having moved there sometime after their father's death. They knew nothing of his work in stained glass, but remembered "two big boxes labelled 'glass' " in the attic, which, when opened, revealed the sketches along with the armorials and several King's Chapel fragments that Jay had rescued from the Hedgeland restorations. After telling the daughters about the windows in Brooklyn, Dr. Dickinson was given the sketches to take back to Holy Trinity. But the good doctor was not only a bearer of exciting information about the father, he was also effective in helping Grace, who had taken to her bed for three years after a bad fall. Knowing that her problem resulted mostly from anxiety, Dr. Dickinson prescribed a regimen of mild exercise, and within three months Grace was able to journey to the United States and walk up the aisle of Holy Trinity to admire the windows designed and made by her father. When Dr. Dickinson returned to Salisbury, at an unspecified date, Grace "was tricycling up [the] gentle hillsides."[178]

In a letter dated 15 December 1924 to Dr. Dickinson, she recounts her visit of that year with Dean Milner-White of King's Chapel, the return of the King's glass fragments, and the gift of her father's copies of sixteenth-century King's and Eton College armorials to the chapel.[179] Later, perhaps as late as the early 1930s, after reading Roscoe Brown's 1922 account of the Holy Trinity windows, Grace Bolton wrote a reminiscence of her father, the

"Notes," which is one of the most valuable documents for his life. This biography was probably written at the request of Dean Milner-White, who quotes from it directly in his article on Jay Bolton, and among whose papers it is kept in the King's College Library. Her great-nephew, Reginald Pelham Bolton, reported that he too "is indebted [to her] for much detailed information regarding her accomplished father," but nothing of her communications with him is documented.[180]

Grace's letter of 8 February 1907 to the National Academy of Design, mentioned earlier, states that many of her father's paintings are in her possession.[181] This encourages the hope that some of these may yet come to light. In the "Notes" she remarks, "He did a good deal of glass for various churches but we have no record of them."[182] She probably refers to the American windows, for by the time she wrote the "Notes," she knew of the Priory and Brooklyn windows from Dr. Dickinson and through Roscoe Brown's book on Holy Trinity.[183] She probably made inquiries of Constable's in Cambridge, and may have learned of additional projects by her father; she certainly found out about his sketches and cartoons that burned in the fire there. It is thus possible that there are Bolton paintings and drawings, and one or more Bolton windows in England, that remain to be discovered.

2

Ideas and Techniques

William Jay Bolton's views on life and art were formed by two potent forces in the nineteenth century, Evangelical Christianity and artistic eclecticism. These views can be known not only through his work in art and as a clergyman but also in his published and unpublished writings. His poetry and religious tracts are not significant as either literature or theology, but can be studied for their contribution to his biography and to an exposition of his thought. Bolton's essays and comments on art, however, are informative documents for the history of stained glass, and as expressions of an artist in the forefront of developments in his medium. A list of Bolton's complete extant writings appears in the Bibliography.

As described in the previous chapter, Jay Bolton was raised in a happy and devoutly religious home. His parents loved and respected their children, and the children were devoted to their parents. Scripture was read and discussed regularly, and the teachings of Christianity were practiced at all times. There was always consideration for others, especially the poor and those in trouble or pain; it was as though the whole community were part of the Bolton family. The Bolton children learned a faith relatively free of intellectual complexities, but rich in instruction for daily life.[1] For Evangelical Christians, salvation could be achieved through faith alone, and it sufficed to love God and one's neighbor, accept the truth revealed through Scripture, and acknowledge one's salvation through Christ as expressed in the sacraments of Baptism and Holy Communion. The very simplicity of their views set the Boltons emphatically against the other great segment of the Anglican and American Episcopal churches. The High Church or Ritualist movement began with the Oxford Tractarians, and was based on traditional theology and on sacramental ritualism. High Churchmen considered Evangelicals to be heretics, and Evangelicals hurled the charge of "popery" at the Ritualists. Jay wrote to his brother James, "Don't you become a <u>tall</u> Churchman. High Churchmen are modern Pharisees" (see Appendix A). Such views play a significant role in his stained glass, as well as in his later books and articles.

Jay Bolton's Evangelicalism is expressed in the directness and intensity of his communion with God on the one hand, and in a lack of theological speculation on the other. His Hulsean Prize topic at Cambridge, which was set by the prize committee as *The Evidences of Christianity as Exhibited in the*

34

Ideas and Techniques

Writings of its Apologists Down to Augustine, was a popular motif for university discussions. His response to the topic is a kind of latter-day collection of *sententiae,* short commentaries that he described as free from "vexed questions, the sad details of civil strife among Christians, and all the disturbing associations that cling to internal and long-continued controversies," and that disavowed an exaltation of the Church Fathers as "authorities coequal with the word of God." The Church of England, he says, is based on the premise that Scripture contains everything necessary for salvation, as stated in the Articles of Faith of the Book of Common Prayer.[2] In seven chapters, entitled "The Argument from Antecedent Probability," ". . . from Antiquity," ". . . from Prophecy," ". . . from Miracles," ". . . from Reasonableness of Doctrine," ". . . from Superior Morality," and ". . . from the Success of the Gospel," he cites the Early Christian Fathers to show in their writings the confirmation, not the rationalization, of scriptural doctrine. In his sixth chapter the Evangelical's practical approach to religion is summed up in a statement that Christianity, unlike other religions, can "make people better and happier." He concludes by saying that the ante-Nicene Fathers "occupied true Protestant ground. They clearly saw the practicability, and at the same time the propriety, of proving the truth of Christianity independently, and without the aid of any tradition or unwritten word."[3] By "unwritten word" he means doctrine that is not specifically scriptural. His theological method, if he had such a thing, is exemplified in his exegesis of Romans 4:11 ("And he received the sign of circumcision, a seal of the righteousness of the faith which he had yet being uncircumcised; that he might be the father of all them that believe, though they be not circumcised; that righteousness might be imputed unto them also"), part of a series of passages relating to justification by faith. Bolton's commentary states:

> A *covenant* (not conditional with *us* children of Eves) but *confirmed* before of God in Christ. The law 430 years after could not disunite, & though it were a *man's* covenant, says Paul, yet if it be *confirmed,* no man addeth or disunites. How much more with God. We are (having faith), & we ought to be proud of it, real children of Abraham & free *and* well as only those Jews who walk in the steps of faithful Abraham.[4]

In other words, gentiles were also promised salvation through the covenant of Abraham, and by faith alone they may walk in the prophet's steps. Jay's is a simple theology based entirely on a literal reading of and an unquestioning belief in Holy Scripture.

To such a man it would be important that sacred art be just as uncluttered and direct in meaning. In the letter noted earlier to Mr. Harison of

Stained Glass Art
of William Jay Bolton

Trinity Church, Bolton says that a proper iconographic program for a large stained glass window would be "a simple, energetic, & natural series of Scripture stories." The culmination of this program might be an "Ascension," because it would afford "so many noble & varied figures" and be "the best subject for a mother Church whose clergy claim a succession from those [the Apostles] who beheld & witness'd to the Lord Jesus <u>Christ</u> all the time." The "Ascension" or a "Crucifixion" would be "a last act, a piece that carries you on from Earth to Heaven." Probably recalling the great biblical windows of King's Chapel, he says that "in the olden time" stained glass windows served to teach Scripture history, and as proper subjects he advocates "those blessed stories we first heard from our mother's tongue & on our mother's knee."

Despite the importance of religion in Bolton's life, his secular writings are more revealing of the man than are his theological discourses, and they are more interesting as cultural history. They include the poems from *The Harp of Pelham,* his biography of his parents, and two articles on art. Not surprisingly, his descriptive writing displays all the effusiveness of a late Romantic. In the letter fragment on the reverse side of the *Castor and Pollux* watercolor, he recalls a rainstorm that occurred during a post-coach trip through the Italian mountains, probably the Apennines:

> [r]ain had just fallen, it was indeed a beautiful vale of tears . . . clouds rose and soon stretched over the hills & over the Heavens, borne on the wings of the wind, they partially obscure the sun who now only shines on the distant landscape. The trees sigh, the brooks murmur with greater distinctness, & the big drops fall, but tis only the edge of the cloud. It will soon be over—a gust comes, the rain follows. The postillions throw sheepskin cloaks over their braided dress of green and red, & the wheels soon throw up mud. Tis gone, blue sky over our heads, the landscape washed glistens in the sunshine, the birds universally strike up a song of joy and my heart resounds though it be a silent verse.[5]

In the letter of 1845 to James he wrote an equally Romantic, though slightly rustic, paean to spring at the Priory: "Oh! that April & her sister May! We even now have fine weather, quite open & mild. The Sound clear, the sun shining, the blue birds & song-sparrows out on their honeymoons, the brooks full and flowing with that <u>gush</u> that goes to your heart & the skunk cabbage swelling." Bolton's poetry can be even more colorful. His daughter describes it correctly when she states that his verses are "unequal, but often very beautiful in thought & always correct in rhyme & scanning."[6] At worst they can be doggerel, as in a poem called "The Evening Dew":

> So sad a thing is sin,
> That if yourself should view
> Eve's silver ewer within
> 'Twould taint the drops of dew.
>
> And so at twilight hour,
> Eve wanders in the wood
> And washes every flower,
> And christens every bud.
>
> But if a foot pass by,
> She hides herself and cruet;
> And this is therefore why
> We never see her do it.[7]

In "The Mourner and the Mourned," however, he shows a sensitivity to both the subject and the language:

> Gentle strangers! which would ye,
> The *mourner* or the *mourned* be?
> Softly, very softly, tread,
>   Round us are
> Those who slumber with the dead,
>   Happier far.
> Sorrow is the one of two,
> See her sit beneath the yew,
> One above, and one below,
> Cruel Earth to part them so.[8]

Jay's sister Abby had not yet died, and the two people described in the poem, one dead, the other mourning, were probably born of his Romantic imagination. In *The Harp of Pelham* he included three of his own long poems written in the medieval romance genre, "Ronan and Ella," "Lady Mellent—A Ballad," and "The Abbot of Reading."[9] Their lines flow nicely and are full of castles, abbeys, crusading knights, and ladies in distress. In "Ronan and Ella," for example, the knight Ronan loves beneath his station, and in consequence is taken crusading by his father. Ella waits for him, but upon hearing that he has been killed, she enters a convent and dies of sorrow. As her funeral cortege is passing along the road, Ronan returns unharmed. In grief he goes to his castle, which is struck by lightning. He is killed, and everything is destroyed except the tower from which he first heard Ella sing. It is easy to imagine Jay reading such poems to the family assembled before a roaring fire in the Priory Armory, surrounded by suits of armor and medieval-revival furnishings.

In other poems by Jay Bolton in *The Harp of Pelham* the reader notes a typically Victorian eclecticism. A poetic description of his journey through the vale of Chamonix, a favorite haunt of nineteenth-century "gothicists," refers frequently to eastern and ancient classical literature.[10] Like many educated people of his day, Bolton had learned Greek, and his daughter Grace reported that in later life it was his custom to read the Greek New Testament every morning. He even used the Greek names for Christ's ancestors in the Jesse Tree at Holy Trinity. Moreover, the "Cinque Cento" style he favored in stained glass is replete with classical references in both style and motif.

The real poet of the Bolton family, however, was James, whose witty verses on animals, katydids, and young lovers vie with more serious poems. In "A Catastrophe - or, an Epitaph on a Cat," he writes,

> Here lies a member of the *mews*;
> A title none will dare refuse,
> Who once has heard the midnight squalling
> Known among men as *cat*-erwauling.
> To put her virtue into rhymes,
> Would be a *cat*-alogue of crimes,
> And yet, to say she'd none at all,
> Would be too *cat*-egorical.[11]

He could at times, however, be a serious lyricist, as in "The Sweetest and the Saddest," a poem about the arts:

> Alas! that all the sweetest things
> Which man has ever said or sung,
> Have issued from desponding wings,
> And from an unintentional tongue.[12]

It is no wonder that James seems to have been Jay's favorite brother, the one to whom Jay described his artistic struggles in 1845, and whom he nursed through smallpox eleven years later.

In Jay's earlier comments on art, that is, in the letters to James and Harison, and his article on the King's Chapel glass, it is interesting that he discusses art without discussing religion, probably not by design, but because his commitment to each in these years, 1844 to 1855, was still more or less separate. Later, in the article of 1872, his comments on architecture

Ideas and Techniques

---

are closely linked to his religious views, as the title indicates, not only because of his many years as a priest, but more interestingly because his arguments address the continuing and widespread controversies over the architectural style that is most appropriate to the needs of Anglican worship. His purpose here is not to take sides, but to define the principles that determine the suitability of a style.

He begins the 1872 piece by criticizing the main trends of his day in Gothic Revival design. Most champions of Gothic, including both John Ruskin and A. W. N. Pugin, viewed the Gothic style as a superficial and purely visual array of pointed arches, gables, vaulted ceilings, and buttresses. Bolton too had no conception of the internal structures of Gothic architecture, and defined it purely in visual terms. Perhaps the most important spokesman for the style was Ruskin, for whom the Gothic was above all ornamental: "[I]n the most characteristic [Gothic] buildings a certain portion of their effect depends upon accumulation of ornament; and many of those which have most influence on the minds of men, have attained it by means of this attribute alone." Ruskin believed that architecture of simple design is of lesser artistic value, and can have the effect of being "haughty."[13] Bolton reacts against this proliferation of ornament on and in churches, attributing the increasing elaboration to the influence of the Tractarians and the Ecclesiologists. He believes that the architects of his day are "extravagant in esthetics and mediaevalism, [threatening] to sweep away all distinctions between the Anglican and Papal Churches," and urges a "New Testament simplicity."[14] Nevertheless, Bolton praises the manner in which Ruskin related architecture to nature, and calls him a "master-mind, to whose enthusiastic and highly moral reflections we owe so much of late."[15] Jay does not mention either the architecture or the ornamental designs by Pugin, but he surely would have disapproved of Pugin's ornate Gothic interiors and, considerably more, of his conversion to Roman Catholicism.

For Bolton the use of Gothic style for churches was justified not by Ruskin's search for beauty or Pugin's for a purity of ecclesiastical design, or even by an assumption that Gothic was a style of English invention. Rather, the pragmatist in him concluded that styles result from the demands of geography and climate, and that these were the proper determinants of an architecture appropriate to a given place.[16] He notes that when architect and public clash over the propriety of a design, the public is more often correct "because the laity are guided by instinct, common sense, and broad national tendencies, to which this question rather belongs."[17] Thus he attributes the development of stained glass windows to climatic demands in northern Europe. In "those countries where architecture was born," that is,

Greece and Rome, windows were kept small in order to reduce the sunlight admitted. Even today, he says, windows in the south, even if large, are designed to admit air, not light. In the north, where long winters bring short days, it is important to have large windows designed to admit light, and it was here that the Gothic style, best characterized by its large windows, was developed. At first, northern windows were high and narrow with wide embrasures, he explains, but the use of glass made it possible for the Gothic window to grow in width as well as height.[18] Thus, climate explains "the history of architecture, giving us the laws of architecture, and deciding our national architecture."[19] Bolton was by no means alone in such views, but one of a number of nineteenth-century theorists who subscribed to the idea of climate as a determining force in the development of styles, a concept that prefigures the functionalism of the next century.[20]

In the 1855 paper on the King's Chapel windows he also notes the increasing amounts of white glass used in English stained glass windows, and suggests that "the art [of stained glass] was imported (say during the sixth or seventh centuries) from southern countries, whence it came glowing with colour suited to the richness of those skies, and necessary to obscure some of their light."[21] The rich color was "soon found inappropriate and inconvenient here" because of the cold and the relative lack of sunlight, and more and more white glass was introduced until it predominated.[22] His observation of the changes that occur in later medieval stained glass are correct: late medieval windows often have vast amounts of white glass. Even the reasons he gives, based on climate differences, have some validity, but they ignore the influence of both aesthetic evolution from medieval to Renaissance and improvements in glass technology on the changing character of designs and color choice. Such matters, however, are outside the scope of this book. Bolton writes that he first grasped the role of climate in determining style during his travels, but whether on the 1841 voyage or the trip following his first wife's death is not specified.[23] It is more likely the latter, for in his Brooklyn windows of 1844 to 1848, which are for a cold climate, the richness of the color even increased as the work proceeded.

If proper design and style derive from the requirements of place, then it follows that one is not limited to a particular canon of design, a view that provided a perfect justification for Bolton's eclecticism. Addressing a matter much discussed in his day, he states that no one can invent a proper Victorian style in architecture, for people do not invent styles: "It is the Providence of God in local arrangements that settles these matters in principle, and it is ours only truly and appropriately to carry them out. . . . [T]he human art

Ideas and Techniques

could not be but for the materials and their adaptations according to circumstances."[24] Bolton further promotes eclecticism in addressing another controversial issue, that of the numerous and often destructive "restorations" being carried out at the time, many by the Ritualists of Cambridge. He decries efforts to destroy the Renaissance classicism of Wren's St. Paul's Cathedral and "restore" the building to its original Gothic. Those in favor of the restoration, he states, "try to force their narrow views upon us—injuring the works of past ages under the plea of restoring them, and slavishly repeating the systems long since discarded."[25] Obviously he had no problem with classical and medieval elements existing side by side in a design. For Bolton, Wren's building was predominantly classical, but was given medieval features by "its painted glass, which never belonged to the classical styles." St. Paul's is, "like most of our public buildings built during the two past centuries, a mixture, or compromise."[26] His only requirement, apart from suitability to the climate, would be that the various parts have functional meaning, for he deplores such things as battlements on a villa or summerhouse, funerary urns as decoration on domestic houses, and gargoyles that do not serve to lead water off a building.[27] Here he risks criticizing the family's Pelham home, with its towers and battlements, and sounds rather like Pugin, who required that a building and its materials be what they appear to be.

In stained glass as in architecture Bolton believes in combining what he considers the best of the medieval styles with whatever else is beautiful and suitable, which in most instances means elements of the Renaissance. The medieval he preferred is the late medieval of northern Europe, which exhibits the impact of the Italian Renaissance. That Bolton as a stained glass artist is nevertheless fundamentally a medievalist is apparent in his article on the King's Chapel windows, which praises the clarity of the potmetal colors and the way in which the leading is harmonized with the design. It is also clear in the letter to Mr. Harison: "[The windows] must be leaded up to suit outlines, folds &c. All the strengthening bars, horizontal or vertical, & every line of lead will melt away at a proper distance, or only serve to distinguish & strengthen the design as well as the colors. This is no uncertain theory, but an actual effect, sought & produced, in all fine windows." He goes on to say that "there is that about pot metals which if in a window, will make it unlike any thing else in the world, a unique & glorious thing." His windows at Pelham, Holy Trinity, and West Lynn are clear demonstrations of these ideas. On the other hand, and surprisingly, Bolton urges the use of glass that is made commercially. He notes that manufacturers have been successful in bringing a "cathedral tint" (a slight yellowing of white glass) to their product, which harmonizes well with old glass:

> But for myself (if I may be allowed to offer an opinion) I believe we shall eventually come to the glass of commerce—the glass of the day. We ought, indeed, only to be too thankful that it is so pure and good as it is; and I feel persuaded that we shall be doing better by giving attention to the essential principles of the art, than to the recovery of this or that tint, which our ancestors were constantly changing, and always—it appears to me—with the hope and determination of getting rid of it altogether.[28]

Here Bolton differs markedly from his famous contemporary in the stained glass revival, Charles Winston, who worked diligently to recover the particular color tones and textural irregularities produced by the medieval method of glass making.[29] Winston believed that true medieval glass was visually more alive than modern glass, and that materials resembling the medieval ones would aid artists in the creation of a new stained glass art based on the medieval.[30]

Unfortunately, Bolton left only an incomplete picture of his procedures for making stained glass windows.[31] He appears to have learned the craft mostly on his own, although for such special techniques as matting, silver staining, and complex leading he may have observed work in stained glass studios during his 1841 trip to Europe, or in the few New York studios mentioned earlier. In making a window he seems to have begun with a small drawing or watercolor, of which several remain for Holy Trinity and for unexecuted or otherwise unknown windows (e.g., figs. 11b, 13). These little preparatory pieces may have been both model for the cartoon and *vidimus* for the patron or architect, although no initials or signatures of approval appear on any; the glass designs he exhibited at the National Academy bear only his own signature. "In his attic room in Pelham Priory WJB made his designs," says his daughter Grace, referring probably to the cartoons.[32] Jay notes in the Harison letter that he built his own kiln, undoubtedly a woodburner, for a cost of $15. In the same letter he notes that he can do his own production work:

> I cut the glass, lead it up, paint it & burn myself here [in Pelham], & find no difficulty. . . . This very Evening I have turn'd out a muffle [kiln] full of excellent burnt pieces. . . . I do not give you this detail to suppose that I would offer to act the practical myself. Others doubtless could do it better & my time would me [=be] more important to me, but to warn you against ignorant or designing person[s].

Ideas and Techniques

The last two sentences are intended to assure Harison of Bolton's knowledge of each step in the stained glass process. They suggest, however, that his Pelham assistants, John Bolton and Thomas Denton, also participated frequently in production.

Some of Bolton's processes in making stained glass windows can be determined from a study of his windows and of extant sketches and watercolors.[33] Only one cartoon fragment is known (fig. 64; Catalog, IX, 11k), but from the repetition of figures in the Jesse Tree at Holy Trinity and in the heads of lights at Holy Apostles (see Catalog III, aisles; IV, all Bolton windows), it is clear that he did prepare cartoons, at least for some of the windows, and most likely all of them. He probably used templates, in the European manner, for cutting the individual pieces of glass.[34] Because modern cutting wheels were not yet invented, Bolton must have cut his glass in the traditional, medieval way, by drawing a hot iron rod along the cut lines to cause tiny cracks that would give when pressure was applied. When the excess was tapped off, however, he would undoubtedly have used a pair of grozing pliers, not the medieval grozing iron, to trim the edges.[35] The reckoning of costs for his Pelham window includes the purchase of leads, indicating that he did not have to make his own. Access to commercially produced leads, as well as potmetal (i.e., colored) glass, enamel pigments (and presumably also stains), obviated for Bolton a number of the more tedious steps of the medieval craft of stained glass, and contributed to his ability, remarked upon in recent times, to produce a great many windows in a short space of time. Other facilitating devices are discussed later.

From the letter to Mr. Harison it is known that for his Pelham altar window Bolton obtained the glass, but probably only the potmetal, from Germany. The potmetal for Holy Trinity and for Holy Apostles is similar to that at Pelham in both quality and tone, and the likelihood is strong that the two later churches were also glazed with German glass. In any case, Bolton's palette of potmetal colors was limited.[36] At Pelham it consisted of only a ruby, deep purple, dark blue, and an uneven olive green (colorplate I); at Holy Trinity, emerald and yellowish green, bright pink, and murrey were added (colorplates III–VII).[37] For all his loyalty to the medieval method, Bolton employed a few enamel colors to increase his color range, and especially to create special landscape effects. At Christ Church, Pelham, the Virgin wears a blouse of pink enamel, and there are a few small passages in red enamel and small amounts of black and light blue in the armorials; these are the only enamels used there. At Holy Trinity he frequently used small strokes of light blue and pink enamel to enhance the soil and rocks in the landscape, and green enamel for the sea in *Christ Stills the Tempest*. Blue,

pink, and yellow-green enamels are sometimes used for clothing: blue on
the tunic of the man to the left of Christ in *Raising of Lazarus,* pink on the
cloak beneath the same man's feet (fig. 34), and yellow-green on Abraham in
Sacrifice of Isaac (fig. 15).[38]

Bolton employed silver stain extensively, beginning with the Priory
armorials, and culminating in the wonderfully decorative effects of the
bright yellows at Holy Trinity and at West Lynn. He had several different
tones of stain, including pale and medium yellow, pale and deep orange. At
Holy Trinity a new stain is added, an unusual russet red.[39] It is used for hair,
for clothing, and for shoes; examples are the hair of the man who holds a
cloak before the donkey in *Christ Enters Jerusalem,* the cloaks of the two
older men in *Christ at the Well,* and what appears to be a hippopotamus in
the *Finding of Moses* (figs. 31a, 29b, 19a). A similar red stain may have been
used by the eighteenth-century English glazier William Peckitt, who, in an
unpublished treatise, described the making of red stain.[40] Jay never mentions the making of any colors himself, and the purchase of "Enamel colors,
&c," mentioned in the Harison letter, probably included stains. Whatever
the source of the stains, Bolton appears to have learned fairly quickly to
control their use, producing an evenness and consistency of tone. Stains in
the Christ Church windows are already, for the most part, of even tone.
One of Jay's grisaille windows there (N5), however, seems to be composed
of pieces in which the tones vary considerably. The pieces might have been
rejected from other windows and used in this one as time ran short for
completion of the series; other shortcuts used at Christ Church are discussed in the Catalog. At Holy Trinity there are a number of intentional
changes in the gradations of tone. For example, in the tower window, now
at the Metropolitan Museum in New York, the silver stain is made to
resemble marble in the panels holding the figures' names (fig. 45).[41] Bolton
stained all manner of objects in a design, from hair, clothing decoration, and
metallic objects to rocks and flowers in the landscape. The lively yellows
and oranges play an important role in the brilliant color harmonies of
Bolton windows.[42]

One of the most interesting technical passages in Bolton's article on the
King's glass concerns the flesh tints for human figures. He observes that
they are

> stained with iron, which allows of its being transparent also, another
> point not to be overlooked in pictorial glass-work; for . . . the flesh . . .
> is a sort of key-note to the whole: if this is dulled with enamels of any
> kind, the entire window has to be dulled too. Thus the glass is shorn of

Ideas and Techniques

---

its glory, its brightness, its first essential property [which is] for the admission of *light*.[43]

In a note Bolton says that three or four years earlier he had succeeded, after much experimentation, "in recovering the cinque-cento flesh stain," which enabled the glass painter to dispense with any sort of flux. From what he says of the King's flesh tones, that they are "stained with iron" and not dulled with enamels, it seems that his paint was some sort of iron stain.[44] A warm, pinkish color appears in the flesh tones at Holy Trinity, beginning even in the Jesse Tree, where it is used inconsistently. In windows such as the *Raising of Lazarus* and *The Crucifixion* where there is intense deterioration of paint, a pinkish cast remains, reinforcing the idea that the tint was a stain of some sort. Bolton provides no further details on his flesh tint, but goes on to say "that Mr. Winston fully approves of it."[45] During discussions following the presentation of his paper to the Section of Antiquities in Cambridge, Bolton commented that one of the faults of modern glazing was the placement of tinted glass where white glass should be, his mind obviously on the brilliant effects of the white glass at King's.[46] It was only at West Lynn that he made full use of white glass as a compositional color.

The Bolton production technique that is best recorded is that for matting and shading. In discussing the King's Chapel windows, Jay states that the glass is "all perfectly transparent" and that stipple-shading is used so that shadows will be "made as diaphanous as possible." These are qualities, he says, of old glass. "It remained for later times to think of obscuring glass with enamels or dirt."[47] At Pelham, he used only badgered matts, but in the vestibule and aisle windows at Holy Trinity, which were apparently the first to be installed, he and John introduced stippling, primarily for the delicate areas of the faces; they increased the use of it as they proceeded. They often added stippled and smeared shadows on top of stroked matt to enhance certain contours, and these, with outlining added for arms and legs, are the areas where so much deterioration has occurred.[48] When the overpaint flakes, it tends to take the matt with it, leaving only the outlines of forms. If well-fired, however, the stippling has a refined appearance, especially when used to make facial shadows (figs. 29a, 55). In the Priory armorials, there are numerous crudities in handling both matt and trace paint, underscoring the experimental nature of these windows. With the Christ Church windows, completed by about 1843, such awkward techniques have all but disappeared.[49] From the Pelham *Adoration of the Magi* to the gallery windows at Holy Trinity and the altar window at West Lynn, Jay's working of matt became increasingly skillful and is generally finer and more subtle than John's. Already in the south clerestory at Holy Trinity, there are great refinements of shading, such as that in *Joshua Stills the Sun and Moon* (fig. 22), which are further enhanced in the gallery windows (fig. 29a) and at Holy Apostles (colorplate VIII) and West Lynn (fig. 55).

On the south side at Holy Trinity, in both gallery and clerestory, Bolton laid on extra-heavy matt, undoubtedly to control the bright sunlight that even today, despite surrounding buildings, streams in on that side. The deep shadows and dense painted surfaces of these windows sometimes obscure the details of the scene, as in the *Coronation of David* and the *Reading of Deuteronomy* in the clerestory, and the *Transfiguration* and *The Trial of Christ* in the galleries (figs. 24, 26, 35a, 37). One wonders how Jay might have felt about this heavy painting after renewing his contact with the King's windows.

The Boltons knew several refined techniques developed by late medieval and Renaissance glass painters, among them quilling and stick-lighting, damascening, and abrading. In quilling and stick-lighting, the painter uses a sharp pointed instrument or a stick to remove matt, producing sometimes delicate, fine-lined patterns of light (fig. 1d). Jay used quilling to create exquisitely subtle grounds in some of the armorials at Pelham. Damascened backgrounds consisting of floral patterns painted in trace paint on potmetal or in color on white glass are frequently employed by the Boltons. They often abraded the color on red flashed glass, probably using a wheel, to make the white centers for red roses in traceries at Holy Trinity and in the frames at Holy Apostles, sometimes filling in with silver-stain yellow. Decorative slashes are abraded in the red tunic of the man pouring water in the center foreground of *Marriage at Cana* at Holy Trinity (fig. 30a). Along the man's shoulders silver-stain "braid" has been inserted in the abraded area. The *Marriage at Cana* window is, in effect, a study in Bolton's color techniques: in addition to ruby, blue, purple, pink, and green potmetals and yellow silver-stains, arranged in harmonious combination, there are pink enamels on the garments of several figures, the pourer's hair is done in the russet red stain, and the guitar near him in a deep orange silver-stain.

Modern glaziers express amazement that Jay Bolton was able to produce so many windows in such a short period of time: some sixty major windows in five years, with the help of one brother, a local youth, and on occasion perhaps a sister or another brother, although no family member but John is recorded as helping. The reuse of cartoons at Holy Trinity and at Holy Apostles has already been mentioned as one way in which production was expedited. The use of paintings and prints as models for parts of

Ideas and Techniques

---

compositions in many windows must also have facilitated the process. There is evidence that speed may sometimes have taken precedence over care in the Bolton shop. Although the loss of trace and matt paint from a number of windows, beginning at Pelham, could indicate inferior pigments or wrong amounts of flux, it is more likely that poor firing was the problem, and no one took the time to inspect firings for problem pieces. In so experimental an operation, perhaps Jay and his crew did not even notice the problems.

Another means the Boltons had of reducing production time has only recently been discovered. When the first three bays of Holy Trinity windows were dismounted for restoration, it was learned that the tracery and lancets were slid into a system of double wooden frames with mullions, then nailed and puttied in place. Raw combed cotton padding was stuffed into the spaces between the panels. With this system it was no longer necessary that panels be measured exactly to fit individual openings, and in some instances there is considerable discrepancy between panel and opening measurements.[50] It was a simple system that must have enhanced the speed not only of installation but, because of the latitude in panel measurements, of production as well. As the restoration at Holy Trinity proceeds, more will undoubtedly be learned of the various methods used by Jay Bolton and his assistants in the production of stained glass windows.

3

Style and Pictorial Sources

Bolton's style and compositions derive in part from the Renaissance, but overall his art belongs to the Gothic Revival, and all but one of his glazing programs was made for a building in the Gothic style. His conception of that style is summarized in the following statement:

> [A]ny kind of windowed, storied, sloping roofed building, is essentially Gothic, and essentially not Grecian. You may take a regular classical and Eastern building, and by lopping off all that is peculiar and necessary for its existence in a hot climate—its exterior verandah or portico, its columns, its cupola, its flat roof, its latticed kiosk—and in their place put the serial window . . . , the chimney, the raised roof, and so on, but then it becomes a legitimate Gothic building . . . whether it be a summer house, a railway station, a gas work, an asylum, or a cathedral.[1]

He goes on to say that the "serial" window, that is, a large stained glass window or group of windows with related designs, such as the one he had suggested for Trinity Church, Manhattan, was essential to the style. Because of such windows the buttress became necessary "as a support for the weakened wall," which led to the "finials and turrets, and all the beautiful but rather barbaric display of flying buttresses and minarets, so common in some Gothic cathedrals."[2] His aversion to overabundant architectural detail, noted also in the previous chapter, is consistent with the simplicity he advocated in religious thought and practice.

Bolton's concept of good design was directed not by artistic theory or archeological truth, but by the eye and the heart. Like John Ruskin in *The Stones of Venice,* he defines Gothic architecture as a collection of surface details, both classical and medieval. In the same way his stained glass demonstrates an almost carefree assemblage of stylistic elements. Along with many of his nineteenth-century contemporaries, Bolton adored the Italian Renaissance, especially the art of Raphael. Yet national pride aroused in him, as it did in so many Romantics, a need to promote the arts that were indigenous to his homeland. One of the charming features of the Gothic Revival in Europe is that each country, in its nationalistic fervor, thought that the Gothic style was its own invention, so Bolton could look at a

48

Style and Pictorial Sources

traditional English parish church or rural dwelling and exclaim, "that is Gothic, because English!"[3] Because his conception of Gothic style was dictated not by rules, but by taste, in a single work of art he could cheerfully combine what he knew of the Gothic with elements of that other style that so greatly pleased him, the Italian Renaissance. This eclecticism could be justified in his mind, as in the minds of many of his contemporaries, solely on the grounds of Beauty, a quality rendered virtuous by its mixture of Gothic spirituality and Renaissance grace.

In his art lessons at Mill Hill, Jay was probably taught to draw in the classical manner. Unfortunately, nothing of this childhood work survives, but an appreciable degree of classicism marks all his later work, especially his treatment of the human figure. The first extant drawing is the Bath cityscape made when he was eighteen, and it is probably significant that he went early in the morning to make the various sections of the drawing in order to avoid the haze created by cookfires across the city. Consequently not a wisp of Romantic smoke or cloud mars the clarity of his presentation (fig. 60). The only hint of Romanticism is the picturesque fence and vegetation of the foreground. Nothing is known of the circumstances in which Bolton undertook to make the drawing of Bath. It may have been intended for use in a topographic engraving, which would have required precision such as this.

Bolton's training in New York was thoroughly academic, as reflected in the baroque treatment of light and shadow in his portraits. Only four of the reportedly numerous family portraits he painted are presently known, three of those self-portraits. The earliest are the oil he did of himself for the National Academy of Design and a pencil drawing that was probably a study for this painting (frontispiece; fig. 61). Both show in three-quarter view a rather self-possessed young man in his early twenties, his blue eyes looking confidently from beneath slightly tousled, dark hair. In each work the face is fully illuminated. In a later self-portrait in clerical collar, from about 1853 or 1854, stronger shadows have replaced the more lucid tones of the earlier pictures, covering one side of the face and defining a hollow in the cheek and a furrow between the eyebrows (fig. 2c). The head now tilts slightly downward, a lock of hair hangs limply on the forehead, and the eye is moist. This small but compelling portrait undoubtedly expresses Bolton's anguish over the recent deaths in his family, and ranks among his best and most Romantic works. The portrait of his sister Abby, known only in an engraving, is almost as fine. It stands between the two self-portraits in oil, and may have been done as late as 1848, during her last visit to England before she died in 1849 at age twenty-two (fig. 62). It is more assured than the first self-portrait, but less poetic than the second. As though in conver-

sation, the young sitter turns her head to one side and touches her left hand
to the scarf at her neck. The graceful beauty of this portrait recalls paintings
by the two major artists whom Jay knew personally, his National Academy
teacher Samuel F. B. Morse, in such works as the portrait of the artist's first
wife, Lucretia Walker; and family friend William Etty, especially in the
informal portraits of Jay's mother and aunt as young women.[4]

Bolton's academic training is equally apparent in a small, undated
watercolor of a combat subject, perhaps St. Michael and the Devil (Rev.
12:7–9), which is the only other significant work by him not related to
stained glass (fig. 63). The two heroic figures exhibit classical formalities of
pose and modeling, and the harsh, rocky setting, the irregular, constricted
spaces, and the strong contrasts of light and shadow create a "Gothic"
environment. The warrior on the left stepping forward with both knees
bent derives probably from a figure in Raphael's *Entombment* (Rome,
Borghese Gallery), and is a type seen in several Bolton windows (e.g., fig.
12). The small rabbit at the lower left, scurrying away from the scene, is one
of many apparently extraneous landscape details that Bolton liked to include
in his designs. They are visual expressions of the trees, brooks, birds, and
small animals of which he writes so fondly in both his poetry and his prose.
The combat drawing also reveals a basic weakness in his draughtsmanship,
for the figures appear stiff, their actions frozen. In his oil paintings and his
stained glass this stiffness is mitigated by the softening effect of the one
medium and the absolute rigidity of the other.

Most of Jay Bolton's sketches preserved in the Long Island Diocese
Archives are related in one way or another to stained glass. Many of them
are for Holy Trinity windows. Another large group consists of pencil
sketches or watercolors of King's College Chapel glass, often of details, and
some with notations about and drawings of the armature (fig. 70). They
were done almost surely while Jay was a restorer at King's in 1848–49.

In order to understand his style in stained glass, it is important to see
the role that the sixteenth-century windows of King's Chapel played in his
visual thinking, both before and after his return to England. He viewed
them as "painted at a period when the 'Ars Vitraria' had attained its
perfection, that is to say, when it exhibited grand and instructive designs
without tampering with the nature of any of its materials . . . the latest
example of a style of glass, ere the degeneracy or rather eclipse com-
menced." It is a "free and pictorial" style produced by artists who

laid aside the older and more conventional styles. . . . Refreshed from
the fountains which Michael Angelo and Raffaelle had just opened to the

Style and Pictorial Sources

---

world, they approached their material with . . . [hands that] seem to have forgotten the trammels of lead and of arming, and to have swept over the glass with grand and flowing lines, that can scarcely be outdone, and every bold contrast of colour and composition.[5]

The English, German, and Flemish artists who designed the King's windows transformed their Renaissance models, by intensified compositional and color rhythms, into a northern style that harmonizes with the ever-multiplying ribs and mullions of the late Gothic architecture.[6] This is the "Cinque Cento" style extolled by Charles Winston as representing the finest period of glass painting. Windows in this style, says Winston, display "the most gorgeous effects of colour, and the greatest contrasts of light and shade that have hitherto been attained in painted glass without sacrificing the transparency of the material, whilst they often possess at the same time considerable merit both in their drawing and composition."[7] Winston disliked early medieval styles, which art historians and glaziers today often prefer, saying that the figures are flat and stiff, and the pictures so small that they are illegible at a distance.[8] Bolton's stained glass art, already formed by the time Winston's book appeared in 1847, is in agreement with Winston's negative attitude toward older medieval glass. Jay makes his views explicit later, in the article on the King's windows, when he discusses the grid effect of supporting iron bars in stained glass, and notes that "in older glass, [the bars] may be mentioned as an apology for stiff necks and other contortions [in the figures]."[9]

Both Winston and Bolton, like many art theorists and commentators of the period, urged an "art for our time," which Winston assumed would reflect late medieval art and derive from the English Perpendicular Gothic, which he dated from 1380 to 1530, and of course from the "Cinque Cento."[10] Bolton concurs in his King's article of 1855:

> [W]e see the folly of going back to ancient times, when circumstances were so different, and taking thence, in too slavish a manner, our model, either of architecture, or of any of its parts.
>
> Eternal principles of taste of course there are, and principles based upon climate, materials, and habits, equally binding; but their application should ever be left to the independent impulses of genius, under the direction of present exigences.[11]

In the article of 1872 he is more direct:

> We cannot go back to the 13th or 14th centuries for anything, and we need not. Those days are gone, with their law, and literature, their

costumes [i.e., customs], and language, and failures. We want something fresh, varied, and adapted to our times. . . . If Gothic we must have, let it be an enlightened, progressive, 19th-century Gothic . . . when we possess better materials, a less superstitious religion, and a more cheerful taste, with all the experience and examples of the past to guide and correct.[12]

Although this last statement appears in 1872, it could be a comment on Bolton's approach to stained glass as early as the Pelham *Magi* window. It is the statement of an optimistic pragmatist who was eclectic enough to defend Wren's St. Paul's Cathedral as an English church Gothicized by its height, its stained glass, its carved woods, and its exterior pilasters.[13]

Jay Bolton's first windows are among the armorials for the Pelham Priory, most of which are based on late medieval drawings of family arms copied by his older brother Robert from sixteenth-century manuscripts in the British Library.[14] The Priory armorials are done in potmetal glass, silver stain, and a few enamels, with the shields often set on grisaille patterns of a late thirteenth-century type (fig. 1c). Only the execution of the armorials in the south tower can be assigned to a particular hand, that of Jay Bolton. The shields appear on quilled and damascened grounds and are surrounded by delicately hatched leaves (fig. 1d). As mentioned earlier, the tower may have been an addition, and these armorials later than others in the house. The damascene on the outer, blue ground is identical with that in the *Agnus Dei* oculus window in Christ Church, which is attributed to Jay by his brother Winter. A Schuyler family armorial similar to the tower windows in all respects except the heraldic charge is owned by Francis T. Chambers of county Mayo, Ireland, a descendant of John Bolton and his wife, Katherine Schuyler;[16] it too may be by Jay Bolton.

Jay's authorship of the *Adoration of the Magi* window in the family church at Pelham is confirmed not only by style but also by the testimony of Winter Bolton.[17] It is here that Jay's personal style is first clearly defined in stained glass (colorplate I). The figures are large and naturalistic in the "Cinque Cento" manner, and are placed in an illusionistic spatial context, although the space is more confined here than it will be at Holy Trinity, to suit the scale of the little country church. It is typical of Bolton that his design paraphrases rather than copies its probable Renaissance model, noted later. Charles Winston would have approved both the model and its transformation for use at Christ Church. He felt that stained glass designs should suit the architecture, and when he described one of several "modernisations" of medieval glass design for a small church in early medieval style, he could be describing the Pelham window:

Style and Pictorial Sources

> [One may] occupy the whole, or some part of the window with a group
> of large figures. The last arrangement, though it may be unsupported by
> any ancient authority, would in skillful hands, be unobjectionable in a
> glass painting avowedly of the nineteenth century. . . . I presume that the
> artist would consider it proper to impart to his figures . . . that grand,
> severe, and classical character, borrowed from the Antique, which belongs
> to the figures in the glass paintings of the Early English style; without
> however imitating their rudeness, or imperfect drawing; and that he
> would select for their execution the deepest and most powerful colours.[18]

Winston would undoubtedly have viewed Bolton's art as conforming to his
ideal of a "new and independent style . . . suited to the exigencies of the
present age."[19]

To judge from Jay Bolton's drawings and other stained glass, all figures
in the Christ Church *Adoration of the Magi* window, except for two replacement or redrawn heads, are his. With their large volumes and rich colors
they are good examples of his "Renaissance" figure types. The tendency to
stiffness noted in his draughtsmanship is obscured here not only by the lead
lines but also by the brilliant colors. At the same time his Renaissance
modeling softens the faces and drapery, giving the figures an appealing
warmth. The faces are rather full, with arching brows over eyes enlivened
with one or two dots of light. The noses are straight and the mouths turn
up slightly at the corners. In his later windows, there is often a feeling for
the individuality of the figure, and as so often in the work of Victorian
artists, it is not difficult to recognize the example of Raphael in Bolton's
figures, not only in the placid faces of the women and the strong charac-
terizations of the older men, but also in the imposing size he gives them all.
The prominent foreshortening in the *Magi* design is somewhat distracting,
and will be more subdued at Holy Trinity, probably because in his later
designs Jay is further along in time from his Italian journey, and thus less
preoccupied with Renaissance devices. In fact, at Holy Trinity he will be
seen as increasingly intent upon integrating the Renaissance and the Gothic
qualities of his art.

Here in the *Magi* window the composition is almost entirely Renaissance, consisting of a triangle with its apex at the Virgin's head, and an
enclosing circle of secondary figures. The scene is illuminated from its
center, from the Christ Child, in the manner of a Renaissance painting well
known in the nineteenth century, Correggio's *Adoration of the Shepherds*
(1522, Dresden, Gemäldegalerie). The actual model for Bolton's design
might well be the *Adoration of the Magi* in the upper section of the *Life of the*

Virgin window at the Church of St. Martin, Liège, designed about 1527 by an unknown glazier of the Liège school (fig. 4).[20] The positions of the Virgin and the two men kneeling beside her in the Pelham window are similar to those of the Liège figures, and the prominent Mannerist columns at Pelham closely resemble columns that appear in profusion in sixteenth-century Belgian glass, including the Liège window. In contrast to the elaborate vaults and classical background structures at Liège, the Pelham scene has a shed and haymows, features well suited to the rural environment of Christ Church. Bolton was unable, however, to reconcile this rustic element with the structural formalities of the window, and the relationship between the straight lines of the painted shed roof and the curving arches of the window's mullions remains awkward. If the *Magi* window's model was the panel at Liège, Bolton must have visited that city during his 1841 trip to Europe, for the window was not available to him in reproduction.[21] Whether or not this window and Correggio's *Adoration* were in fact Bolton's sources, they could have been. Such a variety of both style sources and design models is characteristic of his eclecticism and adds to the art historical as well as the visual interest of his work.

What seems to be a preliminary drawing for the Christ Church altar area may shed further light on the place of the *Magi* window in Jay Bolton's artistic development (fig. 3b). The drawing shows the window with tracery, and with three more figures, one of which stands above the Virgin's head, as Joseph does in the Liège scene. The design is even more pictorial than the one in the completed window, with a curving architectural backdrop and a large area of sky. If this design represents Bolton's initial idea for the window, the final version, with its simpler composition and more compact spaces, already shows him working to reconcile the Renaissance elements of his taste with the medieval nature of stained glass and the Gothic design of the building.

In the sixteenth-century stained glass that Bolton admired, the amplitude of figures was enhanced by the use of large pieces of glass. Such pieces intensify the viewer's sensation of color, and cause the colors to carry for great distances, an effect that is appropriate to the expanse of space at Holy Trinity, but that at Christ Church tends to overwhelm the limits of the small chancel in which the window was placed (fig. 3c). The use of large pieces of glass began in the late fourteenth century, and Charles Winston attributed it to an increase in transparency and evenness of tint, which made the glass less suited to the "mosaic" effect of earlier medieval windows.[22] The glass used by the Boltons has this same uniformity, which Jay praised in his article on the King's Chapel windows, and which must have been

Style and Pictorial Sources

another justification for his adopting the large-figure style.[23] Large pieces also facilitate leading and reduce production time, which further helps to explain the Boltons' considerable output in a short span of time.[24]

The uncomfortable relationship of scale between the *Magi* design and its architectural setting is not the only problem of the *Magi* window. Jay also had difficulty in the composition of his colors. The light colors tend to isolate the darker ones and produce a somewhat splotchy effect. There seems to be too much white glass, due perhaps to his meager palette of potmetal colors, which was limited to ruby, blue, purple, and green, all in deep tones. The pink enamel in the Virgin's blouse and an ornamental use of silver stain do not provide transition tones sufficient for counteracting the whites. He will again use white or light-toned glass extensively at West Lynn, but there he displays the mature artist's mastery of tonal relationships, arranging the colors in an integrated harmony of values.

At Christ Church, Holy Trinity, and St. Peter's, West Lynn, Bolton's pictorial designs extend the scenes continuously behind the mullions (e.g., fig. 14, colorplate X). He always designs so that lead lines are integrated into the composition; and from Holy Trinity on, he is equally successful in dealing with the design properties of tracery, mullions, and metal supports. Even in the *Magi* window he handles lead lines well. As he said in the letter to Mr. Harison of Trinity Church, "All the strengthening bars, horizontal or vertical, & every line of lead will melt away at a proper distance" if the window is designed correctly. Otto Weir Heinigke, an important American glazier of this century, praised Bolton as an artist who "made his drawings with his mind fixed on the material at hand, and he left no difficult or contorted forms, and no lead line to interrupt or cut across an important light."[25] Bolton comments in the Harison letter on his pictorial style as a whole, saying that "Mr H[oppin], I think, unjustly condemns a pictorial distribution of light & shade. If it were not proper, I would not have it, but I do not see how he can as he would allow a natural light & shade for a single figure & yet not extend the same rules to the light & shade of a group."

The other Bolton windows at Christ Church, grisailles by both Jay and John, have a visual strength that allows them to hold their own with the *Magi* window. They combine vine-scrolls in trace paint on a lightly stippled ground with colored geometric forms (fig. 6; colorplate II). Four of the eight grisailles can be attributed to Jay (Catalog II:T1,4, N4,5), and four to John (Catalog II:T3, N1–3); the attributions are confirmed by their brother Winter Bolton and by style comparisons. According to Winter, John made the windows flanking the chancel (Catalog II:T3 and probably what is now

N1), basing his design on thirteenth-century grisaille windows at Salisbury Cathedral.[26] The broad arum vine-scrolls with their characteristic fruit are similar to vine-scrolls in grisaille windows of the Salisbury Lady Chapel, but otherwise the heavy geometries, somewhat awkwardly distributed, have little in common with the supposed models (fig. 6). Winter's comment on their source seems to be more flattery than fact.

The design of the grisaille windows credited to Jay is more subtle and has a more satisfactory balance of elements (colorplate II). The background foliage consists of finely drawn three-pointed leaves on tendrils that curve with a playful freedom (fig. 5). Jay's foliage has precursors in the grisaille ornament of the Decorated period of English Gothic. In two of his windows the careful observer will find tiny drawings among the foliage, in one case a smiling face and a frowning face, in the other a smiling face and a squirrel, and in both a tiny caterpillar (fig. 5). It is a surprise, however, to find an element of sham in Jay's windows: the curving lead lines have been drawn with trace paint on large, rectangular pieces of glass to simulate the leading patterns of thirteenth-century grisaille designs (colorplate II). It may have been haste to complete the project before the opening of the church that prompted the otherwise sincere functionalist to resort to painted "leading."

In the windows of Holy Trinity (now St. Ann and Holy Trinity), Brooklyn, where again John collaborated with Jay, it is likely that the older brother created most or all of the designs. For some windows, there are signed preliminary drawings by Jay; almost all have the mark of his composition and figure types. It is possible that two designs, *The Brazen Serpent* and *The Trial of Christ* (colorplate III and fig. 37), are by John, for he used them in the only large figural windows he is known to have executed independently. The former appeared in a window now lost, but seen and photographed some years ago by Leland Cook (fig. 77);[27] the latter is seen in John's window of ca. 1863 at Grace Church, City Island, New York (fig. 74). On the other hand, these same two designs were executed by Jay at Holy Trinity, and *The Trial of Christ* was used by him at Holy Apostles, which makes John's authorship of the two compositions less likely.

Jay's roots in the Renaissance, both northern and Italian, are again revealed in the models he used for a number of Holy Trinity designs, as well as in compositions there that are entirely his. Among the models are Raphael (1483–1520), several sixteenth-century Flemish artists of King's College Chapel, including probably Dirk Vellert (ac. 1511–1544); Albrecht Dürer (1471–1528), and Hans Holbein the Younger (1497–1543) (see especially Catalog III:C2, 5, 10, 13–15; G2, 4, 6, 7, 14). Jay was aware of the need

Style and Pictorial Sources

---

to reconcile his compositions based on these sources and his own classical tendencies in design and color with a Gothic setting. Looking at the windows in chronological sequence, the viewer can see clearly the maturing of his style and the growth of his understanding of the medium and its relationship to the architecture. The compositional character of the Holy Trinity designs and their color harmonies gradually change, and the more or less classical clarity of the Pelham *Magi* is replaced by designs closer in spirit to the "mosaic" of high-medieval stained glass. The addition of new pot-metal colors to the palette Jay used at Pelham gives him increased flexibility as his ideas develop. He also adds the interesting red stain discussed earlier, and several new enamel colors that he sometimes uses for clothing, but more often as color highlights in the landscape.

Production of the Holy Trinity program may have begun with the vestibule windows. The one Bolton window still in place there is an Old Testament scene depicting Hannah gently turning her small son Samuel toward the inner recesses of the Temple (fig. 46). As with figures in the Pelham *Magi,* the Hannah is almost too large for the picture space she occupies; but unlike them she fits comfortably into the actual architectural space. Again the main scene is flanked by Mannerist columns, and the architecture and the open spaces at either side of the figures could derive either from the Belgian windows that seem to have inspired the *Magi,* or from other sixteenth-century glass, such as that at King's Chapel. The blue of Hannah's cloak is striking against the white glass and grisaille surroundings, producing, however, a composition less harmonized with its Gothic surroundings than are others at Holy Trinity, but which may have had the purpose of supplying light to the entryway. The single figure of Hannah is one of Jay's most beautiful creations, with its graceful gestures and the soft volumes of deep blue cloth. The pleasure that he often takes in coordinating tracery motifs with the scene below begins in this window, the clouds, stars, and angels representing the sacred realm that the child is about to enter. If the second vestibule window, now filled with opalescent glass, were originally by Bolton, even it would have had difficulty competing with the beauty of the *Hannah* window.

In the main vessel of the church, there are three groups of windows: the Jesse Tree and narrative windows of the nave; the great chancel (altar) window, with figures of larger scale than the rest; and the lesser chancel and tower windows, with allegorical figures and decorative quarries. It is obvious that, in keeping with Bolton's functionalist theories, the location and the function of the Holy Trinity windows govern the nature of their designs. In the nave windows the figures are lively actors in a biblical drama played at

---

three levels of the congregation's space (figs. 9 and, e.g., 22, 28). Seen at a greater distance, and in the reserved precinct of the sanctuary, the figures of the altar window take on an almost sculptural quality (colorplate VII). In the tower and side chancel windows, none of which are seen easily by the congregation, the scenes are more decorative than they are dramatic (figs. 43–45).

At first a viewer might agree with one noted authority on stained glass who exclaimed upon entering the church, "But there are quite a number of different styles here!" This effect results from the variety of models used, as well as from the changes brought about as Jay matured as a stained glass artist. His development is observed best in the nave group, where both internal and external evidence reveal, with a measure of certainty, the chronology of installation: first the aisle windows, then those of the clerestory, and finally those of the gallery, where, at the time of the church's consecration, the *Brooklyn Daily Eagle* noted only boards covering the openings.[28] In terms of design, the nave windows can be subdivided into three groups: 1) the dark-colored aisle windows showing an eclectic mix of sources and a constantly repeated design; 2) the earlier clerestory windows, with large figures and a strong Renaissance character; 3) and the later clerestory and the gallery windows, which have somewhat smaller figures and a more complex, and thereby more medieval, appearance. The series demonstrates clearly a talented artist's experiments with both the techniques and the design requirements for a medium in which he could expect little or no help from others or from recent tradition. Bolton's success at Holy Trinity, both artistic and technical, was noted by Otto Weir Heinigke when he wrote that the "color compositions are masterly and full of grandeur, with none of the glitter and sparkle which, in the windows of the present vogue [about 1930], destroy wallspaces more ruthlessly than do the windows of any other historic period."[29]

Before further discussion of the Holy Trinity windows, it is important to define the differences in figure style between Jay and John Bolton. These differences are fully demonstrated for the first time in the aisle windows of Holy Trinity, which together form a Tree of Jesse. The basic design is probably Jay's but it was executed by both brothers (figs. 10a,b,d,e). It consists of seven angels repeated exactly or in mirror image in the side lights, a large, gnarled tree in the center, and in the tracery, busts of the Ancestors holding phylacteries inscribed with their names. The Josaphat angel painted by Jay and the Christ angel by John provide good examples of work by the two painters (figs. 10a,b). In Jay's angel the shadows are rich yet subtly modeled, producing a gentle facial expression and flowing drapery (fig. 10a). With John the shadows are hard, the mouth pouting, and the drapery folds arranged in patterns, such as the circle on the raised arm of the Christ angel (fig. 10b). The differences became even more pronounced as work on the program progressed. Two heads in gallery windows demonstrate the changes. Jay's shows fine modeling of flesh about the eye, nose, and mouth, with delicate highlights on the eyelid (fig. 29a); in John's, shadows tend to form conventionalized patterns (fig. 32b). The eyes of John's figures sometimes have a staring or bulging appearance—for example, in the two men plowing in *Man Labors,* pharaoh's daughter in *Finding of Moses,* and Christ in *Christ Stills the Tempest* (figs. 12, 19a, 33a). It is helpful to compare these figures with the albeit much smaller ones in John's altar window at St. Mary's Church, Scarborough, New York (fig. 73). At Holy Trinity, John is probably responsible for some of the work in at least four windows of the clerestory and at least seven in the gallery series, and for all the painting in six of the aisle windows (see Catalog III). Because of the heavy matt on the south gallery and south clerestory windows, definition of individual hands there is difficult. In the north clerestory windows, however, the distinctions are obvious, in *Expulsion* and *Cain and Abel,* for example. The former is a design by Jay, seen in its original form in a drawing that shows the three figures clearly defined against the brick wall of the Garden (fig. 11b). As executed by John, however, the Adam and Eve are slightly larger than the angel, the drapery is stiff, the movement of the figures awkward, and the white figures are ill-defined against what has become a grey stone wall (fig. 11a). In *Cain and Abel,* on the other hand, which was executed by Jay, the figures are smaller than those of the *Expulsion,* but have more life, and while white glass is still dominant, the shading creates a clarity of form that is further enhanced by the slight turn of each figure out of the picture plane (fig. 14).

To return to the Jesse Tree at Holy Trinity, a comparison of its basic design with the Pelham *Magi* and the *Hannah* windows demonstrates already a change in Jay's concept of stained glass design (colorplate IV; figs. 10a,b,d,e). The compact composition of interwoven linear rhythms and deep colors produces a still closer harmony between the northern late Gothic and Renaissance elements in his art. In the head of each light is the bust of an Ancestor richly dressed and supported by leafy "bases" (fig. 10e). These figures bear such a striking resemblance to the late medieval woodcut busts in Hartmann Schedel's *Nuremberg Chronicle* (Nuremberg: Anton Koberger, 1493), which survives in many copies, that it is hard to deny a direct link (fig. 10f). The angels, on the other hand, recall allegorical figures by Raphael and his shop in the ceiling of the Stanza della Segnatura at the

*Stained Glass Art
of William Jay Bolton*

Vatican, especially the *Justice* and *Philosophy* figures (figs. 10a,b,c). Bolton uses heavy drapery, deep color, and abundant curvilinear plant forms to compress the angels' space and blend the Raphaelesque figures into their medieval setting. In contrast to Raphael's statuesque women, however, Bolton's angels look like sturdy sixteenth-century Flemings; even so, some of the angels are graceful, truly beautiful figures, among them the Josaphat and Asa angels (figs. 10a,d). The horizontal arrangement of the fourteen windows along the aisle walls, in a scheme very different from the usual single-window Jesse Tree, recalls at considerable distance the Ancestors in the clerestory windows of Canterbury Cathedral,[30] as well as those in the lunettes of Michelangelo's Sistine Chapel ceiling. Jay Bolton must have known both programs, the one from his childhood in England, the other from his 1841 trip to Italy.

The first of the nave windows at Holy Trinity was installed most likely in the north clerestory. Here Bolton accommodated Old Testament designs to both the distance at which they would be viewed, and to the somber light on that side of the building. To judge from these designs, his initial idea must have been to fill the northern clerestory scenes with large, classically derived figures in bright landscapes, a scheme that would have brought in considerable light, but that would not have looked very Gothic. Even though such a plan was not fully carried out, Bolton based half the designs there on paintings by Raphael, and as elsewhere, most of the compositions reflect an Italian Renaissance influence. In the *Sacrifice of Isaac,* for example, uncluttered spaces open out on either side of the figures (fig. 15). Abraham twists around in an exaggerated contrapposto pose, while the Isaac is not only a classical nude, but is dramatically foreshortened. Renaissance illusionism prevails; only the colorism of Abraham's eastern costume expresses a Gothic spirit. On the other hand, the preceding *Noah's Sacrifice* window is better reconciled with the architecture. It anticipates Jay's mature designs in its crowded composition, activity close to the picture plane, and richness of color (colorplate IV). From *Jacob's Blessing,* the sixth window in the north clerestory, to the end of the whole program, this is the style that will be developed and transformed. It is, of course, the "Cinque Cento" style, blending Renaissance figure types with ornamental qualities more in keeping with the late Gothic surroundings.

On the south side of the clerestory, the three Moses windows show the artist still somewhat uncertain of his means, perhaps because of the problem of direct sunlight at this location. Undoubtedly to control the increased light he intensified the visual activity in *Finding of Moses,* but small figures and an almost kaleidoscopic treatment of color make the scene difficult to

Style and Pictorial Sources

---

read at a distance (fig. 19a). Yet in *Moses with the Tablets,* the principal figure is large and clothed in bright red; the surrounding areas of color are broader, and the whole more readable (fig. 20a). A comparison of the even more open, illusionistic sketch for this window with the busy landscape of the finished version is a witness to Bolton's increased understanding of how to design for a Gothic space (fig. 20b). In *The Brazen Serpent,* third of the Moses windows and designed possibly by John, the figures and the color areas are all large. Moses, in white, is defined by the red that appears behind him. The colors occur in the outer portions of the scene, so that the slender serpent, in an orange silver stain, is highlighted at the center above the silvery rocks (colorplate III). There is a balanced rhythm of forms and color that is more in tune with the Gothic rhythms of the architecture than in the other Moses windows. *Samson with the Gates of Gaza* demonstrates still another way of reconciling Renaissance and medieval elements. The central figure, which is probably modeled on one by Raphael (see Catalog III:C5), dwarfs everything else in the scene. This essentially classical figure is placed in a complex jumble of rocks and bushes, with the visually active lines of a townscape in the near distance. Rich color patterns of red and orange-yellow in the center light are surrounded by blues and greys, giving to the whole a distinctly medieval decorativeness. It is instructive to compare Samson's painterly environment with the open spaces in *Sacrifice of Isaac* on the north, where the main figures also dominate the scene (figs. 23, 15).

Among the windows of the clerestory Jay Bolton's mature style is at its best in *Joshua Stills the Sun and Moon* (fig. 22). The large figures of Joshua and his horses occupy most of the space, with only the faces of accompanying people seen beyond the main group. Again Bolton uses color to focus the viewer's attention. The central figures are emphasized not only by the light on the horses and on Joshua's armor but also by his red sleeves and the startling murrey blankets on the horses. The reds and reddish purples are both balanced and enhanced by the bright blues that appear like a frame around the edges of the scene. Areas of color are more numerous here than in *The Brazen Serpent* and the *Samson* windows, but so well placed among the large silver-grey forms of man and horses that they neither threaten the whole nor decrease the dramatic readability of the window.

The main chancel window was probably the next to be installed. It embodies the best "Cinque Cento" qualities of the clerestory designs, and again Raphael has a prominent role as figure model (colorplate VII). Because the window is on the west, Bolton chose deep colors and applied heavy shadows to control the brilliant afternoon light, less so in the upper, "celestial" registers than in the lower one. The *Brooklyn Daily Eagle* reported, in its account of the opening of Holy Trinity, "It would be still better if the upper range of glass in which the glorified Savior appears, were also tempered down: the sunshine makes the light through there quite painful."[31] Perhaps so, but Bolton's use of light in this window is narrative and symbolic, with the darkest areas in the earthly space below, and an increase in illumination as the eye follows Christ into a Heaven filled with cherubim and angels, and glowing with silver-stain yellow. In fact, a similar increase in light occurs from the aisles to the gallery level to the clerestory, also a symbolic progression from earth to Heaven (fig. 9). Bishop Hopkins implied a like symbolism when he wrote of church architecture, "[T]he light has always the best effect when it enters the building as near to the top as possible, consistently with true proportion."[32] It is interesting that forty years after the Holy Trinity chancel window was installed, the fashion for "Gothick gloom" in churches had so declined that *The Standard's Pictorial History* for 7 February 1885 could state, while praising Holy Trinity's architecture, that the "light, even on bright days, struggles through the dark glass in the windows and gives a somewhat cheerless air to the church."[33]

Last to be installed was the New Testament series in the galleries, where the bottoms of the windows are almost at floor level. They are viewed close at hand by those making their way into the gallery pews, and in several instances Bolton took advantage of this to invite the viewer's participation in the scene. At the beginning of the series, events in the *Birth of Christ* take place in a small barn realistically provided with the rafters, haymow, and stall-partition that a rural lad such as Jay would have seen many times (colorplate VI). The shepherds make their way from an upper level supported on an arch to the hay-strewn floor on which the Christ Child's manger is placed in the lower foreground. The viewer is thus invited to stand beside the manger itself, across from a kneeling shepherd. In *Christ in Gethsemane* the viewer is so close to Christ as to feel uncomfortable (fig. 36), and in *The Crucifixion* the viewer must stand directly in front of the cross (fig. 38). As in the south clerestory designs, the gallery compositions exhibit strong visual action and bold use of color. A comparison of the lively *Birth of Christ* window with a far simpler and quieter, and probably earlier, watercolor study of the subject shows the distance Bolton has put between his classical leanings and the requirements of Holy Trinity (colorplate VI; fig. 27).

In the gallery windows Bolton's ability to portray individualized character in a face can be seen. Undoubtedly his experience as a portrait painter contributed to the humanity he portrayed in the three men to the upper left in *The Birth of Christ,* or the man with short white hair and beard, the traditional description of St. Peter, in *Christ Stills the Tempest* (fig. 33a).[34]

Style and Pictorial Sources

Jay's use of "framing" colors to accentuate the main figures in a scene continues in the gallery series. Within the "frame," large color areas weave the composition together like a richly colored cloth (colorplate VI; figs. 28, 29b, 31a, 32a, 33a, 37). In a window such as *Christ at the Well,* where the composition is uninspired, visual interest is nevertheless provided by the combination of Christ's deep ruby cloak, the russet stain and deep blue potmetal of the other figures' robes, and the bright emerald-green potmetal of the grass (fig. 29b). It might be noted also that this window affords an instructive comparison between the lively style of Jay Bolton in the left light, and his brother John's more static painting in the other two lights. Only in *Christ in Gethsemane,* where the red of Christ's robe overwhelms the grisaille surroundings, is there an unsatisfactory treatment of color relationships (fig. 36).

One of the curiosities of the gallery windows is the presentation of three different versions of Christ. The beardless youth of *Christ Stills the Tempest* and the slender, ethereal blond of *Christ at the Well, Marriage at Cana,* and *Christ Enters Jerusalem* were all executed by John (figs. 33a, 29b, 30a, 31a). This type resembles the Christ figure in Vellert's designs at King's College Chapel. The dark-haired, heavily bearded Christ of the other New Testament windows can be assigned to Jay's hand. The Christ of the *Transfiguration,* with hair rather like a baroque wig, and the subordinate figures also seem to be by Jay (fig. 35a). It is odd that with so few workers in the shop, these inconsistencies in the appearance of an essential figure could occur, but perhaps once again the speed of production is at the root of the problem.

The tracery motifs in the clerestory and gallery windows are often closely coordinated with the main scene: a rainbow for *Noah's Sacrifice* (colorplate V), Passion symbols for *The Crucifixion,* and so on. Otherwise, one of three combinations of symbols is used, two of them at both levels. Most of the stock motifs relate to the Crucifixion (red rose, passion flower, grapes), but there are also references to Heaven (angels) and to Holy Writ (scrolls, quills, and inkwells). For particulars, see Catalog III.

Among the minor delights of the Bolton stained glass at Holy Trinity are the many sometimes extraneous objects and details of nature, elements that are often present in late medieval glass. A variety of plant and flower forms, executed usually in paint, can be found in the immediate foreground of the windows. Most of this ornament appears to have been done freehand. While some flora are identifiable, such as the passion flower of *Cain and Abel* (fig. 14), the majority are generalized forms, and all have the appearance of wildflowers. Some of the more interesting incidental objects are the snake (perhaps not so incidental) that slithers along at Eve's feet in the

Expulsion (fig. 11a); culinary still-lifes on the tables in *Marriage at Cana* (fig. 30a) and *Christ at Emmaus* (fig. 40); and a cat and a tray with pitcher and glass beneath Isaac's bed in *Jacob's Blessing* (fig. 16). In *Moses with the Tablets,* there is a curious little hollow tree stump with what appears to be a hinged cover at the base of the right-hand light (fig. 20a). Perhaps a Bolton family member had constructed such an object, and it was thought attractive enough to be included in the design of a window. In the West Lynn window, however, some scattered details of this sort are an integral part of the story—the Magdalen's unguent jar, the skull, the chalice and paten—while the delicate flowers and little blue bird in the far right foreground are more of Jay's charming irrelevancies (colorplate X).

The windows on either side of the chancel, and the large window of the tower (now at the Metropolitan Museum of Art), once again exhibit strong classical qualities, although in a manner different from the classicism of the north clerestory windows. The side chancel windows are most likely part of the last phase of glazing. They represent the two Anglican sacraments of Holy Communion and Baptism. The angels wear tube-fold gowns of a distinctly classical character, and the altar and the font are once again Mannerist architectural elaborations of a Flemish type (figs. 43, 44). In both designs there are large areas of silver stain on white glass, producing a highly decorative effect. It is this decorativeness that once again reconciles the classical elements with the medieval style of the architecture.

The same kind of decorativeness is featured in the tower window, which, however, is explicitly Renaissance in its references and its overall spirit. The window would have been seen rising behind the organ pipes at the very back of the church, and at considerable distance from viewers. Its design is therefore simple: musical motifs in the tracery and two very large biblical musicians, Jubal and Miriam, at either side in the register below (fig. 45).[35] Between the two figures are patterned quarry panels, which were originally covered by the pipes. Bolton's models for these figures appear to be in the curiously "Gothic" art of Botticelli. Miriam's pose resembles that of Flora in *Allegory of Spring* (ca. 1482, Florence, Uffizi Gallery); Jubal, dressed in Renaissance clothing, has kinship with some of the Medici youths in Botticelli's *Adoration of the Magi* (1470s; Florence, Uffizi Gallery). The two figures are placed under round-headed, Renaissance arches of glass that mask the real ogee arch of the frame. The colors are particularly striking: rich purple grounds and yellow silver-stain musical instruments in the tracery, and large amounts of bright silver-stain below. The colors and the patterned quarries provide the necessary medieval element in the design.

Style and Pictorial Sources

The northern Renaissance replaces Raphael as Bolton's favorite source for both figures and compositions in the gallery windows at Holy Trinity. The figure of Christ, with his billowing cloak, in *The Baptism of Christ* (fig. 28) resembles the St. Christopher in any number of German sixteenth-century prints of that subject.[36] Two King's College Chapel windows were the apparent sources for parts of *The Trial of Christ* (fig. 37; Catalog III:G4), and a stained glass panel attributed to the shop of Dirk Vellert, one of the designers at King's, may be reflected in Bolton's *Christ Stills the Tempest* (figs. 33c,a). Most of the design in a roundel attributed to Jan Swart van Groningen (ac. 1520–1540) and traced by Bolton at Holy Trinity Church, Bradford-on-Avon, appears in *Marriage at Cana* (figs. 30b,a).[37] *Christ at Emmaus* is taken from a Dürer woodcut.[38] The 1841 trip would have given Bolton access to the Bradford roundel; Bradford is only a short distance from Bath, where his grandfather Jay lived. The Dürer, Holbein, and other northern prints would have been available to him in any number of European libraries, and probably also in New York.

Still other compositions at Holy Trinity can be traced to sixteenth-century art. Many works of this period were available to him in the recently initiated and already numerous publications of Old Master reproductions, and Bolton ranged widely in his borrowings. Compositions by Raphael in the Vatican Logge vaults are reflected in *Sacrifice of Isaac* (fig. 15), *Jacob's Dream* (fig. 17), and *Moses with the Tablets* (fig. 20a). In the last, Bolton's preliminary sketch follows the model more closely than does the completed window, where the design has been adapted to its new setting (figs. 20a,b,21). The *Golden Calf* of the Logge may also be the source for the Holy Trinity *Noah's Sacrifice* (colorplate III), and the horses and chariot in *Joshua Stills the Sun and Moon* may depend on the Raphael shop's *Triumph of David* in the Logge (fig. 22). The male figures in *Man Labors* and *Samson with the Gates of Gaza* derive from the same source as the warrior in Bolton's early combat drawing (figs. 12, 23, 63), probably the young man holding Christ's legs in Raphael's *Entombment* (Rome, Borghese Gallery).[39] On the other hand, a northern woodcut, from Holbein's Old Testament series, probably served as model for the *Jacob's Blessing* window (fig. 16). One of Bolton's most interesting sources in the Holy Trinity windows is for his *Transfiguration* composition, based almost certainly on the first known preparatory version of Raphael's *Transfiguration,* seen in a drawing by Giulio Romano (Vienna, Albertina), and available to Bolton in lithographic reproduction (figs. 35a,b; Catalog III, G2). The Apostles and especially Moses holding up the tablets in Bolton's design closely resemble figures in the drawing. That perennial favorite of Victorian painters, Raphael's completed *Transfiguration* (1517;

*Stained Glass Art
of William Jay Bolton*

Vatican Gallery), is the source of the figure of Christ in the *Ascension* window over the altar at Holy Trinity (colorplate VII). If Bolton did not see the painting in 1841, it was certainly available to him in numerous reproductions and copies. Noteworthy for his absence among Bolton's sources is Michelangelo, the other great Renaissance favorite of Victorian artists. Jay's preference for the placid beauty in human form that he saw in Raphael's paintings undoubtedly precluded any interest in Michelangelo's herculean figures.

Among Jay Bolton's northern sources, the designs of Dirk Vellert are of particular interest. The *Flight into Egypt* roundel at Holy Apostles is based on a design (after Dürer) attributed to Vellert in another roundel traced by Bolton at Holy Trinity Church, Bradford-on-Avon (figs. 50a,b). His model for *Christ Stills the Tempest* in Brooklyn may also be based on a Vellert design, or one used by Vellert (33a,b,c). In these models Bolton may have recognized the style as closely related to that of the King's Chapel windows. If so, it was long before art historians determined that Vellert was a principal figure among the artists at King's.[40] Unfortunately, in Bolton's writings about the King's Chapel windows he does not mention Vellert, the Bradford roundels, or the *Tempest* design, so it cannot be known if his use of these sources is merely coincidental, or a tribute to his connoisseurship.

Raphael was again the *fons et origo* of Bolton's ideas for the ten original windows of Lafever's "Tuscan" Renaissance Church of the Holy Apostles in Manhattan. The subjects of the windows, now depicted in roundels, are an abbreviated Life of Christ and a longer series from the Acts of the Apostles. There is evidence among the sketches in the Long Island Diocese Archives that Bolton's initial idea for Holy Apostles was for traditional single-scene figural windows, which may have been too costly for the building committee to approve. A sketch for a large *St. Peter Distributing Alms* (fig. 66), for example, with its Raphaelesque figures and classical balance of solids and voids, would have suited the architecture, just as its subject matter suited the vocabule of the church. Instead, Jay created an all-purpose window design composed of roundels painted in grisaille and silver stain, and surrounded by colored and grisaille flowers, acanthus leaves, and ogee fillets; in the round head of each window is an angel (colorplate VIII). For the roundel scenes his obvious choice was Raphael's Acts of the Apostles tapestries (e.g., fig. 51), but he also used several of his own Holy Trinity designs (fig. 52), the *Flight into Egypt* attributed to Vellert (figs. 50 a,b), and designs newly composed for Holy Apostles. As in the Jesse Tree at Holy Trinity, the angels are executed from only a few cartoons, here three, repeated as exact or mirror images (figs. 47–49; cf. fig. 47 and colorplate IX).

Style and Pictorial Sources

In the scenes for this classical context, Bolton emphasizes spatial illusion by giving architecture a prominent role, both as backdrops for action and to create space (e.g., figs. 53, 54). To some extent the illusionism reflects the influence of the Raphael tapestry designs that figure so prominently here as sources. Set among the acanthus-leaf surrounds, even the Holy Trinity designs lost their Gothic flavor (fig. 47 top, center). Although in some roundels the paint, even prior to the fire, had deteriorated badly, making the scenes difficult to read, where the style was still clear the work appeared to be by Jay himself. The scale is of course much smaller than that at Holy Trinity, and the painting therefore more refined. There are a number of examples of excellent glass painting, such as *The Deliverance of St. Peter & St. John* (colorplate VIII) and Bolton's version of the *Flight into Egypt* design (fig. 50a), demonstrating that he had also mastered the late medieval and Renaissance art of grisaille painting.

Bolton's last known major window, *The Angel at the Tomb* at St. Peter's, West Lynn, is both a sequel to the later windows at Holy Trinity and testimony to the invigorating effect of renewed direct contact with King's Chapel. The figures are large and clothed in bold colors, yet they are in perfect harmony with an increased use of white glass in the landscape (colorplate X). This new color balance reflects a distinctive characteristic of the King's windows, which Bolton describes as follows:

> But I believe the great charm of these windows lies in their restricted and careful use of colour; quite three-fourths, in some cases seven-eighths of the whole surface, being white glass, or white glass shaded. This reservation gives intense value, by contrast, to the colours employed, greatly reducing their gaudiness, and enhancing their depth. And then the colour that *is* used is collected into nosegays, as it were, and not spotted or diluted by being spread over the picture.[41]

By proceeding in the same manner at West Lynn, Bolton increased the drama of the scene, using the white glass almost as spotlights to focus attention on the actors in the main drama, much as he had used color at Holy Trinity. He placed warm colors, red and yellow, at two focal points: the kneeling Magdalen and the ladder leaning against the cross. The surrounding purple, blues, and greens further intensify the impact of the warm colors. The white glass around the cave mouth forms a halo for the main scene, while the white of the distant hills illuminates the cross. Although the angel appears rather stiff, the women have a gentle sadness in their looks and gestures, the result of some of Bolton's finest glass painting (fig. 55). The two standing women are modeled directly on two women in the window of the same subject designed by Dirk Vellert at King's Chapel, of which Bolton made a watercolor copy (fig. 56).[42] It is perhaps a mark of his Victorian puritanism that he replaced the fancy headdress of the profile figure at King's with a prim bonnet. His wonderful color sense takes a particularly bold turn in the light green cross and the yellow ladder, on the right, which command the viewer's secondary attention and invite reflection on the events that led to the circumstances of the main scene. His potmetal palette is the same as at Holy Trinity, but enlarged by light blue, mostly for parts of the sky, and light green; there are no enamels.

In the tracery the curious but decorative red cherubim on wheels seem out of place above the grandiose landscape, but the blue ground on which they are placed joins the blue sky below and provides a link between the two otherwise disparate parts of the window (colorplate X). The cherubim were evidently a stock tracery motif in the Cambridge shop, for they appear in designs for two other churches. One of these designs is a sketch for an unidentified window, a five-light *Ascension,* based on the completed version of Raphael's *Transfiguration* and on *Messenger* figures from the King's windows (fig. 69). In this version of the cherubim tracery, musical notation appears on the scroll; the same design was used in a gallery window at the Church of St. Andrew the Great, Cambridge. Remarkably similar although less stylized angels on wheels appear in later fifteenth-century tracery glass at the Church of St. Lawrence at Combe (County of Oxford),[43] which may have been known to Bolton, or to whomever it was in the shop who designed the cherubim, for they bear little resemblance to Bolton's other work. A second tracery design at West Lynn appears in the head of a nave window, the only nave light with painted glass (fig. 57). It shows repeated figures of youthful angels in oriels, a motif used again in a gallery tracery at St. Andrew's (fig. 58). An assistant, perhaps Constable, did the West Lynn oriel angels, but those at St. Andrew's are by Jay himself. The only other windows known to have been completed in England by Jay Bolton, and which are still extant, are copies of Eton and King's College armorials formerly in the Provost's Lodge at King's (fig. 59); and copies made apparently for a Gothic Revival house at Christchurch, Hampshire. The high quality of the copies was noted by Dean Milner-White of King's Chapel, who had them installed in two chantries on the north side of the chapel.[44]

It remains to assess William Jay Bolton's style in relation to the styles of contemporary glaziers. There were two principal style trends in stained glass of the 1840s: one in which the glaziers more or less imitated earlier medieval styles, with scenes in medallions surrounded by diaper patterns, or at least confined to a single light; the other, more pictorial and closer to the

Style and Pictorial Sources

Renaissance spirit of academic easel painting. In the first group the most important pioneers were the English artists A. W. N. Pugin, John Hardman, William Wailes, and Thomas Willement; in the second, Charles Winston, Charles Clutterbuck, George Hedgeland, and Thomas Wilmshurst in England, and William Jay and John Bolton in the United States.[45] None of the other pictorialists approach Jay Bolton's effective draughtsmanship or the balance of form and color he achieved in both the figures and their surroundings in his later windows at Holy Trinity and at West Lynn. Winston's figures are awkward; Clutterbuck and Hedgeland tended to dull their designs with enamels. The little that remains of Wilmshurst's work is compositionally not unlike that of Bolton, but with uninteresting backgrounds and overly intense colors.[46]

Early in their campaign for archaeological purity in medieval-revival design, the Ecclesiologists had attacked the pictorial style, and by the late 1850s proponents of pictorialism were no longer receiving commissions, or were turning to the more "correct," high-medieval manner.[47] In his essay on the King's glass in 1855, Bolton is still committed to the "Cinque Cento" style, but it is likely that already in 1849 he had felt the pressures of Ecclesiological taste, and that this was another factor in his decision to cease making stained glass and enter upon theological studies at Cambridge. If so, he left the field as perhaps its outstanding practitioner, regardless of stylistic allegiance, but with so little accomplished while in England that he remained unknown there, his achievements, as in the United States, awaiting discovery in the next century.

Appendix A

Three William Jay Bolton Letters

1. William Jay Bolton to his brother James
Addressed to J. Bolton, Esq., in care of W. G. Ashton, Esq., Cambridge; redirected to Henry Byles, Esq., Henley-on-Thames, Oxon. Postmarked upon receipt at Cambridge, 6 April 1845. In Long Island Diocese Archives, Garden City, N.Y.

Feb. 7, 1845

Dear Jim,

Thank you for your thoughtfulness & trouble about the prospectus. I soon after found my own & because of its early stipulation gave up the first project - on the second I shall probably try. I think "an attack of British Chariots on a Roman legion". What think you of the subject? I have now finished three quarters of my windows, and am satisfied that I shall be able to do something in the "Ars Vitraria". Dr. [Jonathan] Wainwright & Mr. Harris [read: Harison, William H.] have promised to wait about Trinity Window til they have seen mine. This is something, but I have not much hope of the job. What a mercy it is that I am beginning to be able to appreciate & try high finish. I was wrecked once on the beautiful coast of <u>color</u>. <u>Design</u> now is all I sail for. And if I can only by the bribes of industry & perseverance induce some of the dignified figures who walk to & fro in my chambers of imagery to let me take their portraits, I will astonish the natives yet. Talking of "natives", Here's a good joke. Harper is the "native" mayor you know, who with his party promised such improvements in the city, especially to <u>strict</u> <u>cleaning</u>. After as wild a snow storm as many remember, came a thaw & then <u>such</u> a pool by the <u>Park</u>! and what do you think some wag had stuck up on a board: "Harper's ferry". But a little about that snow storm. For 24 hours it blew a vehement East Wind, "snow & hail fulfilling his word". It came horizontally, not in waves & gusts, but like a swift river of wind & wet, and at midnight the tempest wheel'd round & the battle came from the other way. For 24 hours more. Oh! the drifts - walls & fences were buried & 140 gents from this county blockaded in New York, Pa among them. They met at Hull's 3 times a day with such long faces & great coats. But no go for 4 days.

Ayres is still great on ducks & fishes. I see he call[s] you <u>his esteemed</u> <u>friend</u> in art. on "Cottas [?Cottage] hobbis" [?hobbies]. He goes out every day, finds some blossom, paces Bob Morse's island, or lies on the rocks for 3 hours without getting even an old [i.e., ale] wife. I don't consider him <u>deep</u> in his

71

Appendix A

<u>affections</u> or <u>reflections</u>. Otherwise he is a delightful companion & a very volume of Natural History. I much miss my friends, Ellis & Pitt who "knew me even as they were known" & I miss you too & Win[ter] & if it were not for <u>John</u>, I should advertise for wife & the first requisition should be "fond of reading aloud". John is certainly a fine fellow. He <u>will</u> give an oyster supper to the girls every other Wednesday at <u>our</u> house, in spite of Ma's denunciations & sundry symptons of "angina pectoris" the next day. His store is doing well, to others & himself too. You know where it is - opposite Irving Flandereau's. The schoolhouse is about 200 feet <u>south</u> of <u>our</u> gate (by Madame Lanny's or Roosevelts Cottage) on the road, <u>lengthwise</u>. Jackson is to be our teacher in the spring. The very mention of spring makes the babe of Hope leap in its womb. Only think of it! 5 weeks & the 1st of April. Oh! that April & her sister May! We even now have fine weather, quite open & mild. The Sound clear, the sun shining, the blue birds & song-sparrows out on their honeymoons, the brooks full and flowing with that <u>gush</u> that goes to your heart & the skunk cabbage swelling.

Touching Poetry I have not much time now & perhaps less ambition. Still she is like the "voice of one that playeth well on an instrument" and I shall never forget her kindness to me in my youth. I speak to you who will understand me. Though we may not be ever <u>great</u> poets, yet we may please each other & our friends. I still feel the pure delight she gives, by a remembered verse or a quoted line. How often is dull prose enlivened by ryhme [*sic*] and ryhthm [*sic*] & one of those glances of ideal light which Poetry can only throw. So you have been in the Poet's Corner [at Westminster Abbey]. It really is a sad and solemn spot. The bards (& such bards) of our country. Their old harp is all we have of them. <u>They</u> are sleeping after the feast & who shall wake them? I do not admire the confusion or crowdedness of Westminster. It is more like a tomb than a chapel. Otherwise what a place it is. There is (I think) a fine window in the church <u>close</u> by [St. Margaret's]. Did you find Milton's tomb. Its somewhere near where the old London Wall & milestone stood. Also the "Labors" over the Surrey side of one of the bridges. Shakespeare's Tavern I never could find.

Don't you become a <u>tall</u> Churchman. High Churchmen are modern Pharisees (Socinian Sadducees). That is to say they both put their <u>trust</u> in a certain system of order & ceremony; at least they told & tell <u>only</u> that to the people. I mean, & now you will comprehend me, a high Churchman does not & would not preach Paul's doctrine of "faith alone" one Sunday, though he were allowed to preach James' explanation of faith, a <u>living</u> faith, on the following Sunday. To all such systems, justification by works whether of Hindoo, Turk, Komunist, or high Church I would bring the light of Abraham's <u>faith</u>. His justification took place while he was <u>uncircumcised</u> & unbaptised. Look further at 11 verse of Rom. IV & you will see the two Abrahams

---

contrasted & also his two families. I think the parenthesis in the <u>sense</u> begins at "a seal" & extends to the end of the verse, while "and he rec'd the sign of circumcision" refers to the <u>next</u> verse. Look also at 13 & 14 verses. Dr. Coit believes in justification by baptism because faith without it is imperfect. He forgets the 3 of Galatians 8 & 15 & 17 verses. A <u>covenant</u> (not conditional with <u>us</u> children of Eve) but <u>confirmed</u> before of God in Christ. The law 430 years after could not disunite & though it were a <u>man's</u> covenant, says Paul, yet if it be <u>confirmed</u>, no man addeth or disuniteth. How much more with God. We are (having faith), & we ought to be proud of it, real children of Abraham & free <u>and</u> well as only those Jews who walk in the steps of faithful Abraham. And the fact is this is the only way of preaching a . . . [page missing]

. . . works and included <u>under</u> faith - other works are dead, as the article says. I am glad you voted against monachism among those silly boys - always remember this, that <u>primitive</u> marriage (by which I mean one man & one woman) is a <u>Divine</u> ordinance & also that man is <u>naturally</u> inclined to it. Witness XT's [i.e., Christ's] conversation with the Jews about divorce. When you take a sufficient interest & have more leisure I could say a great deal on this subject, both from Scripture & reason which would explain very much the ridicule & levity with which such a sacred matter is treated everywhere & by all. Write to me soon. Don't get in with that "Roe" near King's, he is sure to cheat you. Rather get large books than prints. We are all well. Nnt [Nanette] is writing to Aunt. Give her my love & so to Uncle. I often think of them & theirs.

W.J. Bolton

2. William Jay Bolton to William H. Harison
At the time of this letter, Bolton had already submitted a sketch of an Ascension window to the building committee, of which Harison was a member, at Trinity Church, Manhattan, in the hope of receiving a commission for the altar window there. It seems that Harison had asked Bolton to comment on the ideas for the window put forth by Thomas F. Hoppin, who is probably responsible for the design that was eventually chosen; see Chapter 1, n. 130. The other person named is the Rev. Jonathan Mayhew Wainwright, assistant rector of Trinity Church. In Trinity Church Parish Archives, Manhattan. (With gratitude to the Rector, Church Wardens, Vestrymen, and Parish Archives.)

Pelham Priory, Oct. 19, [1844]

My dear Sir,

I thank you sincerely for your kind thought of me. Mr. Hoppins letter is quite to my mind & well deserves all your attention. It is right as to the <u>style</u> of

Appendix A

---

the <u>work</u>. It <u>must</u> be <u>leaded</u> up to suit outlines, folds &c. All the strengthening bars, horizontal or vertical, & every line of lead will <u>melt</u> <u>away</u> at a proper distance, or only serve to <u>distinguish</u> & <u>strengthen</u> the design as well as the colors. This is no uncertain theory, but an <u>actual</u> <u>effect</u>, sought & produced, in all fine windows. He rightly recommends also the <u>natural</u> before the <u>grotesque</u> figure. Those who persist for the latter have not careful eyes or thoughtful minds. If the architecture solemnizes & awes, why should one of its parts caricature & disgust us. Depend upon it that what you want in Trinity, is a simple, energetic, & natural series of Scripture stories & this brings me to the subject of them. If I might be so bold as to say what I think I should suggest that the Baptism of our Savior might be too <u>small</u> a subject for the great window. Not because it is less important, but because it would only allow of two <u>special</u> figures. As <u>mention</u> is made of others present & though they <u>might</u> be allowed they would still be et ceteras. I had thought much before I chose the "Ascension" & my reasons finally were these. 1. That it was (as I could recollect) an <u>unusual</u> subject for a window & I presumed <u>originality</u> in every thing to be an object. 2. Because it afforded so many noble & varied figures (our Savior, angels & all the apostles &c) both below & above, & I thought a unity of subject better even for so large window, than any broken designs, & 3rdly that it was (as the Trinity cannot be personified by any subject, for one was only a <u>voice</u> at the Baptism) the best subject for a mother Church whose clergy claim a succession from those who beheld & witness'd to the Lord Jesus Christ all the time, "beginning from the Baptism of John <u>unto</u> <u>the</u> <u>same</u> <u>day</u> <u>that</u> <u>he</u> <u>was</u> <u>taken</u> <u>up</u> <u>from</u> <u>us</u>" Acts 1.22. But need the "<u>Baptism</u>" be <u>excluded</u> because it is not so artistically fit for the large window? Certainly not. Take up the quotation just made from the Acts, put the <u>Baptism</u> by John (unless you would begin with the birth &c) as the <u>first</u> of a <u>series</u> in the <u>Easternmost</u> <u>lower</u> <u>side</u> window, & by a procession of subjects, <u>alternating</u> from left to right, & including how many glorious matters! you would be brought <u>gradually</u> & <u>happily</u> to the "<u>Ascension</u>". Don't think me visionary when I assure you that this can be done at no great expense (I will shew you how presently) & beg you <u>then</u> to consider whether a delightful necessity does not arise of having either a "Crucifixion" or an "Ascension" as an end, a last act, a piece that carries you on from Earth to Heaven. As to the other windows you will of course be wise to wait, but do not reject large designs for one or the other because emblems & effigies will be less costly. It need not be so. I could paint a head as soon as I could a cup, but listen. Glass stainers or [= are] often men of natural genius, it is true, but they as often want a <u>refined</u> & <u>general</u> <u>education</u> & so suppose it a wiser plan to mistify themselves & others. I was told that it was impossible without years of practise, I could attain the art, & should have believed it till now, but that for our little Church window's sake I obtained what information

Three Letters

I could, built a furnace, procured leads & German glass & set to work myself. The result enables me to say that the whole matter is quite easy (& <u>therefore</u> it is secreted) & that notwithstanding the different estimates you have had, the large window of Trinity need not cost $1000. Let our window witness.

It is 12 × 8 feet.	
The white glass for limbs, heads & white parts	$2
German glass for draperies from	$30 to 40
Leads at 12 $ per cwt.	12
Enamel colors &c	6
	$60

My own time is the only other item. My furnace cost me 15$. I cut the glass, lead it up, paint it & burn myself here, & find no difficulty. The only true difficulty in the case is to be able to design & draw well enough! This very Evening I have turn'd out a muffle full of excellent burnt pieces & the cutting & leading are mere knacks. I do not give you this detail to suppose that I would offer to act the practical myself. Others doubtless could do it better & my time would me [=be] more important to me, but to warn you against ignorant or designing person[s]. Of course I don't refer to your man. He seems very pleasant & conversable, but to others. On stained windows generally I would humbly ask whether Mr. Hoppin sufficiently appreciates one of the important ends they served "in the olden time" that of teaching Scripture History. Many a poor hind (denied his Bible) has been the better or the worse for a stain'd window! & though the Scriptures like a Sun shine full on us it can do no harm, may do some good & must <u>delight</u> all the lovers of Sacred art (if I may say so) to reflect some of the refulgence upon the noble windows of your noble Church. Apostles & saints in niches, with gloves and swords seperated [*sic*] & allegorized may be made sublime & solemn doubtless, but they will not <u>interest</u> the people, they will not <u>interest</u> you or me, or any one else, so much & so long as one of those blessed stories we first heard from our mother's tongue & on our mother's knee. As to ornate work, tabernacle work, canopies, borders &c I allow that there ought to be a plenty of them in their proper places. An out of doors incident surely requires a consistent back-ground & painted windows have their conventional trees & skies & rocks & grass, as well as their pedestals & rich floors & other architectural display. In the upper part of the Ascension there is a fine opportunity for one & in the lower for the other [i.e., architecture and landscape]. Of course a design should not be <u>copied</u> but <u>made</u> for your window, or as Mr Hoppin observes, amputation will be necessary. Otherwise not. Mr H, I think unjustly condemns a pictorial distribution of light & shade. If it were not proper, I would not have it, but I do not see how he can as he would allow a natural light & shade for a single figure & yet not extend the

---

same rules to the light & shade of a group. Still it need not in the least imitate a transparency. The Leading is visible though not offensive, & there is that about <u>pot metals</u> which if in a window, will make it unlike any thing else in the world, a unique & glorious thing. I appeal to King's Chapel - all Scripture stories! done in this way. I saw Dr. Wainwright on this subject during the summer, but the whole seemed much in dubio. I should like if I might be allowed, before the matter is settled to give in a careful & finish'd design (my first was but a sketch) better suited in its upper (Heavenly) part by its details to ornament such a fine Gothic pointed window. I would also add a practical estimate of what it <u>should</u> cost, done in good style.

In any way, if I could be [of] use to you or your Committee, let me know, but I should not like to trouble the Doctor any more, for though I feel free from any mercenary desire of getting a job, yet I am young & cannot expect to have much weight with my elders. Indeed when I consider how important this business is, I feel diffident about it, but that Professor Morse (the President of our Academy) gave me so much encouragement to proceed & also that I might have both his & such a tasteful gentleman as Mr Hoppin's advice. Nothing should be done as to fixing upon a design, I think, without the <u>united</u> counsel of <u>artists</u> <u>with</u> <u>architects</u>. If you chance to meet the Dr & think this might remind him of me in the matter, please ask him to trouble himself to read it. He has my sketch of the Apostles which I am to call for some day, but I can scarce find time to get to the city. Excuse these desultory remarks, present my kind regards to Mrs. Harison & permit me to subscribe myself your sincere friend & humble ser^t.

W. Jay Bolton.

3. William Jay Bolton to unknown recipient, National Academy of Design. The dates given for this letter are suggested by internal evidence. Another hand wrote "April 1845" at the top of the letter, but the tone of the last sentence suggests that May 1845 is more than just a few weeks away, and the letter could be from 1844. In the Long Island Diocese archives, Garden City, N.Y.

Pelham New Rochelle
n.d. [1844 or 1845]

Dear Sir,

I am sorry that your academy should have cut me so quick, for want of a little explanation. I much respect you all, & as I was pleas'd a year ago to hear that my name was among the associates, so I feel vex'd now at its excision & hasten to disabuse your minds of any <u>slight</u> on my part. Not having a last year's catalogue by me, I cannot refer to it; but the impression has always been on my

Three Letters

---

mind that in one place, instead of an A (associate) there is an H (honorary) or something of that kind. Hence I had a <u>doubt</u> as to my election, and this has been strengthened by the fact I have never received the least <u>official</u> or <u>private</u> communication of it to this day, that is [until] your letter. Being a little modest I have never taken any notice of it myself, & living altogether in the country & seeing so few artists, I suppose, it has never been notic'd to [*sic*] me. As to the <u>condition</u>, I never <u>saw</u> it <u>before</u> & if I have heard of it, it has been forgotten or attributed to the higher grade. This is the <u>simple</u> truth, & may suggest to you, why your rule is sometimes neglected; for want of an <u>official</u> notification. You mean now, I presume, that I am not an associate & that I am to wait until May (45 when if re-elected, I am to send the academy my portrait, before (46? If otherwise please to let me know.

I remain
Your obt. servant
W. J. Bolton.

Appendix B

John Jay Bolton
1818–1898

John Bolton began his career in stained glass by serving as assistant to his older brother, who was probably also his teacher in the art. After Jay returned to England in 1848, John made several interesting programs of windows on his own, mostly nonfigural, but at least two large figural windows. His strength as a glass artist was in decorative design, especially in his grisaille windows that postdate the Pelham ones. There are no finer Victorian grisailles anywhere than John's five slender lancets in the west facade of St. Mary's Church, Scarborough, New York (figs. 71, 72).

Like Jay, John was born in Bath. When the family moved to the United States in 1836, he remained behind with his aunt Arabella Jay Ashton in Cambridge, and joined the family the following year.[1] It is reported, without documentation or particulars, that John became an architect, designed the Bartow mansion in Pelham Park, and entered the competition for the enlargement of City Hall in Manhattan.[2] In addition to his documented work assisting Jay in the stained glass at Christ Church, Pelham, and (St. Ann and) Holy Trinity, Brooklyn, he is also said to have done some of the carving of furniture and other appointments for Christ Church and the Priory.[3] He kept a store for a time in Pelham, although the nature of its merchandise is not recorded.[4] He must have been a charming, fun-loving person, for his brother Jay reports that he hosted an oyster supper for "the girls" every other Wednesday at the Priory, which was denounced by his mother, who complained next day of "sundry symptoms of 'angina pectoris.' "[5] "The girls" were probably the Bolton sisters, because Jay indicates that the other brothers are away when he says that he misses James "& Win[ter] & if it were not for <u>John</u>, I should advertise for wife & the first requisition should be 'fond of reading aloud.' "[6]

When Jay returned to England in 1848, that left John for a short time as perhaps the only serious stained glass artist at work in the United States. He continued to produce stained glass for at least five more years, and was an exhibitor at the New York Exhibition of the Industry of All Nations in 1853, by which time, however, six other glaziers were exhibiting figural windows.[7] In 1850, John completed his two best programs of windows, at St. Mary's Church, Scarborough, New York,[8] and the Church of the Holy Innocents, Albany, New York.[9] The windows for these two churches are quite similar. Both have triplets of colored figural medallions, symbols and diaper patterns—the popular "emblems & effigies" window that Jay decried in his letter to Mr.

John Jay Bolton

Harison—over the altar. The same principal medallion design is used at both churches, with differences in smaller motifs and symbols (fig. 73). Both churches also contain grisaille patterned quarry windows in the nave, and handsome tall floral grisaille lancets on designs from Pelham in the west facade (figs. 71).[10] Oculi with geometric Trinity symbols appear in the gables of the transepts at St. Mary's. The effect of the five western lancets at St. Mary's is reminiscent of the *Five Sisters* at York, but their design is based on Jay's Christ Church, Pelham, grisailles. The designs of the western windows at Holy Innocents are like John's "Salisbury" designs at Pelham. Both sets of grisaille windows include potmetal and silver stain; at Holy Innocents the potmetal red is extremely hot, and balances poorly with the blue. Interestingly enough, two of the five western grisailles at St. Mary's, both on Jay's design, have lead lines drawn in, as at Pelham, while the other three are partially leaded. John achieves a shimmering and mysterious effect in the St. Mary's lancets by omitting the matt, thus allowing the light to flow through the lacy grisaille forms, and bringing the shadowy shapes of trees beyond into the composition (figs. 71, 72). Frank Wills, architect of Holy Innocents, said of John's windows at Albany:

> All the windows are filled with colored glass, without doubt the best imitation of old English art yet executed in this country. The east window is a rich mosaic pattern with subjects of our Lord's life and sacred symbols enclosed within foliated and geometrical borders. The side windows of [the] Chancel are taken from [i.e., based upon] some remains of ancient glass in Salisbury Cathedral. Those of [the] Nave are of a modified design [i.e., quarries].[11]

John's next commission, the windows of the Church of St. James-the-Less, Scarsdale, New York, finished in 1851, produced designs evidently similar to windows at Albany and Scarborough, to judge from the remaining openings and from the brief description of them by Robert Bolton:

> The chancel is lighted by a triplet of richly stained glass, the middle lancet of which contains a cross within the *vesica piscis,* the south, a dove and font, and north, a paten and chalice. The rest of the glass, excepting the west end of the nave, which is richly grisailed [*sic*], and the southern windows of the chancel, which have colored borders, is plain enameled [?quarries]. The whole of the stained glass was manufactured by Mr. John Bolton of Pelham. Over the central lancet in the chancel, and in the middle of the west gable are triangular trifoliated lights with colored glass.[12]

These windows were completely destroyed in a fire of 1882.

Frank Wills states that John was commissioned (as of 1850) to make

Appendix B

windows for the House of Prayer in Newark, New Jersey, but the original windows of this church were removed in 1965, and there is no visual or other record of them to provide a clue to their appearance or maker.[13] It is possible that a large, three-light window found and photographed by Leland Cook some years ago in a restorer's studio is a remnant of John's program at Newark. It is executed on the Holy Trinity design of *The Brazen Serpent* (fig. 77; cf. colorplate III).

John's next windows were an entirely secular series: painted quarries for the drawing room and front doors of the Gothic-style villa built by A. J. Davis in 1850–52 for Francis Key Hunt in Lexington, Kentucky. Only sixty-four of the original one hundred twenty quarries of the doors remain, and none from the drawing room.[14] The door quarries are painted to resemble, collectively, a large grape arbor, with purple, blue, and green enamel and silver stain (fig. 75). A letter of 26 May 1852 from Hunt to Davis suggests that Bolton had not thoroughly mastered the art of firing enamel painting, for he writes that he had been satisfied with the first glass that John sent, and gave him a further order for glass for the front door. When this order arrived, however, Hunt was not "pleased with the design or execution" and sent it back. He complains that

> it is most wretchedly made; not only unsuitable to go with the others, but unfit for any use. Mr. Bolton seemed to be a well disposed, honest man; and if he is so, I can only suppose that he confided in others, and did not see the glass before it was sent. . . . The glass seems to have been overheated, and thereby blistered, and the colors run together, so as, on the outside to shew, instead of a purple bunch of grapes, an ugly yellowish-green or blue blotch.

Hunt must have been a man of generous disposition, for although he wanted the order done over, he was willing to pay additional costs so that Bolton would not realize a loss.[15] It is possible that the forgiving Mr. Hunt was correct that someone else did the firing, or even the painting to Bolton's design, but there is no evidence one way or the other. Hunt's description of the "wretchedly made" windows, however, calls to mind the shoddy workmanship on one of the ca. 1850 armorial windows (Catalog II:N2) at Christ Church, Pelham.

Meanwhile, in 1848 John Bolton married Katherine Schuyler, daughter of Philip and Grace Hunter Schuyler, who were Westchester neighbors. They lived for a time at the Priory, and in 1859 John, following the example of his older brothers and his younger brother Winter, took holy orders. He was ordained to the deaconate at Christ Church, Pelham, served the parish as deacon for two years, and was ordained priest there in 1862.[16] On 22 November 1861 he was chosen rector of the Church of the Redeemer, Morristown, New Jersey, where he would remain until 9 May 1863. When he left the Vestry recorded his resignation as accepted with

John Jay Bolton

deep regret and a Vestry's high regard for his character as a man and as a Christian Minister [and their] sense of the faithful manner in which he has discharged every duty of his high office and his untiring efforts in the field of humanity and that he will carry with him into his new and more promising scene of labor the best wishes of this Vestry and Congregation.[17]

A return to stained glass may have been the "new and more promising scene of labor" for which he left Morristown. It was at this period that John Bolton made a large figural window on his own, for the altar of the newly built Grace Church on City Island, New York. His brother the Reverend Cornelius Winter Bolton had held services in make-shift quarters on the island for a number of years, beginning in 1849, and later his sister Adele, with the help of the other ladies at the Priory, raised funds to erect a church there. Shipwrights were engaged to do the building, and by 1862 Grace Church was under construction. John's window, installed probably sometime in 1863, may have been a gift by him to the church; church records do not comment. The design he used is *The Trial of Christ* from Holy Trinity (also Holy Apostles), with only a few minor variations, but a somewhat less felicitous balance of color and white glass. A comparison of the Grace Church and Holy Trinity versions demonstrates the differences between Jay's richly modeled, lively figures and John's stiffer, less volumetric ones (figs. 37, 74). A few of the City Island figures are very awkwardly drawn and appear to be by a second hand; the tracery is John's own design. The lost *Brazen Serpent* window is another example of his tendency to see in linear patterns (fig. 77). Typically, the drapery looks flat, especially that on the figures standing on either side of the serpent.

Whatever it was John had in mind when he resigned his post in Morristown, it must not have been the success he anticipated, for on 31 October 1863 he was called to and accepted the pulpit of the Church of the Holy Trinity, West Chester, Pennsylvania. John's talent for design would soon serve him again, however, when a larger church was needed. Although times were hard, and it was not until January 1868 that the new church could be started,[18] the architect chosen was none other than John Bolton himself, which adds weight to comments about his earlier activities in architecture. His design shows the influence of Frank Wills's Holy Innocents in Albany. He also designed and made the stained glass windows, which consist of pairs of lancets (doublets) in the nave and vestibule, decorated with a single but handsome design of silver-stain circles overlaid with stenciled patterns and set on a grisaille ground. Once again, some of the leading is painted sham. The western gable holds a roundel similar to one at St. Mary's, Scarborough. The space over the altar is now filled by an early John La Farge memorial window (1889) dedicated to Bolton's by then deceased wife and daughter; no record exists of what was there before.

Appendix B

For the vestibule of the adjoining rectory, John made two more lancets that combine several grisaille devices from St. Mary's, Scarborough, and include an *Agnus Dei* and a pelican-in-piety on colored shields (fig. 76).

John Bolton was much loved at West Chester, and when he resigned his duties in 1891 at age seventy-three, he was given the title of Dean, which was mostly honorary, but which expressed the high esteem in which he was held by the people whom he had served. He died in West Chester in 1898.

Notes

1. The early facts of John's life are reported by R. P. Bolton, "A Heritage of Piety." The first published biography of John is a brief résumé in Maxon, "The Stained Glass in St. Mary's," 49–51. Somewhat more information is provided in Skinner, "The Stained Glass of the Brothers . . . Bolton."

2. R. P. Bolton, "A Heritage of Piety," 120.

3. For John's work with Jay in stained glass, see Chapter 3 and the Catalog. For his participation in the sculpture at Pelham, R. P. Bolton, "A Heritage of Piety," 120, who says that he carved some of the Christ Church corbels, which closely resemble corbels in the Church of the Holy Sepulchre, Cambridge.

4. W. J. Bolton to James Bolton, 7 February 1845, Long Island Diocese Archives, Garden City, N.Y.; text in Appendix A.

5. Ibid.

6. Ibid.

7. *New York Exhibition of the Industry of all Nations. Official Catalogue* (New York: Putnam & Co., 1853), 80–81. I am indebted to Virginia Wright of the Corning Museum of Glass for this interesting reference. The other exhibitors were: Bauman & Winter, Atlantic Street, Brooklyn; William J. Hannington, 364 Broadway, New York City; Sharp & Steel, 216 Sixth Avenue, New York City; Charles J. Thurston, Buffalo, N.Y.; Matilda C. Stephenson, East Brooklyn; E. K. Collins (whose entry was painted by Hannington), 56 Wall Street, New York City; H. L. Bidwell (with painting by Hannington), Hartford, Conn.

8. The Rev. Edward N. Mead drew the plans, based on the north aisle chapel of St. Mary's, York; Henry, *St. Mary's Church of Scarborough,* 2. See Maxon, "The Stained Glass in St. Mary's"; and Robert Bolton, Jr., *History of the Protestant Episcopal Church,* 717.

9. Frank Wills was the architect of Holy Innocents. See Wills's *Ancient English Ecclesiastical Architecture,* 117. The church was opened for services on 3 February 1850. James R. Hobin of the Albany Institute of History and Art was kind enough to furnish a summary of the church's early years. See also the Sunday *Albany Times Union,* 26 June 1983, pp. D-1, D-2.

10. St. Mary's: 19 windows, all by John Bolton. Central altar medallion: Last Supper; lesser medallions in center and side lancets: Evangelists' symbols, pelican, dove, St. Andrew's cross, *Agnus Dei.* Nave and transepts: 9 patterned quarry lancets with medallions holding symbols of the Passion; roundels in transepts with Trinity symbols.

John Jay Bolton

West facade: 5 slender grisaille lancets on a Jay Bolton design at Pelham. St. Mary's remains an active Protestant Episcopal parish.

Holy Innocents: 11 windows by John Bolton, over altar, in west facade, and in two western bays of nave. Central altar medallions: Crucifixion below, Trinity diagram above; medallions in side lancets: Evangelists' symbols. Nave: 4 patterned quarry lancets. West facade: 4 slender lancets of John's "Salisbury" type at Pelham. Until recently, Holy Innocents was used by a Russian Orthodox congregation; efforts are presently under way to preserve this historic building and its important windows.

11. Wills, *Ancient English Ecclesiastical Architecture,* 117. The side chancel windows are no longer visible.

12. Robert Bolton, Jr., *History of the Protestant Episcopal Church,* 713; he notes that the entire cost of the church, including the glass, was $5,000.

13. Douglas Eldridge, Senior Warden of the church, in a letter of 8 July 1977 reported that the windows, which consisted of nine doublets in the nave and two in the east end, were badly damaged by vandals, fires, and weather, and were removed by a contractor and probably scrapped. Mr. Eldridge recalled that the windows appeared to be from various periods.

14. Patrick Snadon made me aware of the Bolton windows in the Hunt house, and of their condition. The house is now the headquarters of the Lexington Art League, which was kind enough to furnish the photograph that illustrates the windows here.

15. Hunt to Davis, 26 May 1852, A. J. Davis Collection, New York Public Library. I am grateful to Professor Snadon for a transcript of this letter. He also sent a copy of entries from Davis's Day Book for 18 June 1851 ("John Bolton, glass stainer & left order for Hunt glass. Visited Miss Bolton [Nanette?], Pelham Priory") and 13 October 1851 ("Bill of John Bolton for 159 lights of stained glass border at 80 ct, settled with Bolton"). Snadon notes that these last would have been for the drawing-room windows.

16. R. P. Bolton, "A Heritage of Piety," 120.

17. Vestry minutes quoted in a letter of 26 June 1975 from the Reverend F. Sanford Cutler of the Church of the Redeemer.

18. *The Church of the Holy Trinity, West Chester,* 32. I am grateful to Caroline H. Rubicam, a member of the congregation, for much useful material on the church.

Appendix C

The Bolton Family in the United States

Robert Bolton (1688–1742) m. Ann, widow of Robert Clay
of Phila.; arr. Phila. 1718 or 1720
.

Robert Bolton (1722–1789) m. Mrs. Stirk (d. 1794)
.

Robert Bolton (1757–1802) m. Sarah McClean (1757–1806)
of Chestertown, Md.
.

Robert Bolton (1788–1857) m. Ann Jay of Bath (1793–1859)
.

Robert (1814–1877)
Ann (Nanette) (1815–1884)
WILLIAM JAY (1816–1884)
JOHN JAY (1818–1898)
Cornelius Winter (1819–1906)
Mary Statira (b. 1820)
Arabella (1822–1860)
James (1824–1863)
Rhoda (1825–1887)
Abby (1827–1849)
Meta (1828–1828)
Adele and Adelaide (1830–after 1895)
Frances Georgianna (b. 1831)

The Family of William Jay Bolton

William Jay Bolton (1816–1884) (m. 1) Susannah Welch
(d. 1850) of King's Lynn
.

Susannah (1850–probably after 1907)
(m. 2) Margaretta Elizabeth Jones Wilkinson (1827–1903)
of Sudbury, Suffolk
.

William Henry (1859–1902)
Arabella Sarah (1860–1861)
Margaretta Grace (1861–after 1933)
James Edward (1863–1928)
Robert Wilkinson (1865–1896)

Glossary

ABRADE (ABRASION). To remove some of the surface of the glass to create a decorative effect; used often with FLASHED GLASS to reveal the color below.

AGNUS DEI. "Lamb of God," a motif depicting a lamb, often with a cross, representing Christ as a sacrifice.

AISLE. In a church, the passageways, often with seating, on either side of the NAVE.

ARMATURE. The supporting framework of a stained glass window; made of iron, bronze, or wood.

ARMORIAL WINDOW. A window whose principal design is a heraldic device or coat-of-arms.

ART GLASS. Decorative and figural glass mass-produced and often sold through catalogs; see OPALESCENT GLASS.

BADGERING. The working of MATT with a firm brush to remove areas of paint in order to create highlights.

BORDER. The outer frame of glass, usually colored and decorated, in a stained glass window; see FILLET.

CAME. See LEAD.

CARTOON. The final drawing for a window; it is the full size of the window (or panel in a window).

CHANCEL. The sanctuary or main-altar area of a church.

CHARGE. The symbols on the shield of a coat of arms.

CLERESTORY. The uppermost window level in a building.

DAMASCENE. Dense floral patterns, often with an oriental character, painted or scratched into the MATT in a stained glass design as an ornamental background.

DIAPER PATTERN. A repeat-pattern background design, usually consisting of square or lozenge shapes.

DOUBLET. A window consisting of two main lights.

ENAMEL. Vitreous paint, either the browns and blacks of MATT and TRACE, or, in later periods of glass painting, a variety of colors. The colors usually become more or less transparent when fired on the glass.

FILLET. Any thin edging strip of glass in a stained glass design.

FIRING. The process of heating painted glass so that the ENAMEL paints or the SILVER STAIN will adhere to or fuse with the glass.

Glossary

FLASHED GLASS. Glass in which a thin layer of color has been fused to the surface of glass of another color, usually WHITE GLASS.

FLUX. The substance, usually borax, added to enamel paints to assist the paints' adherence to the glass when fired.

GALLERY. The middle window level in a building; architecturally, a covered, arcaded area or open tier of seats above the aisles of a church.

GLAZIER. A maker of glass windows; here, a maker of stained glass windows.

GRISAILLE. "Grey-tone" windows; clear, or WHITE, glass with a decorative design in brown or black enamel paint to tone down the light passing through; the effect of the whole window at a distance is greyish.

LANCET. A tall, narrow window.

LEAD, LEADING. Extruded lead strips, usually in an H shape, used to hold together the pieces of glass in a design.

LEAD LINES. The opaque lines created by the leading in a stained glass design.

LIGHT. A single opening in a window; stained glass windows often have several lights.

LUNETTE. A window, or window area, shaped as a half-circle.

MATT, MATTING. A thin wash of brown enamel painted on the glass before details of faces, drapery, etc., are added, and which can be worked with brush, quill, or stick to create shadows and highlights.

MEDALLION. A geometric panel of leaded colored glass usually combined with other such panels to create a window design; typical of earlier medieval windows; compare ROUNDEL.

MULLION. A vertical member of stone or wood that divides a window into LIGHTs.

MURREY. A reddish purple color; can vary in intensity.

NAVE. In a church, the large central area for the congregation.

OCULUS. A circular, usually small window.

OPALESCENT GLASS. Glass invented in the late nineteenth century; semi-opaque and characterized by a mottled color effect. Often used in making ART GLASS windows.

OXIDES. The metallic oxide pigments of colored glasses; see POTMETAL.

PAINT. In stained glass, the ENAMEL colors, including MATT and TRACE paint.

PANEL. A division of a window, usually rectangular and set horizontally, that is part of the support system rather than the design.

PATINA. A film created on the exterior surface of glass by the action of weather and, more recently, pollution.

POTMETAL. Glass colored in the molten state by metallic oxide pigments.

Glossary

QUARRY. A square or diamond-shaped pane of glass.

QUILL WORK, QUILLING. A design scratched in a MATT or other ENAMEL color with a fine-pointed tool.

REGISTER. A range of scenes in a window.

ROUNDEL. A circular glass panel on which the design is usually painted rather than carried out in potmetal; it usually has a minimum of leading.

SILVER STAIN. A yellow to orange, and even red, transparent color stained on the glass by painting it with a silver nitrate pigment and firing the glass.

SMEAR-SHADING. The laying on of MATT in a WASH to create shadows; can be carried out in layers to create degrees of darkness.

STENCILING. The production of repeated decorative designs, often in borders and usually in TRACE paint, by means of cut-out patterns.

STICK-LIGHTING. The removal of MATT using a fine-pointed stick, to create subtle highlights.

STIPPLE-SHADING. The creation of highlights in a MATT by dabbing with the blunt end of a thick, stiff brush.

TRACE, TRACING. The painting of facial features, outlines, and other details in opaque brown or black ENAMELS.

TRACERY. Ornamental cutwork designs of stone or wood in the top of a window opening.

TRANSEPT. In a cross-shaped church plan, the crosspiece at the sanctuary end (occasionally at both ends).

TRIPLET. A window consisting of three main LIGHTS.

VIDIMUS. Latin, meaning "We have seen it"; sketch of a stained glass design presented to the patron or shop master for approval.

WASH. A thin coating of paint.

WHITE GLASS. Clear, essentially colorless glass.

YELLOW STAIN. See SILVER STAIN.

Catalog of the Art
of William Jay Bolton

The known works in all media by William Jay Bolton appear in this catalog. The introductions to the stained glass projects provide a summary of each building's history, of the iconographic program of the windows, and of significant technical matters. A plan of the building, showing window locations, can be found just before the colorplates. Iconographic details of individual windows are described in the entry for each window. Most designs can probably be attributed to Jay, except for the Priory armorials; attributions given here for individual windows relate to execution. Windows are numbered by location in the building, reading clockwise from the main entrance. Location symbols are as follows: for churches, N=nave, T=transept, Ch=chancel, A=aisle, G=gallery, C=clerestory, L=loft or stairwell, V=vestibule, Tw=tower; for the Priory, F=first floor, S=second floor, Tw=tower. Titles and inscriptions written in the window itself are printed here in capital letters. Colors are potmetal unless stated otherwise. The symbol * indicates that a preparatory sketch exists for the window.

I. Pelham, N.Y.: The Priory (glazed ca. 1838–43)

The house was almost certainly designed by a family member, and was built in 1838 of dark grey, local granite, with a brick south stairwell tower, probably added after completion of the main building (fig. 1a). The Priory's English castellated style is complemented on the interior first floor by carved chimneypieces and oak paneling (fig. 1b). There are six sets of stained glass armorials, most on the first floor, with arms of various branches of the Bolton family (fig. 1c). For some of the armorial designs, see Robert Bolton, Jr., *Genealogical and Biographical Account,* 28–31. The designs for most of the armorial windows are most likely by Robert, Jr., who is reported to have had a keen interest in heraldry. The earliest of the Priory armorials are perhaps the relatively crude ones at the head of the stairs on the second floor; the latest and best are those attributed to Jay in the south tower (fig. 1d).

Main house

> *Date:* armorial windows ca. 1838 and after. *Colors:* all include blue and red potmetal, silver stain, and some black enamel in the charges. *Condition:* good, but with flaking and deterioration of paint.

I F1 (Northeast room): 5 armorials in transoms, 3 with ground patterns in grisaille similar to those attrib. to Jay Bolton in Christ Church.

I F2: White glass only.

I F3 (Southeast room): 6 armorials in transoms, with grisaille as well as damascene grounds.

fig. 1c I F4 (Library): 5 armorials in transoms, set on grounds of grisaille and colored glass.

I F5 (Armory): 2 large armorials in transoms.

I S1 (Stair landing): 2 armorials in transoms. *Colors:* as on first floor, but cruder workmanship.

I S2 (Joining of south tower to main house): an interior wall half glazed with clear-glass quarries and patterned colored-glass borders. Probably made about the same time as the south tower armorials.

South tower stairwell

Two armorials attributable to Jay Bolton. Arms on shields set in quadrilobes on quilled grounds, Gothic foliate manteling; in Tw2 the Bolton dove is set on a shield of delicate quilled damascene on a sepia ground. *Date:* ca. 1843. *Colors:* ruby and dark blue potmetal, silver-stain yellow, pink-brown matt.

I Tw1: Arms of Pelham Manor, inscribed THE MANOR OF PELHAM.

fig. 1d I Tw2: Arms of Bolton family, inscribed BOLTON OF BOLTON.

REFERENCES

R. P. Bolton, "William Jay Bolton," 29, 31; W. B. Clark, "America's First Stained Glass," 35.

II. Pelham, N.Y.: Christ Church (glazed by 1843)

Christ Church was built by the Bolton family and presented to the Diocese of New York in 1843. Again the design was most likely by a family member, probably John, and was described as "transitional second pointed" (i.e., early 14th c.) by Winter Bolton in his revision of Robert, Jr.'s *History of the Several Towns* II:96 (figs. 3a–c). It is built of local granite in an English parish-church manner, and was designed as a single vessel without aisles, covered by a timbered ceiling decorated with corbel figures carved by Bolton sons, who also carved the pulpit, former gallery and altar rail, and chancel furniture (fig. 3c). Ornamented altar panels, now in the transept, are by John Bolton. The church originally measured 65 × 22', but was enlarged in 1910, the original nave, on a north-south axis, becoming the transept for a longer, east-west nave. There are 10 stained glass windows

---

by the Boltons, 6 by Jay and 4 by John. The only figural window (T2; colorplate I), by Jay, is a simple opening divided by the mullions supporting three slender wooden arches; it was made for a cost of $50 to $60 (see Chapter I). For the altar area, there is what appears to be a preparatory drawing—perhaps by John, whose descendant now owns it—showing that the original design for the window may have included modest tracery (fig. 3b); the present north transept window (with modern glass) contains tracery in this design. The change in the window design is discussed in Chapter 3. Other Bolton windows in the church consist of single grisaille lancets. According to Winter Bolton, both Jay and John donated the windows they made. The potmetal colors used at Christ Church are few but rich, and include ruby, dark blue, purple, and an olive green; these are enhanced by a variety of silver-stain yellows and oranges. Enamels are used for one color in the *Magi* window, and to achieve the proper heraldic color in several armorials. The grisaille windows all have a thin, stippled matt to control the light. The Christ Church windows have recently been releaded, and both repainting and replacement pieces occur.

II T1,4; N4,5: Grisaille windows by Jay Bolton   *fig. 5*
> *Date:* ca. 1843. *Measurements:* 28¾ × 68½″. *Iconography:* small squirrel and small smiling face in foliage of T4, small smiling and frowning faces in N5, tiny caterpillars in T1, N5. *Colors:* dark blue, ruby, medium to light olive green potmetals, silver stain. *Technical features:* all curving and diagonal lead-lines drawn in trace paint except in lower part of N4, where they are real; vines made from a stencil, leaves freehand. *Condition:* moderate deterioration of paint, sometimes repainted; small piece missing lower rt of T1. *Comments:* N5 has a wide variety of silver-stain tones, and could be made of panels rejected from other windows, which may have occasioned the whimsical sad and happy faces painted in the foliage. The finest painting is in T1, perhaps the last of Jay's Pelham grisailles to be made.

II T2: Adoration of the Magi, by Jay Bolton   *plate I*
> *Date:* completed 1843. *Measurements:* 10 × 9′. *Iconography:* Mary at center holding Babe, Joseph upper lf, shepherd upper rt, three Magi kneeling (Matt. 2:11). The original idea for the scene may have included several more figures, a curving architectural backdrop instead of the shed, and simple tracery, as seen in a drawing (fig. 3b). *Source:* ?St. Martin, Liège, Life of the Virgin window, lower panels of upper register. *Colors:* Virgin: pink enamel, white; male figures lf to rt: purple, dark blue, and white; ruby; ruby and purple; dark blue; ruby and white

with silver-stain trim. Columns with silver stain matted to resemble gilt. *Inscription:* at bottom, MATT.H 2 CHAPT 11 VER (hidden by carved wooden rail across bottom of opening). *Condition:* heads of Babe and of turbanned Magus to rt replaced or redrawn.

fig. 6   II T3, N1: Grisaille windows by John Bolton
Date: ca. 1843. *Measurements:* 20³⁄₄ × 68¹⁄₂". *Source:* said to be based on windows of Salisbury Cathedral (C. W. Bolton's revision of Robert, Jr. *The History of the Several Towns* II:96). *Colors:* ruby and blue potmetal, some red enamel in border of N1, silver stain. *Condition:* deterioration of paint, some repainting, small replacement pieces in border of N1.

fig. 7   II N2, 3: Floral quarry windows with armorial insets, by ?John Bolton and unknown assistant
Date: 1850 or after. *Measurements:* 15¹⁄₄ × 45¹⁄₂" *Colors:* ruby and blue potmetal, silver stain, black enamel. Arms: N2 Bolton, N3 Pelham Manor with inscription R 1850 AD B, meaning probably that Robert Bolton, Jr., gave it. Quarry designs: N2 rose and lily alternate; N3 rose and stylized flower. *Comment:* borders of N2 by unskilled and unknown painter.

II TC3: *Agnus Dei* oculus by Jay Bolton (C. W. Bolton's revision of Robert, Jr.'s *History of the Several Towns* II:96).
Date: after 1843 (physical evidence of installation after completion of building). *Colors:* white glass on bright green damascened potmetal, red enamel cross on banner.

II NC1: Large figural window by Meyer of Munich, 20th c.
II TC2,4: Later memorial windows
II TC1 and 6 chancel windows 20th c.

REFERENCES

C. W. Bolton's revision of Robert Bolton, Jr., *The History of the Several Towns; Christ Church at Pelham;* Mead, "If You Like Historic Spots. William Jay Bolton's Studio"; Barr, *A Brief . . . Account,* passim; Roberts, "William Jay Bolton—Artist in Glass"; Edgar H. Browne, "It Happened in Pelham," *Pelham Sun,* 25 June 1964; Larsen, *A Handbook on the Symbolism of Christ Church;* Reeves, "Bolton Priory and Christ Church"; A. C. Downs, "Stained Glass in American Architecture," 56; W. B. Clark, "America's First Stained Glass," 35–36, 38–40, and "Gothic Revival Stained Glass of William Jay Bolton."

III. Brooklyn, N.Y.: Church of (St. Ann and) the Holy Trinity (glazing begun ?1844, completed 1848)

The Church of the Holy Trinity was begun as a private institution in 1844, funded entirely by Edgar John Bartow of Pelham and Brooklyn, but was admitted into the Diocese of New York in 1852;[1] with the rest of Brooklyn, it is now in the Diocese of Long Island. The building is constructed of red sandstone in the Decorated style (English, late 13th–14th c.), with numerous pinnacles and ornamental gables, and a large single tower over the entry vestibule; the window tracery style is Flamboyant (French, late 14th–15th c.; fig. 8).[2] The interior of the church measures 57 × 170', including the aisles and the vestibule; the crown of the elaborate tierceron and lierne vault reaches a height of 63' (fig. 9). There is a broad (42') but relatively shallow chancel at the western end, and a wooden choir loft over the nave entry in the east; both the chancel and the choir loft have been somewhat altered, but without disturbing their glazing. A large wooden gallery flanks the nave on both sides and obscures the heads of the aisle windows (fig. 9). Although this gallery appears in Lafever's posthumous *Architectural Instructor* (1856, pl. XCVII), the awkward relationship to the aisle windows suggests that it might have been added as an afterthought.[3] The church's interior is enlivened with an abundance of elegant detail: clustered (plastered) piers, a profusion of plaster ornament, and carved black walnut wainscoting.

Jay and John Bolton made all but a few windows at Holy Trinity, for a total of 49, or 50 if the opalescent window of the north vestibule wall replaces a Bolton one.[4] These consist of 3 ranks of large, mostly figural windows distributed across the 7 bays of the main vessel, and in the chancel, vestibule, and tower. Most windows are composed of 3 lancets with trefoil heads, surmounted by Flamboyant tracery;[5] frames, mullions, and tracery are of wood. The aisle and gallery windows are joined by transoms of white-glass quarries behind the wooden galleries, an arrangement that appears somewhat awkward on the interior, but that permits the two levels to be viewed as a single opening on the exterior (figs. 8,9). This exterior effect was aided by the Boltons' unusual but practical manner of installation that allowed protective glazing to be continuous behind the mullions.[6] In November 1985 the tower window was dismounted, most of it to be installed in the American Wing of the Metropolitan Museum of Art.[7]

The program of the Holy Trinity windows relates to Evangelical Anglican doctrine, which emphasizes justification by faith alone, the believer's communication directly with God, and a polarity of sin and salvation. The narrative series of the nave begins with a Tree of Jesse and Christ's ancestors along the aisles and continues as follows:

Catalog:

Holy Trinity

Clerestory	*Gallery*
(Untitled)	(Titled by Bolton)
Expulsion from Eden (C9)	The Birth of Christ (= Adoration of
Man Labors (C10)	the Shepherds) (G8)
Cain and Abel (C11)	The Baptism of Christ (G9)
Noah's Sacrifice (C12)	Christ at the Well (G10)
Sacrifice of Isaac (C13)	Marriage at Cana (G11)
Jacob's Blessing (C14)	Christ Enters Jerusalem (G12)
Jacob's Dream (C15)	Christ Heals the Blind Man (G13)
Jacob Meets Joseph (C16)	Christ Stills the Tempest (G14)
Finding of Moses (C1)	Raising of Lazarus (untitled) (G1)
Moses with the Tablets (C2)	Transfiguration of Christ (G2)
The Brazen Serpent (C3)	Christ in Gethsemane (untitled) (G3)
Joshua Stills the Sun and Moon (C4)	The Trial of Christ (G4)
Samson with the Gates of Gaza (C5)	The Crucifixion (untitled) (G5)
Coronation of David (C6)	Resurrection of Christ (G6)
Building the Temple (C7)	Christ at Emmaus (G7)
Reading of Deuteronomy (C8)	

There is no significance to vertical alignment of windows in the clerestory and gallery.[8] The narrative begins in the north clerestory with the *Expulsion,* humankind's separation from God as a consequence of sin, and chronicles Old Testament expressions of faith (*Noah's Sacrifice, Sacrifice of Isaac*); contact with God (*Jacob's Dream,* which also prefigures the cross); prefigurations of Christ (*Samson with the Gates of Gaza* and *Coronation of David*) and of the Crucifixion (*The Brazen Serpent*). It concludes with a rare, perhaps unique, scene, *Reading of Deuteronomy,* which probably had a special meaning for Evangelicals. The window portrays the finding of the Book of Law, its presentation to King Josiah, and his subsequent banishment of false gods from the Temple. Evangelicals would have seen in these events an analogous banishment of "popery" from the Church. The gallery windows, again beginning on the north, recount the life of Christ, from his birth to the post-Resurrection supper at Emmaus, the latter reconfirming Holy Communion, one of the two Anglican sacraments (the other is Baptism), both of which are depicted in the side windows of the chancel. It was at Emmaus that Christ reiterated for his traveling companions the prophecies of his life and work (Luke 24:27), thus linking the New Testament to the Old. It is Christ himself as Savior who forms the ultimate link between the Old and New Testament subjects at Holy Trinity, and reference to him is made throughout. Supporting both upper ranks, literally and symbolically, is the Tree of Jesse in the aisle windows. Its unusual serial arrangement of repeated designs includes portraits of the ancestors of Christ.⁹ The Jesse Tree series begins at the back of the south aisle and concludes with the Joseph-Mary-Christ window in the baptistry at the back of the north aisle. Because of the location chosen for the baptistry, this series runs counter to those of the upper stories. The great chancel window depicts Christ's ascent to Heaven, the final act of his earthly life.¹⁰ The scene is flanked by windows symbolizing the Anglican sacraments, Holy Communion and Baptism.

In many windows the tracery contains motifs related to the scene below, such as a rainbow for *Noah's Sacrifice,* cherubim and a star for *The Birth of Christ* (colorplates V, VI), pillars of cloud and fire for *Joshua Stills the Sun and Moon* (fig. 22), an ax for John in the *Baptism,* marine motifs for *Christ Stills the Tempest,* symbols of the Passion for *The Crucifixion.* Occasionally the meaning of tracery images is not clear—for example, the urn, swords, and teapot in *The Trial of Christ* (fig. 37). Where there is no specific iconographic relationship between tracery and main scene, one of three tracery programs is used:

> Type 1: passionflowers, red and white roses, non-specific flowers
> (fig. 23)
> Type 2: angels; quill, inkwell, and scroll; lily; ?cloak; red roses
> (fig. 29b)
> Type 3: grape arbor with yellow grapes, red birds (fig. 26).

Obviously the dominant theme in all three is the Passion (passionflower, red rose, lily, grapes). Type 1 is the most frequent; Type 2 appears in both gallery and clerestory; Type 3 in the clerestory only. It is surely not coincidental that the red roses in Types 1 and 2 are virtually identical with the Lancaster roses seen in the great east window at King's College Chapel.

Although there are many reminiscences of the King's College Chapel windows in Jay Bolton's designs for Holy Trinity, none of the latter are based specifically on King's windows, and it is almost certain that he was working from memory and not from sketches. As an example, the color at Holy Trinity is increasingly intense and pervasive in the compositions, but, as Bolton noted in his later article on the King's glass, the King's artists "collected [the color] into nosegays" surrounded by large amounts of white glass. In some instances where Bolton's designs seem to concur with those at King's, such as the *Entry into Jerusalem* (King's Chapel, B12), the King's window uses a popular compositional motif. Where a Holy Trinity design recalls one that is unique to King's, it is at some remove. For example, Bolton's *The Trial of Christ* (fig. 37) appears to combine motifs from the *Mocking of Christ* (by the Fairford painter) and *Christ before Caiaphas* (by

---

Dirk Vellert) at King's,[11] without being a convincing copy of either. In one instance, *Christ at Emmaus* (fig. 40), the King's artist (Vellert) and Bolton used as model the same Albrecht Dürer print, Bolton's version being closer to the original than is Vellert's.[12] By contrast, Bolton's major design after returning to England, the one for West Lynn (colorplate X), draws directly on passages in King's Chapel windows, as if to confirm the fact that in the United States, Bolton had only his recollections of the Cambridge glass to call upon. A watercolor for an Ascension window that has direct borrowings from King's was probably also made after Jay's return (fig. 42). The most important source of Holy Trinity designs was Raphael and his shop in the Vatican Logge, with Bolton drawing either on his sketches of these or on published reproductions. Designs based on work attributed to sixteenth-century Flemish artists, including Vellert, appear in two, probably three Holy Trinity windows (G4,G11,G14); other sources are, each in one window, Dürer (G7), probably Hans Holbein the Younger (C14), and possibly a painting by the seventeenth-century Dutch artist Pieter Lastman (G1). The Ancestor portraits of the Jesse Tree bear a close resemblance to figures in Hartmann Schedel's *Nuremberg Chronicle* (figs. 10e,f).

The color at Holy Trinity is spectacular. The potmetal colors used at Pelham—ruby, dark blue, deep purple, and olive and yellow-green—are increased by the addition of emerald green, pink, and murrey (rose-purple). The wide range of stains at Pelham is further enriched by the very interesting russet red (see Chapter 2). Abraded passages in the ruby and murrey indicate that they are both flashes. To extend his color range even further, Bolton used a light blue and a pink enamel, mostly in small amounts, to enliven the effects of soil and rocks in the landscape, but occasionally also for clothing; in one case (G14) there is a green enamel used for water. For shaping contours Bolton employed both badgered and stippled matts, and smear-shading; stippling predominates for the shading of the face.

The Holy Trinity windows have sustained heavy damage over the years, and are presently undergoing thorough cleaning and restoration.[13] The deterioration of matt as well as trace paint at Holy Trinity is discussed in Chapter 2, where it was noted that, whatever the cause, the effect is more pronounced on the south side of the church. For many years Otto Heinigke and his son Otto Weir Heinigke saw to the preservation of the Holy Trinity windows. It is probably the father who painted several new pieces in a Jesse Tree window, where severe breakage was caused about 1904 by a fire during construction of a subway directly beneath the church;[14] damage to other aisle windows has resulted from the opening and closing of a tilt panel in each center light. All windows continue to suffer from the vibrations of the

---

trains passing below. During the period of anti-Communist hysteria in the 1950s, the liberalism of the Holy Trinity clergy came into conflict with the diocesan hierarchy, resulting in a decline in the parish's fortunes and its eventual dissolution in the summer of 1957. For a brief time a Spanish Protestant congregation took over, after which followed a period of complete closure. In 1967, St. Ann's School moved to a site around the corner from Holy Trinity and since 1969 has used the church for theatrical productions. Meanwhile parishioners of Holy Trinity and the nearby Church of St. Ann joined together and began to use Holy Trinity for services, and its name was changed to St. Ann and Holy Trinity. The vicissitudes and varying uses all took their toll on both the building and its stained glass windows. By the time I began studying the windows in 1975, some were in a desperate condition. Pieces were lost, others broken, many pulling away from the leads, and all were covered with soot and grime; rain fell through holes in the roof to wet the gallery seats and harden the filth between glass and leading.[15] The cost of preservation, let alone restoration, was prohibitive for a small school and a tiny congregation, and it looked as though these monuments of American stained glass would be lost. Then in 1976 the parish was reconstituted, and St. Ann and Holy Trinity was designated a diocesan church. The long-vacant post of rector was filled by the Reverend Franklin Vilas, Jr., who, being persuaded of the signal importance of the stained glass, together with members of the Vestry initiated the restoration program. In 1979 the New York Landmarks Conservancy took the church and its windows as a special project, and with generous grants from several private foundations and the World Monuments Fund, the building has been repaired and the precious windows are gradually being restored.[16] The restorer, The Greenland Studio of New York City, is taking an appropriately conservative approach to the task, replacing and repainting only those pieces that had been lost by the time the restoration began; all original glass is being mended and conserved as is. In November 1988 a national center for the study of stained glass conservation was established at St. Ann and Holy Trinity.

Measurements (glazed area, height by width):
    Vestibule (*Hannah* window): 10′6″ × 5′6″
    Aisle windows: 5′6″ × 5′7″
    Gallery windows: 8′2″ × 5′6″ (transom 2′8″ high)
    Clerestory windows: 10′6″ × 5′6″
    Main chancel window: 40 × 20′
    Side chancel windows: 10′6″ × 5′6″
    Tower window: 40 × 20′

Vestibule

Two windows, the one on the north side by Jay Bolton, the other a late nineteenth-century opalescent window by an unknown glazier. Both have three lancets with trilobe heads and Flamboyant tracery.

fig. 46 III V1: HANNAH BRINGS SAMUEL UNTO THE HOUSE OF THE LORD, by Jay Bolton, lower tracery angels by John, the columns by John or another assistant.
Date: ca. 1845. *Iconography:* Hannah and Samuel in Temple vestibule as she gives him to God (1 Sam. 1:24). *Colors in main scene:* Hannah in blue cloak, white dress, pink hat; green and ruby curtains; the rest in grisaille and silver stain. *Condition:* damage, probably from 1904 fire in subway beneath the church to lower panel of each light, replacement in lower rt corner, base of lf column repainted. *Comment:* while the columns in the Pelham *Magi* window are painted with great precision, these are not, and either John or another assistant must have done them.
III V2: late 19th–early 20th c. opalescent memorial window

Aisles

Tree of Jesse (Isa. 11:1–2) with angels/Ancestors of Christ (Matt. 1:1–16)—14 windows. *Date:* first installations probably by August 1845 (Bartow letter to WJB). Angels flanking heavy tree, Ancestors of Christ in the branches; some angels appear to derive directly from Raphael and his shop (fig. 10c), others more generally; Ancestor figures closely resemble woodcut busts in Hartmann Schedel, *Nuremberg Chronicle* (1493) (fig. 10f). Seven angel cartoons in mirror images in A1–7, repeated in A8–14; the grounds are always damascened dark blue, but by at least two hands; the tree is brown enamel with a ruby, white, blue, or purple passionflower at its base; all Ancestors named on phylacteries, using transliterated Greek form. Windows composed of 3 lancets with trilobe heads (partially hidden by gallery).
III A1: ABRAHAM-ISAAC-JACOB, by Jay Bolton
Iconography: Abraham with scroll inscribed COVENANT; angel below Jacob holds ladder. *Source:* perhaps Raphael's *Philosophy* figure in the ceiling of the Stanza della Segnatura, Vatican. *Colors:* angels in ruby, white, blue, silver stain; Ancestors, respectively, in blue, ruby, white. *Condition:* lf angel head, shoulders, and other pieces to lf replaced; rt angel head and shoulders replaced, most or all of costume from peplum down replaced. Restored 1983 by Greenland Studio.

III A2: JUDAH-PARES-EZROM, by Jay Bolton
Iconography: Judah with crozier-scepter (Gen. 49:10). *Colors:* angels in white with green cloaks; Ancestors in ruby, ruby, blue. *Condition:* minor replacements lower middle light, rt angel's head repainted. Restored 1983 by Greenland Studio.

III A3: ARAM-AMINADAB-NAASON, angels by Jay Bolton, Naason by John
Iconography: Naason, meaning "Enchanter," with hands raised as if casting spell. *Colors:* angels in white with ruby cloaks; Ancestors in ruby, purple, blue. *Condition:* replacements at rt in center and lower panels of middle light; replacement, repainting in lower rt light; much fracturing in rt light; deterioration of brown enamel on upper tree. Restored 1985 by Greenland Studio.

III A4: SALMON-BOOZ-OBED, by Jay Bolton
Iconography: no distinguishing features. *Colors:* angels in white with purple and ruby cloaks; Ancestors in green and white, murrey, white. *Condition:* most of Obed replaced; replacement in lower lf light; large stopgap in center and lower panels of middle light. Restored 1990 by Greenland Studio.

III A5: JESSE-DAVID-SOLOMON, by Jay Bolton   *plate IV*
Iconography: Jesse with shepherd's crook, David as king, Solomon as young king with scepter and orb; Jesse angel holds branch, Solomon angel holds scepter. *Source:* perhaps Raphael's *Justice* in the ceiling of the Stanza della Segnatura at the Vatican (fig. 10c). *Colors:* angels in blue and purple; Ancestors in white and blue, ruby and green, white and green. *Condition:* good. Restored 1990 by Greenland Studio.

III A6: ROBOAM-ABIA-ASA, by Jay Bolton.   *fig. 10d*
Iconography: Roboam with ?scourge to humble himself (2 Chron. 12:12); Abi[j]a as king (1 Kings 15:1); the pious Asa in prayer (1 Kings 15:11–14). *Colors:* angels in green and blue, green and ruby; Ancestors in ruby and green, ruby, white. *Condition:* replacement to lf of Roboam; stopgap for lf angel's head; serious deterioration of matt in lower middle light; replacement in skirt of rt angel. Restored 1990 by Greenland Studio.

III A7: JOSAPHAT-JORAM-OZIAS, by Jay Bolton   *fig. 10a*
Iconography: ancestors as kings, Josaphat (Jehoshaphat) holding book of kings inscribed ASA (2 Chron. 16:11). *Source:* perhaps Raphael's *Justice* ceiling figure in the Stanza della Segnatura, Vatican (fig. 10c). *Colors:* angels in white and blue; Ancestors in ruby, ruby, purple and white. *Condition:* piece missing at center of middle light; replacements in head

of rt angel and at bottom rt of rt light. Restored 1990 by Greenland Studio.

III A8: JOATHAM-ACHAZ-EZEKIAS, angels by John Bolton, Ancestors by Jay
Iconography: Achaz and Ezekias (Hezekiah) as kings. *Source:* see A1. *Colors:* angels in ruby blouse, white and purple skirt (lf angel has red wings, and green not red sleeve, which seems to be original); Ancestors in ruby, ruby, blue. *Condition:* stopgap to rt of lf angel, small missing piece lower rt of lf light; missing pieces upper middle light; small missing pieces upper and bottom rt light; replacement pieces below Joatham; deteriorated matt in tree lower middle light.

III A9: MANASSES-AMON-JOSIAS, angels by John Bolton, outer Ancestors by Jay
Iconography: Josias with scroll of the law (cf. C8). *Colors:* angels in white and ruby; Ancestors in white and purple, ruby and purple, ruby. *Condition:* small pieces missing upper middle and lower rt lights.

III A10: JECHONIAS-SALATHIEL-ZOROBABEL, angels by John Bolton, Ancestors by Jay
Iconography: Jechonias seen from back with hands tied and scroll with BABYLON, because he was born as captivity began (Matt. 1:11); Zorobabel with Book of Law (Ezra 3:2). *Colors:* angels in green cloaks; Ancestors all in ruby. *Condition:* stopgaps to rt of lf angel, a replacement lower lf light; large piece missing lower middle light; deterioration of matt in upper tree and lower rt light.

fig. 10e   III A11: ABIUD-ELIAKIM-AZOR, by Jay Bolton
Iconography: Abiud with flower, Azor as king. *Colors:* angels in white, ruby, medium blue; Ancestors in purple, purple, ruby. *Condition:* damage and cracks in lf light; replacement or repainting of tree in center of middle light; deterioration of matt and trace lower lf of rt light.

III A12: SADOC-ACHIM-ELIUD, angels by John Bolton, Ancestors probably by Jay
Iconography: Eliud as desert tribesman. *Source:* as in A5. *Colors:* angels in motley dress of green, white, ruby; Ancestors in white and purple, purple and white, purple and white. *Condition:* replacement head on lf angel; all of two lower panels of center light probably replacements.

III A13: ELEAZAR-MATTHAN-JACOB, by Jay Bolton
Iconography: no distinguishing features. *Colors:* angels in motley dress of olive green, ruby, purple; Ancestors all in ruby and green. *Condition:* upper tree and scroll repainted; third panel from bottom of center light replaced; large stopgap lower rt light.

III A14: JOSEPH-MARY-CHRIST, by John Bolton   *fig. 10b*
Iconography: Joseph with walking stick; Christ with scepter and crown of thorns. *Source:* see A7. *Colors:* angels in white; upper figures in purple and white, white, ruby and white. *Condition:* tree and scroll of upper panel of middle light replaced; matt and trace deteriorated in Mary; large pieces missing in two lower panels of middle light; lower part of skirt of rt angel replaced.

Gallery

New Testament—14 windows. *Date:* completed in 1848 (date on exterior of tomb base in *Resurrection* window G6 and at top right in *Christ at Emmaus* window G7). Windows composed of three lancets with trilobe heads surmounted by Flamboyant tracery. Either a title or a biblical citation is given in each window.

III G1: Raising of Lazarus (ST. JOHN XI:38–44), by Jay Bolton, with   *fig. 34*
some figures by John in side panels
Iconography: Christ calls Lazarus out of the tomb; tracery: nonspecific Type 1. *Source:* possibly Pieter Lastman's painting of this motif (The Hague, Mauritshuis), which has the same basic composition, in reverse, and a similar large tomb with coping. *Colors in main scene:* Christ in ruby and blue, man far lf and woman to rt in blue enamel; pink enamel on cloth lower and turban upper lf panel; elsewhere purple, medium blue, green, white. *Condition:* deterioration of matt and esp. trace paint in middle and rt lights. Restored 1983 by Greenland Studio.

III G2: TRANSFIGURATION OF CHRIST (Matt. 17:2–3; Mark   *fig. 35a*
9:2–4; Luke 9:29–30), by Jay Bolton
Iconography: Christ lifted up in light, Moses holding tablets lf, Elias rt, several Apostles lower lf and rt; tracery: triangular Trinity monogram, scepter and palm, harps, trumpets, tent, floral forms; meanings unclear. *Source:* probably Giulio Romano's preparatory drawing for Raphael's *Transfiguration* (Vienna, Albertina), which Bolton could have seen in J. Pilizotti, *Lithographierte Copien von Original Handzeichnungen* . . . (Vienna, 1826), where it is attributed to Raphael himself; see Konrad Oberhuber, "Vorzeichnungen zu Raffaels 'Transfiguration,' " *Jahrbuch der Berliner Museen* 4 (1962): 116 (fig. 35b). *Colors in main scene:* Christ in white with medium purple cloak; Moses in silver stain and blue; Elias in ruby (lower part of cloak in red stain); Apostles in purple, ruby, green, silver stain; blue stream. *Condition:* good. Restored 1983 by Greenland Studio.

III G3: Christ in Gethsemane (ST. LUKE XXII.41), by Jay Bolton, tracery   *fig. 36*
angels by a hand not recognized elsewhere

Iconography: Christ kneels to pray, bathed in heavenly light; tracery: stars, chalice, 2 adorsed angels with multicolor wings, blue bird, cherubim, book inscribed MARK XIV CHAP 34, 35, 36TH VERSES, flowers. *Colors in main scene:* Christ in ruby, blue cloak; blue enamel on sleeping figures rt and chalice lf; all else grisaille, except green trees and grass. *Condition:* deterioration of matt in lf panel. Restored 1985 by Greenland Studio.

fig. 37 III G4: THE TRIAL OF CHRIST (Christ before Pilate: Matt. 27:11–24; Mark 15:1–14; Luke 23:1–16; John 18:29–38), ?design by John Bolton, executed by Jay

Iconography: Christ, hands bound in front, stands among mockers and faces Pilate, who is offered a gold washbasin; tracery: sun and moon, swords, funerary urn, hourglass, all of which prefigure Crucifixion, and a fancy teapot that so far defies interpretation. *Source:* appears to combine elements of the *Mocking of Christ* and *Christ before Caiaphas* at King's College Chapel, Cambridge. *Colors in main scene:* Christ in purple and white, Pilate in dark green; others in blue, white, purple, ruby; much silver stain; hair of man rt in balcony is stain; blue enamel on ax and on drapery in lf panel. Very heavy matt. *Condition:* good. Restored 1990 by Greenland Studio.

fig. 38 III G5: The Crucifixion (ST. MARK XV.22–44), by Jay Bolton, with Magdalen and figures to rt probably by John

Iconography: Mary Magdalen embraces cross; Virgin and St. John rt, Longinus and soldiers casting lots lf; tracery: symbols of the Passion. *Colors in main scene:* figures on lf, the Magdalen's cloak, and the Virgin's garment all blue; St. John in olive green and ruby; Longinus's blouse ruby; blue enamel on clothing lf and shirt of man to Christ's rt, pink enamel on ground lf and on Christ's loincloth; all else grisaille. *Condition:* serious deterioration of matt and trace paint throughout. Restored 1990 by Greenland Studio.

fig. 39a III G6: RESURRECTION OF CHRIST (Matt. 28:6; Mark 16:6; Luke 24:6), by Jay Bolton

Iconography: Christ emerges from the tomb to astonishment of soldiers standing guard; tracery: hands with loosed bonds, wrapped corpse, trumpets, angels, urn, flowers. *Source:* Christ figure recalls one of the avenging *fig. 39b* angels in Raphael's *Expulsion of Heliodorus* in the Vatican. *Colors in main scene:* Christ all white, soldiers in blue, ruby, silver stain, shield silver stain, blue, ruby with abrading. *Condition:* pieces missing lf tracery, at Christ's foot, below shield. Restored 1990 by Greenland Studio. *Comment:* date 1848 in silver stain on exterior of tomb base, seen in reverse on interior.

III G7: CHRIST AT EMMAUS (Luke 24:30), by Jay Bolton   *fig. 40*
Iconography: Christ breaks bread for his disciples, who are dressed as travelers; tracery: Type 1. *Source:* adapted from Albrecht Dürer's *Christ at Emmaus* (*Small Passion*, 1509–11). *Colors in main scene:* Christ in white, disciples in ruby and blue, much silver stain, blue enamel shoe on rt figure, red stain strap lower lf. *Condition:* good. Restored 1990 by Greenland Studio. *Comment:* "N. Rochelle/ May 23/ 1848" found in upper rt corner during restoration.

III G8*: THE BIRTH OF CHRIST (Adoration of the Shepherds: Luke   *plate VI*
2:15–16), by Jay Bolton
Iconography: shepherd kneels by manger, Mary and Joseph (or magus?) to rt, probably a magus to lf, who brought box examined by other men (?shepherds), through wall to rt the INN, which refused the couple lodging; tracery: cherubim in cloudy night sky, star shines lower lf. *Colors in main scene:* Mary in pink and blue, Joseph in ruby and green, kneeling shepherd in white and purple, ?magus in blue, ruby, and silver-stain braid, others in white, blue, ruby, much silver stain, blue enamel crib blanket. *Condition:* serious large fractures on figure of Babe and in lower rt light. *Comment:* radical change from what appears to be a preliminary sketch (Catalog IX:11k), only known Bolton cartoon is the one for the Babe (fig. 64).

III G9: THE BAPTISM OF CHRIST (Mark 1:9; Luke 3:21), by Jay Bolton   *fig. 28*
Iconography: John the Baptist baptizes Christ while others watch; pelican with her chicks, a symbol of the Resurrection, to rt; tracery: inscription: THIS IS MY BELOVED SON (partly obscured in the design), two angels with books, dove of the Holy Spirit, ax (symbol of John's later beheading), gold salver holding John's head, inscription on banner above: LAMB OF GOD. *Source:* Christ, holding blowing cloak, resembles various figures of St. Christopher in German sixteenth-century prints. *Colors in main scene:* Christ in white with silver-stain borders, ruby cloak, John in red stain; others in blue, ruby, purple, silver stain, blue enamel on water and hat top lf, pink enamel area on ground; silver-stain pelican. *Condition:* large pieces missing from Christ's tunic.

III G10: CHRIST AT THE WELL (Christ and the Woman of Samaria: *fig. 29a*
John 4:7–26), middle and rt lights by John Bolton, lf light by Jay
Iconography: in a multiple narrative scene, Christ with raised arm teaches the Samaritan woman about the water of everlasting life, his teaching symbolized by the Bible at his feet; the woman approaches rt; on lf, perhaps the man to whom she recounted the conversation; tracery: nonspecific Type 2. *Colors in main scene:* Christ in white and ruby,

woman in white and blue; cloaks of older men on either side in red stain; other colors: blue, green, silver stain; small passages of pink and blue enamel. *Condition:* good.

fig. 30a III G11: MARRIAGE AT CANA (John 2:1–9), middle and rt lights by Jay Bolton, lf light by John

Iconography: in his first miracle, Christ orders water poured into wine jars, to be made into wine, which the governor of the feast samples at lf; tracery: Type 1. *Source:* based largely on a roundel design attrib. to the circle of Jan Swart van Groningen, and traced by Jay at Holy Trinity, Bradford-on-Avon (see Catalog IX:11f). *Colors in main scene:* Christ in purple, pourer in ruby tunic, blue and silver-stain pants, russet-stain hair; bride in pink, bridegroom in silver stain with russet-stain dots; others in blue, green, purple, ruby; guitar in deep-orange stain; unusual salmon-pink potmetal on hat far rt; blue enamel cups, frequent small blue and pink enamel passages; much silver stain. *Condition:* crack lower center mended, otherwise good. Bar obscuring Christ's face was added, apparently as structural support.

fig. 30b

fig. 31a,b III G12: CHRIST ENTERS JERUSALEM (ZACH. IX CH. 9VE) figure with cloak lf (said to be a self-portrait of Jay, cf. fig. 31b and frontispiece) and 2 figures behind him by Jay Bolton, all others by John

Iconography: Christ rides donkey into Jerusalem, man places cloak before donkey, child in tree watches (for this motif, Eleanor Greenhill, "The Child in the Tree . . . ," *Traditio* 10 [1954]: 338–71); tracery: a crown probably foretelling Christ's return to Heaven, lyres, angels with scrolls, books with prophecies, shield inscribed ZACH IXCH.9VE ("thy King cometh unto thee . . . and riding upon an ass"). *Source:* possibly the same subject at King's College Chapel (B12), especially in the small boy turning toward the donkey's head, but most of the scene is traditional; Jay made a drawing of the King's window, but uncertain if after his return to England. *Colors in main scene:* Christ in purple and murrey, man with cloak in dark green, white, and blue, his hair in red stain; donkey caparisoned in mottled silver-stain damascene; child walking in pink and ruby; others in ruby, blue, olive green, purple, silver stain with red-stain dots. *Condition:* head of Christ and piece just above, and 2 heads far rt repainted.

fig. 32a,b III G13: CHRIST HEALS THE BLIND MAN (Mark 8:22–26), foreground figures by John Bolton, background ones by Jay

Iconography: Christ gestures toward the blind man dressed as a traveler; tracery: cornucopias, floral forms, a star, ewers, chalice, bag of grain, sheaf of wheat. *Colors in main scene:* Christ in murrey, blind man in

---

white and silver stain, others in ruby, pink, blue, green, orange silver-stain, silver stain with red-stain dots; small passages in pink enamel. *Condition:* large pieces missing lower rt light; repainting of some faces; hand foreground rt and pieces above it replaced; serious cracks lf light.

III G14*: CHRIST STILLS THE TEMPEST (Matt. 8:23–26; Mark 4:37– 39; Luke 8:23–24), rt light by John Bolton, the rest by Jay   *fig. 33a*
Iconography: beardless, youthful Christ, unique in the series, stands at back of boat with rt hand raised, loose sail flaps in the wind, probably Peter at tiller; tracery: sun, trumpets, anchor, cherubim, plant forms, dove, sea bird. *Source:* ?design used by Dirk Vellert for panel of the same subject, now at The Cloisters, New York City (fig. 33c); see M. H. Caviness et al., *Stained Glass before 1700 in American Collections: New England and New York,* Corpus Vitrearum Checklist I (Washington, D.C.: National Gallery of Art, 1985), 145. In the Holy Trinity version the figures are reversed from Jay's sketch version (fig. 33b), differently arranged in boat, and Christ is beardless, changes perhaps to give greater prominence to Christ. *Colors in main scene:* Christ in purple robe, blue gown; others in ruby, blue, white, red stain; boat is silver stain on a sea of matt brown with touches of green enamel; silver stain on dove lf, ruby potmetal on sea bird rt. *Condition:* badly cracked lower rt light.

Clerestory

Old Testament. Windows undated, but completed probably by second half of 1847. Tracery of most has Bible citations for the scene below. Windows composed of three lancets with trilobe heads, surmounted by Flamboyant tracery.

III C1*: Finding of Moses (EXODUS II.6), possibly all executed by John   *fig. 19a*
Bolton
Iconography: Pharaoh's daughter and court in lf light, infant Moses and his sister in middle light, Nile scene with ?hippopotamus to rt; tracery: Type 2. *Colors in main scene:* daughter in purple, others in ruby, green, blue, silver stain, red-stain ?hippopotamus. *Condition:* good. Restored 1991 by Greenland Studio.

III C2*: Moses with the Tablets (EX. XXIV.3–5), by Jay Bolton
The Bible verses cited mention the promulgation of the Law, the twelve pillars for the Twelve Tribes of Israel, and Tribes motifs appear to dominate the tracery. Not all the Hebrew inscriptions form real words (all were interpreted by Carney Gavin, Semitic Museum at Harvard).

Iconography: Moses about to throw Tablets, people worship golden calf to rt; tracery: green and yellow flag inscribed *RA'ANU* ("he has looked upon [or seen] us"); hart inscribed *NAPHTALI,* golden vase (?Asher), sword (?Gad) inscribed *?M'N,* wolf (?Benjamin) inscribed *?H,* inscription *?LVIII,* lion (?Judah), book, sailing ship (?Zebulun), flowers (?Joseph); cf. simpler version in preparatory sketch (fig. 20b). *Source:* a close adaptation of the same subject by Raphael's shop in the Vatican Logge (fig. 21). *Colors in main scene:* Moses in ruby receives Tablets, throws them down wearing blue with ruby cloak; other colors green, blue, ruby, purple, much silver stain, deep blue sky; small passages in blue and pink enamel. *Condition:* small replacement in tracery, otherwise good. Restored 1991 by Greenland Studio.

plate III III C3: The Brazen Serpent (NUMB. XXI.9), ?design by John Bolton, executed by Jay

Iconography: people bitten by snakes in lf light, the curative bronze serpent on the pole (prefiguring the Crucifixion) in middle light, Moses to rt; tracery: Type 1. *Source:* woman and children on lf possibly modeled on woman and children in center background of *Fire in the Borgo* (Vatican, Stanza d'Eliodoro) by Raphael's shop. *Colors in main scene:* woman at lf in ruby, purple and blue, Moses in white, other figures in ruby, blue, and white, much silver stain; small passages in blue and pink enamels. *Condition:* good. Restored 1991 by Greenland Studio.

fig. 22 III C4: Joshua Stills the Sun and Moon (JOSH. X.12), by Jay Bolton
Iconography: Joshua raises hands to still the sun and moon, which appear in the heads of the lf and middle lights; tracery: sun and moon, pillars of cloud and fire (Ex. 13:21), spears, shields, armorial, swords, chain length (?broken bondage). *Source:* reminiscent of Raphael shop's *Triumph of David,* Vatican Logge. *Colors in main scene:* Joshua in ruby and white, elsewhere murrey, white, silver stain; small landscape passages in blue and pink enamels. *Condition:* piece replaced in upper tracery. Restored 1991 by Greenland Studio.

fig. 23 III C5: Samson with the Gates of Gaza (JUDGES XVI.3), by Jay Bolton
Iconography: Samson carries off gates under a night sky; tracery: Type 1. *Source:* Samson recalls figure holding Christ's legs in Raphael's *Entombment* (Rome, Borghese Gallery; cf. C10). *Colors in main scene:* Samson in ruby with light blue cloak, green bushes rt, dark blue sky, rest is white and silver stain; small landscape passages of pink and blue enamels. *Condition:* small pieces missing in tracery.

fig. 24 III C6: Coronation of David (I SAM. XVI.13), by Jay Bolton
Iconography: David kneels at center, Samuel pours anointing oil, David's

sword and crown to lower rt; note Renaissance loggia; tracery: Type 2. *Colors in main scene:* David in dark blue with ruby cape, Samuel in dark blue, others in ruby and blue, surroundings in matt brown and silver stain. *Condition:* good. Recent technical study revealed poor firing and extensive amounts of cold paint, explaining the window's relative opacity.

III C7: Building the Temple (I KINGS VI.1), by Jay Bolton   *fig. 25*
Iconography: workmen in foreground, Solomon in background with plans; tracery: Type 1. *Colors in main scene:* man to lf in medium blue and white, man in middle light in motley ruby, white, blue, purple, others in dark green, ruby, pink, blue, purple, white, surroundings in matt brown and silver stain. *Condition:* pieces missing in tracery.

III C8: Reading of Deuteronomy (II KINGS XXIII.2), by Jay Bolton *fig. 26*
Iconography: rare, perhaps unique scene showing King Josiah listening as newly discovered Book of Law is read; tracery: Type 3 (but with blue birds). *Colors in main scene:* Josiah in purple and white, man lf in olive and white, man rt in ruby and blue, surroundings in brown matt and silver stain; passages of pink enamel on floor. *Condition:* good.

III C9*: Expulsion from Eden (GEN. 3.24), by John Bolton *fig. 11b*
Iconography: angel with sword, Adam and Eve in animal skins, serpent; tracery: large tree with serpent around trunk, butterfly, rabbit, squirrel. *Source:* same subject by Raphael's shop in Vatican Logge. *Colors in main scene:* silver-stain hair and serpent, angel's scarf blue, otherwise all grisaille. *Condition:* good.

III C10*: Man Labors (GEN. 3.19)—by John Bolton   *fig. 12*
Iconography: Adam and Abel plow, Cain hunts deer in background; tracery: Type 3. *Source:* figures of Adam and Abel resemble man holding Christ's legs in Raphael's *Entombment* (Rome, Borghese Gallery; see Clark, "America's First Stained Glass," 49–50; cf. C5). *Colors in main scene:* Adam in white and murrey, Abel in white, ruby, and blue, Cain in white and red stain, one steer white, the other red stain; small landscape passages in blue enamel. *Condition:* good.

III C11: Cain and Abel (GEN. 4.4), by Jay Bolton   *fig. 14*
Iconography: a brooding, dark-haired Cain with scythe to lf, his altar cold, blond Abel with shepherd's crook to rt, his altar burns brightly as ray of God's acceptance shines on it, passion plant in foreground as symbol of final sacrifice in Christ; tracery: angels adorsed, crook, hammer, sheep, basket of fruit, on book: HEB. XICH. 4V. *Colors in main scene:* blue mountain, green landscape background, olive green plants foreground, silver-stain fire and Abel's hair, all else grisaille. *Condition:* good.

---

plate V   III C12: Noah's Sacrifice (GEN. 8.20), by Jay Bolton
Iconography: Noah kneels before fire on altar, family gather about to pray; tracery: ark, departing storm clouds, dove, raven, large rainbow. *Source:* possibly *The Golden Calf* in the Vatican Logge (fig. 21). *Colors in main scene:* Noah in white blouse, ruby cloak, man lf in abraded murrey tunic with ruby hem, has red-stain hair, women rt in medium blue with silver-stain veil, others in green and purple, fire is silver stain; blue enamel on stream rt. *Condition:* good.

fig. 15   III C13: Sacrifice of Isaac (GEN. XXII.9), by Jay Bolton
Iconography: Abraham dressed in eastern garb, angel catches his arm, Isaac kneels on altar, fire pot and ram caught in bush to lf; tracery: Type 1. *Source:* adaptation of the same subject in Raphael's ceiling, Vatican, Stanza d'Eliodoro. *Colors in main scene:* Abraham in yellow-green enamel, ruby cloak with dark blue lining, yellow-green enamel bushes, all else grisaille. *Condition:* good.

fig. 16   III C14: Jacob's Blessing (GEN. XXVII.27), probably all by John Bolton
Iconography: Rebecca with dish of meats, Jacob kneels to receive Isaac's blessing; tracery: Type 2. *Source:* probably from Hans Holbein the Younger, *Jacob's Blessing* in the Old Testament woodcuts (1508). *Colors in main scene:* Rebecca in white, purple, blue, Jacob in silver stain and ruby, Isaac and covers in white, bed and hangings purple. *Condition:* good.

fig. 17   III C15: Jacob's Dream (GEN. XXVIII.12), by John Bolton
Iconography: Jacob asleep in foreground, angels descending wide ladder; tracery: angels descending ladder, roses. *Source:* same subject by Raphael shop in Vatican Logge. *Colors in main scene:* Jacob in dark blue on ruby cloak, one angel in blue and white, one in white, surroundings in grisaille. *Condition:* good.

fig. 18   III C16: Jacob Meets Joseph (GEN. XLVI.29), by John Bolton
Iconography: father and son embrace in middle light; tracery: Type 1. *Colors in main scene:* Jacob in white, Joseph in blue and white, man to lf in red-stain cloak, others in blue and ruby, surroundings in grisaille. *Condition:* good.

Chancel

Four side windows, each with 3 lancets with trilobe heads and Flamboyant tracery; altar window with 2 registers, each made of 7 lancets with trilobe heads, and Flamboyant tracery.

fig. 43   II Ch1: Eucharistic Angel, by Jay Bolton
Iconography: angel at baroque altar, with ewer, chalice, and sacramental bread; altar medallions of Good Samaritan and ?Joseph of Arimathea

with Grail; inscription: THIS CUP IS THE NEW TESTAMENT IN MY BLOOD (Luke 22:20); tracery: I.H.S. monogram, floral and plant forms, crowns, cherubim, architectural ornament. *Colors:* angel's wings red and blue, all else grisaille and silver stain. *Condition:* good.

III Ch2,5: Grisaille windows made of patterned quarries with ruby and green frames and blue borders, by unknown glazier.

III Ch3*: Ascension of Christ (Mark 16:19; Luke 24:50–53; Acts 1:9–12),   *plate VII* by Jay Bolton

Date: installed by 25 April 1847 (*Brooklyn Daily Eagle*). *Iconography:* in lower register, St. Peter at center, John the Baptist in hair shirt to Peter's rt, and the remaining nine Apostles, with ?St. John on Patmos and ?Adam and Eve in the background, all watching Christ, in upper register, rise to Heaven accompanied by angels and cherubim; tracery: an angel orchestra in an elaborate organ loft, cherubim, lilies, roses, anchor, crucifix, brazen serpent, sword and shield, chalice and round loaf, stars, trumpets, sun and moon, Alpha and Omega symbols, lamb, and over Christ's head the dove of the Holy Spirit; inscriptions: SON OF MAN, MOSES, MELCHIZEDEK, AARON, BRAZEN SER-PENT, BEHOLD THE LAMB OF GOD, OLD TESTAMENT, NEW TESTAMENT, DEATH, HELL; compare description of Ascension window Bolton proposed for Trinity Church, in letter to W. H. Harison (Appendix A). *Sources:* figure of Christ from Raphael's *Transfiguration* (Vatican Gallery); the seated figure in the lowest register resembles figures of St. John on Patmos that appear in many north French and Flemish late medieval books of hours, and could be Bolton's only direct use of a genuinely medieval model. *Colors:* Christ in ruby robe, dark blue cloak, around him mostly grisaille with bits of green, purple, and silver stain; great variety of color in crowd below, dominated by blue, ruby, purple, and red stain; in tracery blue sky, angels in white, inscribed swags in green, murrey, and ruby. *Condition:* good.

III Ch4: Baptismal Angels by John Bolton and (?)a third painter   *fig. 44*

Iconography: angel at font, altar to lf, parents with child rt, Trinity medallion below, inscription: FATHER SON HOLY GHOST; tracery: dove, cherubim, plant and floral motifs. *Colors:* angel in white, wings red and a yellow-green potmetal unique to the series, altar cloth also yellow-green, parents in red and blue, font base purple, red cloth in heads of lights, blue Trinity medallion, all else grisaille and silver stain. *Condition:* strengthening of lines by cold paint; lighting blocked by added vestry.

Catalog:
Holy Trinity

Organ loft

III L1,6: Two windows of the Evangelists, by unknown glazier

Stairwells

III L2–5: Stairwell windows by unknown glazier, each a large landscape, made perhaps ca. 1900

Tower

fig. 45 III Tw1: JUBAL and MIRIAM (Gen. 4:21; Ex. 15:20–21), Jubal by Jay Bolton, Miriam by John

In 1985 this window was installed in the court of the American Wing, Metropolitan Museum of Art, in a somewhat reduced form (omitting one quarry lancet and small portions of the tracery). Designed to be a backdrop to organ pipes, the window celebrates music in the figures of Jubal, "the ancestor of those who play the harp and pipe," and Miriam, the prophetess who "took up her tambourine," danced, and sang; and in the musical instruments of the tracery. It was originally composed of 2 registers, each with 4 lancets with trilobe heads and Flamboyant tracery. There were purple quarries with a single floral design in the 2 inner lancets of the upper register, and in all 4 of the lower. The 2 musicians are in the outer lights of the upper register. The window was designed to accommodate organ pipes that rose in front of the quarries and were flanked by the 2 musicians and surmounted by tracery containing musical instruments. The larger pipes of the organ installed in 1925 obscured all but the top of the tracery.

Iconography: Jubal with bells and trumpet, Miriam with tambourine in outer lights of upper register, inscriptions: JUBAL and MIRIAM below the figures; in heads of upper-register lancets: cogged wheels and ropes (?bell pulls); tracery: musical instruments; inscriptions: SPIRITUAL SONGS, HYMNS PSALMS. *Sources:* Jubal and Miriam recall figures by Botticelli. *Colors:* Jubal in red cap and tunic with silver-stain details; Miriam in white with rose enamel pattern and silver-stain details; patterned and damascened blue and purple grounds behind figures, purple in quarries and in tracery; silver-stain yellow in architecture and in instruments of tracery; black enamel around some instruments. *Condition:* minor fracturing, small replacement pieces; restored 1985 by Greenland Studio. *Comment:* round arch with classical ornament just below trefoil head of each lancet in upper register.

Catalog:

Holy Apostles

Other windows not by the Boltons: floral panels over the doors from the vestibule into the nave and aisles; panels in the vestibule barrier, windows in adjacent church structures.

R*EFERENCES*

Brooklyn Daily Eagle, 26 April 1847; Lafever, *The Architectural Instructor,* 478–81; Heinigke, "The Windows of Holy Trinity Church," 1–3; Brown, *Church of the Holy Trinity;* R. P. Bolton, "William Jay Bolton," 28–29; Dickinson, "Windows and Kings' Ransoms"; Skinner, "The Stained Glass of the Brothers . . . Bolton," 11–15; Lloyd, *Stained Glass in America,* 47–49; *The New Yorker* (21 May 1979), 28–29; A. C. Downs, "Stained Glass in American Architecture," 56; W. B. Clark, "America's First Stained Glass"; W. B. Clark, "Gothic Revival Stained Glass of William Jay Bolton," 30–34; *Preservation News* 20:8 (1980): 3; Sloan, "A New Look," 231–35; Sloan, "Documentation of Stained Glass Window Restoration," 12–19; Sturm and Chotas, *Stained Glass,* 19–20.

IV. New York, N.Y.: Church of the Holy Apostles (glazing ?1846 to 1847)

Unlike Christ Church and Holy Trinity, Holy Apostles was "High Church" in its views and its liturgical practices. This does not appear to have affected William Jay Bolton's stained glass designs in any way, but indicates that the professional artist was not so adamant in his opposition to "tall" churchmen as to refuse a commission from them. The architect for Holy Apostles is once again Minard Lafever, but this time his building is in an Italian Renaissance Revival style. The architectural commission was awarded in July 1845 and construction began the following March.[17] Nothing is known of the arrangements that Lafever or the church made with Bolton, but they probably date from late 1845 or early 1846. Holy Apostles is a relatively small brick structure that was originally a single vessel with aisles and a windowless chancel; there were 10 openings for windows along the aisles. In 1854 the nave was lengthened westward from 89 to 114′; in 1858, two broad transepts were added, causing transposition of some Bolton windows. Of the 10 Bolton windows at Holy Apostles, the 6 nave ones remain in their original location, and the other 4 are now in the western walls of the transepts (see Building Plans).

The classical lines of the building called for round-arched windows, and for these Jay chose an unusual and effective design consisting of 3 roundels painted in grisaille and silver stain, and set in a single light among white acanthus leaves, lilies, and colored flowers; an angel fills the head of each window (colorplate IX). The subjects of the roundels form two cycles: an abbreviated Life of Christ in 4 windows, 12 roundels, stressing the final events; and the principal acts of the Apostles in 6 windows, 18 roundels. Sketches of *The Calling of Peter, St. Peter Distributing Alms,* and musical subjects, all for round-headed windows, could have been early ideas for the Holy Apostles series (figs. 65–67).[18] In June 1846, Vestry minutes chided the building committee for deciding, after plans were complete, to permit installation of an altar window;[19] this, however, was not carried out. If a large window had been under consideration, then perhaps the 3-light *St. Peter Distributing Alms* was intended for this east window. The unusual and beautiful study of musical angels around an open space might have been designed for a western organ loft window, the space to accommodate the organ pipes, as in the tower window at Holy Trinity.[20] Perhaps Jay's first plans for the Holy Apostles windows were more elaborate than Lafever had in mind, or appeared too expensive for the building committee, apparently a major problem in Bolton's bid for the Trinity Church job. The repetitive design of the installed windows at Holy Apostles was certainly quicker and therefore cheaper to carry out than any program of fully colored figural windows he might have preferred.

In its April 1990 issue, *Preservation News* reported on the courageous restoration effort that the parishioners of Holy Apostles had just begun. It is thus bitterly ironic that on the night of 9 April 1990, smoldering embers from a fire set earlier in the day by a careless roofer's blowtorch reignited, and the roof of Holy Apostles, with its wooden supports, went up in flames. Quick and effective action by the fire department saved most of the church, but the water cannons and firemen's axes damaged the windows severely, especially on the north (street) side. The day after the fire, volunteers picked up every piece of glass they could find and plans were initiated immediately to conserve what was left and to cope with what is now a restoration project of overwhelming dimensions. Holy Apostles today is not only an active parish but also runs the nation's second-largest soup kitchen for the poor and homeless, which never missed serving a meal after the fire. The restoration project will need a great deal of help from outside agencies and from individuals who value America's heritage of nineteenth-century stained glass and architecture.

Prior to the fire, the paint in a few of the Bolton roundels had so deteriorated that stylistic details could not be seen, but the rest could be assigned without hesitation to Jay Bolton, who also painted the angels surmounting each window. Employing the production method he used for

---

the Jesse Tree at Holy Trinity, he designed only 3 cartoons for the 10 angels (figs. 47–49). These are repeated sometimes exactly, sometimes as mirror images. While 4 of the Christological designs are reductions of their Holy Trinity counterparts, Bolton's principal source for the other roundel designs was again Raphael—in some cases the Vatican Logge, more often the tapestry designs depicting Acts of the Apostles. He may well have seen the tapestry cartoons (now in the Victoria and Albert Museum) when they were at Hampton Court, for he refers to them in a later publication as being there; he probably also saw the tapestries themselves at the Vatican. Further-more, the tapestry designs had recently been engraved, the edition of which was available to him in the library of the National Academy of Design.[21] As he had done at Holy Trinity, he also drew on northern sources at Holy Apostles, for example, in the *Flight into Egypt* roundel (figs. 50a,b); the Oostsanen roundel (Catalog IX:12,b) may have been intended then rejected as a source. When Jay borrows a design he usually makes changes in it, sometimes substantial ones.

The series at Holy Apostles must have begun originally on the south side of the altar, with the *Annunciation, Nativity, Flight into Egypt* window (T1), proceeding westward back and forth across the nave (see Plan B). More recently the Christological windows, to which those by Sharp and Steel were added, were separated from the Acts windows and made to proceed clockwise around the transept (see Plan A). As he did in most windows of the gallery at Holy Trinity, Bolton clearly identified the roundel scenes, providing titles in the framing.

Jay Bolton achieved a remarkable harmony in these windows by his combination of grisaille and color (colorplates VIII,IX). The roundels are executed in silver stain and matt and trace brown, and each has a border in bright silver-stain yellow. In all but one window the ogee fillets surrounding the roundels are dark blue or purple potmetal, as are the borders surround-ing the whole window; one (N3) has a green fillet and borders. Light is controlled in the fillets and borders by a variety of patterns stenciled in matt. The roses are in a bright red flashed glass and have abraded and silver-stain yellow centers; the lilies are white or pale yellow silver-stain, and the leaves are matt and trace brown. Red, pink, and green potmetal details appear among the leaves and flowers of the frames. The angels are in brown and silver stain, and each has a halo in one of the several potmetal colors. The titles are given in bands above the roundels, usually in silver-stain yellow. There was, before the fire, considerable deterioration of the paint in a number of windows, and obvious repainting and replacement in many of the frame elements; some breakage had occurred and had been repaired.[22]

The variations in tone and the deterioration of the matt and trace paints of both frames and roundels undoubtedly resulted from the same problems that had similar effects at Holy Trinity. At Holy Apostles some of the problems may have been caused by Bolton's rush to complete the job and prepare to sail for England. In this context, the better pre-fire state in general of the Christological roundels might mean that he did them first and supervised all the work himself, but in the Acts series left some steps to a helper.

All Bolton windows measure 11′ × 41½″, the roundels 14½″ to 14¾″ in diameter. The roundels, indicated as a, b, and c in the Catalog entry for each window, are read from top to bottom of the window.

Following the fire, 18 of the Bolton roundels remain whole, 5 survive in two to four pieces, and 5 in many pieces. The surrounding glass of the panels suffered even more, with 2 panels entirely destroyed, 3 from 70% to 90% gone, and others from 5% to 50% damaged. All but one of the angels in the heads of the Bolton windows are intact. Most of the fine Sharp and Steel windows in the east transept were completely destroyed. All of the windows are smoke damaged and show a variety of cracks from both blows and heat. The condition of each panel and roundel is summarized below. Ed Kamper, director of the restoration project, supplied the post-fire condition report.

Transept

IV T1: a. THE ANNUNCIATION TO THE SHEPHERDS (Luke 2:8–14), b. THE BIRTH OF JESUS CHRIST (Matt. 1:25; Luke 2:7), c.* THE FLIGHT INTO EGYPT (Matt. 2:13–14)
fig. 50a
Iconography: a. angel descends to 6 shepherds, angel with harp above; b. shepherds enter through arch to stable, Babe in manger, Mary seated, Joseph to rt; c. Joseph leads Mary and Babe seated on donkey, farm in landscape. *Sources:* a. *Isaac Blessing Jacob* by Raphael's shop (Vatican Logge), adapted; c. slight variation on his tracing of a roundel attrib. to Dirk Vellert (see Catalog IX:12a). *Condition:* angel panel deteriorated; c. roundel large crack, lower lf rose and decoration above it replaced. After fire: a. 20% of panel cracked; b. intact; c. 10% of panel cracked, roundel in 2 pieces.

fig. 52
IV T2: a. CHRIST ENTERING JERUSALEM (Matt. 21:7–11; Mark 11:7–11; Luke 19:35–38; John 12:12–14), b. CHRIST TRIED BEFORE PONTIUS PILATE (Matt. 27:2; Mark 15:1–5; Luke 23:1–15; John 18:29–40, 19:1–16), c. CHRIST BEARING HIS CROSS, roundel probably by Sharp and Steel, framing by Bolton

---

Iconography: a: Christ on donkey, with crowd, man lf with cloak, small child; b. Christ to lf, Pilate on throne rt, 2 men in balcony center. *Sources:* a. from the Holy Trinity design; b. from the Holy Trinity design. *Condition:* roundel c is a replacement, probably for an original Bolton one that was destroyed, as framing is all Bolton. After fire: a. 50% of panel in fragments; b. 90% of panel destroyed, roundel in 4 pieces; c. 35% of panel cracked.

IV T3–T6: All by Sharp and Steel of New York City, 1854

IV T7: a. CHRIST CRUCIFIED (Matt. 27:35; Mark 15:24; Luke 23:33; John 19:18), b. CHRIST RISES FROM THE TOMB (Matt. 28; Mark 16; Luke 24; John 20), c. CHRIST ASCENDS TO HEAVEN (Mark 16:19, Luke 24:51)

Iconography: a. Christ crucified center, women lf, John rt; b. Christ exits rock-cut tomb, 4 soldiers startled; c. Christ ascends, Apostles and kneeling Virgin below. *Sources:* a. adapted from Raphael's *Transfiguration* (Vatican Gallery); b. from the Holy Trinity design. *Condition:* lower part of frame in c replaced and repainted. After fire: a. 5% of panel cracked; b. 35% of panel cracked; c. 10% of panel cracked, roundel in 3 pieces.

IV T8: a. THE BAPTISM OF CHRIST BY JOHN (Matt. 3:15; Mark 1:9), b. CHRIST RESTORES THE BLIND MAN (Mark 8:22; John 9:6–7), c. ST. PETER WALKS ON THE SEA (Matt. 14:29)   *fig. 47*

Iconography: a. Christ and John the Baptist in river, dove above; b. Christ and blind man center of crowd; c. Christ rt lifts Peter, fishermen in boat lf rear. *Sources:* a. figure of Christ from a ?St. Christopher; b. from the Holy Trinity design. *Condition:* good. After fire: a. 30% of panel destroyed; b. 20% of panel cracked; c. 20% of panel cracked.

Nave

IV N1: a. THE SHIPWRECK OF ST. PAUL (Acts 27:41), b. THE MIRACLE OF THE VIPER (Acts 28:3), c. ST. PAUL IMPRISONED IN ROME (Acts 28:16)

Iconography: a. ship with curving prow lf, people and debris in stormy sea; b. Paul behind fire and vipers center, crowd around; c. Paul seated in carved chair, hands chained, cat below chair, soldier rt, in a study with Roman insignia. *Sources:* b. women and children to rt from the Raphael shop's *Fire in the Borgo* (Vatican, Stanza d'Eliodoro). *Condition:* some deterioration of paint in a and b; c. originally very dark paint, serious deterioration of paint decreases legibility, roundel cracked, lower leaves and rt rose replaced, many repaired cracks. After fire: a. intact;

---

b. panel destroyed, roundel in 6+ pieces; c. 30% of panel cracked, roundel in 3+ pieces.

fig. 48   IV N2: a. ST. STEPHEN STONED (Acts 7:59), b. ST. PHILIP AND THE EUNUCH (Acts 8:27–39), c. THE CONVERSION OF ST. PAUL (Acts 9:3–6)

Iconography: a. Stephen in center of group, in classical courtyard; b. Philip in 2-horse chariot, eunuch rt, pyramid behind; c. Paul thrown from horse amid soldiers. *Sources:* a. adapted from tapestry design by Raphael; b. probably from the Vatican Logge *Triumph of David* by Raphael's shop; c. adapted from tapestry design by Raphael. *Condition:* weak tones in angel and c; b. cracked and repaired; c. rose and one small leaf piece replaced lower lf. After fire: a. 25% of panel cracked; b. panel destroyed, roundel in 6+ pieces; c. intact.

fig. 54   IV N3: a. ST. PETER & ST. JOHN HEAL THE LAME (Acts 3:6–8), b. THE APOSTLES THREATENED (Acts 4:21), c. DEATH OF ANANIAS (Acts 5:5)

Iconography: a. in columned house, lame man rises, Peter and John center, another lame man rt; b. Annas the high priest and others gesture at Peter and John, whose ?followers are barred entry at rt; c. Ananias dies, Apostles on a kind of stage look on. *Sources:* b. ?two main figures of Raphael's tapestry *Elymas Struck with Blindness,* and background recalls 15th-c. Annunciations, e.g., Domenico Veneziano at the Fitzwilliam Museum, Cambridge; c. adapted from Raphael's tapestry design of same subject, perhaps from the cartoon (London, Victoria and Albert Museum), cf. Bolton's drawing *St. Peter Distributing Alms* (Catalog IX:12d) perhaps based on figures in the same Raphael design. *Condition:* a. good; b. some paint deterioration in roundel; c. 3 leaves of frame replaced, cracks in lower frame. After fire: a. 25% of panel cracked; b. 90% of panel destroyed, roundel in 6+ pieces; c. 50% of panel cracked, roundel in 6+ pieces.

fig. 49   IV N4: a. THE ACTS OF THE APOSTLES, b. MATTIAS CHOSEN FOR AN APOSTLE (Acts 1:26), c. THE DESCENT OF THE HOLY GHOST (Acts 2:1–4)

Iconography: a. the author in his study; b. Paul lf holds hands over crowd rt, child lower lf; c. Apostles seated in columned room, dove descends in light. *Sources:* b. adapted from Raphael's tapestry *The Preaching of St. Paul,* probably the cartoon version with Paul lf (London, Victoria and Albert Museum). *Condition:* a. some paint deterioration in roundel; b. serious paint and stain deterioration in roundel; c. roundel broken and repaired, one frame leaf replaced or repainted, piece out in upper rt corner. After fire: a. 10% of panel cracked; b. 5% of panel cracked; c. 15% of panel cracked, roundel in 5 pieces.

IV N5: a. THE SEVEN DEACONS CHOSEN (Acts 6:5), b. ST. PETER HEALING THE SICK (Acts 5:15), c. THE DELIVERANCE OF ST. PETER & ST. JOHN (Acts 5:19) *fig. 53* *plate IX*
Iconography: a. a deacon kneels to receive hands-on blessing, others seated on elaborate, high-back bench below 3 arches; b. Peter in classical town square with crowd; c. angel leads Peter and John from prison, soldier sleeps rt. *Sources:* a. recalls background of Alesso Baldovinetti's *Annunciation* (before 1460; Florence, Uffizi Gallery). *Condition:* a. broken and repaired; b. some paint deterioration; c. good. After fire: a. 30% of panel cracked, roundel in 4 pieces; b. 5% of panel cracked; c. 20% of panel cracked.

IV N6: a. ST. PETER'S VISIT TO CORNELIUS (Acts 10:25–26), b. ST. PAUL PREACHING AT ATHENS (Acts 17:17), c. ST. PAUL BEFORE AGRIPPA (Acts 25:23) *plate VIII* *fig. 51*
Iconography: a. Peter lifts kneeling Cornelius, whose kinsmen and friends look on; b. Paul preaches in ?marketplace with well, crowd rt; c. Paul, rt, brought by Festus, lf, before King Agrippa and Queen Bernice. *Sources:* b. combination of tapestries *The Sacrifice of Lystra* and *The Preaching of St. Paul* by Raphael. *Condition:* a. good; some paint deterioration on roundels of b and c; c. paint very light, probably from poor firing. After fire: a. 5% of panel cracked; b. 20% of panel cracked; c. 70% of panel destroyed, roundel in 6+ pieces.

Choir loft

IV L1: Large roundel, uncertain date, unknown designer.

*R*EFERENCES

Edelblute, *The History of . . . Holy Apostles; The New York Times,* 13 October 1966, p. 47, 9 January 1967; *Chelsea Clinton News,* 20 October 1966, 29 December 1975; W. B. Clark, "America's First Stained Glass," 53.

V. West Lynn, Norfolk, England: Church of St. Peter (glazing ?1949–50)

Built in the Perpendicular style of the late Middle Ages, St. Peter's is a small parish church consisting of an aisleless rectangular nave and slightly raised rectangular chancel, the latter rebuilt in 1934.[23] The only two windows containing stained glass are those with designs by Jay Bolton; the others are glazed in white glass. Bolton designed and made the large altar window and the tracery in one north nave window nearest the chancel. The single tracery installation suggests that more extensive glazing was planned, begun, and stopped perhaps by the pressures of Bolton's university studies. Dedicated to Amelia Walker, who died 29 July 1849, the altar window is Jay Bolton's only known example of the memorial genre; it was installed before 8 July 1850.[24] The commission was probably a result of Jay's friendship with the Welch family of King's Lynn, which also led to his marriage to Susannah Welch in September 1849. The subject is the post-Resurrection visit to Christ's tomb by the three women. As in Bolton's other large windows, the design is continuous behind the mullions. The relationship to the King's Chapel windows in both design and handling of color was noted in Chapter 3. His potmetal palette is similar to that at Holy Trinity, with the addition of light blue and light green. In the tiny forget-me-nots in the foreground (2 left lights), Bolton achieves a delicate effect by backing a pale blue potmetal with silver-stain yellow (colorplate X). The refined figure painting and the dramatic use of white and colored glass make this one of Jay Bolton's finest works. Only *The Birth of Christ* at Holy Trinity and *The Deliverance of St. Peter & St. John* at Holy Apostles can stand comparison with the West Lynn design.

Chancel

The altar window is composed of four lancets and Perpendicular tracery under a 4-centered arch; the glazed area measures 8′ 6½″ × 13′ 9″.

plate X

fig. 55

V Ch2: The Angel at the Tomb (Mark 16:1–7), altar window by Jay Bolton
Iconography: Mary Magdalen, Mary mother of James, and Salome greeted by the angel at Christ's empty tomb, with Golgotha and the chalice shown to the right; green of the cross relates to Tree of Life symbolism; small flowers in foreground may have symbolic content; tracery: cherubim on wheels, and grapes, roses, angel with Trinity shield. *Sources:* the two standing women, and the bushes and fence above their heads,

fig. 56

from the same subject in window 17A of King's College Chapel; the angel and the kneeling Magdalen perhaps from the figure of Christ and the Magdalen in King's Chapel window 17B (by Dirk Vellert); tracery: bears a resemblance to the traceries of St. Lawrence, Combe (County of Oxford). *Colors:* angel in white with purple apron, Magdalen in red, two standing women in purple and bright blue; cross, green; ladder, silver-stain yellow; orange silver-stain bushes and fence; green trees and grass; yellow silver-stain in landscape and in the checkered floor of cave. *Inscriptions:* below main scene: "To God and the Church in memory of a beloved sister Amelia Walker of North Lynn who died July xxix a.d. mdcccxlix aged xvi years, this window is dedicated by her three sisters"; tracery: scroll held by cherubim, "Why seek ye the living among the dead." *Condition:* good, but backed by visually disruptive protective wire.

Nave

V N3: First northeast nave tracery only: 4 large and 3 small lights in Perpendicular tracery.

Tracery: Angels in oriels, by Bolton studio assistant, Cambridge   *fig. 57*
    Iconography: angels in oriels surmounted by Christ monogram, floral ornament in 2 small lights. *Colors:* angels in grisaille with green or red wings, on contrasting damascened green or red ground, oriels in grisaille and silver stain, with touches of red, blue, and green potmetal; Christ monogram in silver stain; minor lights in white and blue glass; on scroll held by angels, THY WILL BE DONE. *Condition:* deterioration of matt and trace paints in 2 of the larger lights. *Comment:* compare design of second northeast gallery window at Church of St. Andrew the Great, Cambridge.

REFERENCES

W. B. Clark, "A William Jay Bolton Window Discovered"; Haward, *Nineteenth Century Norfolk Stained Glass;* Pevsner, *Buildings of England. North West and South Norfolk,* 375.

VI. Cambridge, England: Church of St. Andrew the Great (glazing ?1849)

The church was built in 1842–43 on a design by Ambrose Poynter. Its only decorative glazing consists of two 6-light traceries by Jay Bolton in the northern gallery, over 2 registers of white-glass quarries; and 2 armorial windows in the chancel, neither of which is by Bolton. The rest is white glass. St. Andrew's has recently been deconsecrated, and efforts are being made to save the Bolton glass.

Gallery

VI G4: Angels in oriels, by Jay Bolton   *fig. 58*
    Iconography: same design as Bolton's nave window at West Lynn, on scroll held by angels: GLORY TO GOD IN THE HIGHEST, ON EARTH PEACE. *Colors:* as at West Lynn. *Condition:* minor deterioration of trace and matt paint, and pockmarking.

VI G5: Cherubim on wheels, by Jay Bolton
Iconography: same design as West Lynn altar window tracery. *Colors:* as at West Lynn. *Inscription:* 6 times ALLELUIA. *Condition:* some paint deterioration.

REFERENCES

W. B. Clark, "A William Jay Bolton Window Discovered," 54, 55.

VII. Armorials by William Jay Bolton in England and Ireland

Cambridge: King's College Chapel
Twelve armorial windows, with arms of King's College and Eton, copied by Jay from sixteenth-century originals. They were made for the 1828 Provost's Lodge of King's College, and for a Gothic Revival home at Christchurch, near Bournemouth, in Hampshire. All have been installed in a side chapel (Wayment, chapel F, 30a1,a3,c1,c2,d1,d2,e1,e2, f1,f2,h1,h3) of King's College Chapel. An account of their discovery is given by Dean Eric Milner-White (see Chapter 1).

REFERENCES

Milner-White, "William Jay Bolton," 212–15; K. Harrison, *An Illustrated Guide,* 63, 64; Wayment, *King's College Chapel, the Side–Chapel Glass.*

Newport, County Mayo, Ireland, Collection Francis T. Chambers
Armorial window bearing the arms of the Schuyler family of Westchester County, New York. The design is identical, but for the charge, with one of the armorials (Catalog I:Tw1) of the Priory south tower, and can be assigned to Jay Bolton on the basis of stylistic relationship to the *Agnus Dei* window of Christ Church, known to be by Jay. Owner is a descendant of John Bolton and his wife Katherine Schuyler.

VIII. Lost Windows by William Jay Bolton

Brooklyn, N.Y., Church of (St. Ann and) the Holy Trinity: perhaps one window in the vestibule.

Cambridge, England, Church of St. Mary the Less: east window. (*The Builder* 8 [28 December 1850]: 8), removed in 1890.

IX. Paintings and Drawings

Paintings

1. *The Defeat and Capture of Caractacus by the Romans,* fresco (Pelham, N.Y., Priory library), mostly destroyed by fire.

Catalog:
Paintings and Drawings

---

2. Self-portrait, oil on canvas, ca. 1845 (New York, National Academy of Design), for admission to National Academy of Design as an Associate.
3. Portrait of Abby Bolton, before 1849, known in an engraving in Rhoda Bolton, *The Lighted Valley,* frontispiece.
4. Self-portrait, oil on canvas, ca. 1853 or 1854 (Cambridge, King's College Provost's Lodge).

Drawing and Watercolor

Unless otherwise noted, the following are all at the Archives of the Episcopal Diocese of Long Island, Garden City, N.Y.

5. *The City of Bath from Beechen Cliff,* 37″ × 22¹/₂″, pencil and sepia wash, 1834 (Bath, Victoria Art Gallery, presented by Miss Bolton of Salisbury in 1929).   *fig. 60*
6. Self-portrait, pencil, ca. 1845 (Brooklyn, N.Y., formerly Church of St. Ann and Holy Trinity, present location unknown); known from photograph at Long Island Diocese Archives. Probably a preparatory sketch for the first oil version listed above.   *fig. 61*
7. Sketch of so-called Castor and Pollux monument, Rome, pencil.
8. Sketch of Raphael, *Marriage of the Virgin,* Vatican, Sistine Chapel, pencil.
9. Biblical or mythological subject: *Man and devil fighting,* watercolor.   *fig. 63*
10. ?A scholar, pen and ink, signed "WJB."
11. Drawings and sketches intended or possibly intended for (St. Ann and) Holy Trinity.
    a. *Expulsion* watercolor, signed "W.J. Bolton"; compare III:C9.   *fig. 11b*
    b. *Man labors,* pencil; compare III:C10.   *fig. 12*
    c. *Finding of Moses,* pencil, signed "WJB"; compare III:C1.   *fig. 19b*
    d. *Moses with the Tablets,* pencil, signed "W.J. Bolton"; compare III:C2.   *fig. 20b*
    e. *The Adoration of the Child,* watercolor; may not be intended for this church; compare III:G8.   *fig. 27*
    f. *Marriage at Cana,* 10¹/₄″ diam., tracing by William Jay Bolton at Holy Trinity Church, Bradford-on-Avon, of a roundel here attributed to the circle of Jan Swart von Groningen on the basis of resemblance to a glass panel similarly attributed at the Rijksmuseum, Amsterdam (museum catalog no. 130, 16th c.); compare III:G11.   *fig. 30b*
    g. *Christ Stills the Tempest,* pencil, signed "WJB"; compare III:G14.   *fig. 33b*
    h. *Angel with chalice,* watercolor, signed "WJB"; may not be for this church; compare III:Ch1.
    i. *Angel with salver,* watercolor, signed "WJB"; may not be for this church; compare III:Ch4.

Catalog:
Paintings and Drawings

---

fig. 42   j. *Ascension of Christ,* watercolor, signed "WJB"; ? after 1848; compare III:Ch3.

fig. 64   k. A cartoon for the Babe in *The Birth of Christ* (owned by Church of St. Ann and the Holy Trinity, Brooklyn; present location unknown); compare III:G8.

12. Sketches intended or possibly intended for Holy Apostles

fig. 50b   a. *The Flight into Egypt,* 8⅞″ diam., tracing from roundel attributed to Dirk Vellert, after Dürer, at Holy Trinity Church, Bradford-on-Avon; for another version, Hermann Schmitz, *Deutsche Glasmalereien der Gotik und Renaissance. Rund- und Kabinettscheiben* (Munich: Riehn & Reusch, 1923), no. 71, where the Vellert attribution is made. Compare IV:T1c.

     b. *The Kiss of Judas,* 8¼″ diam., tracing from roundel on a design by Jakob Cornelisz van Oostsanen at Holy Trinity Church, Bradford-on-Avon. I am grateful to Prof. Julius S. Held for identifying Oostsanen as the designer; see Kurt Steinbart, *Das Holzschnittwerk des Jakob Cornelisz von Amsterdam* (Burg bei Magdeburg: August Hopfer, 1937), 48. Design does not appear at Holy Apostles.

fig. 65   c. *The Calling of Peter,* pencil, signed "WJB"; compare IV:T8c.

fig. 66   d. *St. Peter Distributing Alms,* pencil, based perhaps on the central figures in Raphael's tapestry design *The Death of Ananias;* does not appear at Holy Apostles.

fig. 67   e. Angelic musicians over an arched space, pencil, using motifs from the Holy Trinity chancel window, but in a more symmetrical arrangement; does not appear at Holy Apostles.

13. Drawings and sketches for or of windows at various locations:

     a. *The Road to Emmaus,* pencil, signed "WJB."

fig. 68   b. *Crucifixion,* watercolor, signed "WJB."

     c. *The Good Samaritan,* watercolor, signed "WJB."

     d. *The Last Supper,* pencil, signed "WJB."

fig. 69   e. *The Ascension of Christ,* pencil, pen and ink, based on Raphael's *Transfiguration.*

     f. An ecclesiastical armorial, watercolor.

     g. Two late medieval Apostles windows with armorials in the church at Stone, Gloucestershire, watercolor.

     i. Ten watercolors and pencil sketches of windows at King's College Chapel, plus several sheets of details of designs and mountings, all probably done between 1848 and 1850 in Cambridge during restoration of the Chapel windows.

Notes

1.—The Life of William Jay Bolton

1. Medieval windows are made of numerous pieces of colored glass that were cut to fit the design contours, and leaded into place. The result is a kind of mosaic of colored light worked into scenes of a decidedly two-dimensional character. Beginning in the sixteenth century, a quicker and easier method of making colored glass designs was developed using vitreous paints, called enamels, on large sheets of clear glass. It was better suited to a contemporary taste for elaborate scenic effects. André Félibien, *Des principes de l'architecture, de la sculpture, de la peinture, et des autres arts qui en dépendent* (Paris, 1699; facs. Farnborough, 1966), chap. XXI (on stained glass), 182, regrets that in his day the rich colors of medieval windows were no longer used because of the costs involved. For a summary of the medieval technique, see Francis Stephens, "Making a Stained-Glass Window," in Lawrence Lee, George Seddon, and Francis Stephens, *Stained Glass* (New York: Crown Publishers, 1976), 177–89. Enamel technique is reviewed by Jerry D. Meyer, "The Painter and Craftsman: Late Eighteenth Century Glass in England," *Stained Glass* 76 (1981): 221–22; and Dorothy L. Maddy, "Glass Enamels," *Stained Glass* 81 (1986): 116–22. See also John A. Knowles, "The Transition from the Mosaic to the Enamel Method of Painting on Glass," *Antiquaries Journal* 6 (1926): 26–35. Arthur Channing Downs, Jr., "Stained Glass in American Architecture," *Nineteenth Century* 3:4 (1977): 56, points out that because plate glass had to be imported into the United States, and was very expensive, large enamel-painted picture windows were never made here.

2. Kenneth Clark, *The Gothic Revival. An Essay in the History of Taste* (London: Constable, 1928).

3. For the history of the English stained glass revival, the fundamental work is Martin Harrison, *Victorian Stained Glass* (London: Barrie & Jenkins, 1980); see p. 10. Charles Winston's pioneering book was published anonymously as *An Inquiry into the Difference of Style Observable in Ancient Glass Painting . . . with Hints on Glass Painting* (Oxford, 1847). Winston also experimented with ways of making glass in the medieval manner; his ideas are explored in Chapter 3. The early history of stained glass in the United States is reviewed by John Gilbert Lloyd, *Stained Glass in America* (Jenkintown, Pa.: Foundation Books, 1963); and by James M. Sturm and James Chotas, *Stained Glass from Medieval Times to the Present* (New York: E. P. Dutton, 1982), chap. 2, which deals with windows in the New York City area of both American and European manufacture. The American revival is surveyed briefly by A. C. Downs, "Stained Glass in American Architecture," 54–60.

4. Window designs by Pugin and Winston are reproduced by M. Harrison, *Victorian Stained Glass,* pl. 4, ill. 11.

5. Bolton's achievements were first chronicled by two eminent glaziers, Otto Heinigke ("The Windows of Holy Trinity Church, Brooklyn, N.Y.," *Architectural Review* 13 [1906]: 1–3) and Orin E. Skinner ("The Stained Glass of the Brothers William Jay Bolton and John Bolton," *Stained Glass* 34 [Spring-Summer 1936]: 1–20), and by Bolton's nephew Reginald Pelham Bolton ("William Jay Bolton, Associate of the

National Academy," *Quarterly Bulletin of the Westchester County Historical Society* 9 [April 1933]: 25–32). Lloyd, *Stained Glass in America,* mentions the Boltons briefly (pp. 47–49).

6. The study is my article, "America's First Stained Glass: William Jay Bolton's Windows at the Church of the Holy Trinity, Brooklyn, New York," *The American Art Journal* 11 (1979): 32–53. The Bolton window, from Holy Trinity, officially went on exhibition at the Metropolitan on 18 November 1985. In November 1988, Holy Trinity, now St. Ann and Holy Trinity, became the site of a national center for the study of stained glass restoration.

7. His sister Abby refers to him as Jay in letters quoted in Rhoda Bolton, *The Lighted Valley, or, The Closing Scenes of the Life of Abby Bolton* (New York: R. Carter & Bros., 1850; London: Hamilton, Adams & Co., 1850), 19ff. The book was reissued in New York (1855, 1872) and in London (1853). The copy in Special Collections, Columbia University, of William Jay Bolton, ed., *The Harp of Pelham* (New York: Windt's Printery, 1844), a volume of poems by Bolton family members, confirms this, for someone penciled in the names of the various authors, including "Jay."

8. Documentation for nineteenth-century stained glass artists is universally scanty, a fact Martin Harrison, *Victorian Stained Glass,* 10, attributes to the glaziers' lack of social standing at the time. It could be added that they also had very little status in the world of art, undoubtedly because stained glass was not accepted into the official world of the academies.

9. A helpful summary of the Evangelical movement, which also encompassed Nonconformist (i.e., to the Anglican Church) groups such as the Wesleyites, Congregationalists, and Baptists, is Ian C. Bradley, *The Call to Seriousness: The Evangelical Impact on the Victorians* (New York: Macmillan, 1976). See also L. E. Elliott-Binns, *The Early Evangelicals* (London, 1953). For High Church–Low Church controversies, Owen Chadwick, *The Victorian Church* (London: Adam & Charles Black, 1966); and Desmond Bowen, *The Idea of the Victorian Church* (Montreal: McGill Univ. Press, 1968).

10. William Jay, *Prayers for the Use of Families* (Hartford: Silas Andrus, 1829), 9.

11. Robert Bolton, Jr., *A History of the County of Westchester from Its First Settlements to the Present Time,* 2 vols. (New York: Alexander S. Gould, 1848); this was revised by a younger brother, Cornelius Winter Bolton, and published as *The History of the Several Towns, Manors, and Patents of the County of Westchester,* 2 vols. (New Rochelle, 1881). Robert, Jr. also wrote *History of the Protestant Episcopal Church in the County of Westchester from Its Foundation* (New York: Stanford & Swords, 1855). For this Robert, see Reginald Pelham Bolton, "Robert Bolton, School-Master, Parish Priest, and Antiquarian," *Quarterly Bulletin of the Westchester County Historical Society* 7 (July 1931): 89–105. James published numerous short moral and religious writings, many for children.

12. The Bolton line to which Jay's family belonged claimed lineage from Oughtred de Bolton, a twelfth-century descendant of the Saxon earls of Mercia; Charles Knowles Bolton, *The Boltons of Old and New England with a Genealogy of the Descendants of William Bolton of Reading, Massachusetts* (Albany, 1889), 1. Another account has the first ancestor as Edwin, Earl of Mercia, lord of the Manor of Bodeltone before and after 1066; Robert Bolton, Jr., *A History of the County of Westchester* II:504.

13. A genealogy of the American branch and of the family of William Jay Bolton is found in Appendix C. The history of this Bolton line is reviewed most completely by Henry Carrington Bolton and Reginald Pelham Bolton, *The Family of Bolton in England and America 1100–1894* (New York: Privately printed, 1895), 267–68. This is a revision and expansion of the family history by Jay's brother Robert Bolton, Jr., *Genealogical and*

Biographical Account of the Family of Bolton in England and America (New York: John A. Gray, 1862). Another source of family history, in its Georgia phase and with particular reference to business affairs, is the Walter Hartridge Collection at the Georgia Historical Society in Savannah.

14. The events of this Robert's life are told by his grandson, William Jay Bolton, *Footsteps of the Flock. Memorials of the Rev. Robert Bolton and of Mrs. Bolton* (London: Hamilton, Adams & Co., 1860), 20–24, as as well as by H. C. and R. P. Bolton, *The Family of Bolton,* chap. 16, where the will (Registry of Wills, Savannah) is printed in its entirety. Robert, the grandfather, married Sarah McClean of Chestertown, Maryland; their portraits, by Walter Robertson, are, respectively, at the Telfair Academy in Savannah and the St. Louis Art Museum. I am grateful to the latter for information on these portraits.

15. H. C. and R. P. Bolton, *The Family of Bolton,* 296–97. It is interesting that Bolton piety did not preclude the ownership of slaves.

16. W. J. Bolton, *Footsteps,* 44.

17. Ibid., 47; H. C. and R. P. Bolton, *The Family of Bolton,* 328. The most useful accounts of William Jay are his own *The Autobiography of the Reverend William Jay,* ed. George Redford and John Angell James, 2 vols. (New York, 1855); his son Cyrus Jay's *Recollections of William Jay of Bath* (London: Hamilton, Adams & Co., 1859); and Rev. S. S. Wilson, *The Rev. William Jay* (London: Binns & Goodwin, n.d. [ca. 1860]). William Jay is the author of *Morning and Evening Exercises for the Closet* (1828; New York: John P. Haven, 1833), home meditations that were popular in both England and the United States.

18. H. C. and R. P. Bolton, *The Family of Bolton,* 267 and passim.

19. Robert's friendship with the Jays and his marriage are recorded in W. J. Bolton, *Footsteps,* 51; and H. C. and R. P. Bolton, *The Family of Bolton,* 329. Ann's brother William Jay, Jr. (1792–1837), was a talented architect who, as a result of his connection with Robert Bolton, visited Savannah and designed several large and important town houses there, in Charleston, and on Sullivan's Island, S.C. His first commission was a house in Savannah for Richard Richardson (now the Owens-Thomas House), who was married to Robert Bolton's sister Frances; Edward V. Jones, "The Owens-Thomas House," *Antiques* 91 (March 1967): 22–26.

20. W. J. Bolton, *Footsteps,* 84–85, 90–97. Reginald Pelham Bolton, "A Heritage of Piety," typescript, Westchester Co. Historical Society, 76, and "William Jay Bolton," 25, states that in 1819 Robert had put up his Savannah inheritance as collateral for notes to meet payments, and instructed relatives of his mother in Savannah to sell the properties to pay debts. The sales took place, but the money was appropriated by the Savannah cousins, and Robert and the English branch of the Bolton firm were forced into bankruptcy. R. P. Bolton does not provide citations for the sources of his information, one of whom may have been Arabella Jay Bolton, daughter of Jay's older brother Robert. She died in the 1950s, and is said by present-day Boltons to have known much family history.

21. W. J. Bolton, *Footsteps,* 85, 107n, 112; H. C. and R. P. Bolton, *The Family of Bolton,* 112.

22. W. J. Bolton, *Footsteps,* 67. The library is undoubtedly reflected in part in the extensive library of Robert, Jr., listed in *Catalogue of the Library of the Late Reverend Robert Bolton . . . to be sold at Auction . . . April 12th, 13th and 14th, 1887 . . . at the Leavitt Art Gallery* (New York, 1887); titles reflect interests not only in theology and church history but also in history, natural history, philosophy, psychology, classics, literature, heraldry,

and art. Robert Bolton, Jr., *A History of the County of Westchester* I:555–57, lists among other treasures in the library a copy of Eliot's Indian Testament, published by Samuel Green in Cambridge, Mass., in 1661; coins of the ancient world; signatures of Elizabeth I and her Council members, of Queen Mary, of Oliver and Richard Cromwell; and letters of many famous people.

23. H. C. and R. P. Bolton, *The Family of Bolton,* 333–34; R. P. Bolton, "A Heritage of Piety," 67–68. Dennis Farr, *William Etty* (London: Routledge & Kegan Paul, 1958), 26n, says that despite the £40,000 average income that, according to Joseph Farrington's diary for 1 April 1799, Robert Bolton had at that date, in 1827 Robert owed Etty £30; Farr is unaware of the financial ruin that had intervened. He also reports the Reverend Jay in arrears to Etty for £15 in 1827, which may have been for the portrait of William Jay himself, which the latter presented to the young Robert Boltons at Liverpool, with an accompanying poem, on 13 September 1817 (*Autobiography* II:220). This portrait is now lost, but is pictured in an engraving in Farr, *William Etty,* pl. 11a. The Etty portraits of Robert Bolton and of Ann Jay Bolton with her eldest children, Nanette and Robert, are at the Owens-Thomas House in Savannah, designed by Ann's brother; see Helena Zimmerman, "The Boltons Return to Savannah," *Savannah News-Press,* 23 March 1975, pp. 1E, 8E. Jay Bolton's daughter Margaretta Grace Bolton, "Notes of the Life of William Jay Bolton" (after 1922; manuscript in the Milner-White archive, King's College Library, Cambridge), 1, says that Etty did several chalk portraits of her father at the age of about six months, but these have not been found.

24. For the friendship between the Reverend Jay and Etty, Cyrus Jay, *Recollections,* 99–104, where several interesting anecdotes about the asthmatic Etty are recorded.

25. The Etty portraits of Jay's daughters are the one of Ann Jay Bolton and children mentioned earlier in n. 23, now in Savannah, and one of Mary Arabella Jay in the National Gallery, London (Farr, *William Etty,* pl. 33). Mary Arabella (d. 1854) became the wife of William Garfit Ashton, a solicitor at Cambridge; they lived at The Limes, near Queens' College. She is mentioned by M. Grace Bolton, "Notes," 1; and by William Jay, *Autobiography* I:107.

26. William Jay, *Autobiography* II:220.

27. M. Grace Bolton, "Notes," 1.

28. The passage quoted is found in W. J. Bolton, *Footsteps,* 79. Ann called her diary her "Record of Mercies." Begun in 1815, when she was twenty-two, it ran to more than nine volumes, and its disappearance is a great loss for Bolton family history.

29. R. P. Bolton, "William Jay Bolton," 26.

30. M. Grace Bolton, "Notes," 3. For Arabella Jay Ashton, see n. 25.

31. William Jay, *Autobiography,* I:28, ed. note; Wilson, *The Rev. William Jay,* 7, reports that the youth would scold the masons for their bad language.

32. William Jay, *Autobiography* II:336. Fonthill Abbey in Wiltshire was an enormous picturesque Gothic manor house designed by James Wyatt for William Beckford in 1796, and redesigned and enlarged in 1807.

33. M. Grace Bolton, "Notes," 3.

34. Ibid.

35. Ibid. 4.

36. R. P. Bolton, "William Jay Bolton," 26; but he does not specify when Jay crossed the Atlantic. William Jay, *Autobiography,* I:105, says that the Boltons' remove to the United States "was one of the greatest trials of my life," but that he understood the reasons, and did not oppose their going.

37. R. P. Bolton, "Robert Bolton [Jr.]," 92–93; he cites a description of the trip in a letter by Robert Bolton, Sr., now in the Hufeland Memorial Library of Westchesteriana, New Rochelle, N.Y.

38. Robert Bolton, Jr., *History of the Protestant Episcopal Church*, 385; W. J. Bolton, *Footsteps*, 159–61; Jay notes that many years before in Savannah, Robert had helped the woman deal with her alcoholic husband. See also H. C. and R. P. Bolton, *The Family of Bolton*, 339; and R. P. Bolton, "Robert Bolton [Jr.]," 93. In 1836, Robert Bolton had succeeded in recovering some of the funds lost in Savannah: he exerted a claim in his wife's marriage contract to a portion of the property sales, and this money was used to buy the farm; R. P. Bolton, "A Heritage of Piety," 76.

39. W. J. Bolton, *Footsteps*, 168–69. See also R. P. Bolton, "The Pondfield Farm—Bronxville," *Quarterly Bulletin of the Westchester County Historical Society* 7 (1931): 26–30.

40. [James Bolton], *Brook Farm. The Amusing and Memorable Account of American Country Life* (London: Wertheim, MacIntosh & Hunt, 1859; MacIntosh, 1863).

41. Sarah Evans, cousin of Robert Bolton, Sr.

42. [James Bolton], *Brook Farm*, 149.

43. The autographs included, among others, those of Henry VII, Elizabeth I, Oliver Cromwell, Lord Nelson, Napoleon, and William Penn; Robert Bolton, Jr., *A History of the County of Westchester* I:556–58, lists many more.

44. [James Bolton], *Brook Farm*, 82, 103–4, 149.

45. *Christ Church at Pelham, Pelham Manor, New York 1843–1943* (Pelham: The Church Vestry, 1943), 14; Barbara Reeves, "Bolton Priory and Christ Church," *Pelham Sun*, 29 April 1954; rpr. 24 November 1975; *Country Life* (June 1948): 30. The parcel was conveyed by Elbert J. Roosevelt to Robert Bolton for $5,847 by a deed dated 18 September, 1838, recorded 16 February 1839; Lockwood Barr, *A Brief . . . Account of . . . the Ancient Town of Pelham, Westchester Co., State of New York* (Richmond, Va.: Dietz Press, 1946), 175. The transfer is confirmed by town records, and I am grateful to Susan C. Swanson, Pelham town historian, for searching these for me. The cottage still exists. None of the articles cites documents; Reeves relies at times on Christ Church clergy. *Christ Church at Pelham*, 15, cites discussions with Arabella Bolton, daughter of Robert, Jr.

46. W. J. Bolton, *Footsteps*, 170.

47. W. J. Bolton, *Footsteps*, 171, notes that the neighbors were astonished by the house's Gothic style. On Old English, see, for example, Charles L. Eastlake, *A History of the Gothic Revival* (1872; rpr. American Life Foundation, 1975), 339–45; and Andrew Saint, *Richard Norman Shaw* (New Haven and London: Yale Univ. Press, 1976), 24–44.

48. Compare the castellated style of Richard Upjohn's Oaklands (Gardner, Me., 1835–36), where the symmetries and simple roofline are purer picturesque Gothic. For Oaklands, E. M. Upjohn, *Richard Upjohn, Architect and Churchman* (New York: Da Capo, 1968), 38–43.

49. *Christ Church at Pelham*, 15. W. J. Bolton, *Footsteps*, 182, noted that Irving was a frequent visitor at the Priory.

50. R. P. Bolton, "William Jay Bolton," 27; *Christ Church at Pelham*, 15; M. Grace Bolton, "Notes," 5. Sir Walter Scott's *Kenilworth* was published in 1831. Letters from Irving to the Reverend Robert Bolton and to Robert, Jr. are printed in Washington Irving, *Letters*, ed. R. M. Aderman, H. L. Kleinfield, and J. S. Banks (Boston: Twayne Publishers, 1982), III: nos. 1264, 1347; IV: nos. 2009, 2542. These contain references to sun blinds about which Robert, Sr. had requested information from Irving, and to an

Irving expedition to the Priory; one is a letter of condolence to Robert, Jr. on the death of Robert, Sr., Irving's long-time friend. The tone of the first two letters is informal and familiar.

51. Robert Bolton, Jr., *A History of the County of Westchester* I:555.

52. A. J. Davis, Day Book (A. J. Davis Collection, New York Public Library), I:224, 257. The drawing appears as fig. 55 in later editions of Andrew Jackson Downing's *Treatise on the Theory and Practice of Landscape Gardening,* first published 1841; Downing describes the Bolton Priory: "A highly unique residence in the old English style. . . . The exterior is massive and picturesque, in the simplest taste of the Elizabethan age, and being built amidst a fine oak wood, of the dark rough stone of the neighborhood, it has at once the appearance of considerable antiquity" (1889 edition by A. O. Moore [New York], 347). Downing goes on to praise the interior decor, but neglects to mention the stained glass.

53. W. J. Bolton, *Footsteps,* 171–72, recalls the problems with the contractor, and tells of the children sleeping in the half-finished house.

54. M. Grace Bolton, "Notes," 6. Heinigke, "The Windows of Holy Trinity Church," 2, noted such reports during his visit with Cornelius Winter Bolton and his niece Arabella, Robert, Jr.'s daughter, the last Boltons at the Priory.

55. *Christ Church at Pelham,* 13.

56. W. J. Bolton, *Footsteps,* 180, describes the making of these forest trails. See also *Christ Church at Pelham,* 15. The style of the gardens is noted by Robert Bolton, Jr., *A History of the County of Westchester* I:558.

57. The house and greenhouse are pictured in Robert Bolton, Jr., *A History of the County of Westchester* I:555.

58. The Priory was sold to a former pupil of the Boltons' Priory School, Adele L. Sampson (Mrs. F. W. Stevens), who presented it to her daughter, Mrs. Frederick H. Allen, in 1883; Barr, *A Brief . . . Account,* 122. Its present owner, who acquired the house in 1969, has been most gracious in giving me and my colleague Leland Cook permission on several occasions to examine locations and make photographs in the house.

59. Reported in *Christ Church at Pelham,* 15.

60. *The Harp of Pelham* (New York: Windt's Printery, 1844). The preface notes the source of the poems in the family newspaper. The price of the paper was "one contribution."

61. The entire letter is reproduced in Appendix A. James Bolton was then a student at Cambridge. The letter is preserved in the Archives of the Episcopal Diocese of Long Island, Garden City, N.Y. The Bolton materials at the Archives include a book of sketches and letters given in 1906 to the Church of (St. Ann and) the Holy Trinity, Brooklyn, N.Y., by William Jay Bolton's daughter (see p. 32); and a scrapbook on the art of William Jay and John Bolton made by their friend Eliza F. Clibborn, and presented to the same church by her grandson, Dr. Henry M. Nicholson, in 1944.

62. M. Grace Bolton, "Notes," 3.

63. W. J. Bolton, *Footsteps,* 192. He devotes chap. XIV entirely to ideas on education.

64. *Christ Church at Pelham,* 23, where operations of the school are described by a former pupil.

65. See above, n. 22.

66. Robert Bolton, Jr., *A History of the County of Westchester* I:559; he refers to the architectural style as "Saxon." By 1848, when the *History* appeared, the public school had eighty to ninety pupils.

Notes to Pages 11–14

67. *Christ Church at Pelham,* 25; Barr, *A Brief . . . Account,* 122, 136.

68. M. Grace Bolton, "Notes," 17–18.

69. National Academy of Design, Register of Students of the Antique School, for the sessions 1839–40 and 1840–41. I am indebted to Abigail Booth Gerdts of the National Academy for help in finding these registers. She notes that the academic year ran from 30 October through 15 March. For Morse, Carleton Mabee, *The American Leonardo. A Life of Samuel F. B. Morse* (New York: Alfred A. Knopf, 1943), 157, 181; Paul J. Saiti, Jr., and Nicolai Cikovsky, Jr., in *Samuel F. B. Morse: Educator and Champion of the Arts in America,* exhibition catalog, National Academy of Design (New York: National Academy of Design, 1982); and Gary A. Reynolds, "New York University's First Professor of Fine Arts," in the catalog of a Morse exhibition, New York University, 1982; I am grateful to Peter Arnade of the university for the last reference.

70. Bolton's living quarters are mentioned in Register of Students; Morse's quarters at the university are described in Mabee, *The American Leonardo,* 181–82.

71. David Hunter Strother of Virginia; see Samuel F. B. Morse, *Samuel F. B. Morse. His Letters and Journals,* ed. Edward Lind Morse (Boston and New York: Houghton Mifflin, 1914), I:162. Strother goes on to recount the time when, for lack of funds, Morse had not eaten for twenty-four hours; on Morse's poverty, see Mabee, *the American Leonardo,* passim, and for this period, p. 181.

72. Morse, *Letters and Journals* I:163.

73. John L. Morton to William Jay Bolton, 18 March 1840, Long Island Diocese Archives, Garden City, N.Y.

74. R. P. Bolton, "William Jay Bolton," 27.

75. The fresco competition for the newly built Houses of Parliament took place in 1843, and the first composition was completed, by William Dyce, in 1846; Christopher Forbes, *The Royal Academy Revisited. Victorian Paintings from the Forbes Magazine Collection* (N.p., n.d.), 153.

76. R. P. Bolton, "William Jay Bolton," 27. Elsewhere he gives the "painful" painting's title as "Canonicus and the Governor of Plymouth," stating that it won a prize, which casts doubt on both his facts and his artistic judgment; R. P. Bolton, "A Heritage of Piety," 112.

77. "Exhibition Record of the National Academy of Design," in *Constitution of the National Academy of Design and Schedule of the Property* (New York: Sackett & Co., 1852), 43.

78. Mrs. G. W. Maynard of the National Academy to R. P. Bolton, 23 September 1932. I am grateful to the National Academy for photocopies of this and other documents relating to Bolton.

79. Morse to W. J. Bolton, 22 April 1843, Long Island Diocese Archives, Garden City, N.Y.

80. The 1907 letter, which gives a brief summary of her father's life, is preserved at the National Academy of Design, New York, N.Y. National Academy records also list a painting entitled *Rhododendron* by Miss A. Bolton of New Rochelle [i.e., the Priory, on the Pelham–New Rochelle border], exhibited in 1845; this could be either Nanette (Ann) or Abby, both of whom are known to have had some skill in painting and drawing.

81. M. Grace Bolton, "Notes," 6–7.

82. Ibid.

83. Ibid., 12.

84. Francis Haskell and Nicholas Penny, *Taste and the Antique* (New Haven: Yale Univ. Press, 1981), 139, comment on the popularity of this monument.

85. M. Grace Bolton, "Notes," 7. So far as is known, all have disappeared.

86. Most of the armorials can be identified in Robert Bolton, Jr., *Genealogical and Biographical Account,* 28–31: drawings of Bolton armorials from British Library MSS Harley 891, 1096, 1468, 1476, 2986; Add. 5533, 5822. Robert also made tracings of armorials in stained glass windows; H. C. and R. P. Bolton, *The Family of Bolton,* 364; also R. P. Bolton, "Robert Bolton [Jr.]," 91, and "William Jay Bolton," 27. Robert's comments on stained glass, *History of the Protestant Episcopal Church,* 649–50, show his knowledge of the techniques and vocabulary of the medium.

87. John Henry Hopkins, *Essay on Gothic Architecture, with Various Plans and Drawings for Churches* (Burlington, Vt.: Smith & Harrington, 1836), 13. On Hopkins, see Lawrence Wodehouse, "John Henry Hopkins and the Gothic Revival," *Antiques* 114 (April 1973): 776–82. A scholarly essay of 1830, appearing in *The American Journal of Science and Arts* 18, no. 2: 220–29, also stated that stained glass belonged to the Gothic; William H. Pierson, Jr., *American Buildings and Their Architects, Technology and the Picturesque, the Corporate and the Early Gothic Styles* (Garden City, N.Y.: Anchor Books, 1980), 169.

88. W. J. Bolton, *Footsteps* 174.

89. Ibid. For a survey of Tractarianism and Ecclesiology, and their influence in America, see Phoebe B. Stanton, *The Gothic Revival and American Church Architecture* (Baltimore: Johns Hopkins Press, 1968), intro. and chaps. I–III.

90. W. J. Bolton, *Footsteps,* 176–77.

91. Ibid., 178.

92. Stanton, *The Gothic Revival,* xviii and passim.

93. In fact, the Boltons' church recalls Pugin's St. Lawrence's, Tubney (after 1842), except for the latter's separately articulated sanctuary. Interestingly enough, while Pugin's interests and clientele were predominantly Roman Catholic, Tubney was one of his churches for Protestants. St. Lawrence's, Tubney, is pictured in Phoebe B. Stanton, *Pugin* (New York: Viking Press, 1972), 131.

94. Robert Bolton, Jr., *A History of the County of Westchester* II:558, and *History of the Protestant Episcopal Church,* 695–96, where the instrument of donation of the land and building to the Diocese of New York is printed. An account of the building of Christ Church, along with other relevant documents, is in *Christ Church at Pelham,* 19–22.

95. *Christ Church at Pelham,* 18, 61, 65; the crucifix was framed by Robert Bolton, Jr., for the chapel in his own home, and given later to Christ Church; the lanterns were given by Arabella Bolton after 1936. Domestic furniture attributable to the Pelham Boltons is now owned by various family members in New York, Vermont, and Ireland. In 1853, John carved, gilded, and inscribed a reredos, which is now under the south transept window; *Christ Church at Pelham,* 61.

96. Robert Bolton, Jr., *The History of the Several Towns* II:96. See Chapter 3 for particulars.

97. For the medieval technique, see n. 1. The possibility of windows in the medieval technique in the United States predating those of Bolton is discussed in A. C. Downs, "Stained Glass in American Architecture."

98. M. Grace Bolton, "Notes," 8. Her information probably came from Dr. Robert C. Dickinson; see comments at the end of this chapter.

99. See Frances G. Mead, "If You Like Historic Spots. William Jay Bolton's

Studio," *Westchester Host* 1:12 (23–30 March 1926). The house was on the east side of Pelham Road, north of Pelhamdale Avenue. Mead says that in earlier times, bits of glass could still be dug in the garden. See also, R. P. Bolton, "A Heritage of Piety," 114.

100. The windows can be assigned by style, as well as by comments in Winter Bolton's revision of Robert, Jr.'s history of Westchester County, *The History of the Several Towns* II:96. See the discussion of styles in Chapter 3 and Catalog II. The booklet *Christ Church at Pelham,* 17, is incorrect in dating the *Agnus Dei* oculus after 1850.

101. *Christ Church at Pelham,* 40.

102. The 1854 lecture was published as "King's College Chapel Windows, Cambridge," *Archaeological Journal* 12 (1855): 153–72.

103. Bolton to William H. Harison, of the building committee of Trinity Church, Manhattan, with the dateline "Pelham Priory, Oct. 19," written almost certainly in 1844, as will be shown; it is now in the Trinity Church Parish Archives. See Appendix A for the complete text. The letter was discovered by James Sturm, who very kindly sent me a copy. I am grateful to Phyllis Barr, archivist of Trinity Church, and to the Rector, Churchwardens, Vestrymen, and the Parish Archives for helpful information relating to this letter.

104. The window is noted in *The Builder* 8 (28 December 1850): 8; it was removed in 1890 to make way for the one by C. E. Kempe. The dollar-sterling exchange rate is from A. Barton Hepburn, *A History of Currency in the United States,* rev. ed. (New York: Augustus M. Kelley, 1967), 62. Steven J. Bell of the Lippincott Library, Wharton School, Univ. of Pennsylvania, very kindly provided this reference; he noted that all such figures should be used with caution.

105. The glass for Richard Upjohn's Trinity Church, Manhattan, glazed not long after the Pelham installations, also came from Germany; A. C. Downs, "Stained Glass in American Architecture," 56.

106. These glaziers are mentioned in *History of Architecture and the Building Trades of Greater New York,* 2 vols. (New York: Union History Co., 1899), II:18–19. Gibson is reported to have made ecclesiastical glass, but Carse & Wert, of 472 Pearl Street, made windows for "steamboat or packet ship lights, transparent signs, window blinds, sky lights and other purposes, for which stained glass is commonly used." The latter production may have been only colored glass, not stained or painted glass.

107. M. A. Gessert, *Rudimentary Treatise on the Art of Painting on Glass or Glass-Staining,* 3d ed. (London: John Weale, 1857), 2.

108. For England, see M. Harrison, *Victorian Stained Glass,* chap. I. The history of the stained glass revival on the Continent remains to be written.

109. Among the available manuals were F. Haudicquer de Blancourt, *De l'art de la verrerie* (Paris, 1697, 1718; rpr. 1973), translated as *The Art of Glass* (London, 1699); Félibien, *Des principes de l'architecture,* chap. XXI; Louis Hautecoeur, *Histoire de l'architecture classique en France* (Paris, 1643), with a chapter on stained glass; Pierre Le Vieil, *L'art de la peinture sur verre et de la vitrerie* (Paris, 1774).

110. [Winston], *An Inquiry into the Difference of Style.*

111. Letter signed "W.J. Bolton" and postmarked Pelham–New Rochelle; it is in Appendix A. The official letter of appointment as Associate is dated 15 May 1845. Both letters are in the Long Island Diocese Archives, Garden City, N.Y.

112. In earlier articles, including my own, the window count has varied. I have now removed the stairwell and organ-loft windows from the Bolton canon, which leaves forty-nine windows: one in the vestibule, fourteen in the aisles and galleries, sixteen in

the clerestory, three in the chancel, and one in the tower. If an opalescent window now in the vestibule replaced one by Bolton, as Otto Weir Heinigke proposed (see Catalog III), the total would be fifty.

113. Jacob Landy, *The Architecture of Minard Lafever* (New York: Columbia Univ. Press, 1970), 105, and on Bartow, p. 267 n. 1, and passim. Also on Bartow, Roscoe C. E. Brown, *Church of the Holy Trinity Brooklyn Heights in the City of New York, 1847–1922* (New York, 1922), 23–24.

114. Landy, *The Architecture of Minard Lafever*, 105.

115. Anne Elliott Roberts, "William Jay Bolton—Artist in Glass," *Pelham Sun*, 22 July 1954. The design of a Regency-style mansion built for Edgar Bartow's brother Robert in what is now Pelham Park is attributed to John Bolton by R. P. Bolton, "A Heritage of Piety," 120. Landy, *The Architecture of Minard Lafever*, gives the dates of its construction as between 1836 and 1842; he too supposed (p. 3) that Bartow "discovered" Bolton. See also Joseph Downs, "History in houses, Bartow Mansion," *Antiques* 55 (April 1949): 274–77, who states that Lafever might be the architect, which Landy disputes.

116. Landy, *The Architecture of Minard Lafever*, 106.

117. Ibid., 105.

118. The same is true of England; A. C. Sewter, "Victorian Stained Glass," *Apollo* (December 1962): 765.

119. *Contributions to the History of the Parish of The Church of the Holy Trinity, Brooklyn, L.I. . . . November 26, 1871* (New York, 1872), 31, cited by Landy, *the Architecture of Minard Lafever*, 41, 106.

120. Minard Lafever, *The Architectural Instructor* (New York: G. P. Putnam & Co., 1856), 478–79.

121. Landy, *the Architecture of Minard Lafever*, 117, 121. Orin E. Skinner, "The Stained Glass of the Brothers . . . Bolton," 15, recalls that when Grosvenor Thomas, a collector of antique stained glass, entered Holy Trinity, he exclaimed, "Kings College Chapel," and added, "I had no idea anything so fine had been done within five hundred years." King's Chapel was a source of architectural design for several other New York buildings of the period, including Lafever's First Baptist Church on Broome Street (1841–42); Landy, *The Architecture of Minard Lafever*, 81, 116–17. An engraving of King's Chapel was widely known in John Britton's *Architectural Antiquities of Great Britain* (London, 1807), I:pl. V.

122. Although attempts have been made to link Bolton's designs specifically to King's Chapel windows, a close examination of the compositions involved proves otherwise. A case in point is the depiction of Christ at Emmaus. The King's artist and Bolton used the same Dürer print, but Bolton's version is more faithful to the model (fig. 40). Another is Bolton's *Entry into Jerusalem*, the composition of which is too common to allow determination that the King's design was his source (fig. 31a).

123. Julie L. Sloan, "A New Look at Bolton Windows of the Church of St. Ann and the Holy Trinity," *Stained Glass* 77 (1983): 235. My former student, Tracy Martin, located the date on the tomb of the *Resurrection* window; the second date was discovered by the restorers.

124. Edgar John Bartow to William Jay Bolton, 16 August 1845, Long Island Diocese Archives, Garden City, N.Y.

125. The angels of A1–7 are repeated in A8–14 (see church diagrams and Catalog, III). The reuse of cartoons was frequent in the Middle Ages and can be seen, for

example, in the Messenger figures of the windows at King's College Chapel, Cambridge. Bolton also devised shortcuts in installation; see Sloan, "A New Look."

126. Despite the kind efforts of Susan C. Swanson, Pelham town historian, the location of "Irving Flandereau's" has not been determined. Ms. Swanson suggests, in a letter of 6 March 1986, that it may have been in the town of New Rochelle, which bordered on the Bolton property.

127. For the Harison letter, see n. 103. Dr. Jonathan Mayhew Wainwright was assistant rector of Trinity Church. The original orthography has been maintained.

128. For an "emblem and effigy" window, see John's design in fig. 73.

129. The large chancel window at Trinity Church, depicting individual figures of Christ and six apostles under canopies in the upper register, with Christian symbols in the lights below, is the only figural window of the program, and is carried out in both potmetal and enamel colors; Sturm in Sturm and Chotas, *Stained Glass,* 16–19, who illustrates it in color (p. 18), discusses what is known of the production, and quotes a critic of the period who refers to the "poverty of the window's original design."

130. Sturm in Sturm and Chotas, *Stained Glass,* 19, credits Hoppin (1816–1872) with the designs, and Abner Stephenson with the actual glazing. See also A. C. Downs, "Stained Glass in American Architecture," 56, who mentions only Stephenson.

131. A. C. Downs, "Stained Glass in American Architecture," 56, seems to suggest that the Trinity window preceded those of Holy Trinity; Sturm in Sturm and Chotas, *Stained Glass,* 16, expresses uncertainty. The window openings at Trinity Church were described as unglazed in April 1844 (Sturm and Chotas, *Stained Glass,* 16).

132. In Morse, *Letters and Journals* I:280 Edward Lind Morse states that in 1845 Samuel Morse retired as Academy president to turn his attention to inventing.

133. John Steegman, *Victorian Taste* (Cambridge, Mass.: MIT Press, 1971), 134.

134. I first learned of the Bolton windows at Holy Apostles from Orin E. Skinner, to whom I am grateful for early encouragement in my study of the Boltons.

135. Holy Apostles' Tractarian leanings are reported by Lucius A. Edelblute, *The History of the Church of the Holy Apostles* (New York: Privately printed, 1949), 60.

136. Landy, *The Architecture of Minard Lafever,* 149.

137. Edelblute, *The History of . . . Holy Apostles,* 58; Landy, *The Architecture of Minard Lafever,* 149. In the 1850s a transept was added and the chancel enlarged; not long after, the nave was extended to the west to accommodate a growing congregation; Landy, *The Architecture of Minard Lafever,* 150. During these renovations, several new windows by Sharp and Steel, a New York City firm, in the same overall design, but with roundels more delicately pictorial, were installed in the transept.

138. "My dear Nanette," a poem written after he saw her when they both visited their relatives in Lausanne, 1883; in *A Consecrated Life, being an account of Nanette Bolton* (New York, [1885]), 31. H. C. and R. P. Bolton, *The Family of Bolton,* 370, state that Jay Bolton was the author of this volume, which would thus have been a posthumous publication.

139. M. Grace Bolton, "Notes," 12; she names another assistant, a boy named Cenoweth. For William Henry Constable, see Birkin Haward, *Nineteenth Century Norfolk Stained Glass* (Norwich: Geo Books, Centre of East Anglian Studies, 1984), 136.

140. Rhoda Bolton, *The Lighted Valley,* 9, 28.

141. *Christ Church at Pelham,* 25. This letter is now lost.

142. Robert Bolton, Sr., "The Pains of Memory," in W. J. Bolton, ed., *The Harp of Pelham,* 45.

143. For Robert, Sr.'s last days, W. J. Bolton, *Footsteps,* 223. Forbidden by English law to serve an Anglican parish because of his American Episcopal ordination, Robert Bolton spent his last days as chaplain to the Earl of Dulcie at Tortworth Court (Gloucestershire). Information on Robert's home at this period, Vittoria Walk, Cheltenham, was kindly provided by Graham H. Baker of the Cheltenham Library.

144. H. C. and R. P. Bolton, *The Family of Bolton,* 373; R. P. Bolton, "William Jay Bolton," 31.

145. For the inscription and newspaper notices, see Catalog V. *The Builder* for 1843 describes a window by William Wailes for a church at Newcastle-upon-Tyne as "the first obituary window in the area"; M. Harrison, *Victorian Stained Glass,* 21.

146. A notice on the West Lynn window was published by Birkin Haward, who identified the work as Bolton's, in his *Nineteenth Century Norfolk Stained Glass,* Gazetteer, "West Lynn." It is discussed in more detail in W. B. Clark, "A William Jay Bolton Window Discovered, 'The Angel at the Tomb' at West Lynn, Norfolk," *Journal of Stained Glass* 18:1 (1983–84): 52–57.

147. The St. Andrew's and St. Mary's windows are recorded without specifics by Sir Thomas Kendrick, "English Stained Glass" (typescript, Royal Institute of British Architects, London), vol. II, sec. 4. *The Builder* 8 (28 December 1850): 8, names Bolton as the maker of the St. Mary's window; it was removed when a window by C. E. Kempe was installed. In my article "America's First Stained Glass," 53 and n. 52, I mistakenly assumed the eastern armorial window at St. Andrew's to be by Bolton.

148. Hilary Wayment, *The Windows of King's College Chapel Cambridge,* Corpus Vitrearum Medii Aevi, Great Britain. Supplementary Vol. I (London, 1972), 41. They cleaned windows 8–12 and 15–19. On J. P. Hedgeland, see M. Harrison, *Victorian Stained Glass,* 36 n. 35. Criticisms of Hedgeland's restoration policies, especially the use of "oil colours" and the replacement of pieces, and his reply, are in *The Guardian,* 7 and 21 November 1849; other criticism of Hedgeland's methods by J. Birkbeck Nevins, "The Secret of Ancient Painted Glass," in *The Builder* 8 (28 December 1850): 616.

149. M. Grace Bolton, "Notes," 12.

150. *The Guardian,* 7 and 21 November 1849, called attention to the excesses of Hedgeland's procedures, and shortly thereafter the job was terminated; Wayment, *The Windows of King's College Chapel,* 41 n. 2.

151. The drawings are now at the Long Island Diocese Archives, Garden City, N.Y.

152. The events surrounding Grace's gifts to King's are discussed later.

153. On the armorials, Hilary Wayment, *King's College Chapel, Cambridge, the Side-Chapel Glass* (Cambridge: Cambridge Antiquarian Society and King's College, 1988), 14–15, 115–21; also Kenneth Harrison, *An Illustrated Guide to the Windows of King's College Chapel, Cambridge* (Cambridge: King's College, 1965), 63.

154. The smaller armorials were sold to King's by F. Sydney Eden in 1927 with unrelated stained glass; correspondence between Eden and Dean Milner-White is preserved in the Milner-White archive, King's College Library, Cambridge. I am grateful to Hilary Wayment for sending me photocopies of these and other documents.

155. W. J. Bolton, "King's College Chapel Windows," 153–72, will be discussed in the next chapter.

156. W. J. Bolton, "King's College Chapel Windows," 171.

157. M. Grace Bolton, "Notes," 13, says that it was in response to his wife's wish that her father began studying for holy orders. She mistakenly assumes that he matriculated after his wife's death.

158. M. Grace Bolton, "Notes," 12.

159. J. A. Venn, *Biographical History of Gonville and Caius College, 1349–1897* (Cambridge, 1898), II:291; J. A. Venn, *Alumni cantabrigienses* (Cambridge, 1940), vol. I, pt. II, p. 31.

160. W. J. Bolton, *The Evidences of Christianity as Exhibited in the Writings of its Apologists Down to Augustine* (Cambridge: Macmillan & Co., 1853; Boston: Gould and Lincoln, 1854; New York: R. Carter & Bros., 1854).

161. W. J. Bolton, "Architecture and its Connection with Religion," *The Christian Advocate and Review,* 2d ser., 6:69 (November 1872): 823. The Camden Society, begun in 1839, had moved to London by Jay's period at Cambridge, and in 1841 became the Ecclesiological Society; see K. Clark, *The Gothic Revival,* chap. 8.

162. The ordination dates are given by Robert Bolton, Jr., *Genealogical and Biographical Account,* 188.

163. In a publication of April 1933 by R. P. Bolton, "William Jay Bolton," she is mentioned as the sole survivor of Jay's family.

164. Robert Bolton, Jr., *Genealogical and Biographical Account,* 189; H. C. and R. P. Bolton, *The Family of Bolton,* 373. All efforts to locate descendants of these children, if they exist, have so far been fruitless. William Henry, who became a "High Church" priest, is listed in Venn, *Alumni cantabrigienses,* vol. I, pt. II, p. 31; his brief obituary notice in *The Times,* 6 August 1902, does not mention a family. Their mother was buried 31 December 1903 in St. Martin's Church, Salisbury (funeral notice, clipping file, Bath Municipal Reference Library), and it was noted that her one daughter was ill and her sons were dead; see also n. 178.

165. *Fireside Preaching. Facts and Hints for Visitors of the Poor* (London: Seeley, Jackson, & Halliday, 1856).

166. M. Grace Bolton, "Notes," 14.

167. The parish locations, dates of incumbency, and the quotation are from M. Grace Bolton, "Notes," 13. As for the number of children, it should be remembered that a girl by Margaretta had died in infancy.

168. W. J. Bolton, "Architecture and . . . Religion," discussed in the next chapter.

169. M. Grace Bolton, "Notes," 15. He published a historical study of the thirteen, *The Stratford Martyrs of the Reformation. A Sermon preached at St. John's, Stratford, E[ast] . . . July 12, 1868* (London, 1868).

170. A copy of Rufus W. Griswold, *The Songs and Ballads of Sir Walter Scott with His life* (New York: Leavitt & Allen Brothers, n.d.,) bears Jay's signature, his address as the Priory, and Christmas 1879 as the date. The book is now owned by Mrs. J. Lewis Bolton of Fishkill, N.Y.

171. M. Grace Bolton, "Notes," 20, says that she did not learn of the American windows until the visit in 1906 of a member of the Holy Trinity congregation.

172. M. Grace Bolton, "Notes," 18.

173. Ibid., 17.

174. Ibid., 15.

175. Ibid., 16.

176. He wrote a poem to Nanette, dated 27 June 1883, with the rubric, "Lines written after a visit to Lausanne, to his sister Nanette"; *A Consecrated Life,* 31–33.

177. M. Grace Bolton, "Notes," 18–19.

178. In an Easter, 1944 address to the Annual Meeting of the Holy Trinity congregation, Dr. Dickinson recalled the Salisbury trips and Grace Bolton's visit to Brooklyn;

copy on deposit at the Long Island Diocese Archives, Garden City, N.Y.; the Reverend William Howard Melish very kindly sent me a photocopy of this interesting text. Susannah may be intended in Grace's use of "we" in her 1907 letter to the National Academy, but nothing more is said of Susannah after that, and it might be supposed that she had died. Grace's long indisposition is also recorded in her mother's death notice of 1903 (see n. 164), which states that only Susannah was present at the funeral, as "the other daughter" was an invalid.

179. M. Grace Bolton to Dr. Dickinson, 15 December 1924, Long Island Diocese Archives, Garden City, N.Y. Dean Milner-White also wrote an account of her arrival at his office carrying some of the ancient glass, and of his visit to Salisbury to collect the rest. He noted only one box in the Misses Bolton's attic, and describes it as containing "scraps of canopies, of borders, of armorials, of colour. Most . . . consisted of essays and experiments after ancient models by Mr. Bolton himself." There were also the Bolton copies, mentioned earlier, of three Tudor armorials, which Milner-White initially took to be originals until he compared them with the smaller copies bought in 1927 from Mr. Eden. He then knew that all were by Bolton. His account is in the Milner-White archive in King's College Library, and is summarized in Milner-White, "William Jay Bolton," 215.

180. R. P. Bolton, "William Jay Bolton," 31.

181. The 1907 letter to the National Academy is preserved there, and I am grateful to the Academy for a photocopy of this document.

182. M. Grace Bolton, "Notes," 12.

183. Brown, *Church of the Holy Trinity*, says only that Bolton "executed some of the windows in Bolton Priory," not mentioning specifically the *Adoration of the Magi* in Christ Church.

2.—Ideas and Techniques

1. Desmond Bowen, *The Idea of the Victorian Church*, 143–44, points out that there was a certain anti-intellectualism even among Tractarians. Bowen's discussions of both groups are complex but informative. Other relevant studies include Bradley, *The Call to Seriousness;* Elliott-Binns, *The Early Evangelicals;* and Chadwick, *The Victorian Church.*

2. W. J. Bolton, *The Evidences of Christianity*, 16.

3. Ibid., 301.

4. Ibid.

5. The watercolor is in the Long Island Diocese Archives, Garden City, N.Y.

6. M. Grace Bolton, "Notes", 3–4.

7. W. J. Bolton, ed., *The Harp of Pelham*, 44.

8. Ibid., 69.

9. Ibid. 26–31, 45–53, 71–75.

10. Ibid. 59–64; the poem is called "Mont Blanc."

11. Ibid, 79.

12. Ibid, 57.

13. John Ruskin, "The Nature of Gothic," in *The Stones of Venice* (London: Smith, Elder, & Co., 1851–53), II: Chap. VI.

14. W. J. Bolton, "Architecture and . . . Religion," 824.

15. Ibid., 829.

16. Ibid., 823. Bolton first enunciated this theory, but did not develop it, in his 1855 article on the King's Chapel windows.

17. W. J. Bolton, "Architecture and . . . Religion," 825.

18. W. J. Bolton, "King's College Chapel Windows," 153–54.

19. W. J. Bolton, "Architecture and . . . Religion," 824; see also pp. 826–27, 831, where he notes similar ideas in Montesquieu, Dugald Stewart's *Elements of the Philosophy of the Human Mind,* the historian Sir James Stephen, and James Fergusson's *Handbook of Architecture* (1855).

20. Georg Germann, *Gothic Revival in Europe and Britain: Sources, Influences and Ideas,* trans. G. Onn (Cambridge, Mass.: MIT Press, 1973), 115; he includes also local materials and national cultural traits as important contributors to style.

21. W. J. Bolton, "King's College Chapel Windows," 172.

22. Ibid.

23. W. J. Bolton, "Architecture and . . . Religion," 826.

24. Ibid.

25. Ibid., 838. Five years later, in 1877, William Morris formed the Society for the Protection of Ancient Buildings to prevent the destructive restoration to which Bolton refers here.

26. W. J. Bolton, "Architecture and . . . Religion," 838.

27. Ibid., 825. In 1888, William Morris still viewed the Gothic style as a combination of classicism and northern "barbarian" culture; "The Revival of Architecture," in Nikolaus Pevsner, *Some Architectural Writing of the Nineteenth Century* (Oxford: Clarendon Press, 1972), 318.

28. W. J. Bolton, "King's College Chapel Windows," 170–71.

29. According to Martin Harrison, *Victorian Stained Glass,* 37, Winston's glass was first used in 1852, for windows in the Temple Church, City of London.

30. A. C. Sewter, "The Place of Charles Winston in the Victorian Revival of the Art of Stained Glass," *Journal of the British Archaeological Assn.,* 3d ser., 24 (1961): 85.

31. For technical terms, consult Glossary.

32. M. Grace Bolton, "Notes," 8.

33. A great deal remains to be learned about the glass, the pigments, the various stages of production, and the installation of Bolton windows. It is expected that a technical report will eventually result from the ongoing restoration at Holy Trinity, and that this will address and clarify some of these issues.

34. The glazier's use of templates is discussed in Lee, Seddon, and Stephens, *Stained Glass,* 179.

35. On cutting tools, Lee, Seddon, and Stephens, *Stained Glass,* 181.

36. By 1865 the production of colored glass had so increased that Clement Heaton could speak of "140 different tints" of potmetal glass available to the glazier; "Ornamented and Stained Glass," *The Builder* 21 (25 February 1863): 139. Heaton's article is an important early survey of the techniques used in the nineteenth century.

37. [Winston], *An Inquiry into the Difference of Style,* 217, says that the making of ruby glass had ceased by the beginning of the eighteenth century, and was only recently (presumably the late 1830s) revived in France, but its production soon became widespread.

38. On enamel colors and fluxes in Bolton's time, see Gessert, *Rudimentary Treatise on the Art of Painting on Glass,* chap. 1; and Emmanuel Otto Fromberg, *A Rudimentary Essay on the Art of Painting on Glass* (London: John Weale, 1851), from his *Handbuch der*

Glasmalerei, Quedlinburg and Leipzig, 1844. The flux, which is often borax, is added to the mixture of pigment and glass dust that constitutes the paint, and, by reducing the paint's melting point below that of the glass, allows the paint to fuse with or adhere to the glass, depending on the chemical structure of the color. Achieving the correct amount of flux can be difficult; Fromberg, *A Rudimentary Essay on the Art of Painting on Glass,* 29.

39. Mary Higgins, conservator at the Greenland Studio, states that she has reproduced this stain with a modern amber stain thickly applied, but that Bolton's color was difficult to match; for this and other technical information conveyed in conversation and by letter, I offer Ms. Higgins my warm thanks. Fromberg, *A Rudimentary Essay on the Art of Painting on Glass,* 53–54, says that if, when a silver-stain paste of ferruginous clay and chloride of silver painted on a piece of glass is fired, a small amount of reduced silver is present and a "siskin yellow" is obtained, but if more silver is used, the color can become "a more or less intense red." It was surely instructions of this sort which Bolton followed, but by whom is not known. The German edition of Fromberg's handbook appeared in 1844, which means that Bolton could have seen it just as he began the Holy Trinity glass; the English edition postdates Holy Trinity.

40. Reported in an important article by Roy Newton and Trevor Brighton, "William Peckitt's Red Glasses," *Stained Glass* 81 (1986): 214–20. Peckitt, like Fromberg, describes his red stain as being made from a combination of silver and ferruginous clay (specifically, yellow ocher), but he calls for silver sulfide rather than silver chloride. He too notes that a greater amount of the silver will produce red, and less will yield yellow.

41. A good explanation of the present-day silver-stain process is Dorothy L. Maddy, "Silver Staining," *Stained Glass* 79 (1984): 258–62, where some of the dangers and errors, and their results, are outlined. See also Albinas Elskus, *The Art of Painting on Glass* (New York: Charles Scribner's Sons, 1980), 97–101. The marbling effect using silver stain can be seen in many late medieval windows.

42. Yellow potmetal was probably not available to him, for as Winston notes, *An Inquiry into the Difference of Style,* 217, its use was abandoned in the seventeenth century in favor of silver stain.

43. W. J. Bolton, "King's College Chapel Windows," 171.

44. Ibid., n. 6. A paint without a flux, when fired, would have to produce a chemical reaction on the surface of the glass, in the form of an ion exchange, and in the manner of a silver-stain color. Iron stains are not presently known, but such a stain would be possible. I am grateful to Frank L. Reusche and David Stanton of L. Reusche & Company, Newark, for information on the chemical properties and functions of enamel paints, fluxes, and stains. A flesh stain has recently been invented by Richard T. Gray; see Norman Temme, "A New Flesh Stain," *Stained Glass* 78 (1983–84): 377.

45. W. J. Bolton, "King's College Chapel Windows," 171 n. 6.

46. A report on the papers and discussions, including a paper by Winston, appears in *Supplement to the Cambridge Chronicle,* 15 July 1854.

47. W. J. Bolton, "King's College Chapel Windows," 170. Winston also condemns the "dirtying" of glass to make it appear old; *An Inquiry into the Difference of Style,* 213.

48. So far, the exact cause of the deterioration at Holy Trinity, and at Holy Apostles as well, has not been determined. One possible explanation is that the pieces for these windows were poorly fired. Another is that too much borax flux was added to the paint, as often happened in the nineteenth century. R. G. Newton, *The Deterioration and*

Notes to Pages 45–53

Conservation of Painted Glass: A Critical Bibliography (Oxford: Oxford Univ. Press, 1982), V, states that the result of too much borax is that the paint can dissolve in condensation on the windows. In either case, the deterioration at Holy Trinity is worse on windows that receive large quantities of sunlight, which apparently exacerbates the problem.

49. An exception at Christ Church is the southwest window of 1850 (N2), where the borders are crudely painted, and even more poorly fired, perhaps by an assistant.

50. The system is explained in Sloan, "A New Look."

3.—Style and Pictorial Sources

1. W. J. Bolton, "Architecture and . . . Religion," 837.

2. Ibid., 833.

3. Ibid.

4. For the Morse portrait, Mabee, *The American Leonardo,* opp. 54; and the Etty portraits, Farr, *William Etty,* pls. 7 and 33.

5. W. J. Bolton, "King's College Chapel Windows," 154, 169.

6. Hilary Wayment, "The Use of Engravings in the Design of the Renaissance Windows of King's College Chapel, Cambridge," *The Burlington Magazine* 100 (1958): 385–88, has shown that Raphael, Dürer, and Lucas van Leyden were among the sources for the designs at King's.

7. [Winston], *An Inquiry into the Difference of Style,* 163. Another of Winston's reasons for preferring the later styles was that with their larger pieces of glass and pictorial designs they were better suited to the purer quality of nineteenth-century glass. The important French theorist of the Gothic Revival, Eugène Viollet-le-Duc (*Dictionnaire raisonné de l'architecture française du XIe au XVIe siècle* [Paris, 1867], IX: 441–42), had views similar to Winston's. He considered the stained glass art that was "reborn" after the Hundred Years' War to be just as medieval as what had gone before; he faulted later glass for its easel painting effects and abandonment of medieval technique.

8. Charles Winston, *Memoirs Illustrative of the Art of Glass Painting* (London: John Murray, 1865), cited by Sewter, "The Place of Charles Winston," 82; [Winston], *An Inquiry into the Difference of Style,* 285.

9. W. J. Bolton, "King's College Chapel Windows," 169. Virginia C. Raguin, "Bolton's Renaissance Sources," *Stained Glass* 77 (1983): 228–29, is an excellent summary of Winston's theories. For an opposing view, see George Edmund Street, "On Glass Painting," *The New York Ecclesiologist* (November 1852): 175–79.

10. [Winston], *An Inquiry into the Difference of Style,* 276.

11. W. J. Bolton, "King's College Chapel Windows," 172.

12. W. J. Bolton, "Architecture and . . . Religion," 838–39.

13. Ibid., 838.

14. Robert Bolton, Jr., *Genealogical and Biographical Account,* 28–31: drawings of Bolton armorials from British Library MSS Harley 891, 1096, 1468, 1476, 2986; Add. 5533, 5822.

15. Robert Bolton, Jr., *The History of the Several Towns,* rev. by C. W. Bolton, II: 96.

16. I am grateful to Mr. Chambers for sending photographs of his panel, and for his kindness in providing information on other Boltoniana in his possession. The Schuylers were neighbors and friends of the Boltons in Pelham.

17. Robert Bolton, Jr., *The History of the Several Towns,* rev. by C. W. Bolton, II: 96.

18. [Winston], *An Inquiry into the Difference of Style,* 286–87.

19. Ibid., 268, 276.

20. Yvette Vanden Bemden, *Les vitraux de la première moitié du XVIe siècle conservés en Belgique,* Corpus Vitrearum Medii Aevi, Belgique IV (Ghent and Ledeberg: Erasmus, 1981), 185, fig. 132.

21. Dr. Vanden Bemden in a letter confirms that nineteenth-century reproductions of the Liège windows did not exist.

22. [Winston], *An Inquiry into the Difference of Style,* 277.

23. The exact nature of Bolton's glass has yet to be determined. It is relatively thin, and may be hardly more than colored window glass.

24. Sloan, "A New Look," 233, notes that the larger pieces also add strength to the individual panels of which every stained glass window is constructed.

25. Otto Weir Heinigke quoted by Skinner, "The Stained Glass of the Brothers . . . Bolton," 13.

26. Robert Bolton, Jr., *The History of the Several Towns* II: 96. John's models may have been lancets in the Chapel of the Holy Trinity and All Saints at Salisbury; see Lewis F. Day, *Windows, a Book about Stained and Painted Glass* (London: B. T. Batsford, 1897), 146. John used another Salisbury-type design at the Church of the Holy Trinity, West Chester, Pa.

27. At the time the window was in a glazier's studio.

28. *Brooklyn Daily Eagle,* Monday, 26 April 1847.

29. Otto Weir Heinigke quoted by Skinner, "The Stained Glass of the Brothers . . . Bolton," 13.

30. On the Canterbury windows and their relationship to Ancestors windows at the former abbey church of St. Yved at Braine in northern France, Madeline H. Caviness, "Stained Glass," in *English Romanesque Art 1066–1200,* exhibition catalog, London, April-July 1984 (London: Arts Council of Great Britain, 1984), 137.

31. *Brooklyn Daily Eagle,* Monday, 26 April 1847. This effect has been greatly reduced by structures built adjacent to the church on the west.

32. Hopkins, *Essay on Gothic Architecture,* 13.

33. This notice was brought to my attention by the archivist of the Cathedral of St. John the Divine, New York, N.Y.

34. From Early Christian times and throughout the Middle Ages, Peter was often pictured with grey hair and beard, both clipped short in the ancient Roman style. Good examples are the beautiful seventh-century icon of Peter with Christ, St. Stephen and the Virgin (Sinai, St. Catherine's Monastery) and the well-known "portraits" of Peter and Paul, the latter with his characteristic long black beard (Paris, Bibl. Nat. MS lat. 12004, fol. IV, from the Abbey of Corbie).

35. Only the tracery and the upper register were installed at the Metropolitan Museum, and these with some reductions.

36. For examples, Ernst Konrad Stahl, *Die Legende vom heiligen Riesen Christophorus in der Graphik des 15. und 16. Jahrhunderts* (Munich, 1920).

37. Two other roundels that Bolton traced at Bradford are discussed later. Bolton's method in reproducing them was to trace the designs in pencil, then add shadows freehand. The twenty-two roundels at Bradford were collected by John Ferret (d. 1770), installed in the first southeast window of Holy Trinity Church about 1760, and reset in white glass in 1954; my thanks to Miss Rosemary Carr of Bradford for this information. For other particulars, Catalog III:G4, G11, G14, and IX:11f, 12a,b. Dr. William Cole very kindly verified the designs at Bradford; Dr. Hilary Wayment took me there to see and photograph them.

38. Catalog III:G7. For the relationship of Bolton's *Christ at Emmaus* to the Dürer, see W. B. Clark, "America's First Stained Glass," 51, figs. 19, 20.

39. See W. B. Clark, "America's First Stained Glass," figs. 12, 13.

40. Vellert's style was first recognized at King's Chapel by Max Friedlaender, in *Ausstellung von Kunstwerken des Mittelalters und der Renaissance aus Berliner Privatbesitz, Veranstalt von der Kunstgeschichtlichen Gesellschaft* (Berlin, 1899), where Vellert is known only as Master D*V; see Wayment, *The Windows of King's College Chapel*, 18. Vellert is not listed in the King's Chapel documents with the other glaziers whom Bolton mentions in his 1855 article on the windows (pp. 156–57). Vellert scholarship, with additions, is summarized by Ellen Konowitz, "The Glass Designer Dierick Vellert," in *Northern Renaissance Stained Glass,* exhibition catalog, Cantor Art Gallery, College of the Holy Cross (Worcester, Mass., 1987), 22–28; see also Ellen S. Jacobowitz and Stephanie Loeb Stepanek, *The Prints of Lucas van Leyden and His Contemporaries* (Washington, D.C.: National Gallery, 1983).

41. W. J. Bolton, "King's College Chapel Windows," 171.

42. See Catalog V. The face of the woman to the right (as well as on the left, which Bolton did not use in his design) at King's is a replacement by Hedgeland; Wayment, *The Windows of King's College Chapel,* 92.

43. Peter A. Newton, *The County of Oxford. A Catalogue of Medieval Stained Glass,* Corpus Vitrearum Medii Aevi, Great Britain I (London: Oxford Univ. Press, 1979), 71, pls. 26, 27.

44. Milner-White, "William Jay Bolton," 212, records that some of the armorials were given to King's Chapel by Grace Bolton, and that those from the house in Hampshire were acquired by purchase; see Chapter 1 and Catalog VII.

45. The two groups are discussed by M. Harrison, *Victorian Stained Glass,* chap. 2.

46. See M. Harrison, *Victorian Stained Glass,* pl. 6.

47. M. Harrison, *Victorian Stained Glass,* 35, notes that the pictorialism in stained glass that had prevailed at the 1851 Great Exhibition was hardly represented at the International Exhibition at South Kensington in 1862.

Catalog of the Art of William Jay Bolton

1. Brown, *Church of the Holy Trinity,* 24.

2. Lafever, *The Architectural Instructor,* 478; Landy, *The Architecture of Minard Lafever,* 113.

3. Landy does not address this matter.

4. It is Otto Heinigke, "The Windows of Holy Trinity Church," 1, who stated that a Bolton window preceded the rather unattractive opalescent now in the north wall of the vestibule. The Boltons were not involved with the glazing of the choir loft, the eastern or western stairwells, the eastern inner and outer portals, and the western chapel.

5. Landy, *The Architecture of Minard Lafever,* 122, refers to cinquefoil lancet heads, but the uppermost lobe is a single ogee opening.

6. Julie L. Sloan, "A New Look," 234, describes the ingenious installation method that not only accelerated the production process but also accommodated panels of varying size; see p. 47.

7. The lower register, containing quarry lancets, one of the two upper quarry

lancets, and a modest amount of the tracery were omitted in the Metropolitan Museum's installation (to meet space requirements).

8. It does not appear that the Rev. William Jay's popular *Morning and Evening Exercises* (1828) had any direct effect on the choice of subject matter at Holy Trinity, although there may be echoes of such meditations as the one for Christ's entry into Jerusalem, where the lesson is to make known one's faith with courage (E. 17 August); or for the woman at the well, who represents the sinner converted by grace (M. 26 June).

9. Bolton's Jesse Tree is a combination of the traditional family-tree of Christ ("And there shall come forth a rod out of the stem of Jesse, and a Branch shall grow out of his roots: And the spirit of the Lord shall rest upon him," Isa. 11:1–2) with the ancestors of Christ as listed at the beginning of the Gospel of St. Matthew. One is tempted to compare the arrangement with Michelangelo's Ancestors of Christ in successive lunettes of the Sistine Chapel, but Jay's design has otherwise nothing in common with Michelangelo's, nor does he ever use works by Michelangelo as models for other compositions.

10. There has been considerable discussion of the subject of the great chancel window, whether it is an Ascension or, with the crowd below and musical angels above, a Glorification of Christ *(Te Deum)*. The Harison letter found in 1984 at Trinity Church appears to remove all doubt about the subject of the scene, for in proposing an Ascension for the chancel window of Trinity Church, Jay Bolton described it as follows: "[i]t afforded so many noble & varied figures (our Savior, angels & all the apostles &c) both below & above."

11. The King's glass attributions are based on Wayment, *The Windows of King's College Chapel.*

12. Dürer prints were a popular source for late medieval stained glass designs, especially in the Low Countries; for another *Supper at Emmaus* based on the same Dürer print, see Madeline H. Caviness et al., *Stained Glass before 1700 in American Collections: New England and New York,* Corpus Vitrearum Checklist I (Washington, D.C.: National Gallery of Art, 1985), 189 (New York, N.Y., Riverside Church, panel by a Flemish artist).

13. By the Greenland Studio of New York City; Julie L. Sloan, "Documentation of Stained Glass Window Restoration. Church of St. Ann and The Holy Trinity, Brooklyn, N.Y.," *APT* 15:1 (1983): 12–19, outlines the procedures being used.

14. Otto Weir Heinigke noted damage to two windows, probably the lower rt light of VI and portions of AI. The Heinigkes' preservation efforts and the son's notes on the glass are recorded by Skinner, "The Stained Glass of the Brothers . . . Bolton," 11–12. Their work began sometime after 1904, with a gift to the church of $45,000 by George Peabody of Brooklyn; Brown, *Church of the Holy Trinity,* 34.

15. I would like to acknowledge gratefully the help of Rudolf Meyer, Master Restorer at The Cloisters, in stabilizing the most damaged windows until preservation work could begin.

16. A summary of the church's history appears in *The New Yorker* (21 May 1979), 28–29. Among those people who were most instrumental in putting the restoration project on course are Father Vilas; Maxwell E. Cox, head Vestryman of the church; Gail T. Guillet of the New York Landmarks Preservation Commission; Brendan Gill, President of the New York Landmarks Conservancy; and Felicia Furman Dryden, formerly of the New York Landmarks Conservancy. A series of concerts and performances, entitled "The Arts at St. Ann's," was instituted to aid the restoration project.

17. Landy, *The Architecture of Minard Lafever,* 149.

18. These sketches are all at the Long Island Diocese Archives, Garden City, N.Y. A watercolor for a large window of the Crucifixion under a round arch is less likely to be related to Bolton's ideas for a church dedicated to the Apostles.

19. Edelblute, *The History of . . . Holy Apostles,* 58.

20. Edelblute, ibid., notes that the organ and choir were originally in a western gallery.

21. R. Cattermole, *The Book of Raphael's Cartoons* (London, 1845), with steel engravings of seven of the cartoons, is listed in the 1852 inventory of the National Academy library, in *Constitution of the National Academy,* 47; according to Abigail Booth Gerdts of the National Academy, to whom I am indebted for information on this publication, it was purchased during the 1845–46 fiscal year.

22. Richard Millard, in a letter of 23 September 1980, wrote that the most recent conservation work at Holy Apostles was a releading, together with protective glazing and some structural reinforcement, carried out in 1967 by the Roemer-Millard Company.

23. Pevsner, *Buildings of England. North West and South Norfolk,* 375.

24. *Bury & Norwich Post,* 8 July 1850, reads as follows: "A very handsome stained glass window, in the cinque cento style has been placed at the altar end of West Lynn Church, in token of remembrance of a beloved sister by the Misses Walker, daughters of Giles Walker, Esq., North Lynn. The design is both chaste and elegant, the subject being 'The Angel at the Tomb', over the painting are the words, 'Why seek ye the living among the dead?' Under it appears the following inscription: [given in Catalog entry, V:Ch2]. The artist (Mr Bolton of Cambridge) has chosen for his design, the moment of interview between the Angel, and Mary Magdalen, Mary the mother of James, and Salome. The whole of the figures are very well executed, and the window forms an elegant ornament to the Chancel of the Church." A similar, but briefer, notice appears in the *Norfolk Chronicle,* 13 July 1850. I am indebted to Birkin Haward for his generosity in making me aware of these notices and providing me with the texts.

Bibliography

Works by William Jay Bolton

Anabaptism or Second Baptism, a Serious Mistake. Bath: Martin Wood, 1883.

"Architecture and its Connection with Religion." *The Christian Advocate and Review,* 2d ser., 6:69 (November 1872): 822–41.

The Constant Presence. London, 1874.

The Evidences of Christianity as Exhibited in the Writings of its Apologists Down to Augustine. Cambridge: Macmillan & Co., 1853; Boston: Gould & Lincoln, 1854; New York: R. Carter & Bros., 1854.

Fireside Preaching. Facts and Hints for Visitors of the Poor. London: Seeley, Jackson, & Halliday, 1856.

Footsteps of the Flock. Memorials of the Rev. Robert Bolton and of Mrs. Bolton. London: Hamilton, Adams & Co., 1860.

The Great Antichrist. Who? When? Where? A contribution for Anxious Times. London: S. W. Partridge & Co., 1869.

The Harp of Pelham. New York: Windt's Printery, 1844. Edited by WJB, with a number of contributions by him.

"King's College Chapel Windows, Cambridge." *Archaeological Journal* 12 (1855): 153–72.

Preface, and poem written to his sister Nanette in 1883, in *A Consecrated Life, being an account of Nanette Bolton.* New York, [1885]. He may also be the author.

Preface to Rhoda Bolton, *The Lighted Valley, or, The Closing Scenes of the Life of Abby Bolton.* London: Hamilton, Adams & Co., 1850, 1853; New York: R. Carter & Bros., 1850, 1855, 1872.

St. James' Court, Bath, a narrative of Events. Bath: Martin Wood, 1884.

The Stratford Martyrs of the Reformation. A Sermon preached at St. John's, Stratford, E[ast] . . . July 12, 1868. London, 1868.

Unpublished Letters from William Jay Bolton
(for texts, see Appendix A)

To James Bolton, 7 February 1845

To William H. Harison of Trinity Church, Manhattan, probably 19 October 1844

To the National Academy of Design, 1844 or 1845

Bibliography

Other Sources

Barr, Lockwood. *A Brief . . . Account of . . . the Ancient Town of Pelham, Westchester Co., State of New York.* Richmond, Va.: Dietz Press, 1946.

Bolton, Charles Knowles. *The Boltons of Old and New England with a Genealogy of the Descendants of William Bolton of Reading, Massachusetts.* Albany, 1889.

Bolton, Henry Carrington, and Reginald Pelham Bolton. *The Family of Bolton in England and America 1100–1894.* New York: Privately printed, 1895. A revision and expansion of Robert Bolton, Jr., *Genealogical and Biographical Account.*

[Bolton, James.] *Brook Farm. The Amusing and Memorable Account of American Country Life.* London: Wertheim, MacIntosh & Hunt, 1859; MacIntosh, 1863.

Bolton, Margaretta Grace. "Notes of the Life of William Jay Bolton 1816–1884." Manuscript in Milner-White archive, King's College Library, Cambridge. Written after 1922.

Bolton, Reginald Pelham. "A Heritage of Piety for Three Hundred Years." Typescript in the Westchester County Historical Society, Valhalla, New York.

———. "The Pondfield Farm—Bronxville." *Quarterly Bulletin of the Westchester County Historical Society* 7 (1931): 26–30.

———. "Robert Bolton, School-Master, Parish Priest, and Antiquarian." *Quarterly Bulletin of the Westchester County Historical Society* 7 (July 1931): 89–105.

———. "William Jay Bolton, Associate of the National Academy." *Quarterly Bulletin of the Westchester County Historical Society* 9 (April 1933): 25–32.

Bolton, Rhoda. *The Lighted Valley, or, The Closing Scenes of the Life of Abby Bolton.* New York: R. Carter & Bros., 1850; London: Hamilton, Adams & Co., 1850. Reissued in London in 1853, and in New York in 1855 and 1872.

Bolton, Robert, Jr. *Genealogical and Biographical Account of the Family of Bolton in England and America.* New York: John A. Gray, 1862.

———. *A History of the County of Westchester from Its First Settlements to the Present Time.* 2 vols. New York: Alexander S. Gould, 1848.

———. *History of the Protestant Episcopal Church in the County of Westchester from Its Foundation.* New York: Stanford & Swords, 1855.

———. *The History of the Several Towns, Manors, and Patents of the County of Westchester.* Edited by Cornelius Winter Bolton. 2 vols. New Rochelle, 1881. Rev. ed. of *A History of the County of Westchester,* based on notes of Robert Bolton, Jr.

Bibliography

Bowen, Desmond. *The Idea of the Victorian Church.* Montreal: McGill Univ. Press, 1968.

Bradley, Ian C. *The Call to Seriousness: The Evangelical Impact on the Victorians.* New York: Macmillan, 1976.

Brown, Roscoe C. E. *Church of the Holy Trinity Brooklyn Heights in the City of New York, 1847–1922.* New York, 1922.

Catalogue of the Library of the Late Reverend Robert Bolton . . . to be sold at Auction . . . April 12th, 13th and 14th 1887 . . . at the Leavitt Art Gallery. New York, 1887.

Chadwick, Owen. *The Victorian Church.* London: Adam & Charles Black, 1966.

Christ Church at Pelham, Pelham Manor, New York 1843–1943. Pelham: The Church Vestry, 1943.

The Church of the Holy Trinity, West Chester, Pennsylvania. West Chester: Church of the Holy Trinity, 1938.

Clark, G. Kitson. *The Making of Victorian England.* Cambridge, Mass.: Harvard Univ. Press, 1962.

Clark, Kenneth. *The Gothic Revival. An Essay in the History of Taste.* London: Constable, 1928.

Clark, Willene B. "America's First Stained Glass: William Jay Bolton's Windows at the Church of the Holy Trinity, Brooklyn, New York." *The American Art Journal* 11 (1979): 32–53.

———. "Gothic Revival Stained Glass of William Jay Bolton: A Preservation Project and Census." *Nineteenth Century* 7:2(1981): 30–34.

———. "A William Jay Bolton Window Discovered, 'The Angel at the Tomb' at West Lynn, Norfolk." *The Journal of Stained Glass* 18:1 (1983–84): 52–57.

Constitution of the National Academy of Design and Schedule of the Property. New York: Sackett & Co., 1852.

Country Life (June 1948): 30.

Davis, A. J. Day Book. A. J. Davis Collection, New York Public Library.

Day, Lewis F. *Windows, a Book about Stained and Painted Glass.* London: B. T. Batsford, 1897.

Dickinson, Robert L. "Windows and Kings' Ransoms." *The Parish News* (Church of the Holy Trinity), n.d. [ca. 1912].

Downing, Andrew Jackson. *A Treatise on the Theory and Practice of Landscape Gardening.* 1841. New York: A. O. Moore, 1889.

Downs, Arthur Channing, Jr. "Stained Glass in American Architecture." *Nineteenth Century* 3:4 (1977): 54–60.

Downs, Joseph. "History in houses, Bartow Mansion." *Antiques* 55 (April 1949): 274–77.

Bibliography

Eastlake, Charles L. *A History of the Gothic Revival.* 1872. Reprint. N.p.:
     American Life Foundation, 1975.

Edelblute, Lucius A. *The History of the Church of the Holy Apostles.* New York:
     Privately printed, 1949.

Elliott-Binns, L. E. *The Early Evangelicals.* London, 1953.

Elskus, Albinas. *The Art of Painting on Glass.* New York: Charles Scribner's
     Sons, 1980.

Farr, Dennis. *William Etty.* London: Routledge & Kegan Paul, 1958.

Félibien, André. *Des principes de l'architecture, de la sculpture, de la peinture, et des
     autres arts qui en dépendent.* Paris, 1699; facs. Farnborough, 1966.

Forbes, Christopher. *The Royal Academy Revisited. Victorian Paintings from the
     Forbes Magazine Collection.* N.p., n.d.

Fromberg, Emmanuel Otto. *A Rudimentary Essay on the Art of Painting on Glass.*
     London: John Weale, 1851, and a number of subsequent editions. First
     published as *Handbuch der Glasmalerei.* Quedlinburg and Leipzig, 1844.

Germann, Georg. *Gothic Revival in Europe and Britain: Sources, Influences and
     Ideas.* Translated by G. Onn. Cambridge, Mass.: MIT Press, 1973.

Gessert, M. A. *Rudimentary Treatise on the Art of Painting on Glass or Glass-
     Staining.* 3d ed. London: John Weale, 1857. First published as *Geschichte der
     Glasmalerei,* 1834.

Harrison, Kenneth. *An Illustrated Guide to the Windows of King's College
     Chapel, Cambridge.* Cambridge: King's College, 1965.

Harrison, Martin. "Contemporary Art Glass 100 Years Ago." *Glass* 6:1
     (1978): 36–39.

————. *Victorian Stained Glass.* London: Barrie & Jenkins, 1980.

Haskell, Francis and Nicholas Penny. *Taste and the Antique.* New Haven: Yale
     Univ. Press, 1981.

Haward, Birkin. *Nineteenth Century Norfolk Stained Glass.* Norwich: Geo
     Books, Centre of East Anglian Studies, 1984.

Heaton, Clement. "Ornamented and Stained Glass." *The Builder* 21 (25
     February 1863): 139.

Heinigke, Otto. "The Windows of Holy Trinity Church, Brooklyn, N.Y."
     Architectural Review 13 (1906): 1–3.

Henry, Rev. Leland Boyd. *St. Mary's Church of Scarborough, New York.* N.p.,
     [1962].

Hepburn, A. Barton. *A History of Currency in the United States.* Rev. ed. New
     York: Augustus M. Kelley, 1967.

History of Architecture and the Building Trades of Greater New York. 2 vols. New
     York: Union History Co., 1899.

Hopkins, John Henry. *Essay on Gothic Architecture, with Various Plans and
     Drawings for Churches.* Burlington, Vt.: Smith & Harrington, 1836.

Bibliography

Irving, Washington. *Letters.* Edited by R. M. Aderman, H. L. Kleinfield, and J. S. Banks. 4 vols. Boston: Twayne Publishers, 1982.

Jacobowitz, Ellen S., and Stephanie Loeb Stepanek. *The Prints of Lucas van Leyden and His Contemporaries.* Washington, D.C.: National Gallery, 1983.

Jay, Cyrus. *Recollections of William Jay of Bath.* London: Hamilton, Adams & Co., 1859.

Jay, William. *The Autobiography of the Reverend William Jay.* Edited by George Redford and John Angell James. 2 vols. New York, 1855.

——————. *Morning and Evening Exercises for the Closet.* New York: John P. Haven, 1833. First published in England in 1828.

——————. *Prayers for the Use of Families.* Hartford: Silas Andrus, 1829.

Jones, Edward V. "The Owens-Thomas House." *Antiques* 91 (March 1967): 22–26.

Kendrick, Sir Thomas. "English-Stained Glass." Typescript, Royal Institute of British Architects, London.

Knowles, John A. "The Transition from the Mosaic to the Enamel Method of Painting on Glass." *Antiquaries Journal* 6 (1926): 26–35.

Konowitz, Ellen. "The Glass Designer Dierick Vellert." In *Northern Renaissance Stained Glass,* exhibition catalog, Cantor Art Gallery, College of the Holy Cross. Worcester, Mass., 1987.

Lafever, Minard. *The Architectural Instructor.* New York: G. P. Putnam & Co., 1856.

Lafond, Jean. *Le vitrail.* Paris: Arthème Fayard, 1966.

Landy, Jacob. *The Architecture of Minard Lafever.* New York: Columbia Univ. Press, 1970.

Larsen, Rev. Lawrence Bernard. *A Handbook on the Symbolism of Christ Church at Pelham.* Pelham, [1965].

Lee, Lawrence, George Seddon, and Francis Stephens. *Stained Glass.* New York: Crown Publishers, 1976.

Le Vieil, Pierre. *L'art de la peinture sur verre et de la vitrerie.* Paris, 1774.

Lloyd, John Gilbert. *Stained Glass in America.* Jenkintown, Pa.: Foundation Books, 1963.

Mabee, Carleton. *The American Leonardo. A Life of Samuel F. B. Morse.* New York: Alfred A. Knopf, 1943.

Maddy, Dorothy L. "Glass Enamels." *Stained Glass* 81 (1986): 116–22.

——————. "Silver Staining." *Stained Glass* 79 (1984): 258–62.

Maxon, John Moore. "The Stained Glass in St. Mary's Church, Scarborough." *Quarterly Bulletin of the Westchester County Historical Society* 11 (July 1935): 49–51.

Mead, Frances G. "If You Like Historic Spots. William Jay Bolton's Studio." *Westchester Host* 1:12 (23–30 March 1926).

Melish, William Howard. "The Great Chancel Window." Sermon-lecture, July 18, 1982, St. Ann and Holy Trinity. Mimeograph by the church.

[?Melish, W. H.] "William Jay Bolton of Bolton Priory." *The Parish News* (February 1944); reprinted in *Stained Glass* 39 (Summer 1944): 42–48.

Meyer, Jerry D. "The Painter and Craftsman: Late Eighteenth Century Glass in England." *Stained Glass* 76 (1981): 221–22.

Milner-White, Eric. "William Jay Bolton, 1816–1884." Manuscript in Milner-White archive, King's College Library, Cambridge.

Morse, Samuel F. B. *Samuel F. B. Morse. His Letters and Journals.* Edited by Edward Lind Morse. 2 vols. Boston and New York: Houghton Mifflin, 1914.

Newton, Peter A. *The County of Oxford. A Catalogue of Medieval Stained Glass.* Corpus Vitrearum Medii Aevi, Great Britain I. London: Oxford Univ. Press, 1979.

Newton, R. G. *The Deterioration and Conservation of Painted Glass: A Critical Bibliography.* Oxford: Oxford Univ. Press, 1982.

Newton, Roy, and Trevor Brighton. "William Peckitt's Red Glasses." *Stained Glass* 81 (1986): 214–20.

Nevins, J. Birkbeck. "The Secret of Ancient Painted Glass." *The Builder* 8 (28 December 1850): 616–17.

New York Exhibition of the Industry of all Nations. Official Catalogue. New York: Putnam & Co., 1853.

Pevsner, Nikolaus. *The Buildings of England. Cambridgeshire.* London: Penguin, 1954, 1977.

————. *The Buildings of England. North West and South Norfolk.* London: Penguin, 1962.

————. *Some Architectural Writing of the Nineteenth Century.* Oxford: Clarendon Press, 1972.

Pierson, William H., Jr. *American Buildings and Their Architects, Technology and the Picturesque, the Corporate and the Early Gothic Styles.* Garden City, N.Y.: Anchor Books, 1980.

Raguin, Virginia C. "Bolton's Renaissance Sources." *Stained Glass* 77 (1983): 228–29.

Reeves, Barbara. "Bolton Priory and Christ Church." *Pelham Sun,* 29 April 1954; reprinted 24 November 1975.

Reynolds, Gary A. "New York University's First Professor of Fine Arts." In Morse exhibition catalog, New York University, 1982.

Reyntiens, Patrick. *The Technique of Stained Glass.* New York: Watson Guptill, 1967.

Roberts, Anne Elliott. "William Jay Bolton—Artist in Glass." *Pelham Sun,* 22 July 1954.

Bibliography

Ruskin, John. *The Stones of Venice.* 3 vols. London: Smith, Elder, & Co., 1851–53.

Saint, Andrew. *Richard Norman Shaw.* New Haven and London: Yale Univ. Press, 1976.

Saiti, Paul J., Jr., and Nicolai Cikovsky, Jr., in *Samuel F. B. Morse: Educator and Champion of the Arts in America,* exhibition catalog, National Academy of Design. New York: National Academy of Design, 1982.

Sewter, A. C. "The Place of Charles Winston in the Victorian Revival of the Art of Stained Glass." *Journal of the British Archaeological Assn.,* 3d ser., 24 (1961): 80–91.

——————. "Victorian Stained Glass." *Apollo* (December 1962): 760–65.

Skinner, Orin E. "The Stained Glass of the Brothers William Jay Bolton and John Bolton." *Stained Glass* 34 (Spring-Summer 1936): 1–20.

Sloan, Julie L. "Documentation of Stained Glass Window Restoration. Church of St. Ann and The Holy Trinity, Brooklyn, N.Y." *APT* 15:1 (1983): 12–19.

——————. "A New Look at Bolton Windows of the Church of St. Ann and the Holy Trinity." *Stained Glass* 77 (1983): 230–35.

Sowers, Robert. *The Lost Art: A Survey of One Thousand Years of Stained Glass.* New York: Wittenborn, 1954.

Stahl, Ernst Konrad. *Die Legende vom heiligen Riesen Christophorus in der Graphik des 15. und 16. Jahrhunderts.* Munich, 1920.

Stanton, Phoebe B. *The Gothic Revival and American Church Architecture.* Baltimore: Johns Hopkins Press, 1968.

——————. *Pugin.* New York: Viking Press, 1972.

Steegman, John. *Victorian Taste.* Cambridge, Mass.: MIT Press, 1971.

Steinbart, Kurt. *Das Holzschnittwerk des Jakob Cornelisz von Amsterdam.* Burg bei Magdeburg: August Hopfer, 1937.

Street, George Edmund. "On Glass Painting." *The New York Ecclesiologist* (November 1852): 175–79.

Sturm, James M., and James Chotas. James. *Stained Glass from Medieval Times to the Present.* New York: E. P. Dutton, 1982.

Temme, Norman. "A New Flesh Stain." *Stained Glass* 78 (1983–84): 377.

Upjohn, E. M. *Richard Upjohn, Architect and Churchman.* New York: Da Capo, 1968.

Vanden Bemden, Yvette. *Les vitraux de la première moitié du XVIe siècle conservés en Belgique.* Corpus Vitrearum Medii Aevi, Belgique IV. Ghent and Ledeberg: Erasmus, 1981.

Venn, J. A. *Alumni cantabrigienses.* Cambridge, 1940.

——————. *Biographical History of Gonville and Caius College, 1349–1897.* Cambridge, 1898.

Bibliography

Viollet-le-Duc, Eugène. *Dictionnaire raisonné de l'architecture française du XIe au XVIe siècle.* 10 vols. Paris, 1854–69.

Wayment, Hilary. *King's College Chapel Cambridge. The Great Windows. Introduction and Guide.* Cambridge: Provost and Scholars of King's College, 1982.

———. *King's College Chapel, Cambridge, the Side-Chapel Glass.* Cambridge: Cambridge Antiquarian Society and King's College, 1988.

———. "The Use of Engravings in the Design of the Renaissance Windows of King's College Chapel, Cambridge." *The Burlington Magazine* 100 (1958): 385–88.

———. *The Windows of King's College Chapel Cambridge.* Corpus Vitrearum Medii Aevi, Great Britain. Supplementary Vol. I. London, 1972.

Wills, Frank. *Ancient English Ecclesiastical Architecture and Its Principles Applied to the Wants of the Church at the Present Day.* New York: Stanford & Swords, 1850.

Wilson, Rev. S. S. *The Rev. William Jay.* London: Binns & Goodwin, n.d. [ca. 1860].

[Winston, Charles.] *An Inquiry into the Difference of Style Observable in Ancient Glass Painting . . . with Hints on Glass Painting.* Oxford, 1847.

Winston, Charles. *Memoirs Illustrative of the Art of Glass Painting.* London: John Murray, 1865.

Wodehouse, Lawrence. "John Henry Hopkins and the Gothic Revival." *Antiques* 114 (April 1973): 776–82.

Zimmerman, Helena. "The Boltons Return to Savannah." *Savannah News-Press,* 23 March 1975, pp. 1E, 8E.

Illustrations

The numbers following many captions refer to the Catalog. Most of the photographs of the (St. Ann and) Holy Trinity windows were made before recent restorations, which are still in progress.

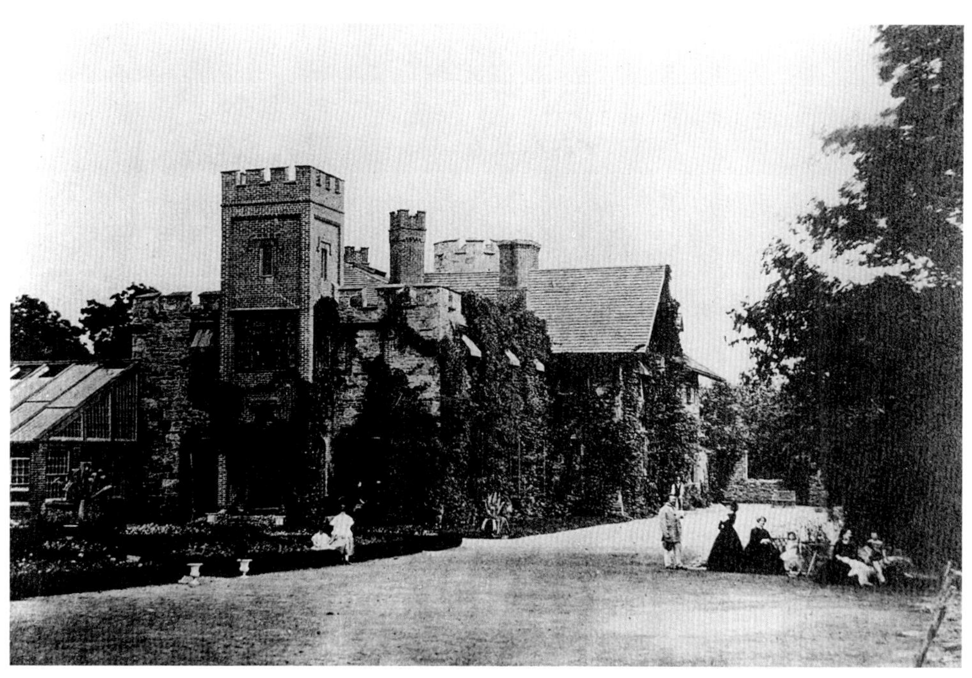

1a. Pelham, N.Y., Priory, begun 1838, seen from the southwest
(Photo: Avery Architectural Library, Columbia Univ.)

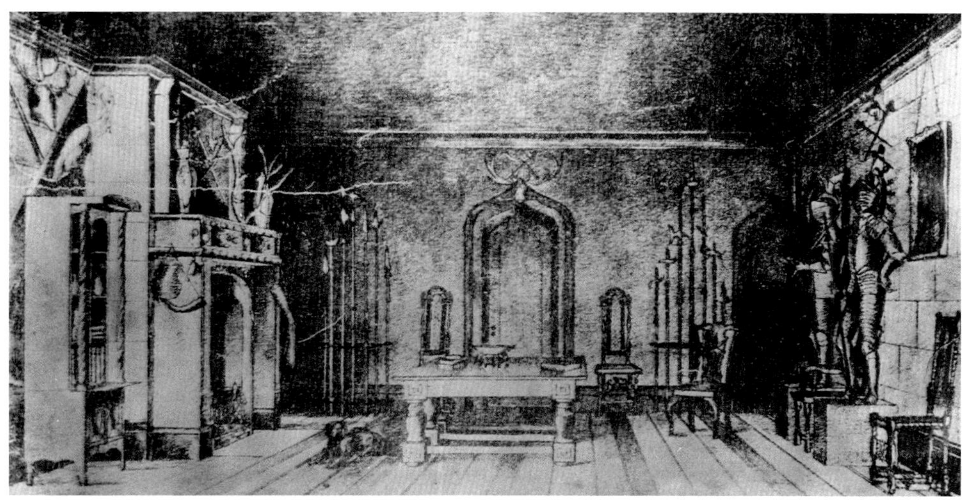

1b. Pelham, N.Y., Priory, the Armory, drawing by Grace De Luze, a Bolton cousin.
Table made from Priory oak by the Bolton brothers. Mantel brought from Venice by
William Jay Bolton. Chairs made by the Boltons in their shop. Chest, base of book
cabinet, brought by WJB from Italy. Upper part made by Robert his brother.
Vases on mantle, Lowestoft from the Bolton home, Savannah. Armor brought from
Europe by William Jay. Old Nero the family Newfoundland.
(Long Island Diocese Archives, Garden City, N.Y.)

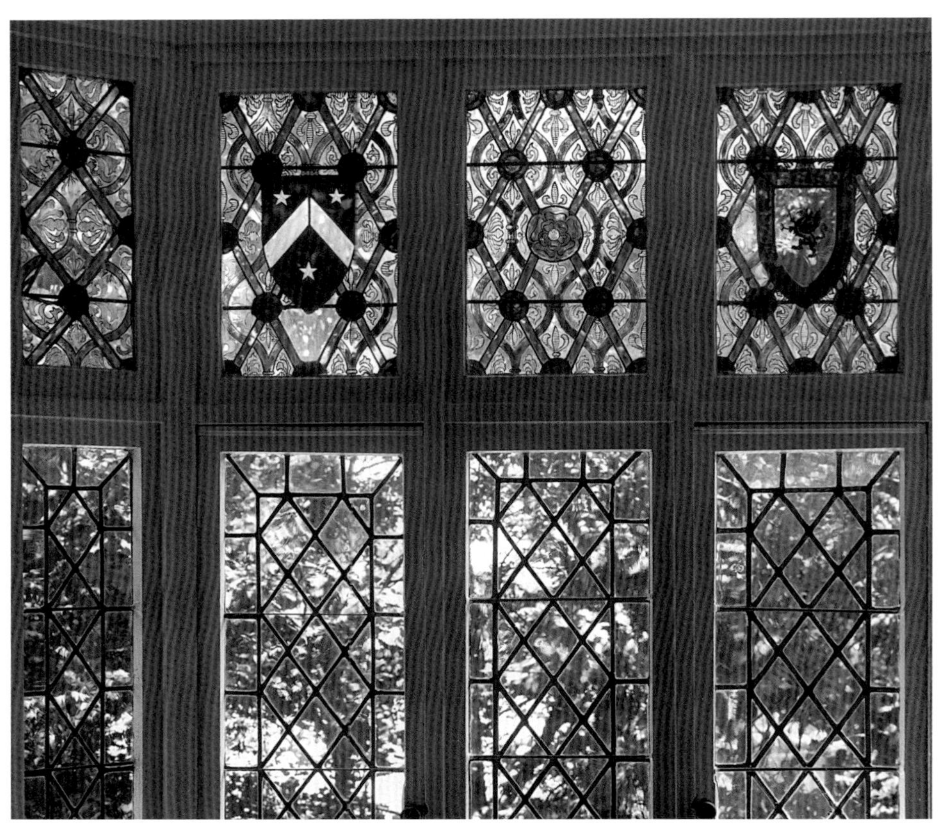

1c. Priory, Pelham: Armorials of the library   Cat. I:F4

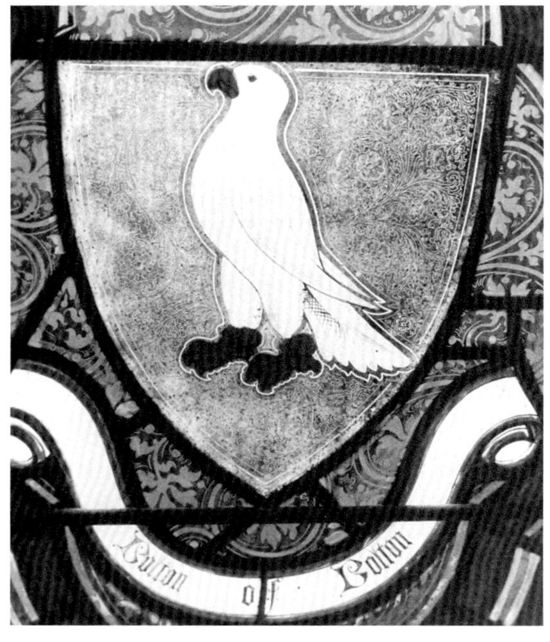

1d. Priory, Pelham:
Bolton of Bolton arms   Cat. I:Tw2

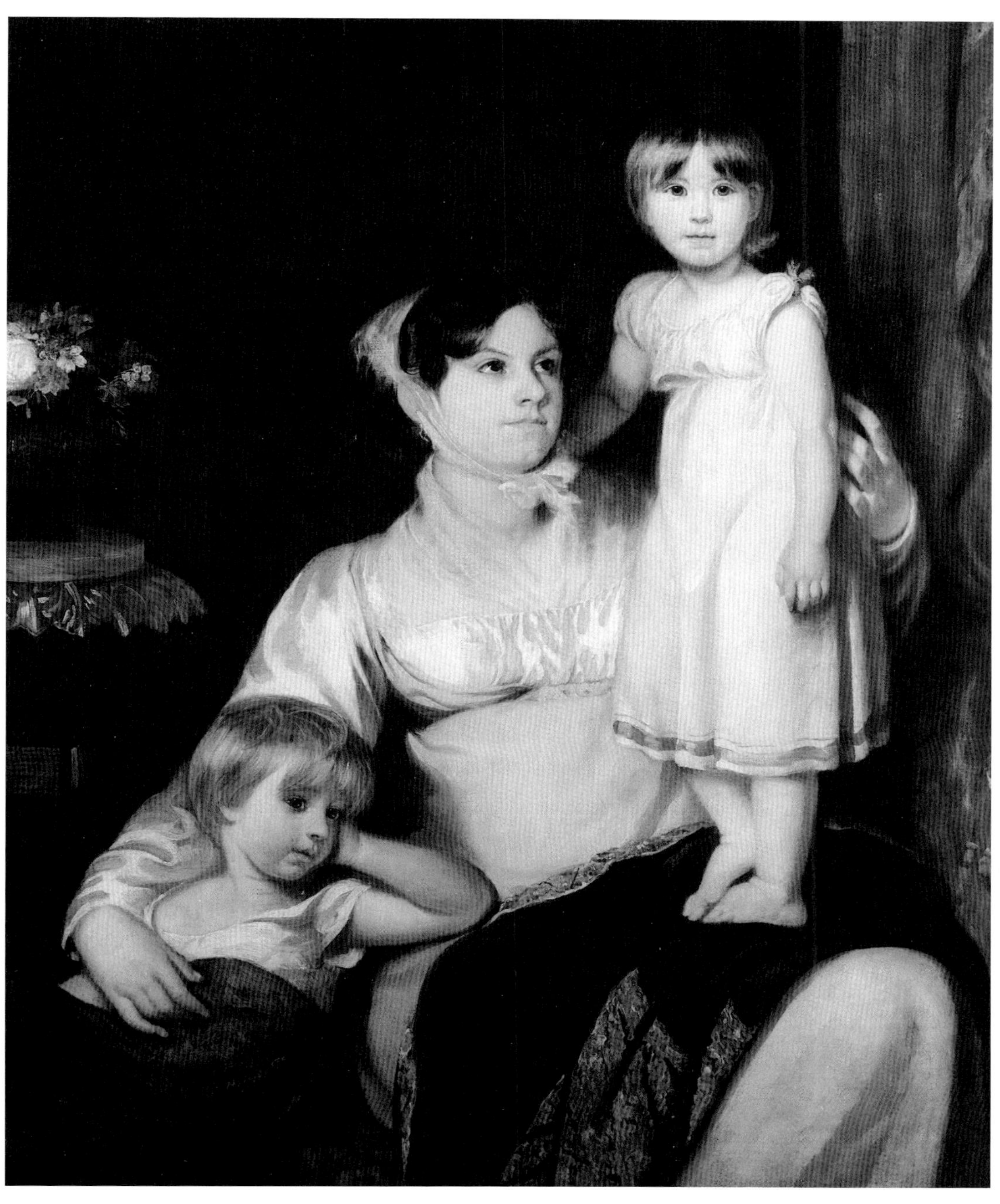

2a. William Etty, portrait of Ann Jay Bolton and children, 1818
(Owens-Thomas House, Savannah, Ga.; courtesy of The New-York Historical Society)

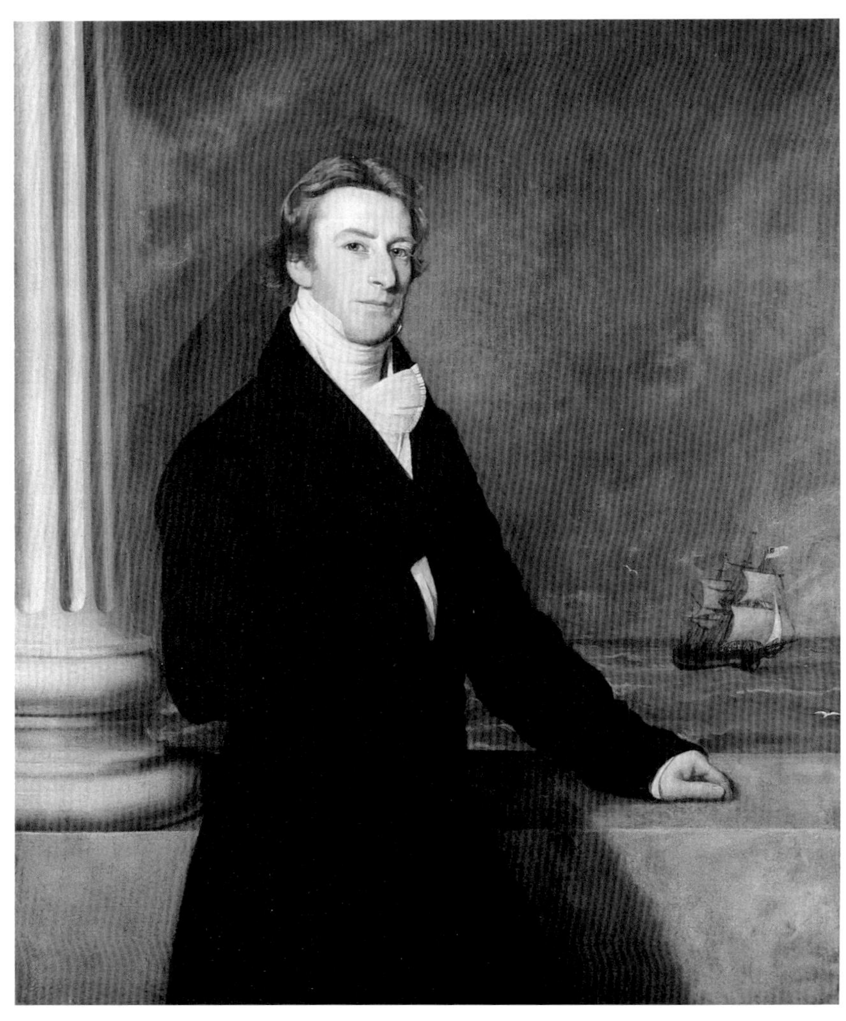

2b. William Etty, portrait of the Rev. Robert Bolton, 1818
(Owens-Thomas House, Savannah, Ga.; courtesy of
The New-York Historical Society)

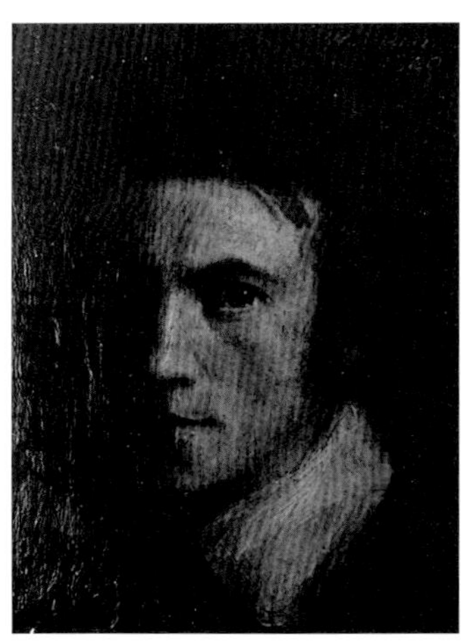

2c. William Jay Bolton, self-portrait, oil
(Cambridge, King's College Provost Lodge)
(Photo: W. B. Clark)   Cat. IX:3

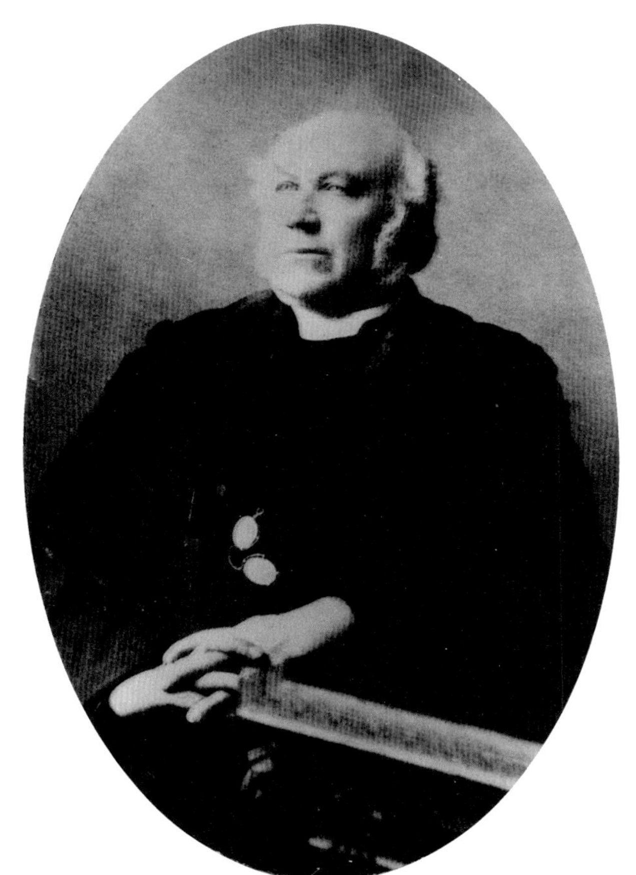

2d. William Jay Bolton in his last years (photograph at Long Island Diocese Archives, Garden City, N.Y.)

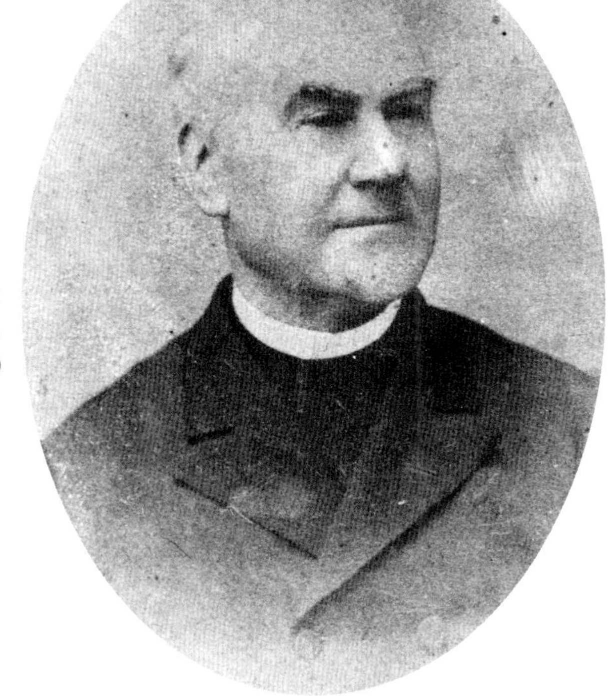

2e. John Bolton (photograph at Long Island Diocese Archives, Garden City, N.Y.)

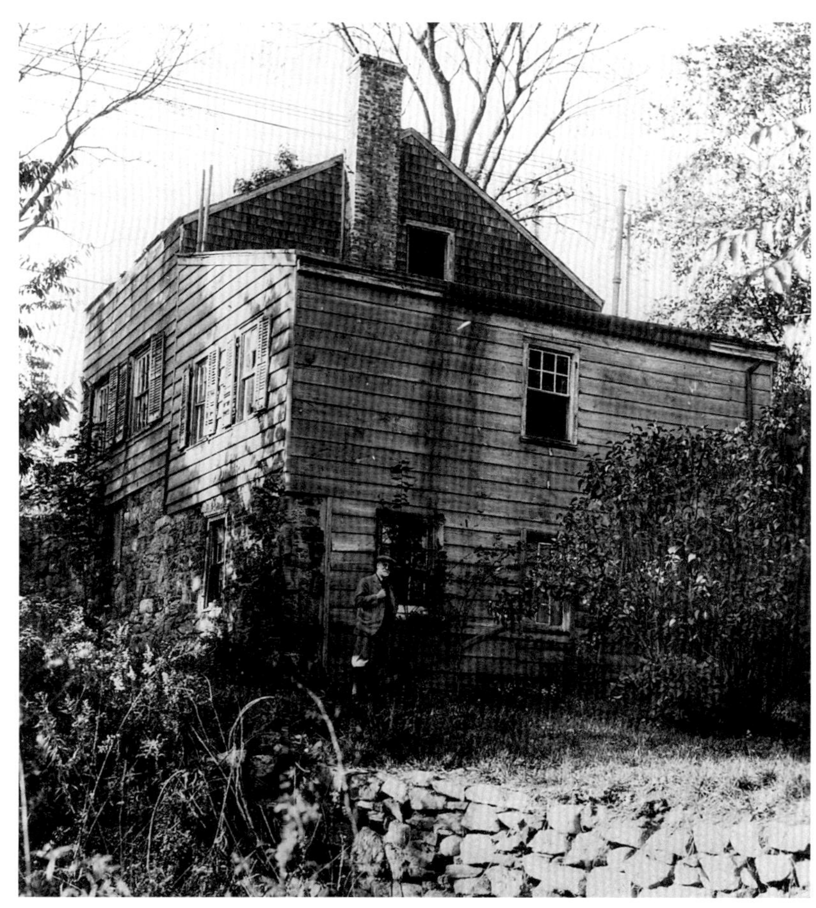

2f. Photograph of the Boltons' glass shop in Pelham, with Reginald Pelham Bolton (Westchester County Historical Society, Valhalla, N.Y.)

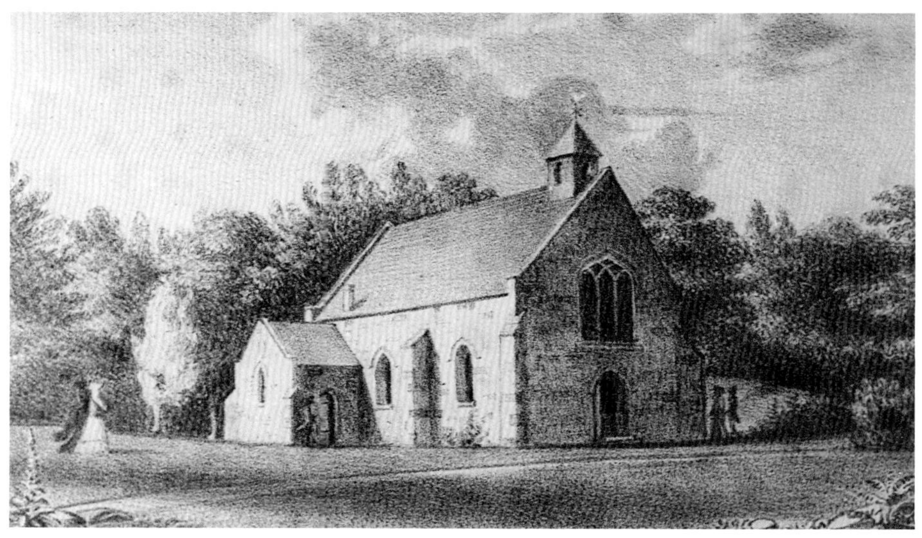

3a. Christ Church, Pelham, seen from the east in perhaps the original rendering (Coll. Francis T. Chambers; photo courtesy Mr. Chambers)

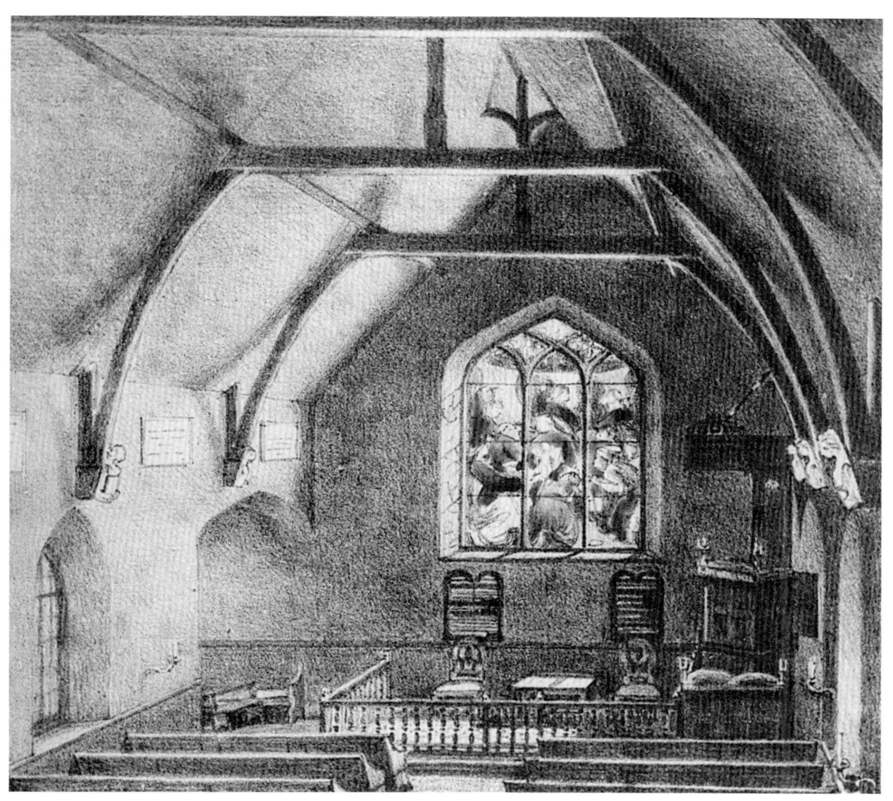

3b. Christ Church, Pelham, interior in perhaps the original rendering
(Coll. Francis T. Chambers; photo courtesy Mr. Chambers)

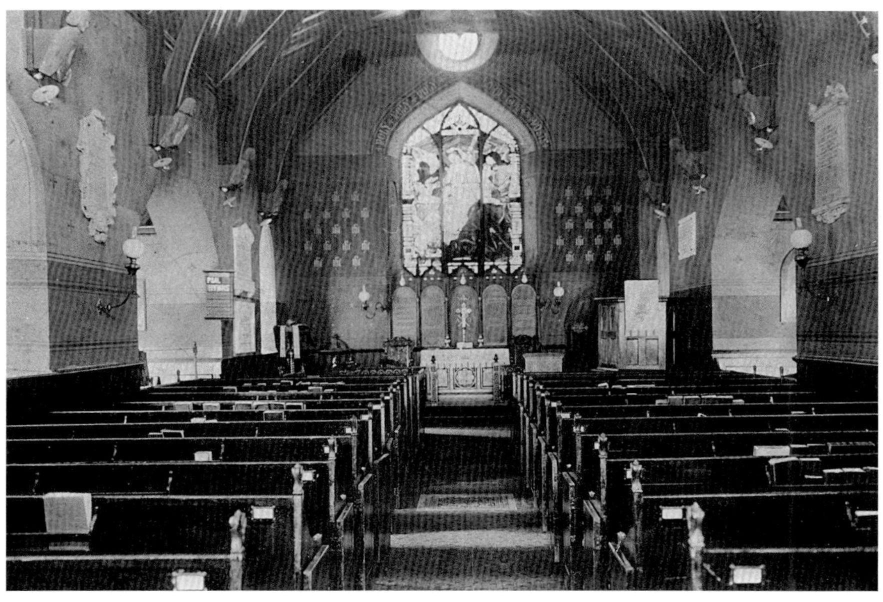

3c. Christ Church, Pelham, interior before 1910 showing
John Bolton's reredos below the *Magi* window, and
corbel figures carved by Bolton sons (Christ Church, Pelham, N.Y.)

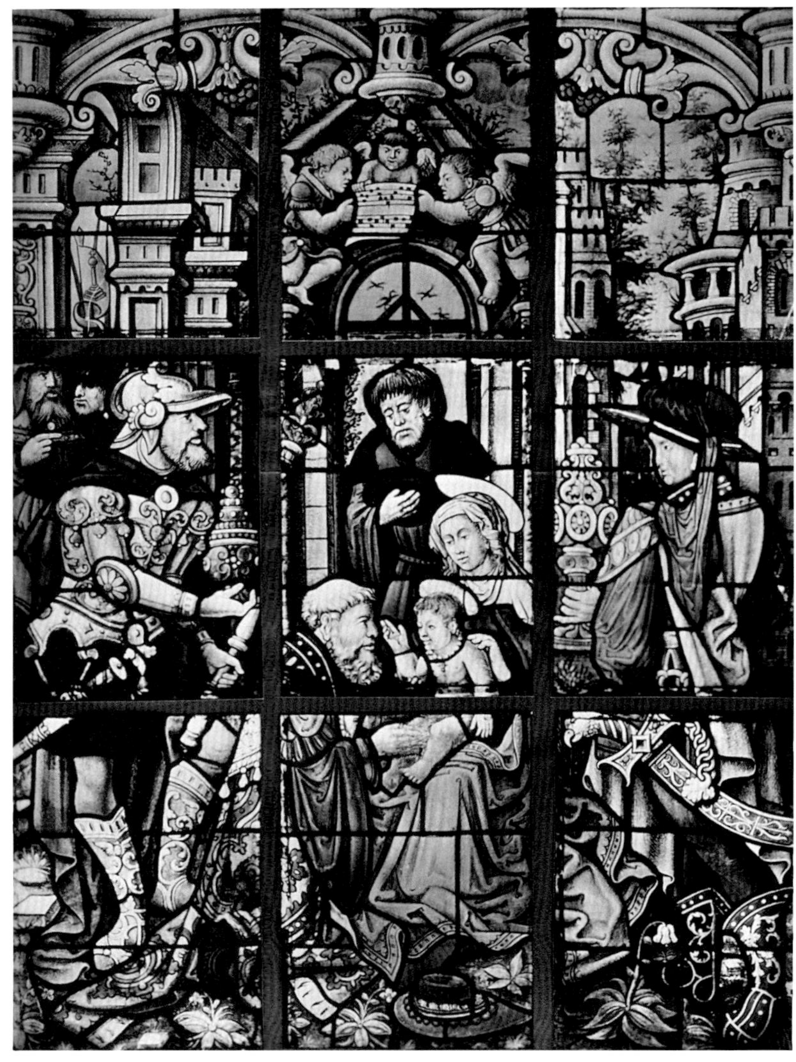

4. Church of St. Martin, Liège (Belgium): Life of the Virgin window, ca. 1527, upper register, bottom panel (Photo: A.C.L. Brussels)

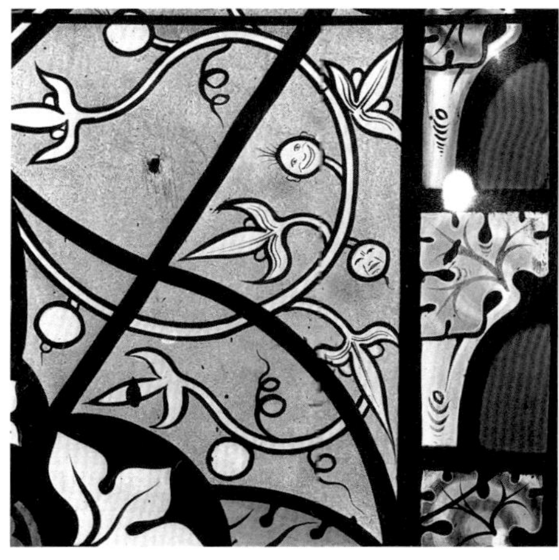

5. Christ Church, Pelham: Grisaille window, with small faces, detail   Cat.II:N5

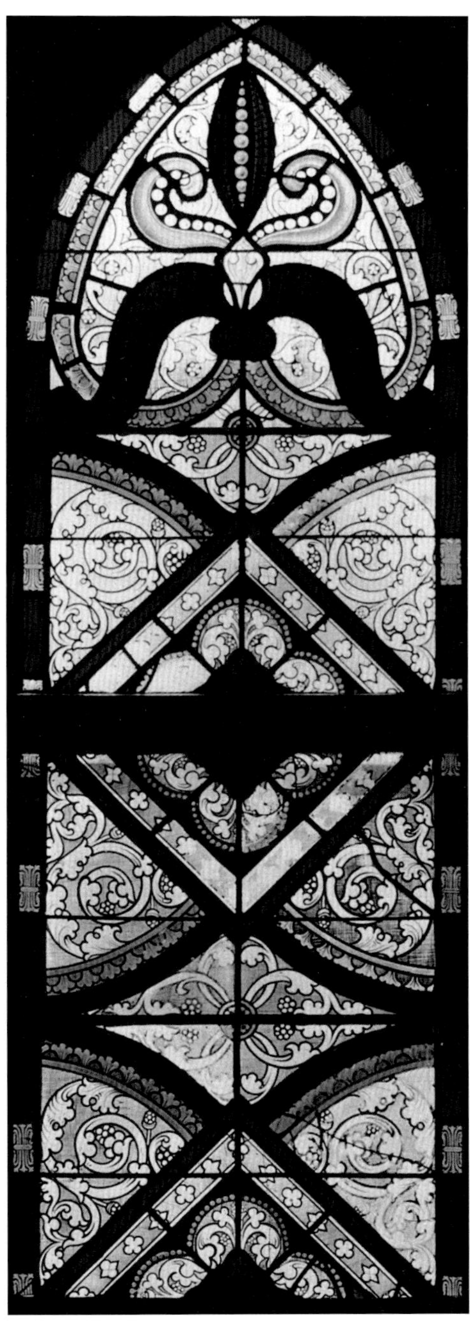

6. Christ Church, Pelham: Grisaille
window by John Bolton   Cat. II:N1

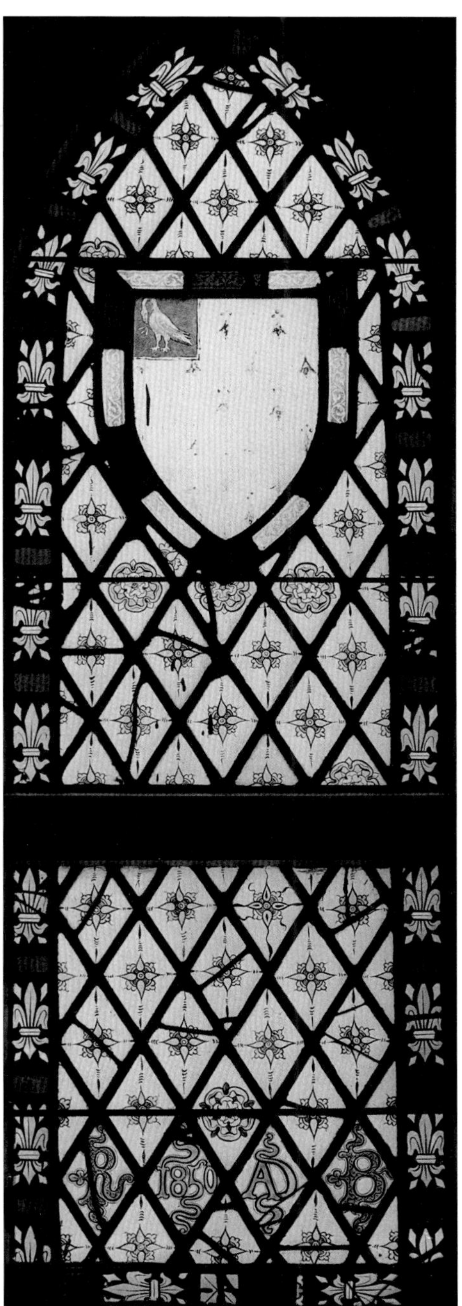

7. Christ Church, Pelham: "1850"
armorial window   Cat. II:N3

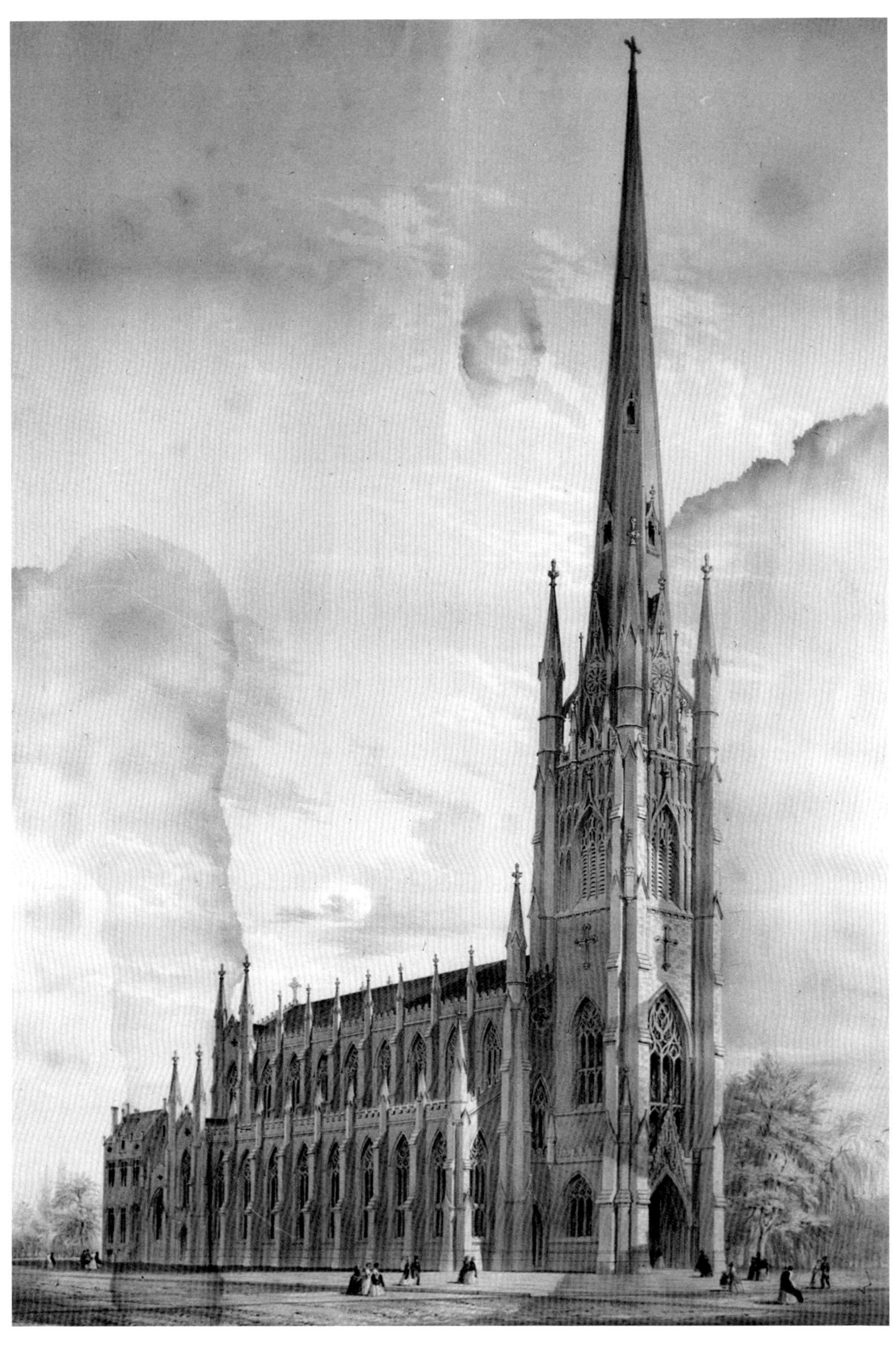

8. Minard Lafever, rendering of Holy Trinity, ca. 1844
(Church of St. Ann and the Holy Trinity, Brooklyn, N.Y.)

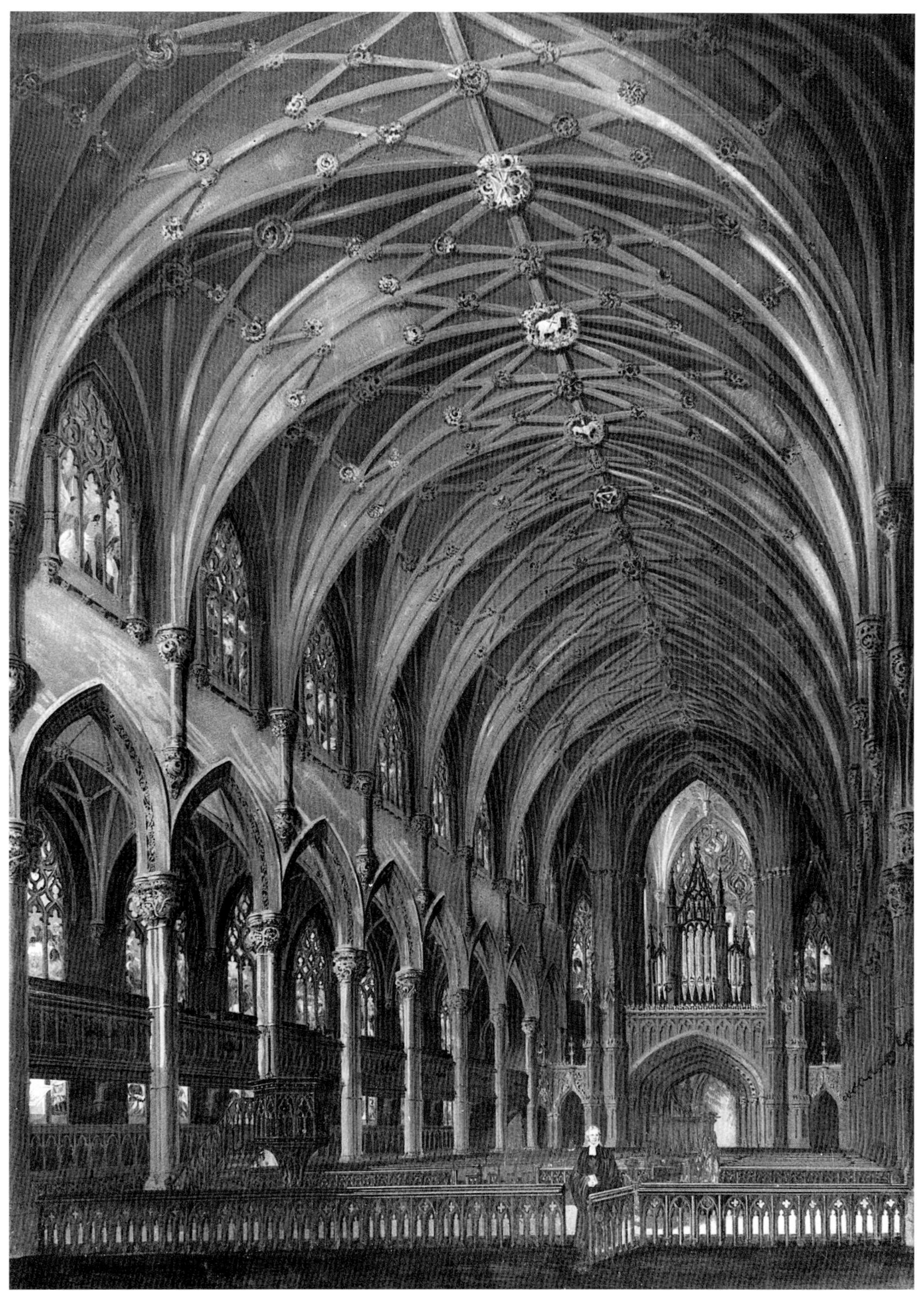

9. Holy Trinity, interior, watercolor of 1860
(Museum of the City of New York; photo: the Museum)

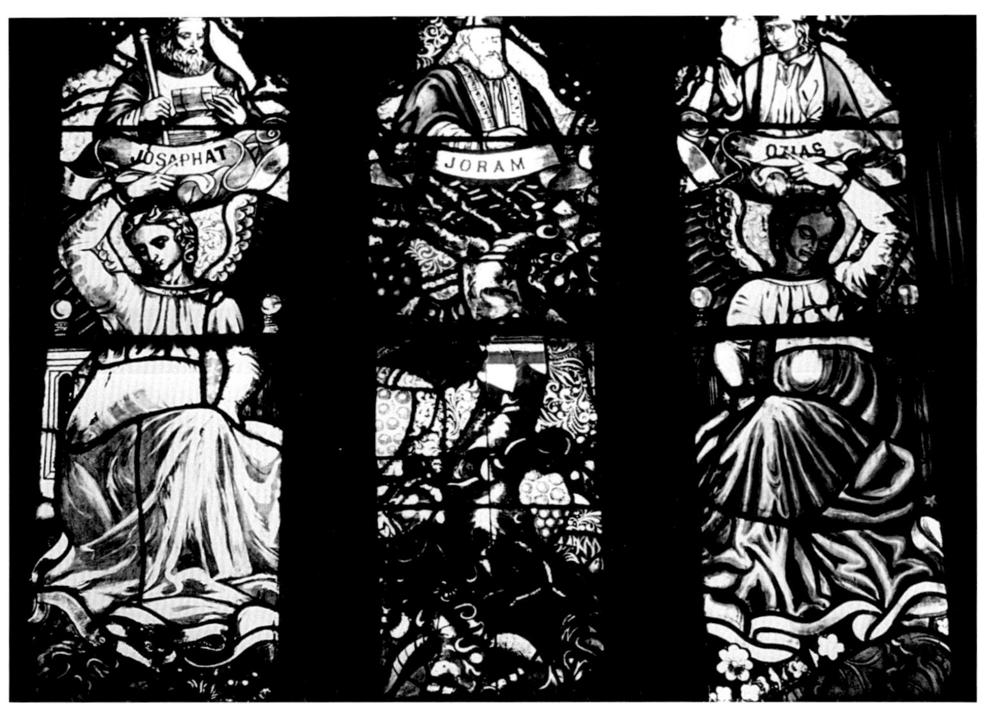

10a. (St. Ann and) Holy Trinity, Brooklyn:
Tree of Jesse, *Josaphat-Joram-Ozias*   Cat. III:A7

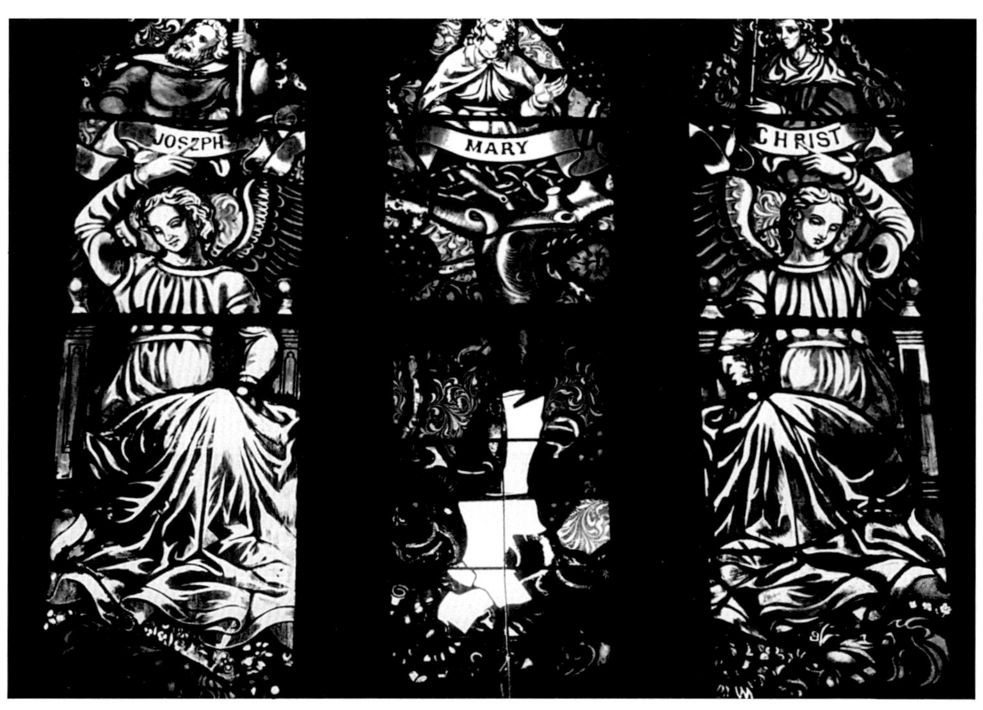

10b. (St. Ann and) Holy Trinity, Brooklyn:
Tree of Jesse, *Joseph-Mary-Christ*   Cat. III:A14

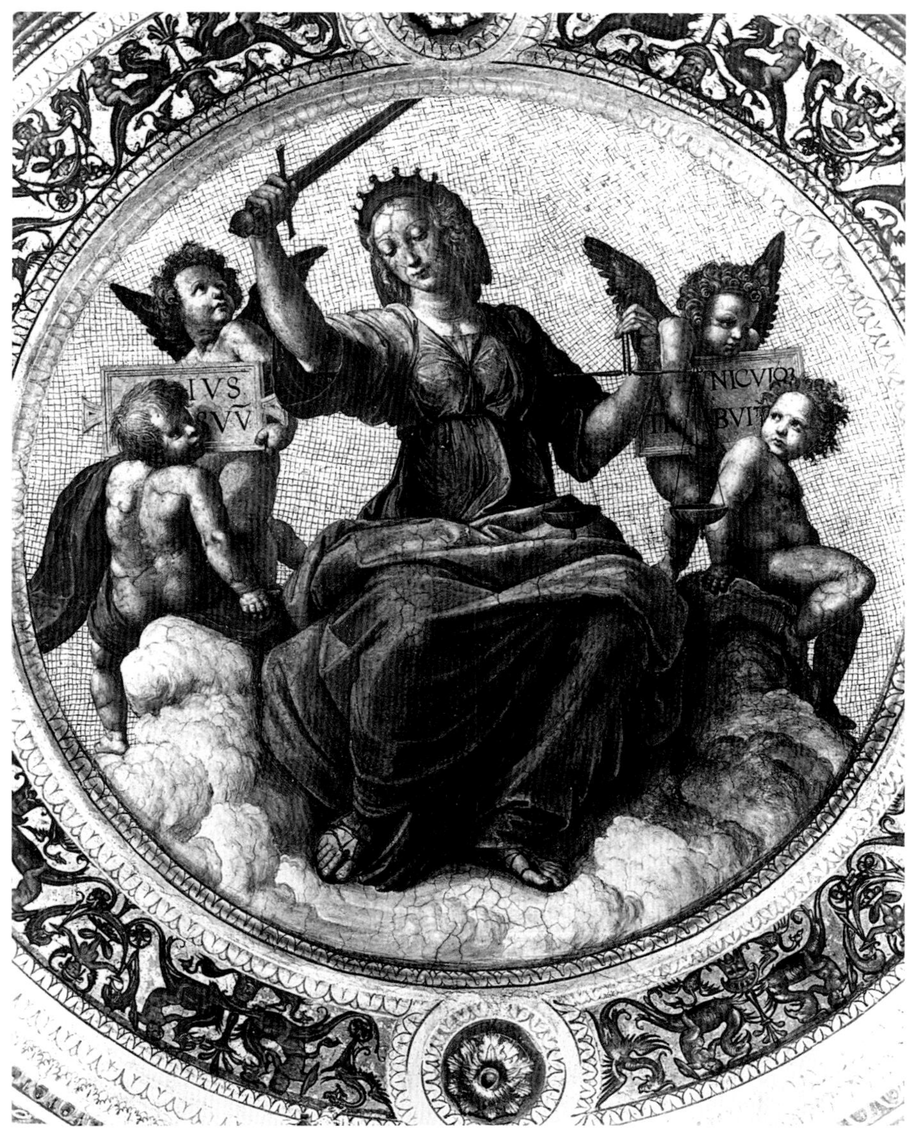

10c. Raphael, *Justice,* Vatican, Stanza della Segnatura ceiling (Photo: Alinari)

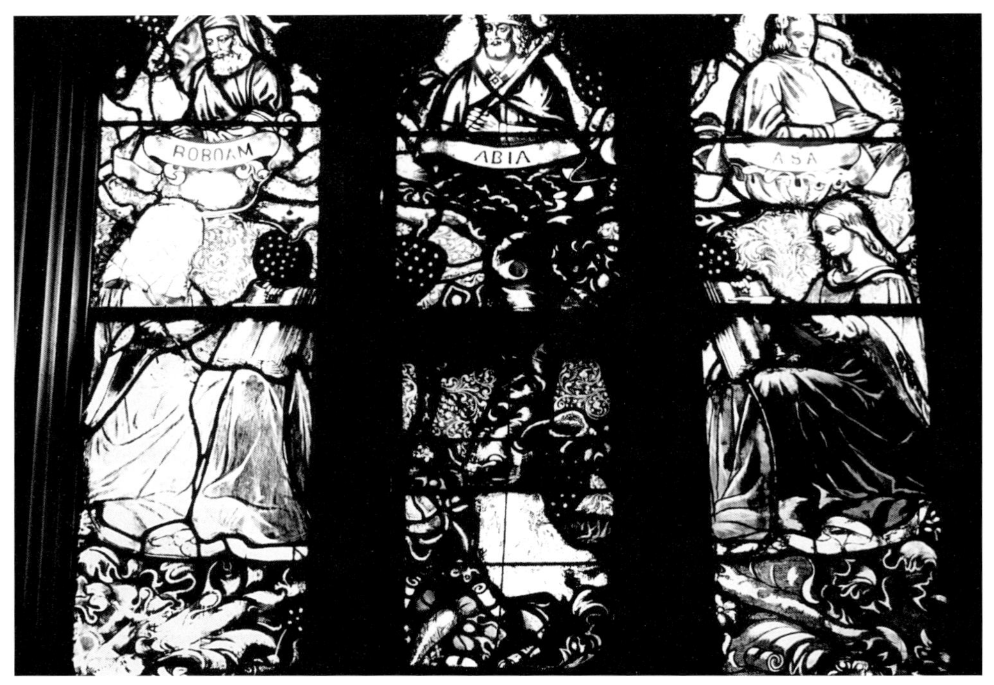

10d. (St. Ann and) Holy Trinity, Brooklyn: Tree of Jesse, *Roboam-Abia-Asa*   Cat. III:A6

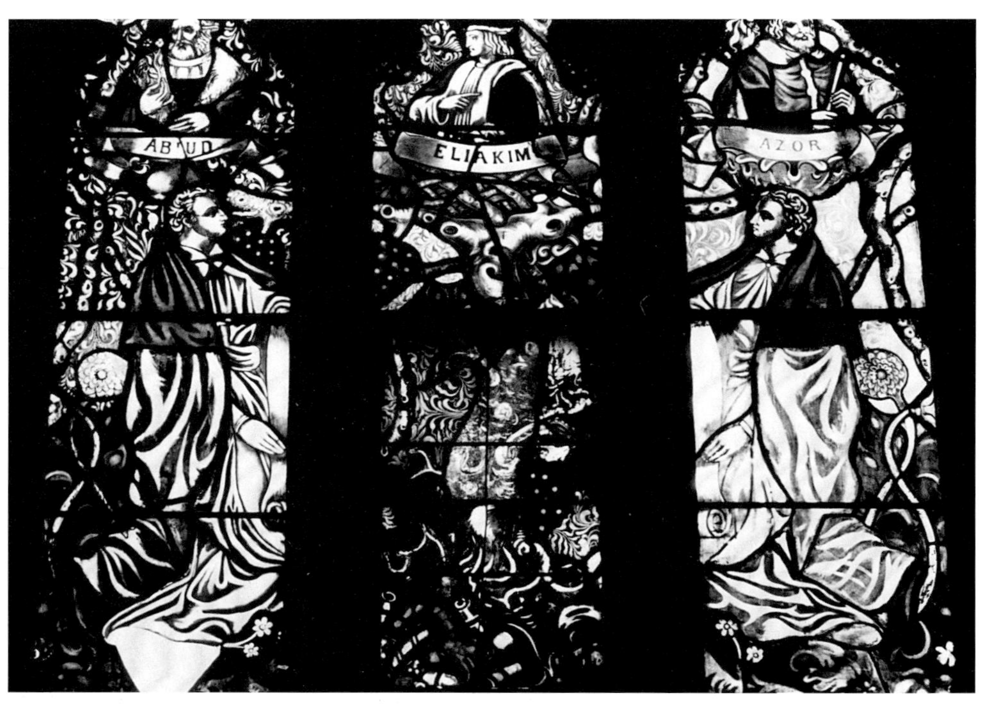

10e. (St. Ann and) Holy Trinity, Brooklyn:
Tree of Jesse, *Abiud-Eliakim-Azor*   Cat. III:A11

1of. Hartmann Schedel, *Nuremberg Chronicle,* 1493: *Pherecides*
(Marlboro College Study Coll.; photo: W. B. Clark)

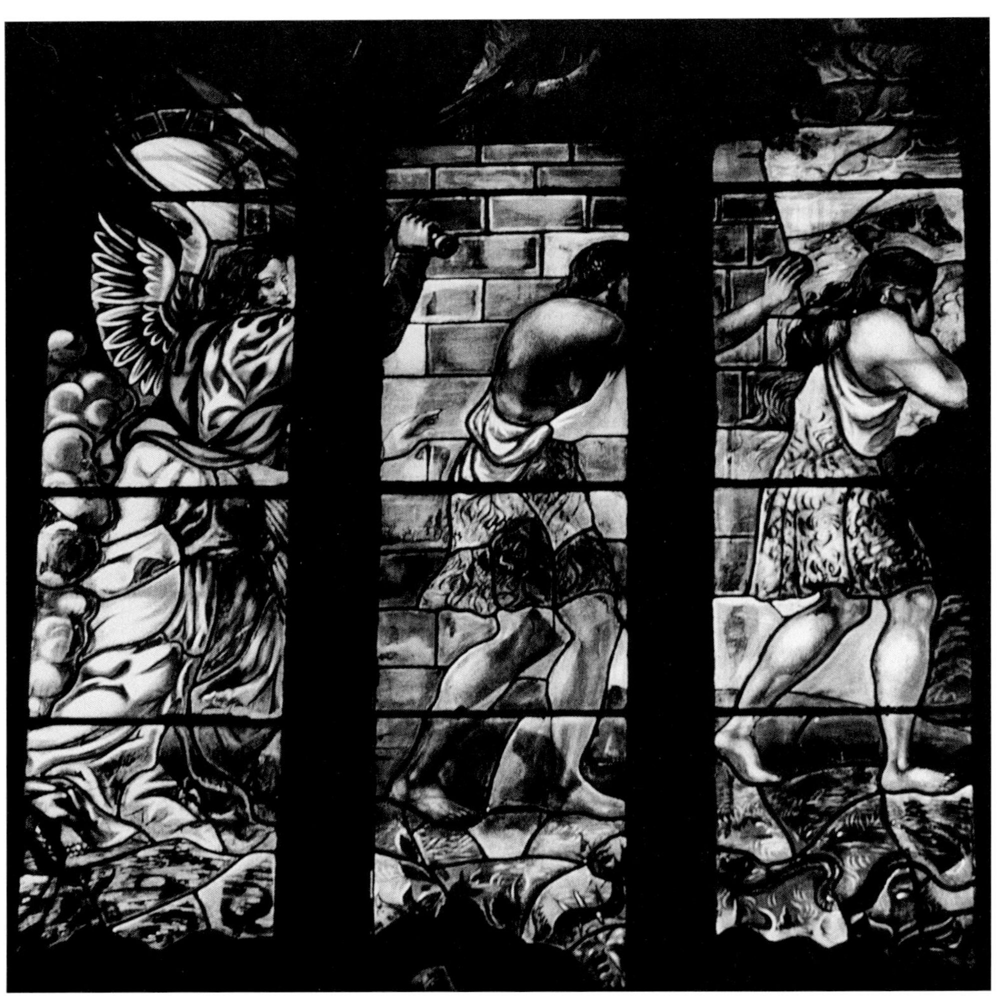

11a. (St. Ann and) Holy Trinity, Brooklyn: *Expulsion from Eden*   Cat. III:C9

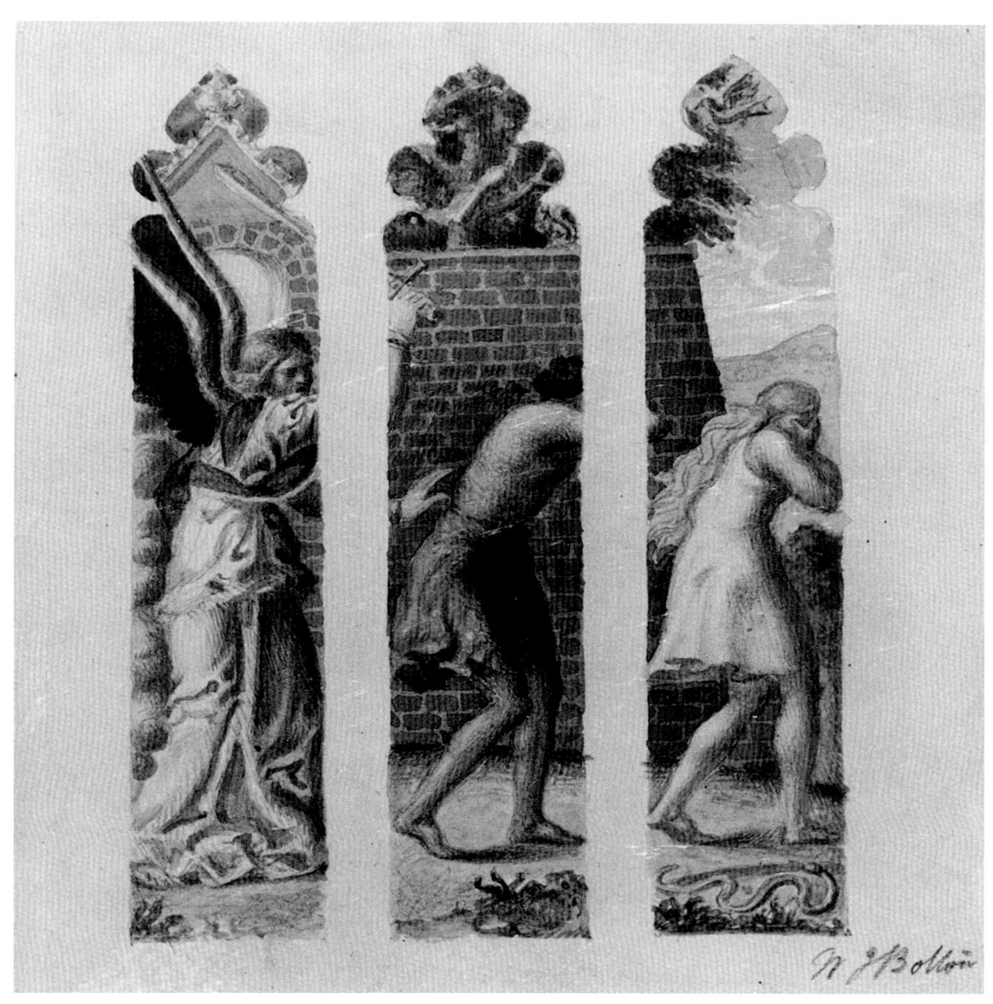

11b. William Jay Bolton, *Expulsion,* watercolor
(Long Island Diocese Archives, Garden City, N.Y.)   Cat. IX:11a

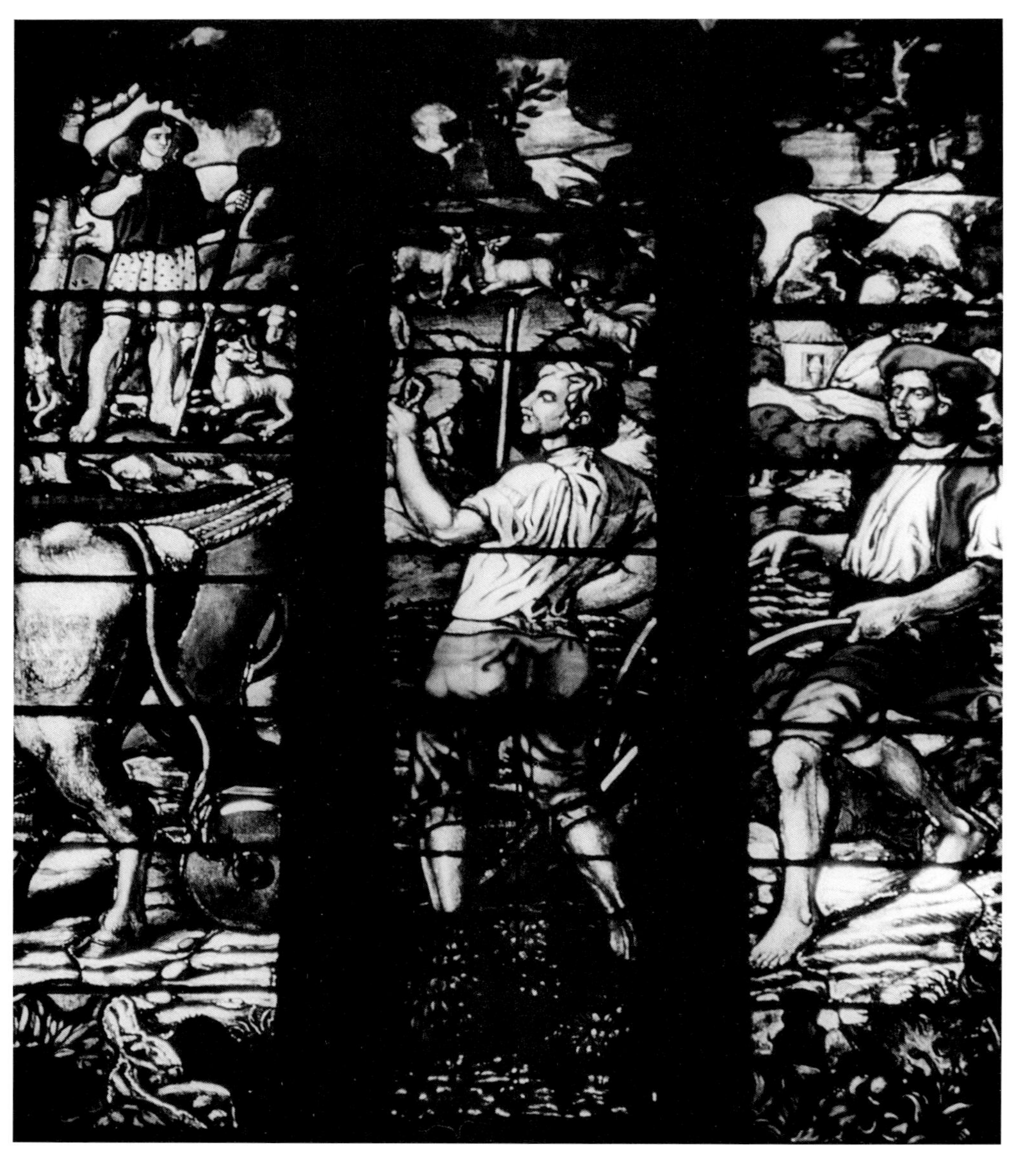

12. (St. Ann and) Holy Trinity: *Man Labors*   Cat. III:C10

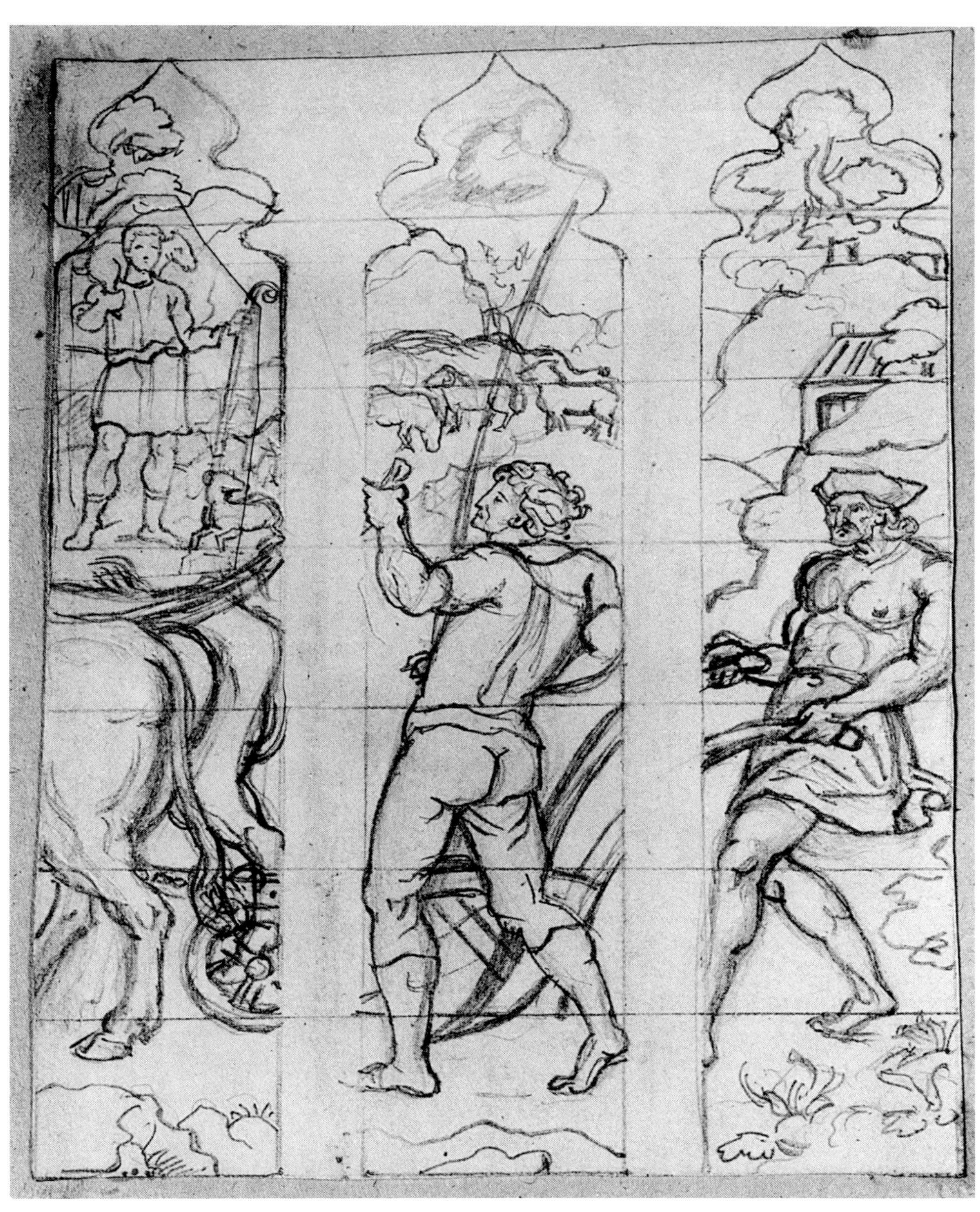

13. William Jay Bolton, *Man Labors,* pencil
(Long Island Diocese Archives, Garden City, N.Y.)   Cat. IX:11b

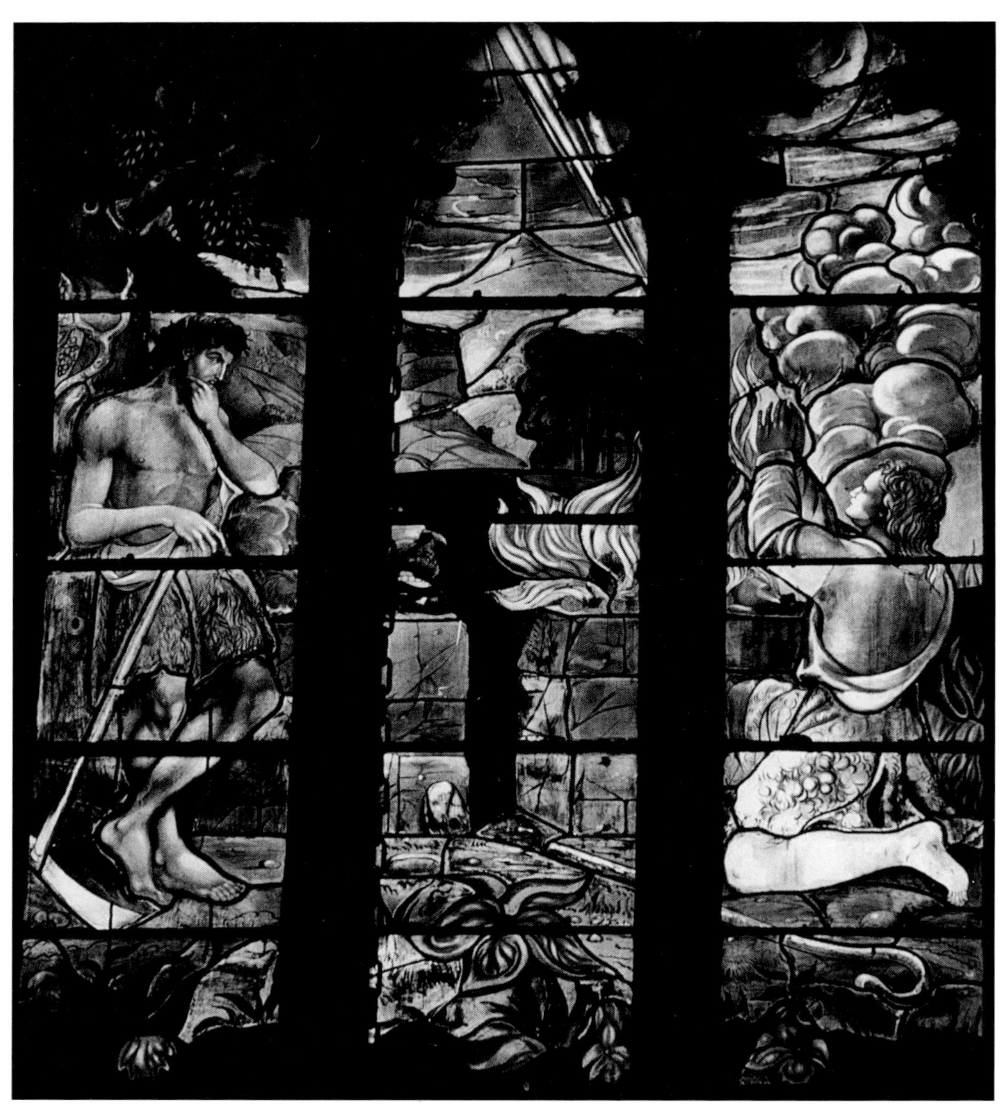

14. (St. Ann and) Holy Trinity, Brooklyn: *Cain and Abel*   Cat. III:Cɪɪ

174

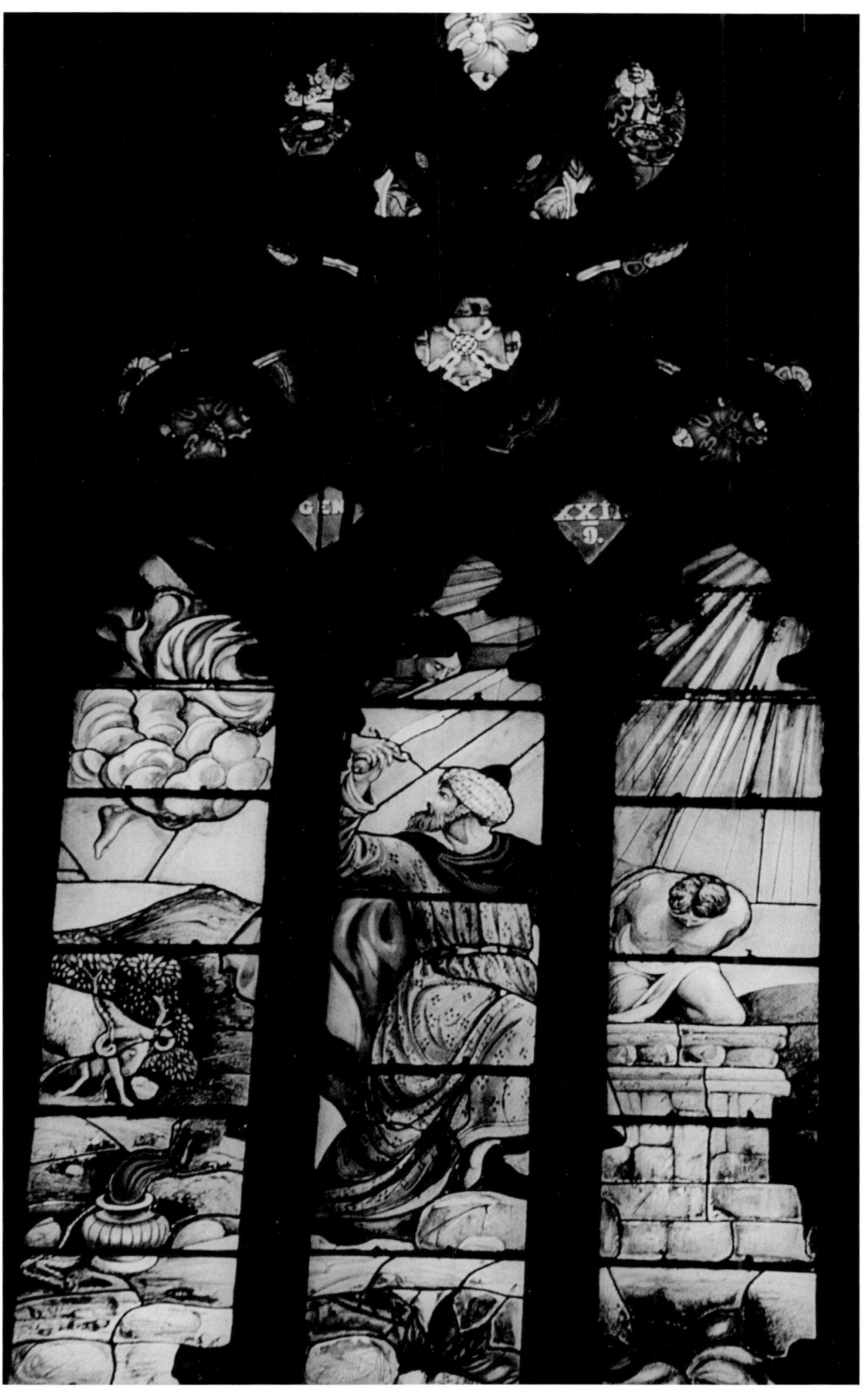

15. (St. Ann and) Holy Trinity, Brooklyn: *Sacrifice of Isaac*   Cat. III:C13

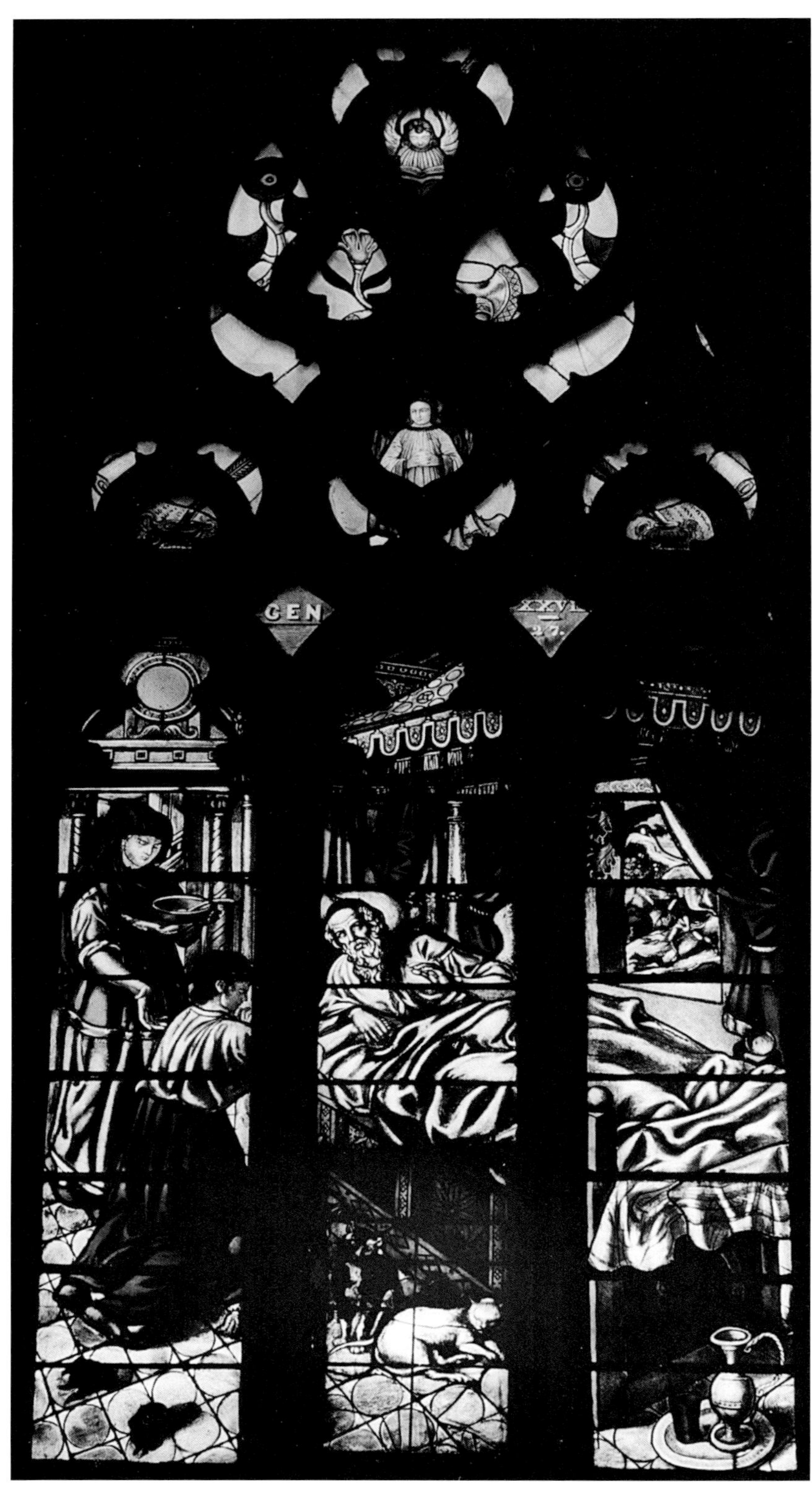

16. (St. Ann and) Holy Trinity, Brooklyn: *Jacob's Blessing*   Cat. III:C14

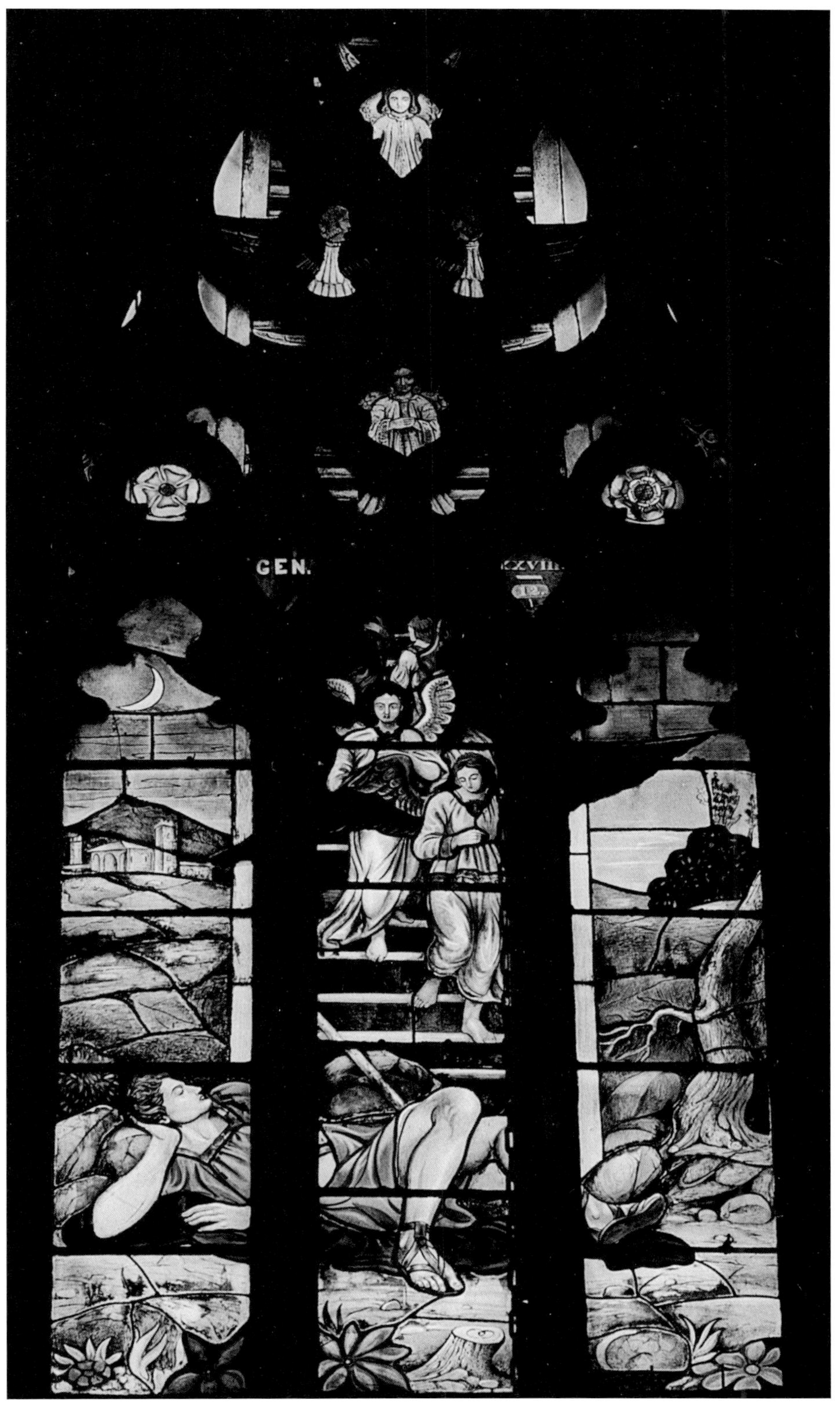

17. (St. Ann and) Holy Trinity, Brooklyn: *Jacob's Dream*   Cat. III:C15

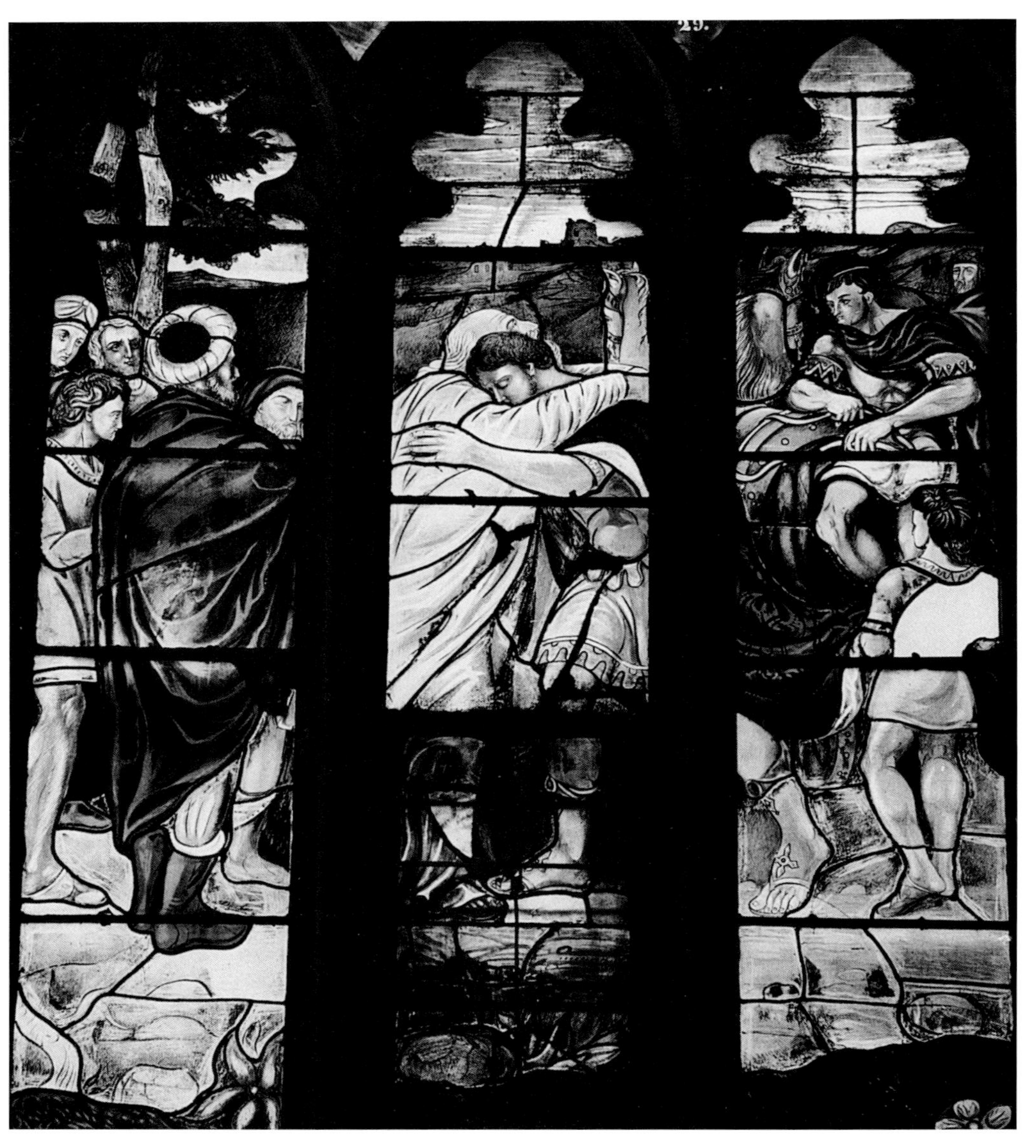

18. (St. Ann and) Holy Trinity, Brooklyn: *Jacob Meets Joseph*   Cat. III:C16

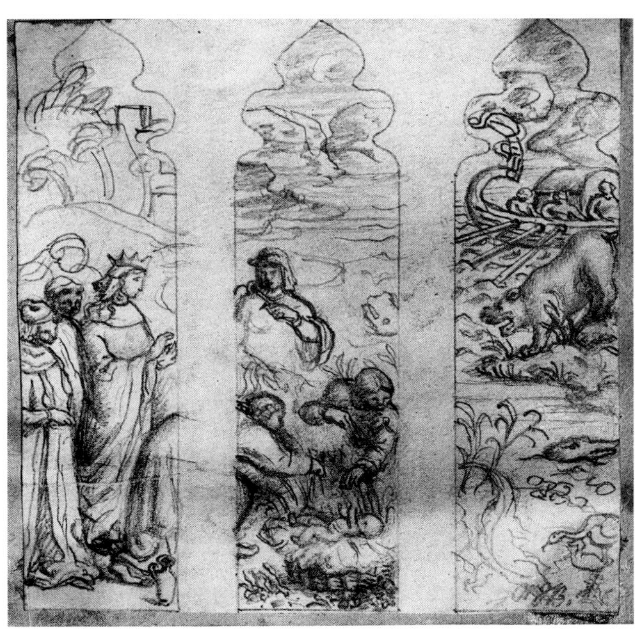

19a. (St. Ann and) Holy Trinity, Brooklyn:
Finding of Moses   Cat. III:C1

19b. William Jay
Bolton, *Finding of
Moses,* pencil
(Long Island Diocese
Archives, Garden
City, N.Y.)
Cat. IX:11c

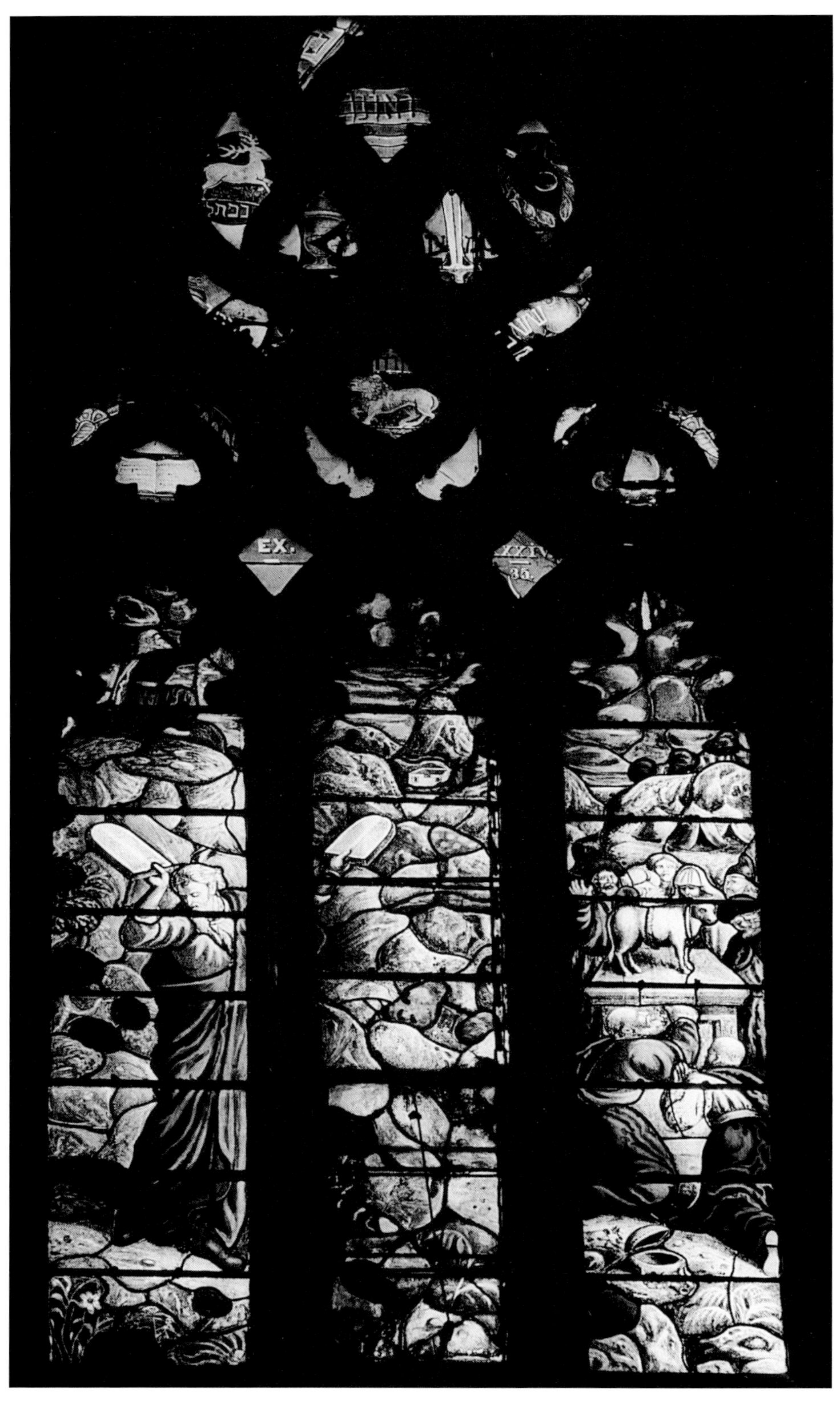

20a. (St. Ann and) Holy Trinity, Brooklyn: *Moses with the Tablets*   Cat. III:C2

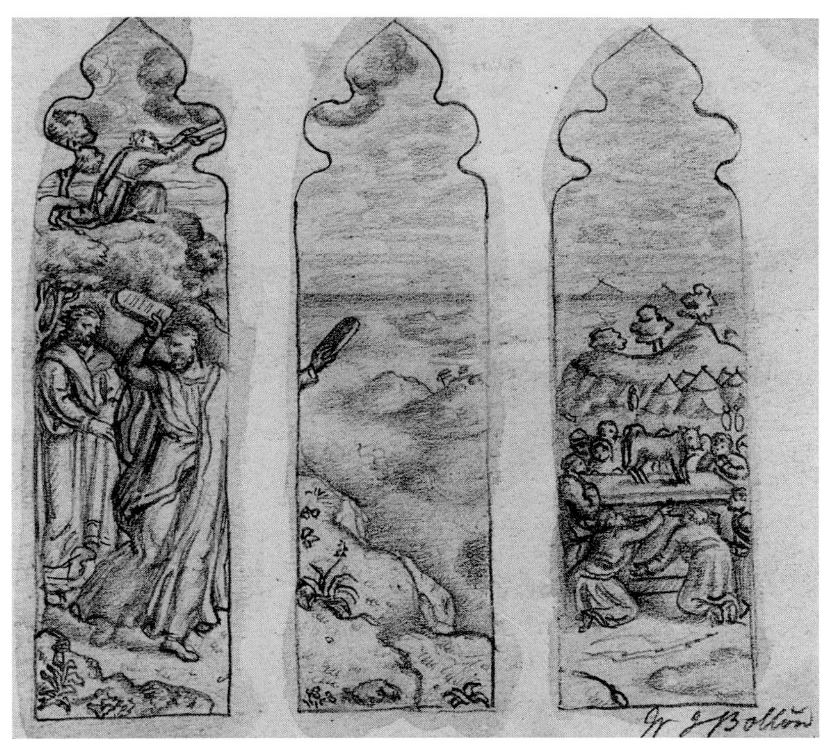

20b. William Jay Bolton, *Moses with the Tablets,* pencil
(Long Island Diocese Archives, Garden City, N.Y.)   Cat. IX:11d

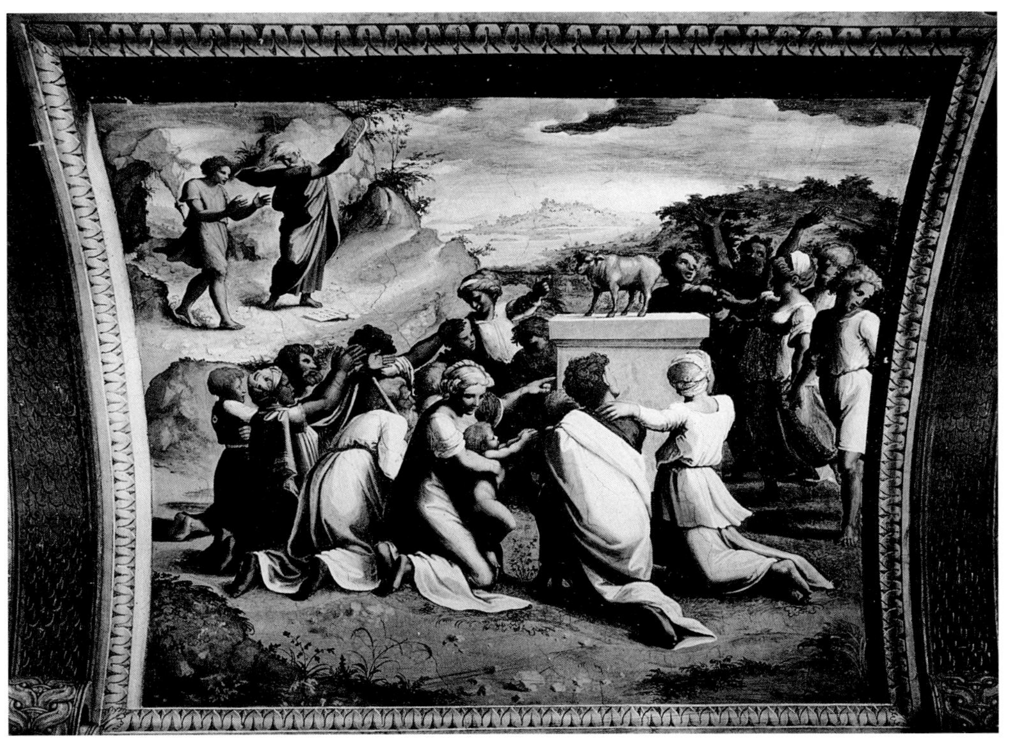

21. Raphael shop, *The Golden Calf,* Vatican, Logge

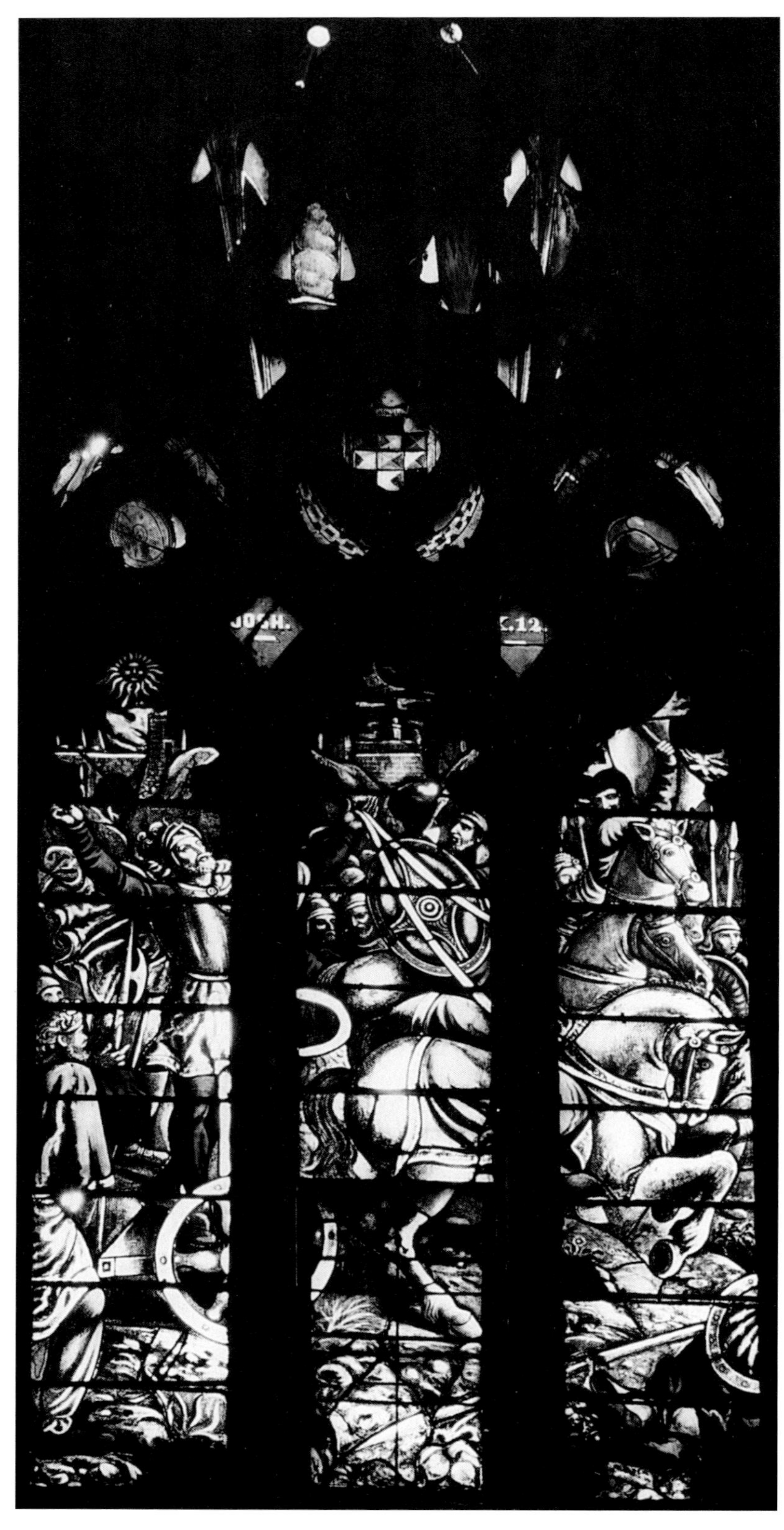

22. (St. Ann and) Holy Trinity, Brooklyn: *Joshua Stills the Sun and Moon*   Cat. III:C4

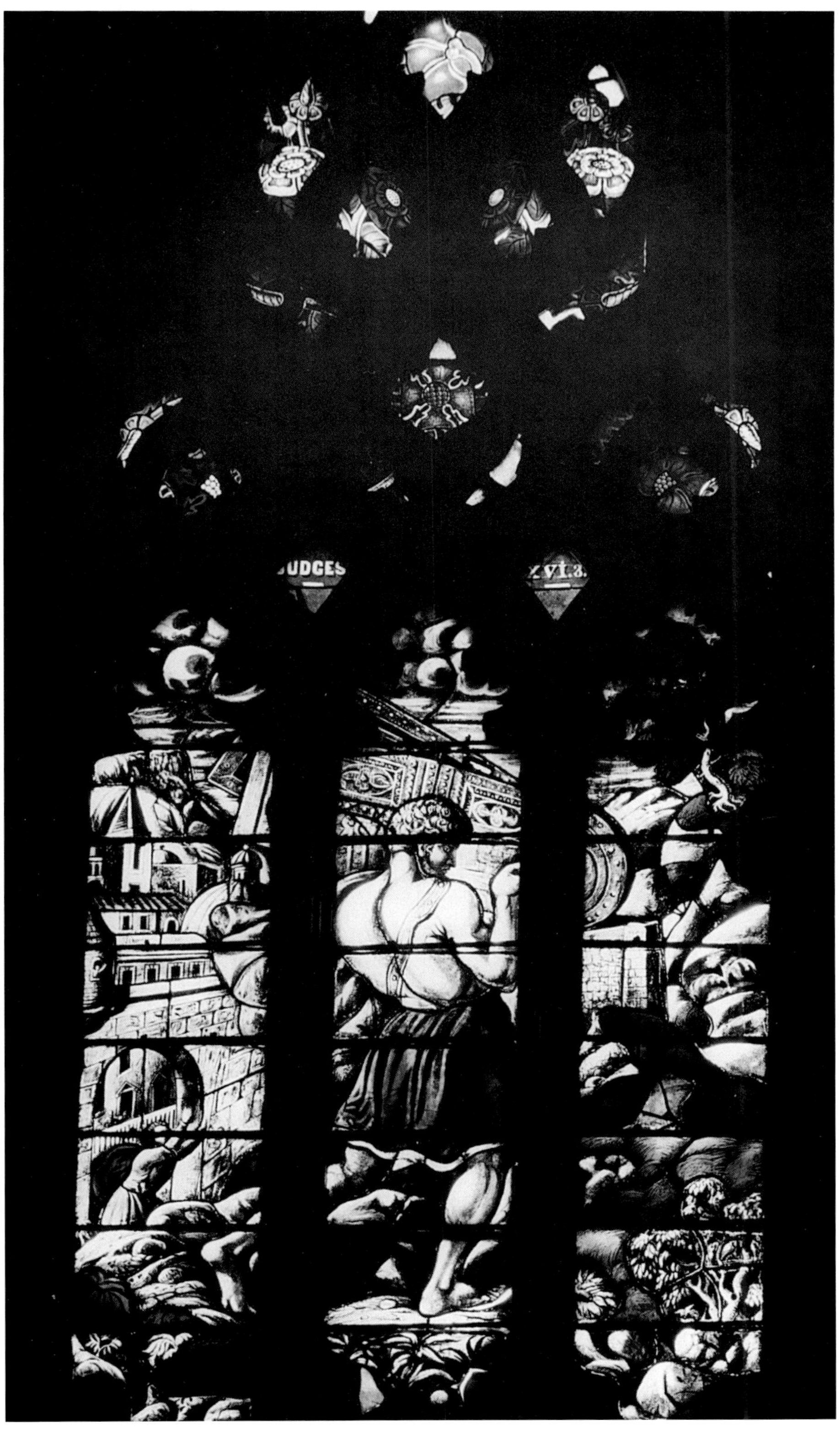

23. (St. Ann and) Holy Trinity, Brooklyn:
Samson with the Gates of Gaza   Cat. III:C5

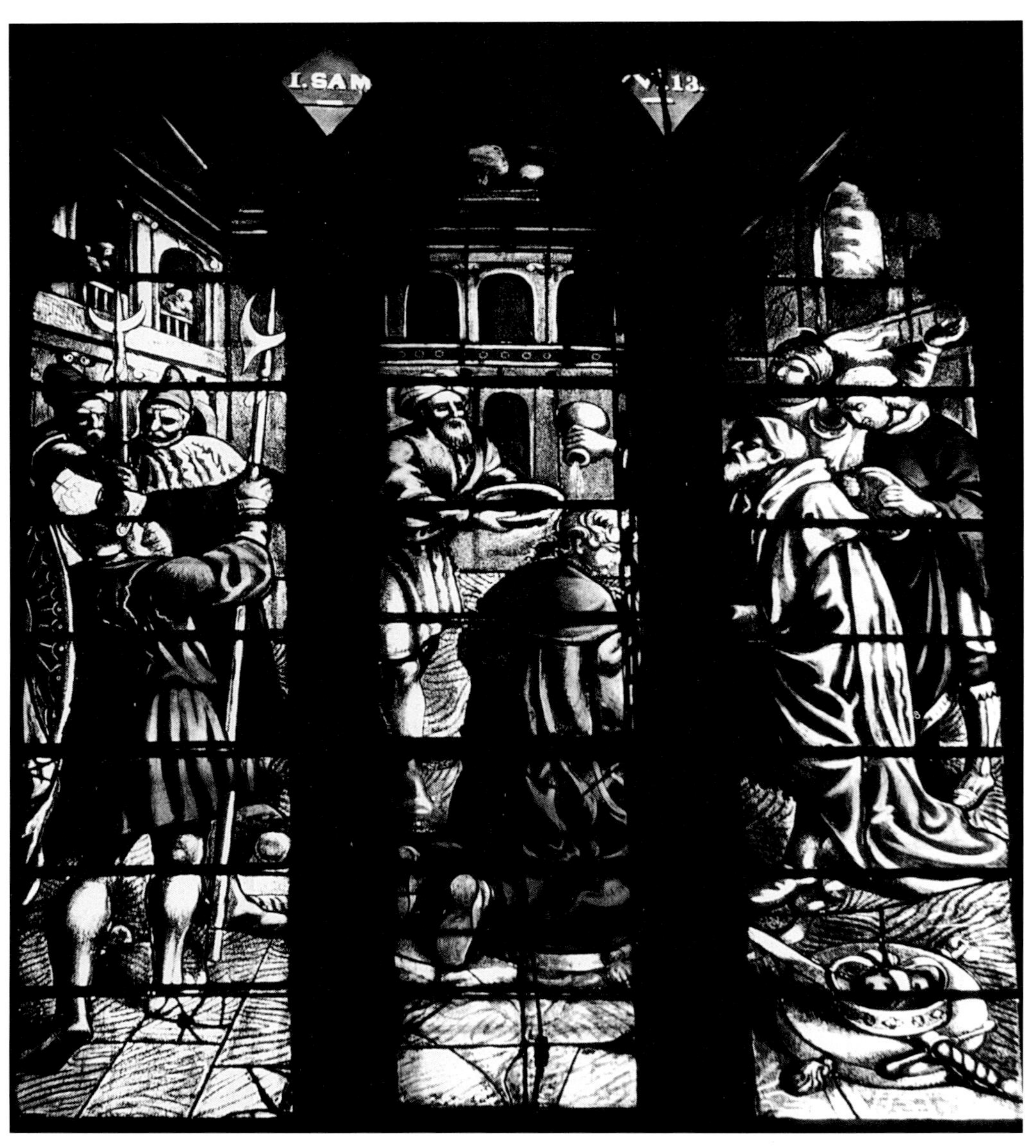

24. (St. Ann and) Holy Trinity, Brooklyn: *Coronation of David*   Cat. III:C6

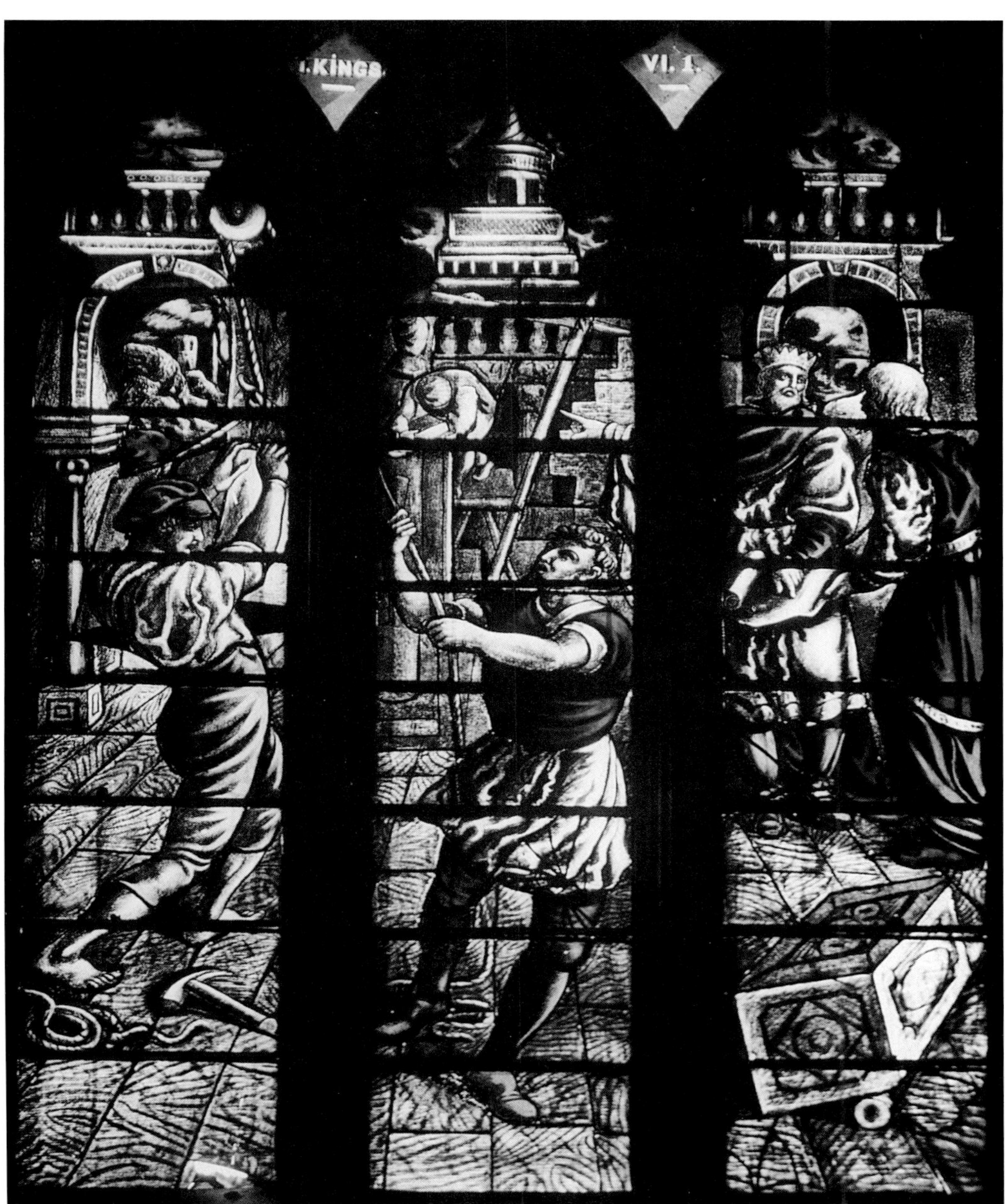

25. (St. Ann and) Holy Trinity, Brooklyn: *Building the Temple*   Cat. III:C7

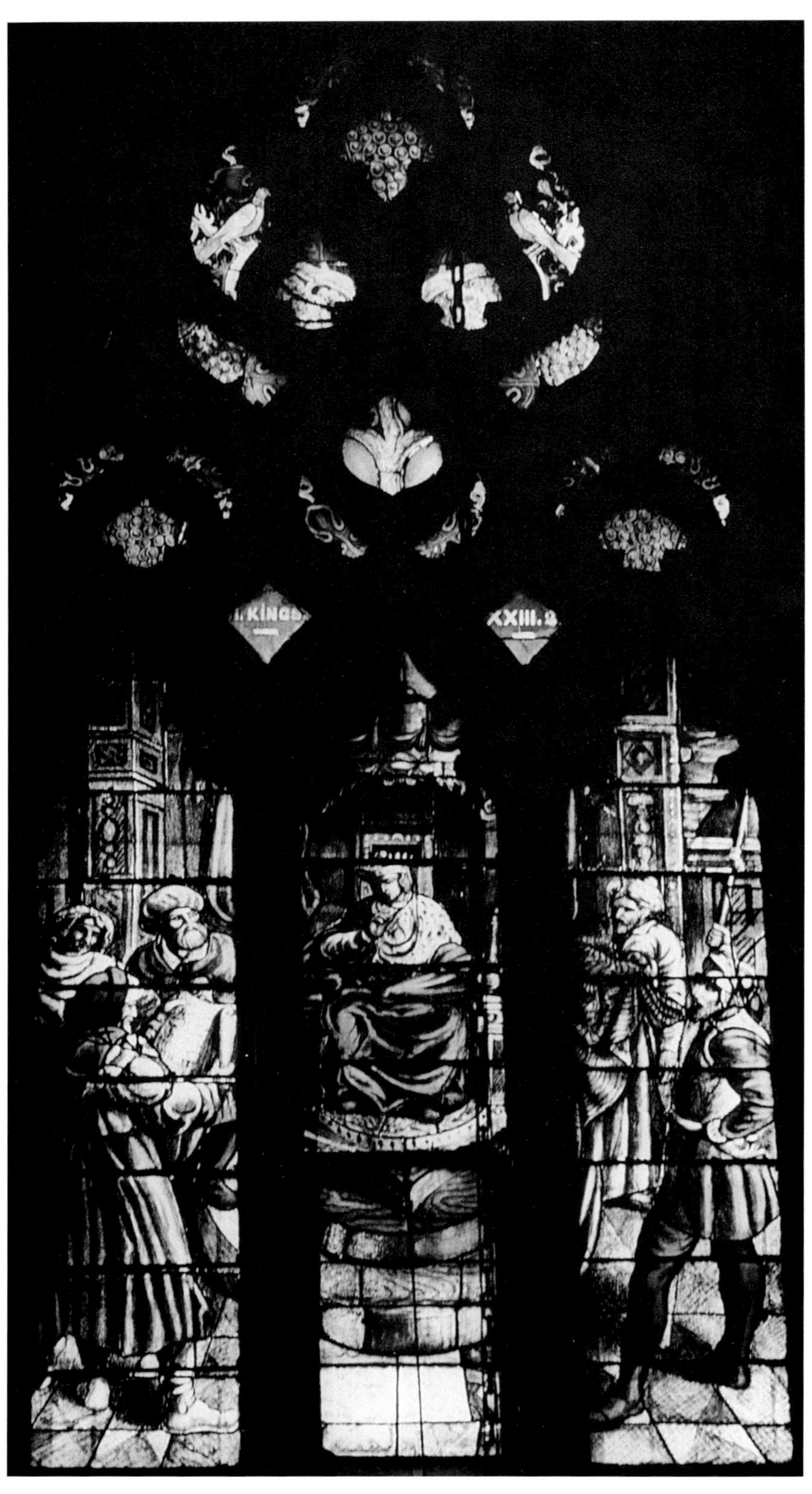

26. (St. Ann and) Holy Trinity, Brooklyn:
Reading of Deuteronomy   Cat. III:C8

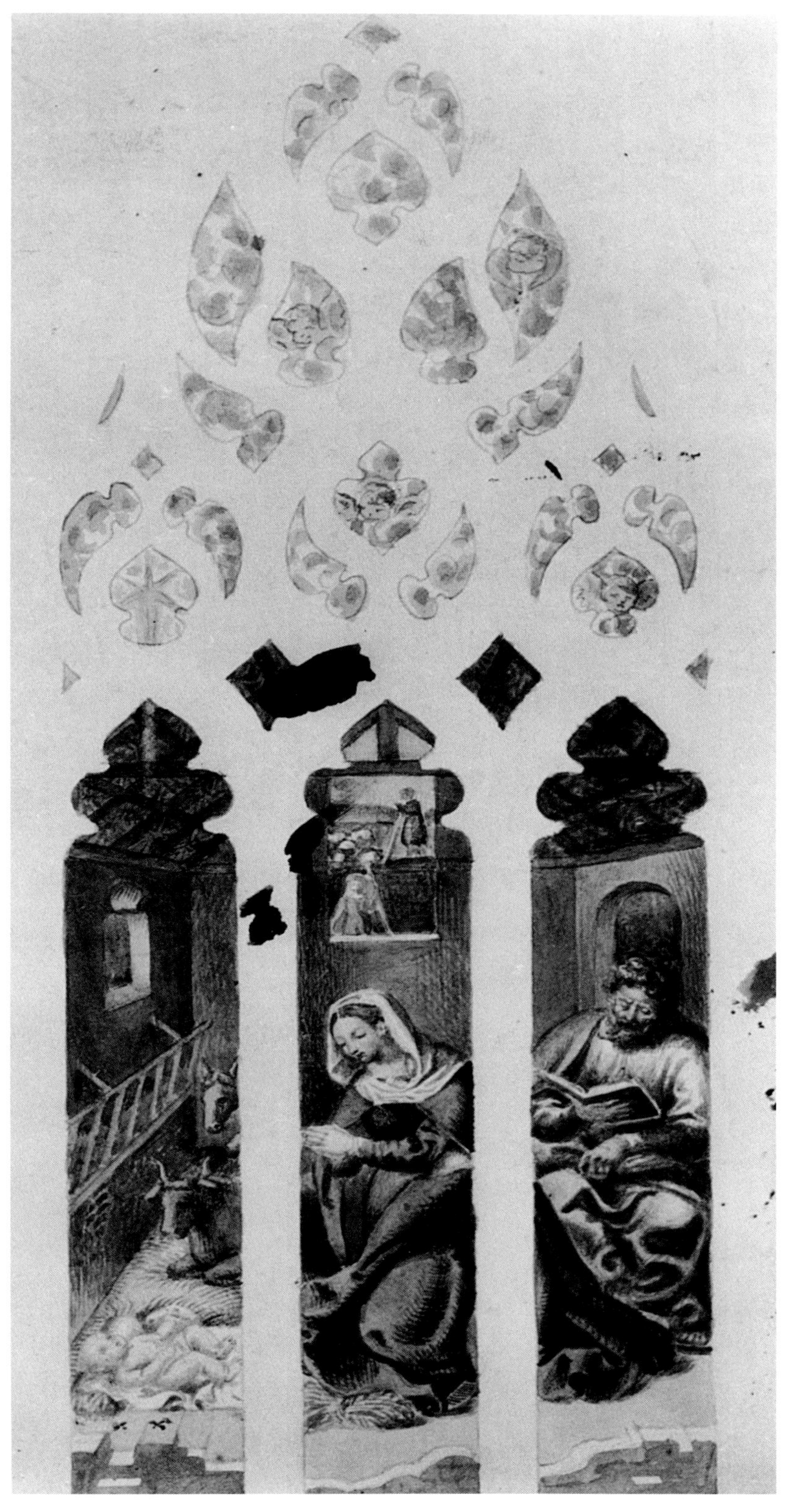

27. William Jay Bolton, *The Adoration of the Child,* watercolor
(Long Island Diocese Archives, Garden City, N.Y.)　Cat. IX:11e

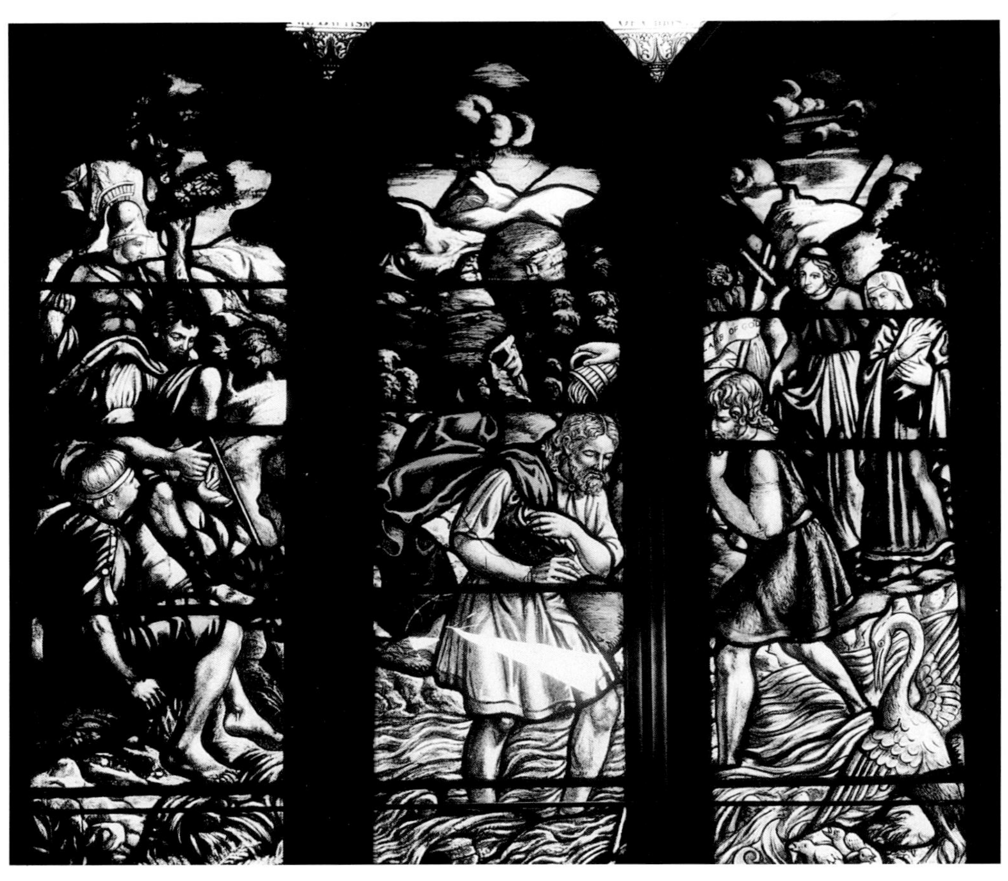

28. (St. Ann and) Holy Trinity, Brooklyn:
The Baptism of Christ (Photo: W. B. Clark)   Cat. III:G9

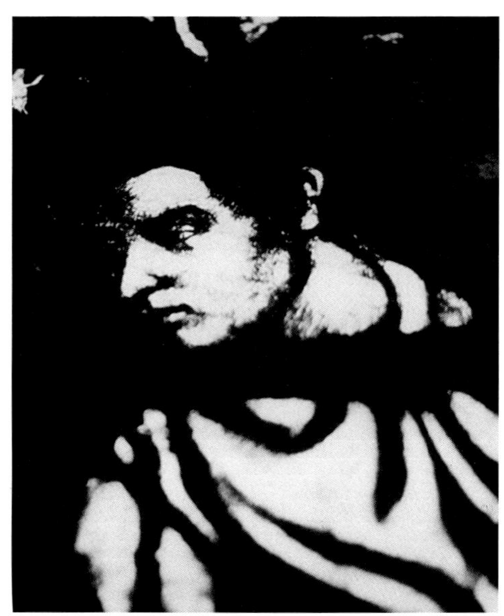

29a. Detail of fig. 29b
(Photo: W. B. Clark)

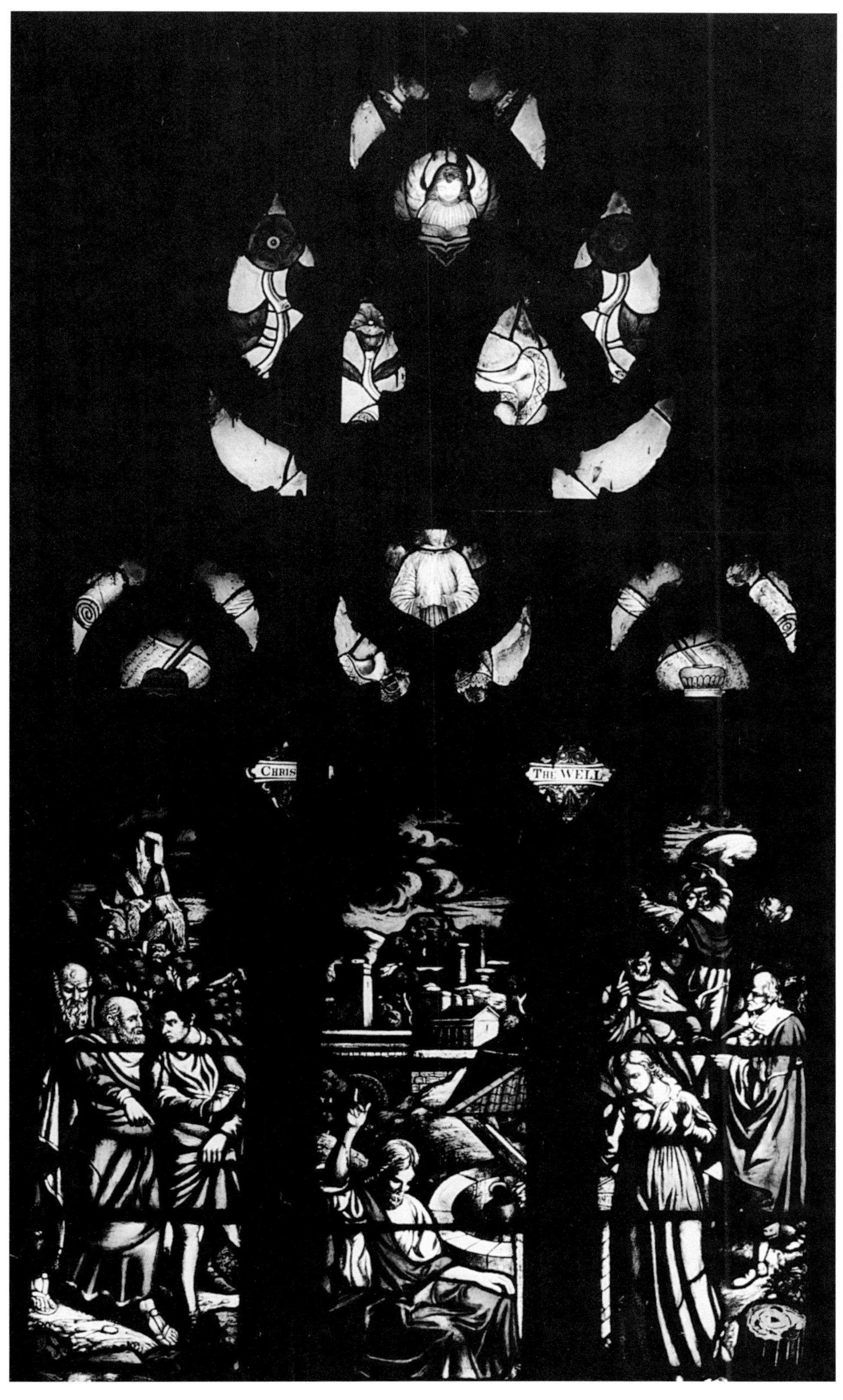

29b. (St. Ann and) Holy Trinity, Brooklyn: *Christ at the Well*   Cat. III:G10

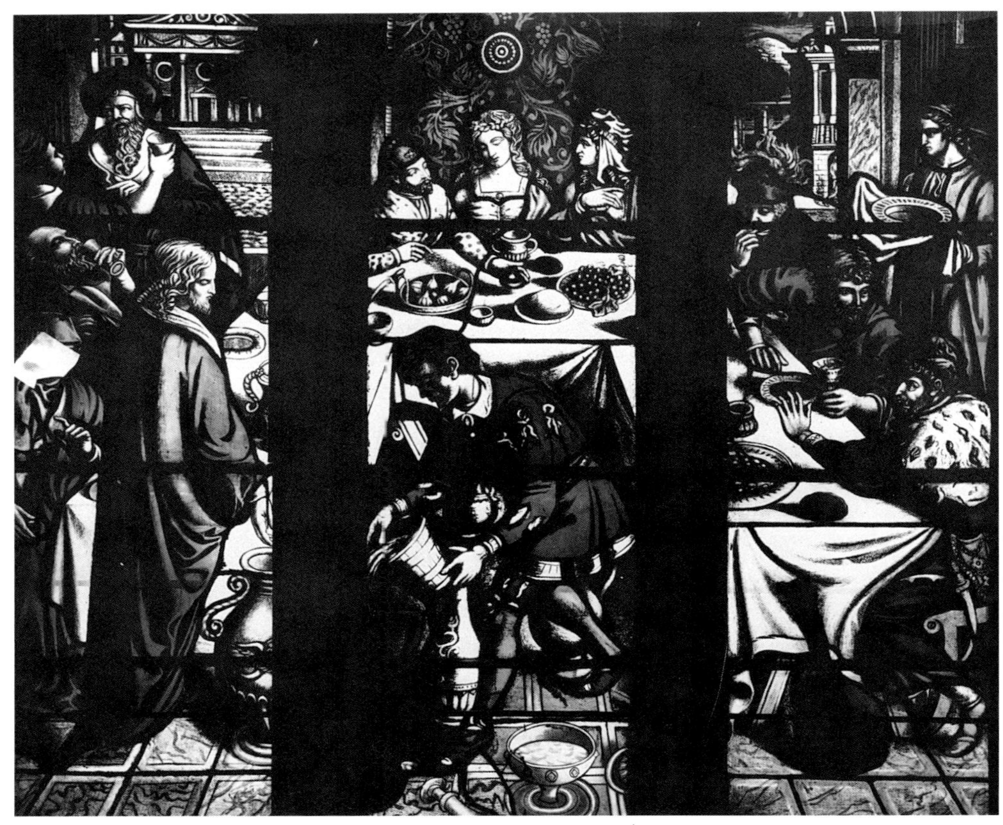

30a. (St. Ann and) Holy Trinity, Brooklyn: *Marriage at Cana*   Cat. III:G11

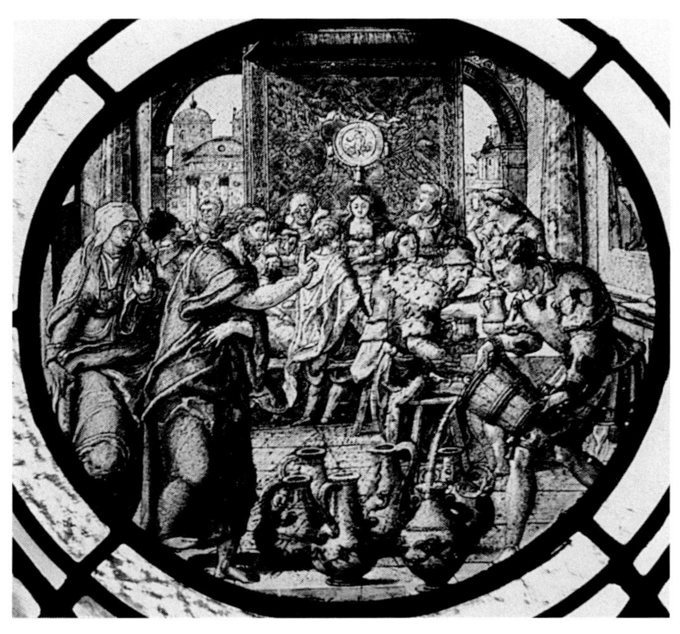

30b. Design attributed to Jan Swart van Groningen, *Marriage at Cana,* in a roundel at Holy Trinity Church, Bradford-on-Avon, tracing by William Jay Bolton (Long Island Diocese Archives, Garden City, N.Y.)   Cat. IX:11f

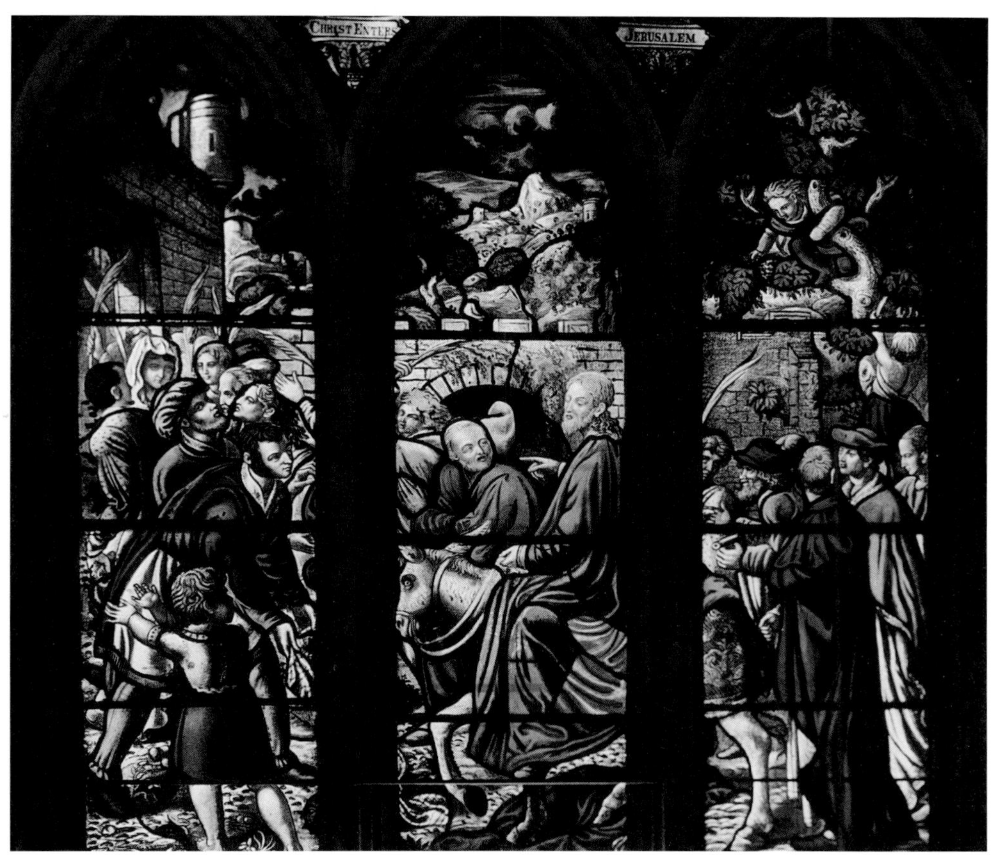

31a. (St. Ann and) Holy Trinity, Brooklyn: *Christ Enters Jerusalem*   Cat. III:G12

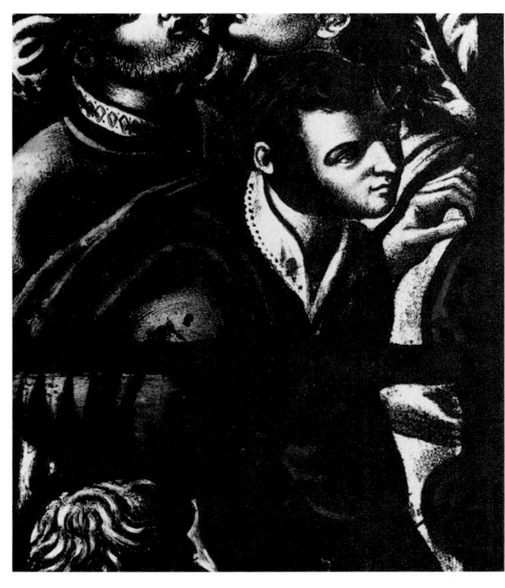

31b. Detail of fig. 31a

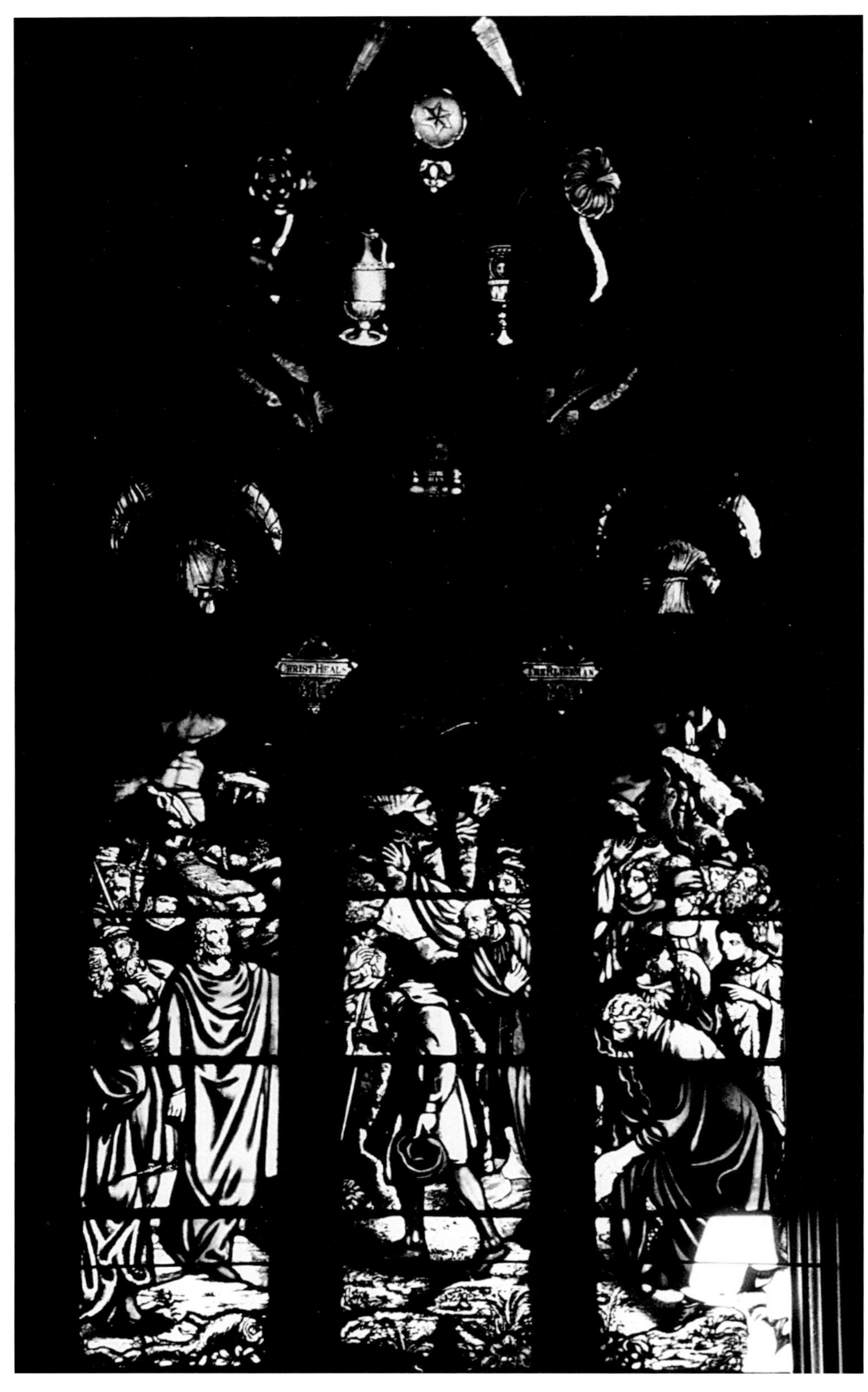

32a. (St. Ann and) Holy Trinity, Brooklyn:
Christ Heals the Blind Man (Photo: W. B. Clark)   Cat. III:G13

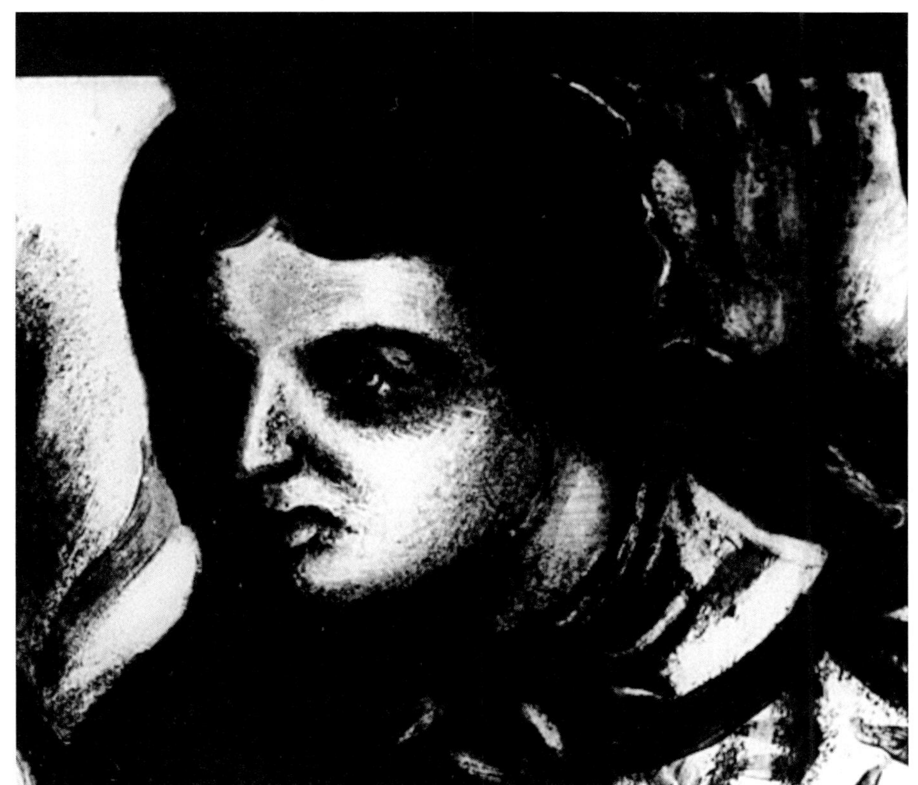

32b. Detail of fig. 32a

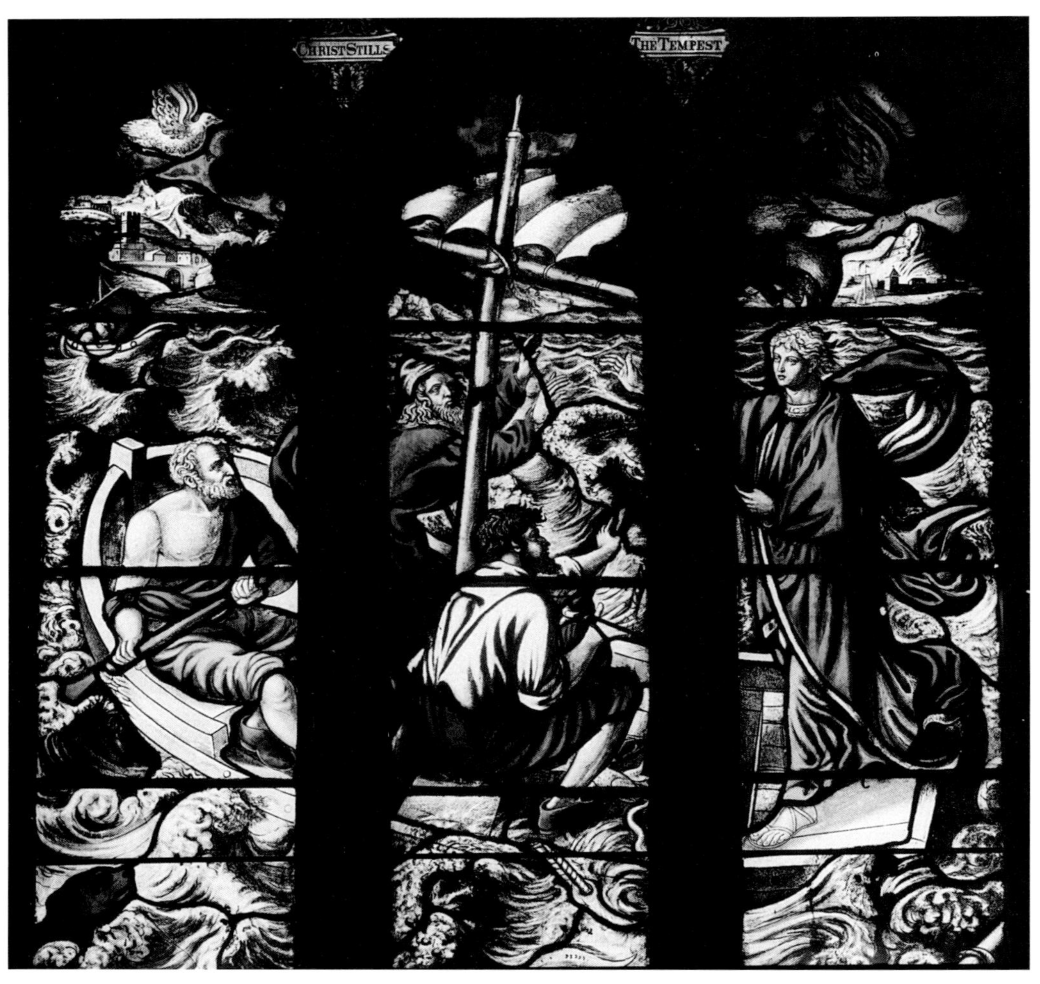

33a. (St. Ann and) Holy Trinity, Brooklyn: *Christ Stills the Tempest*   Cat. III:G14

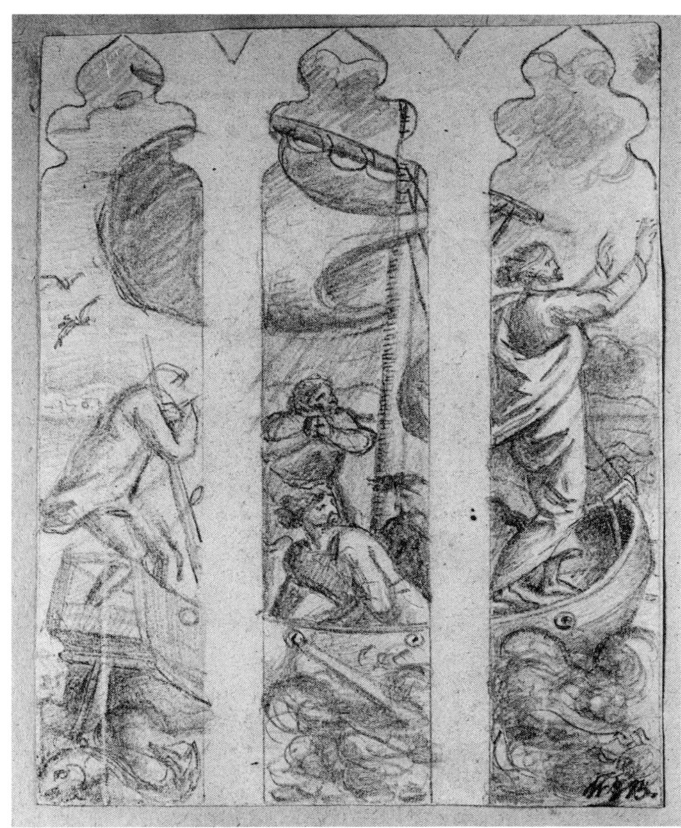

33b. William Jay
Bolton, *Christ Stills the
Tempest,* pencil
(Long Island Diocese
Archives, Garden City,
N.Y.)   Cat. IX:11g

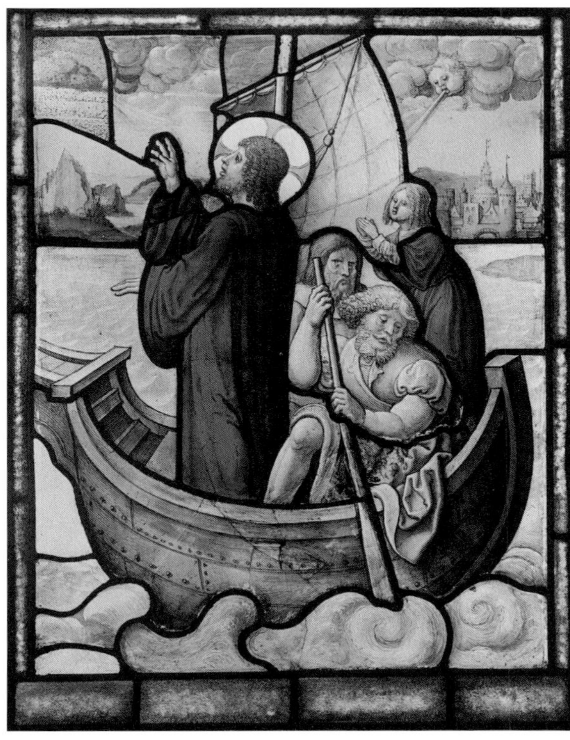

33c. Shop of Dirk Vellert,
Christ Stills the Tempest, panel
(New York, Metropolitan
Museum of Art; photo:
all rights reserved, The
Metropolitan Museum of Art)

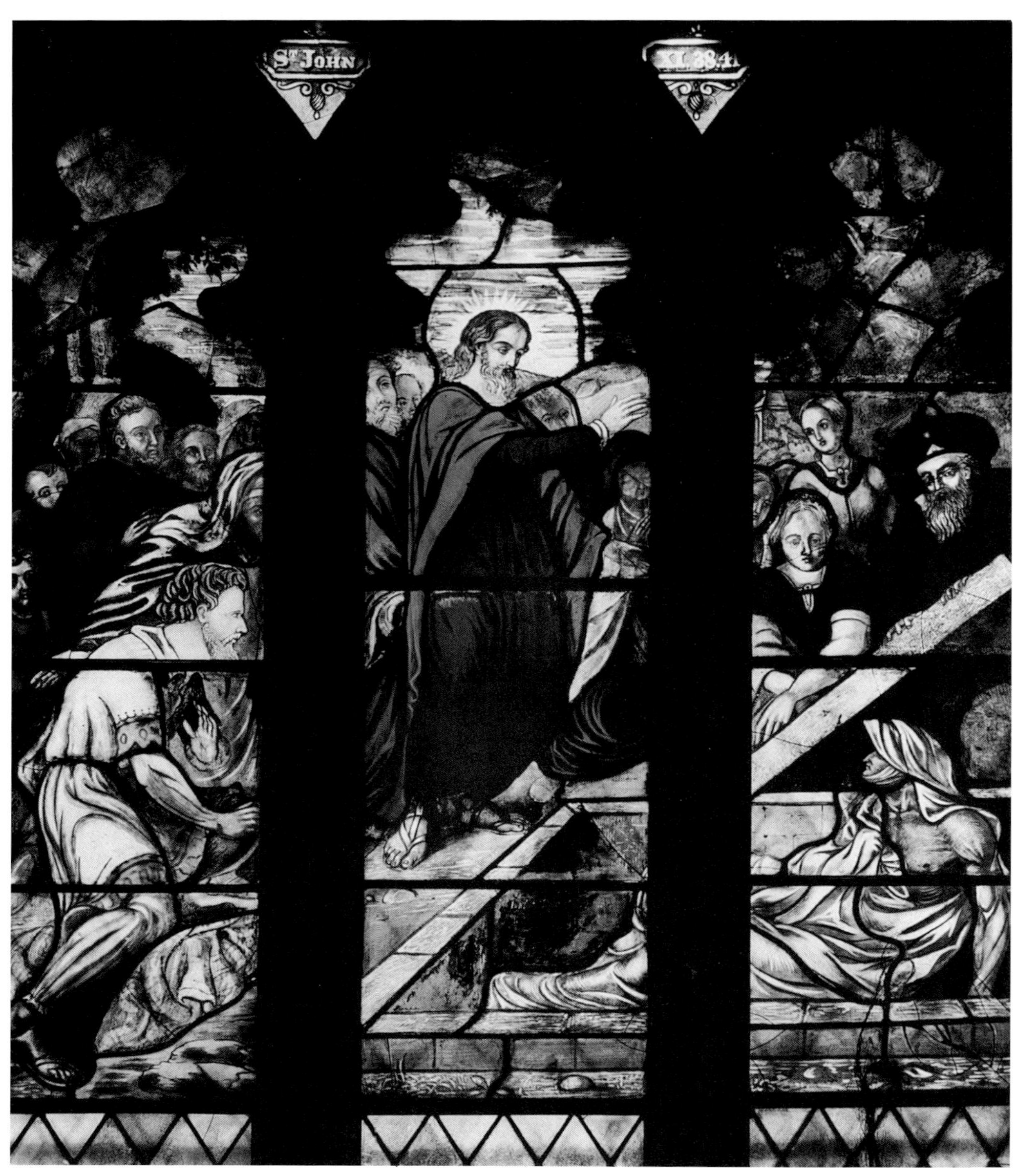

34. (St. Ann and) Holy Trinity, Brooklyn: *Raising of Lazarus*   Cat. III:GI

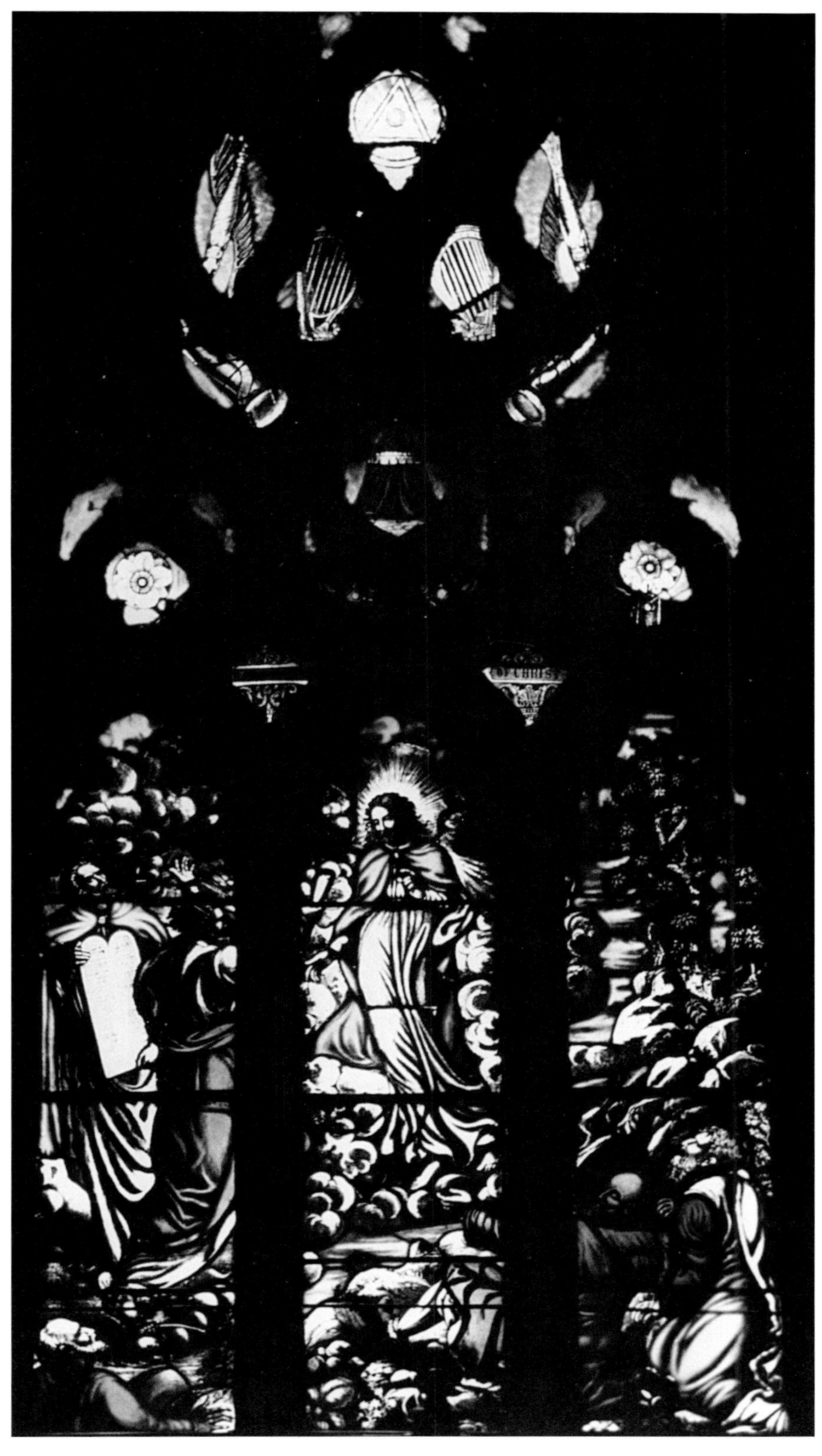

35a. (St. Ann and) Holy Trinity, Brooklyn:
Transfiguration of Christ (Photo: W. B. Clark)   Cat. III:G2

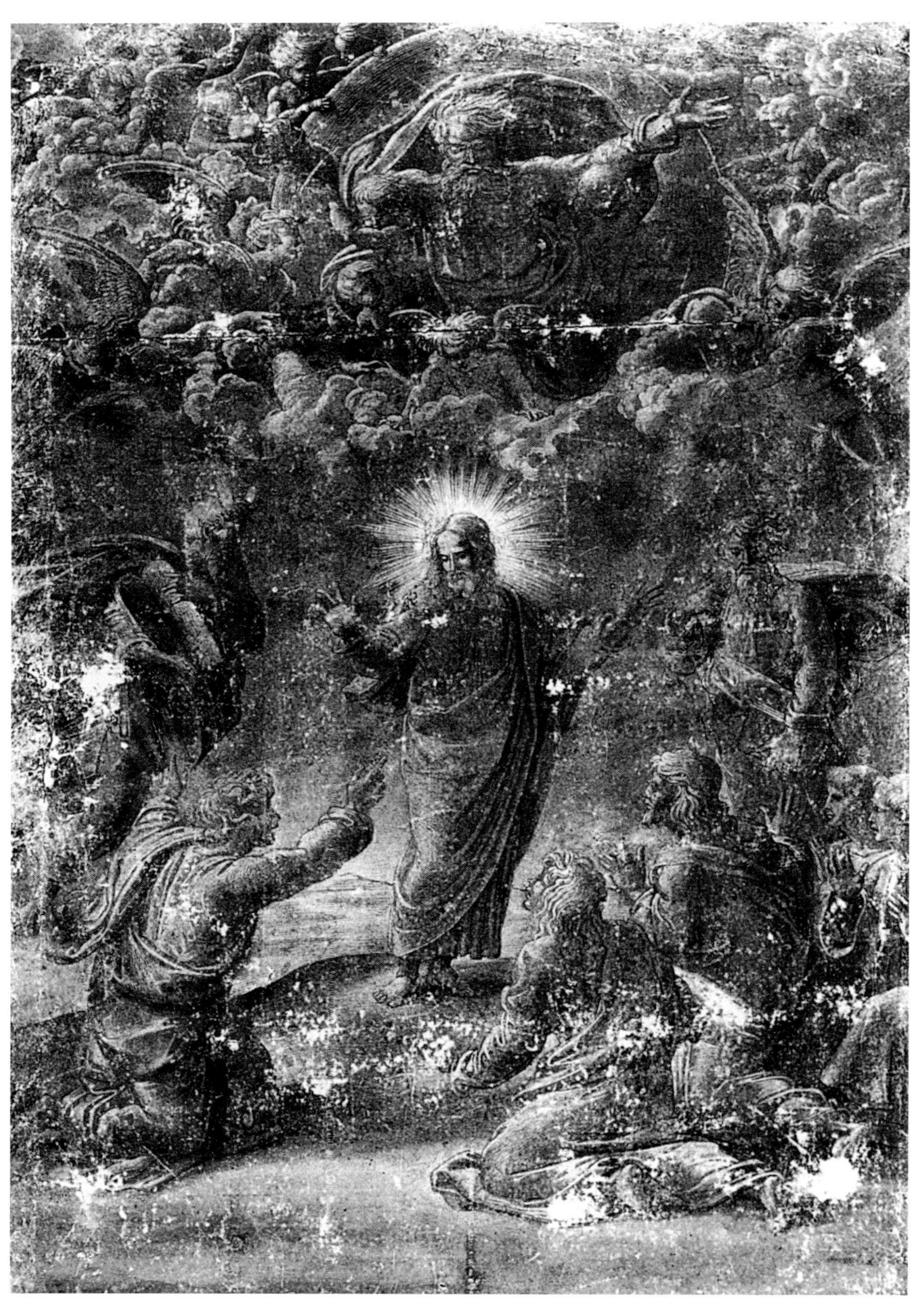

35b. Raphael, *The Transfiguration,* preparatory drawing by
Giulio Romano (Vienna, Albertina; photo: the museum)

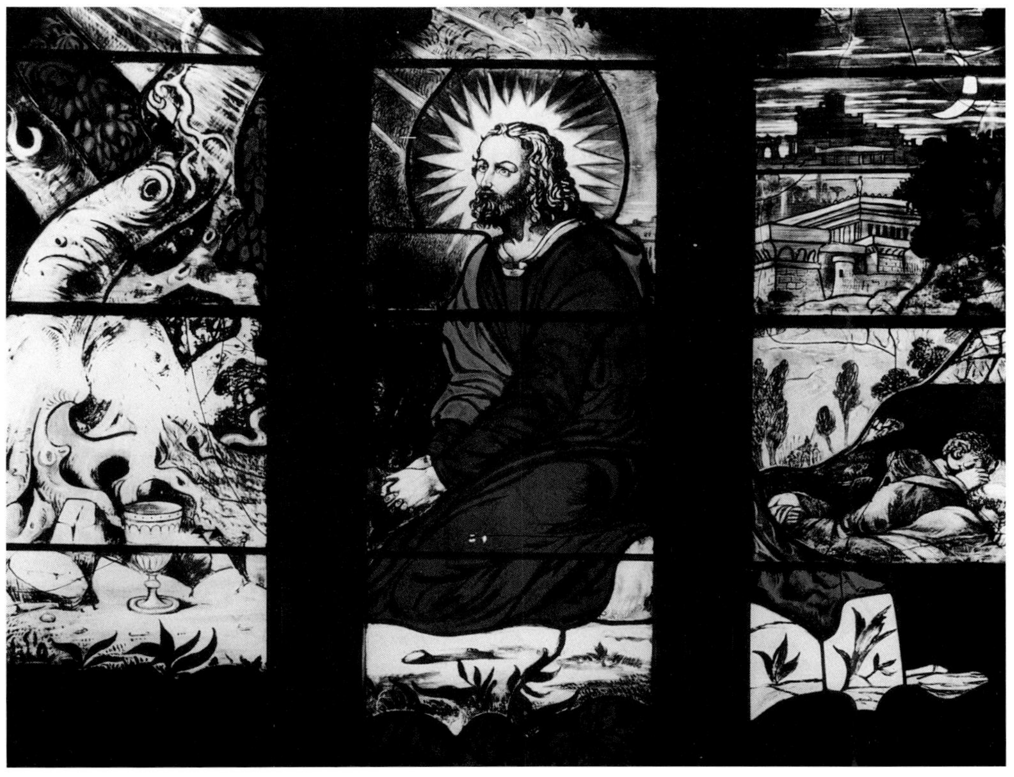

36. (St. Ann and) Holy Trinity, Brooklyn: *Christ in Gethsemane*   Cat. III:G3

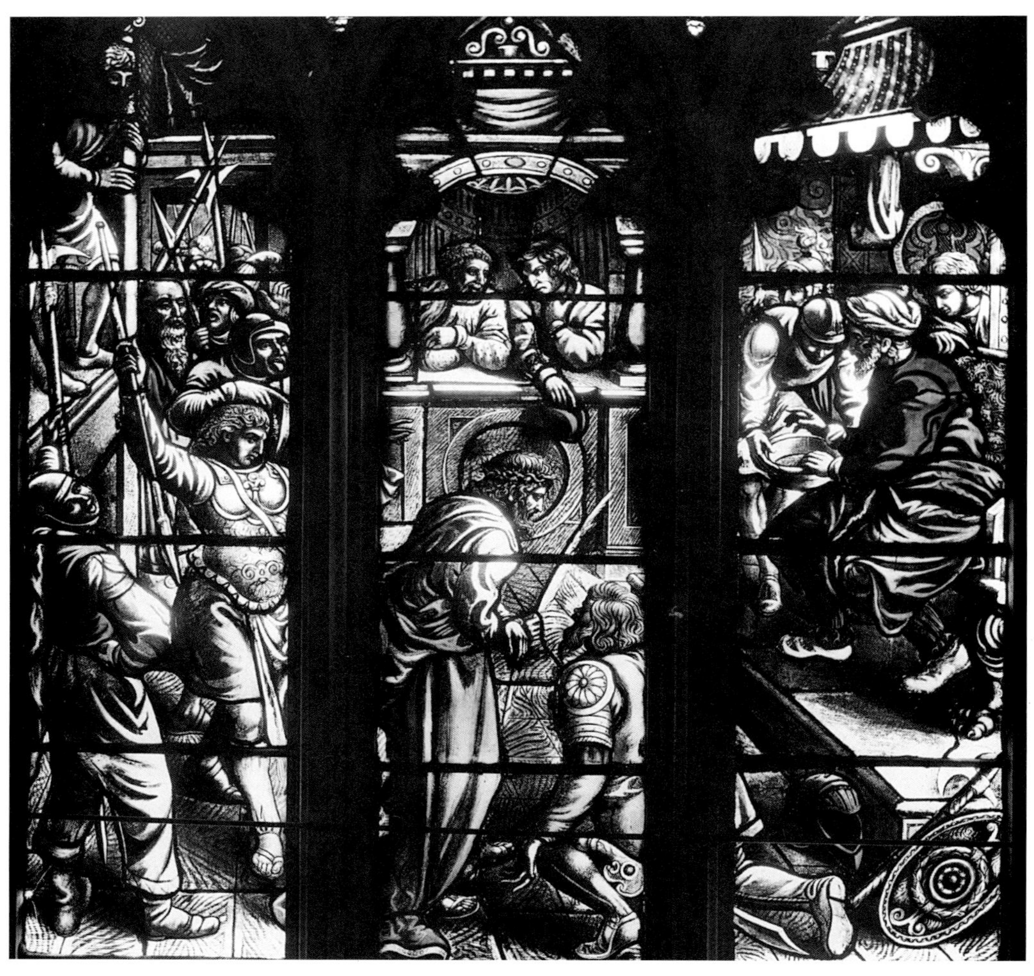

37. (St. Ann and) Holy Trinity, Brooklyn: *The Trial of Christ*   Cat. III:G4

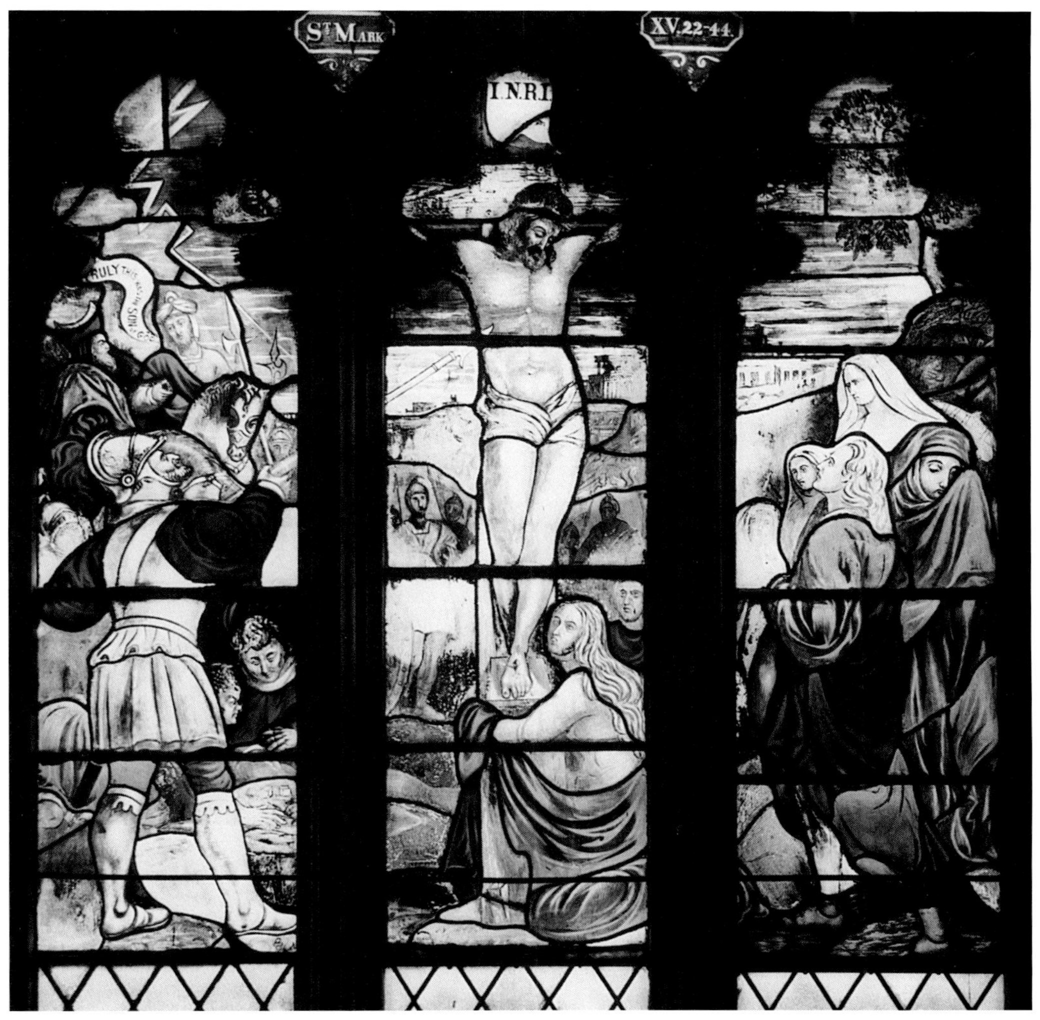

38. (St. Ann and) Holy Trinity, Brooklyn: *The Crucifixion*   Cat. III:G5

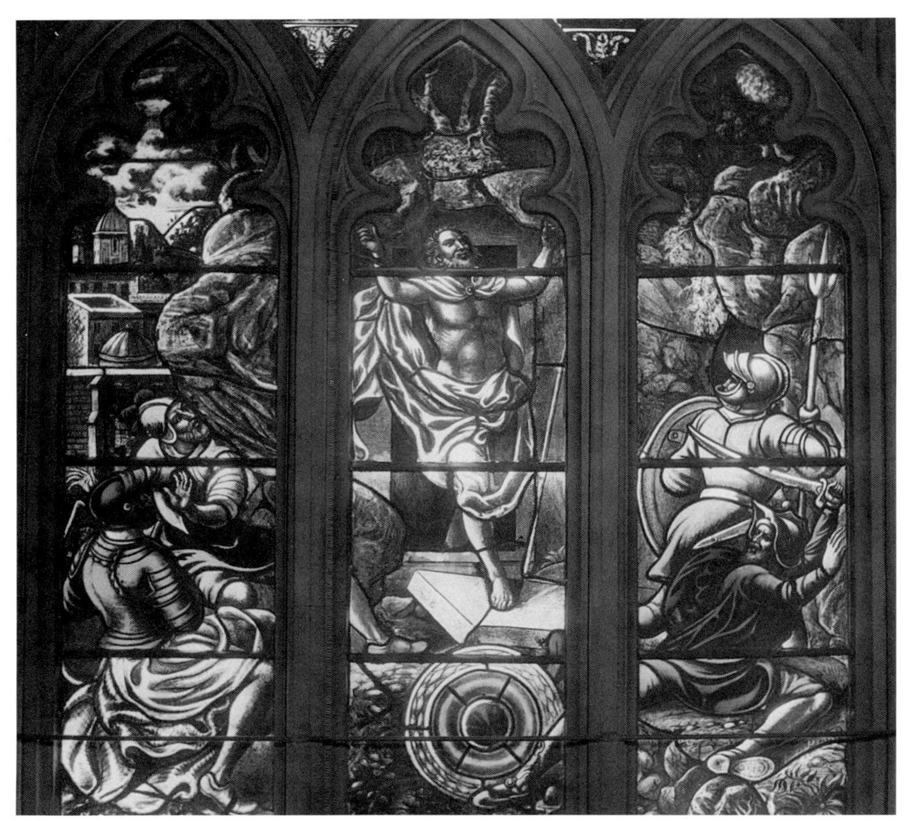

39a. (St. Ann and) Holy Trinity, Brooklyn: *Resurrection of Christ*   Cat. III:G6

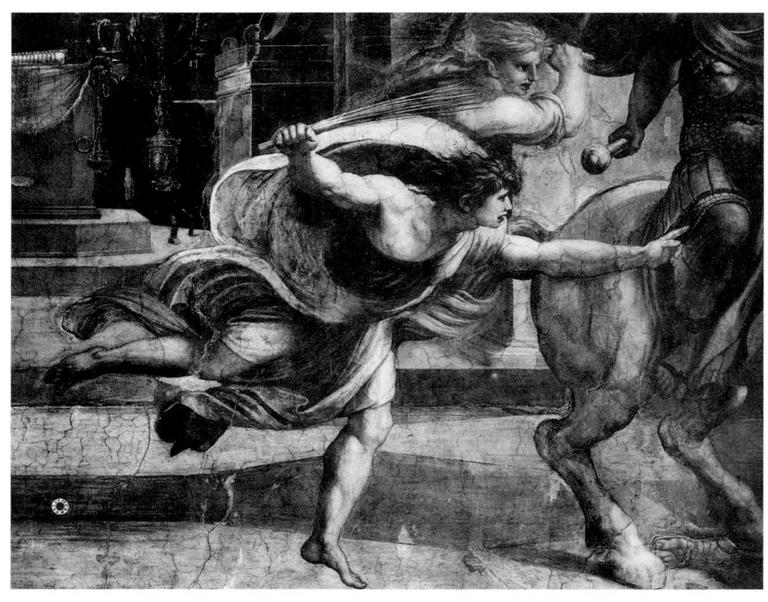

39b. Raphael, *The Expulsion of Heliodorus,*
detail (Vatican, Stanza d'Eliodoro)

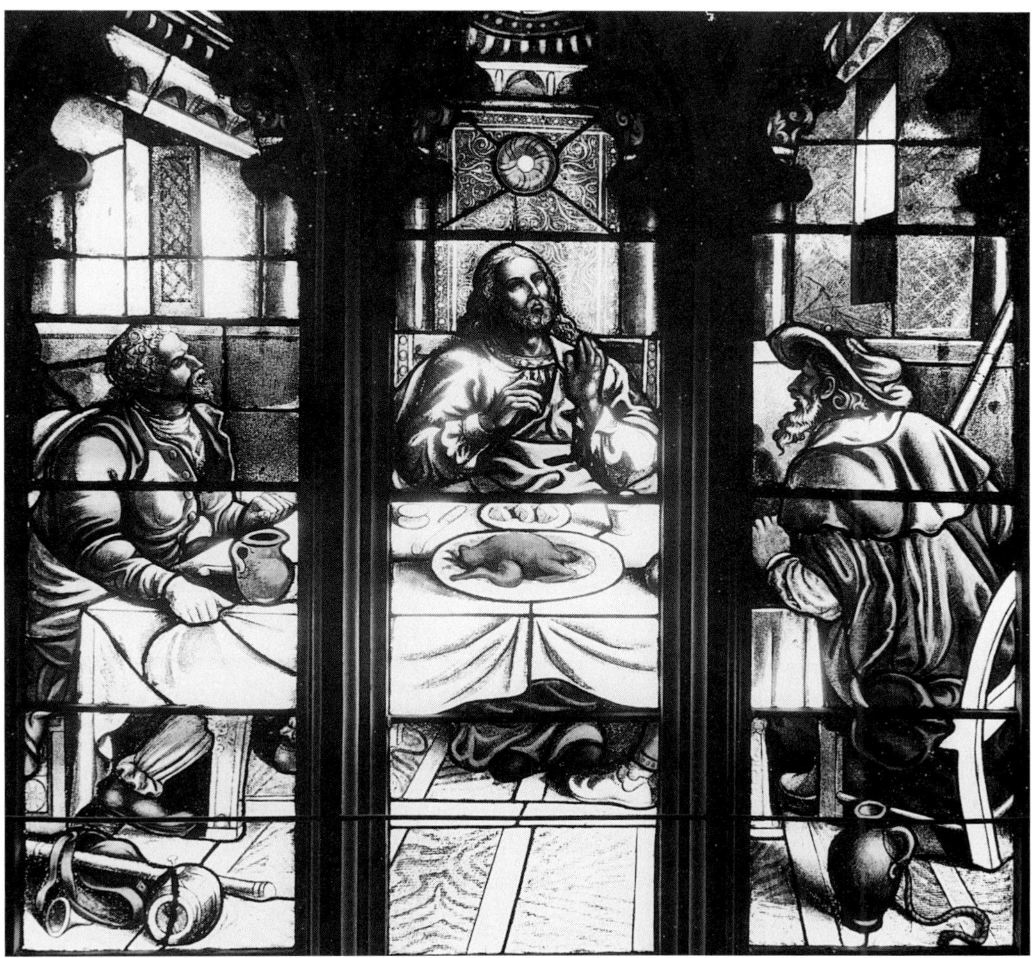

40. (St. Ann and) Holy Trinity, Brooklyn: *Christ at Emmaus*   Cat. III:G7

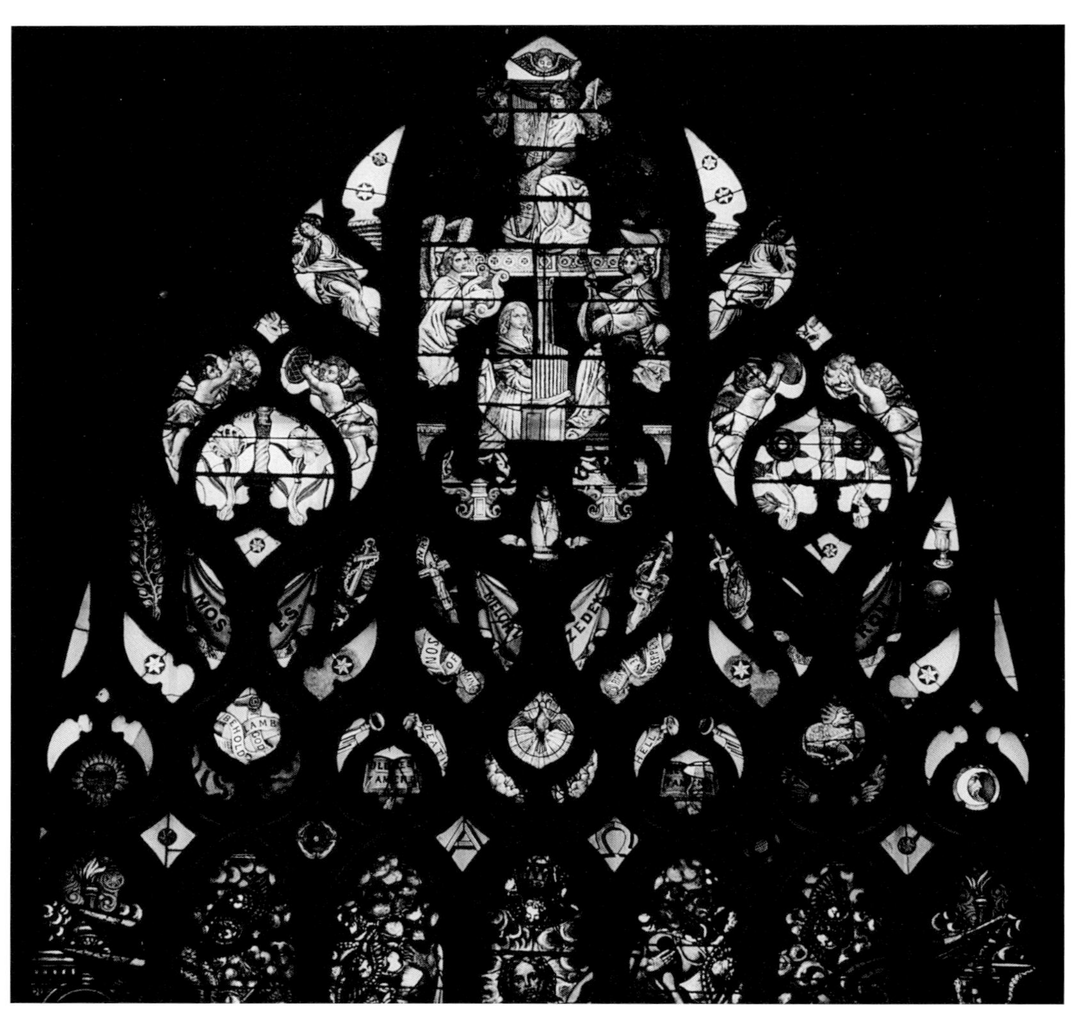

41. (St. Ann and) Holy Trinity, Brooklyn: *Ascension of Christ,* tracery

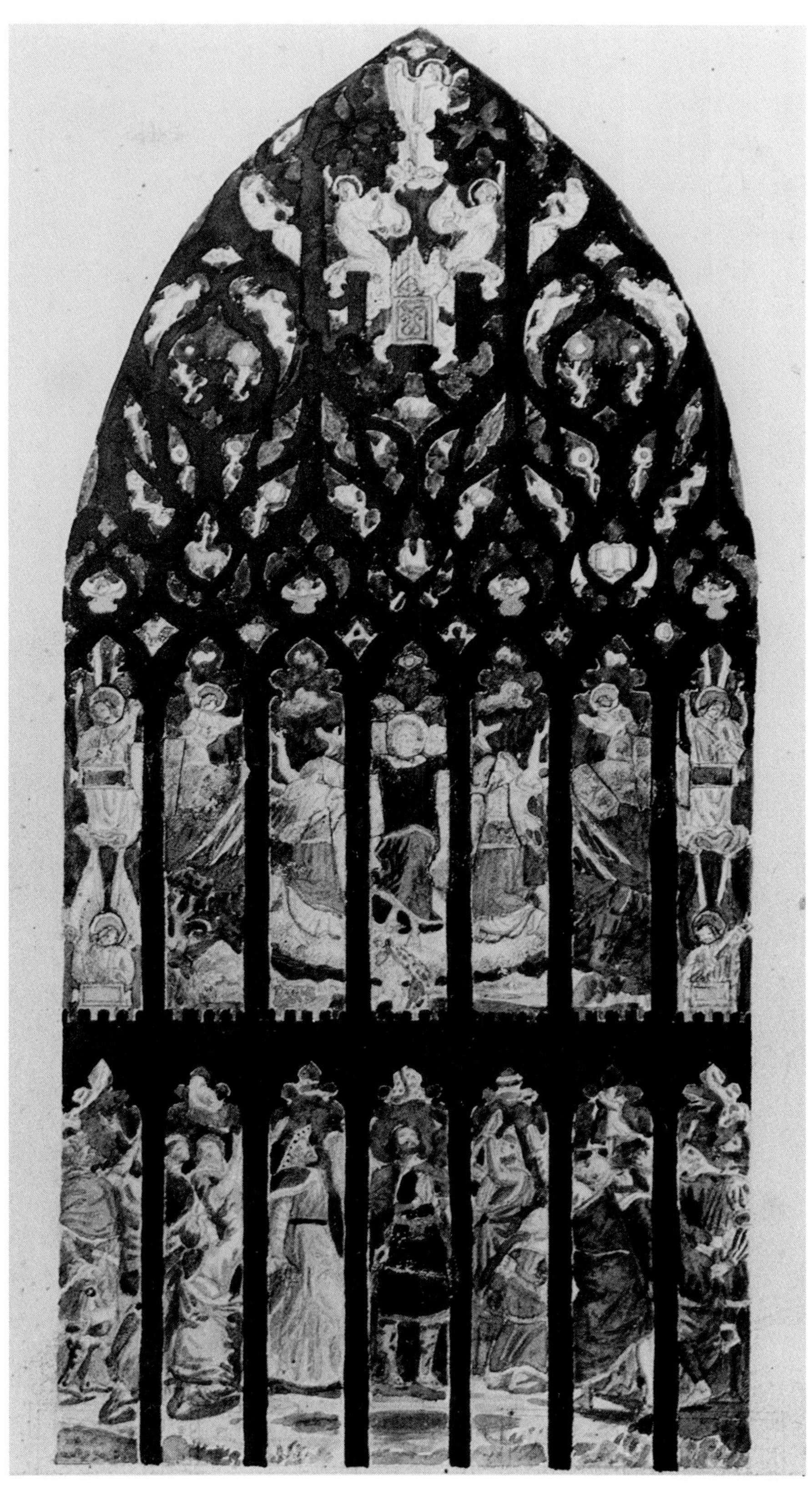

42. William Jay Bolton, *Ascension of Christ,* watercolor
(Long Island Diocese Archives, Garden City, N.Y.)   Cat. IX:11j

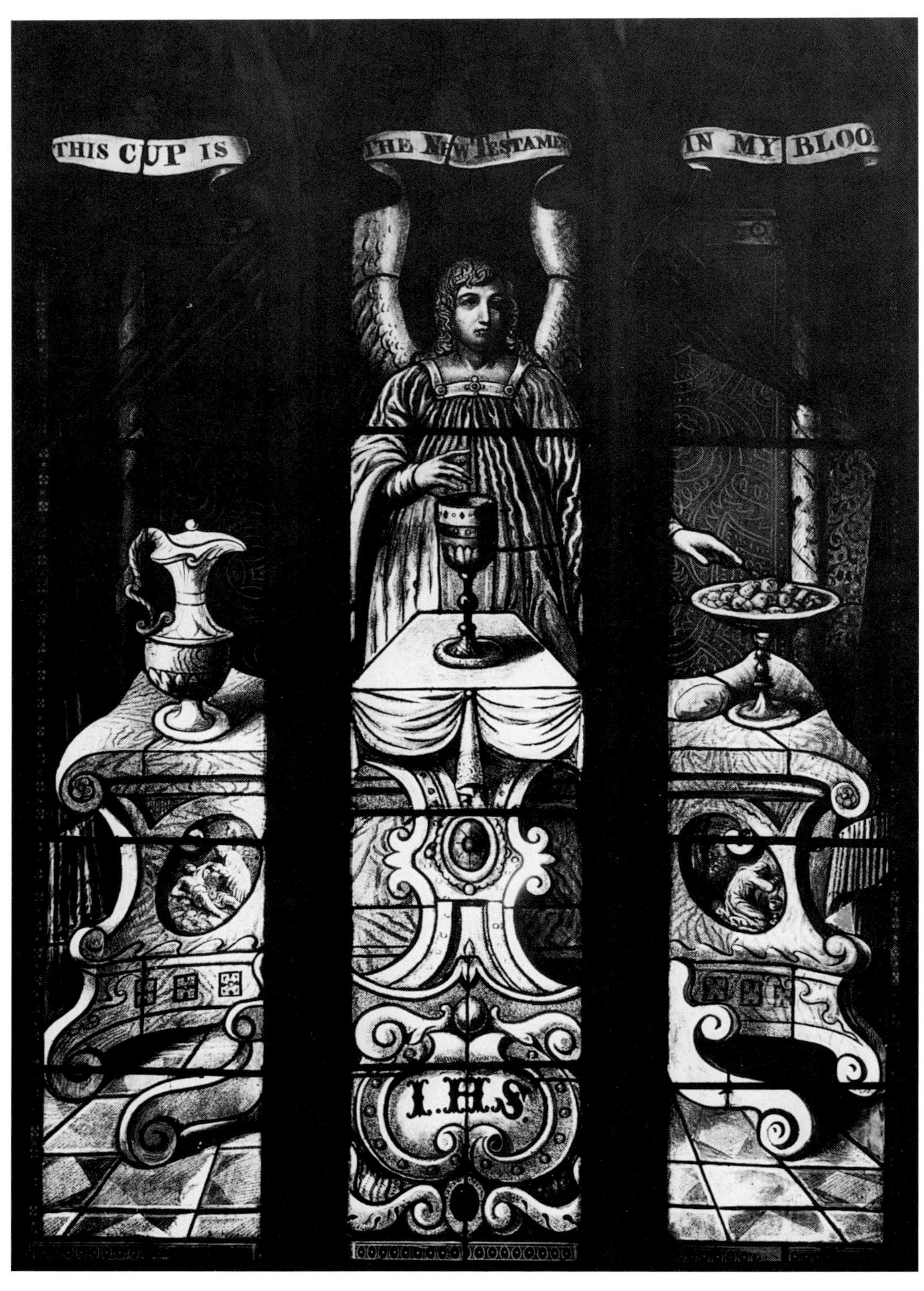

43. (St. Ann and) Holy Trinity, Brooklyn: *Eucharistic Angel*   Cat. III:Chi

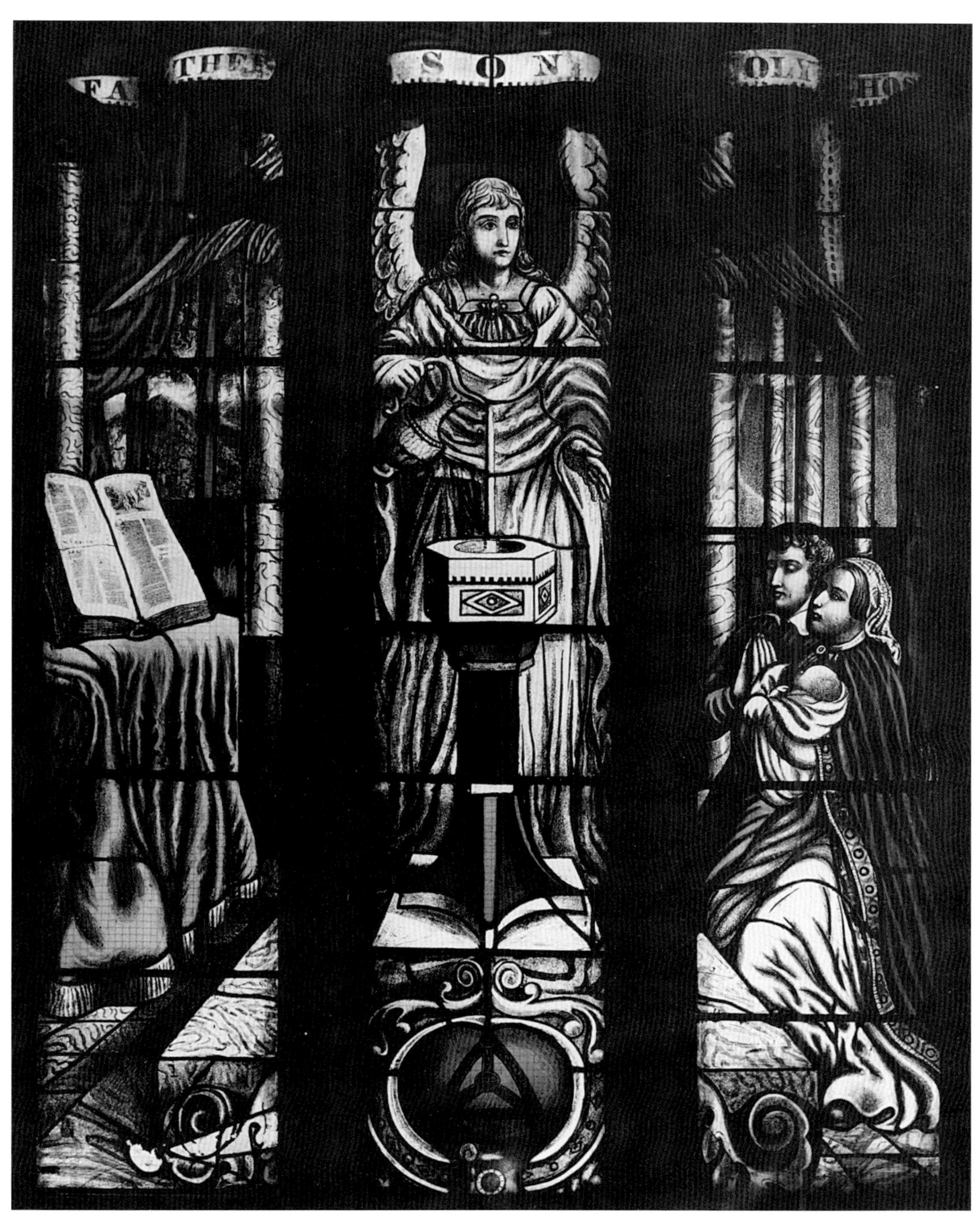

44. (St. Ann and) Holy Trinity, Brooklyn· *Baptismal Angel*   Cat. III:Ch4

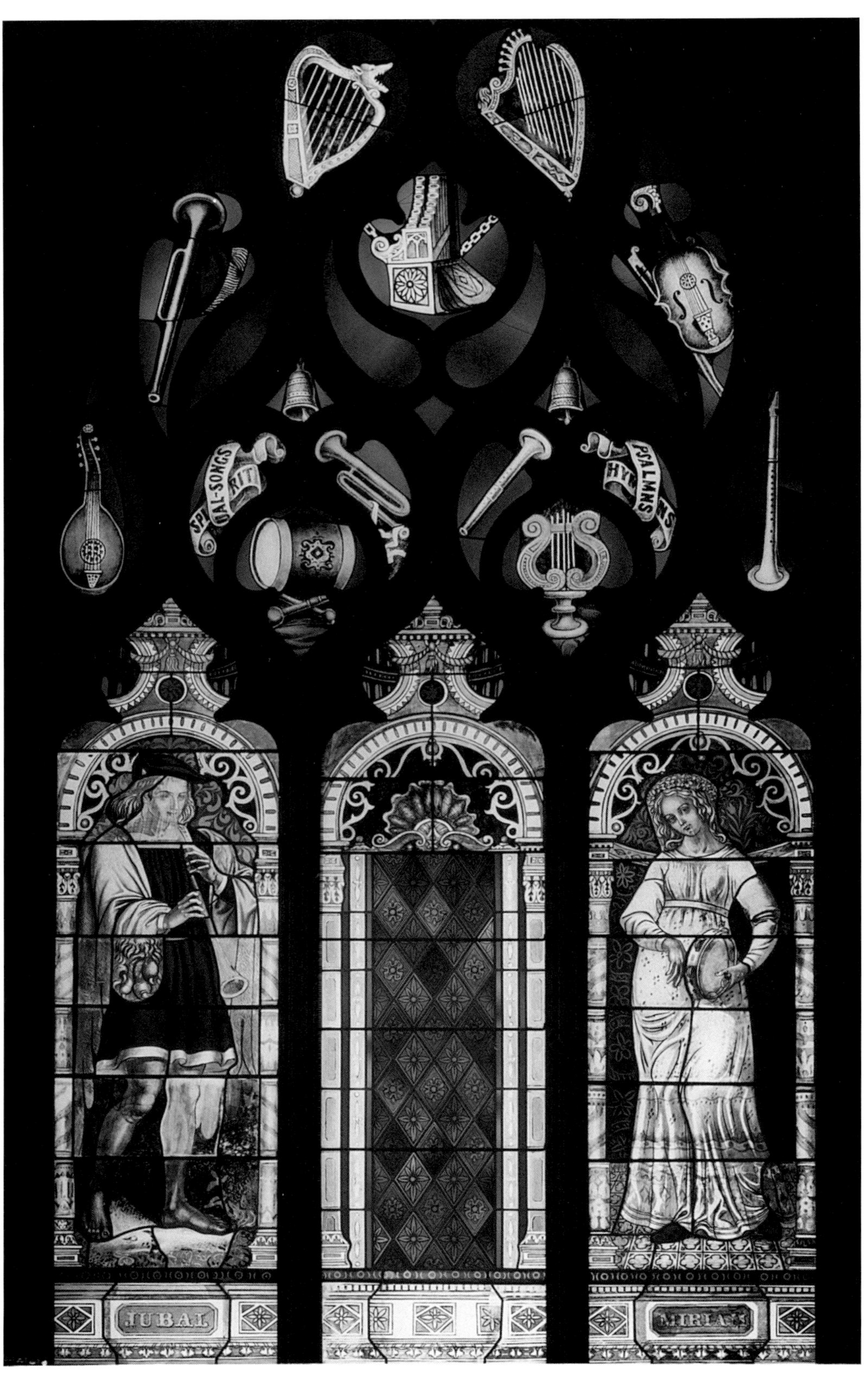

45. (St. Ann and) Holy Trinity, Brooklyn: *Jubal and Miriam*
(as installed at Metropolitan Museum of Art, American Wing)   Cat. III:Tw1

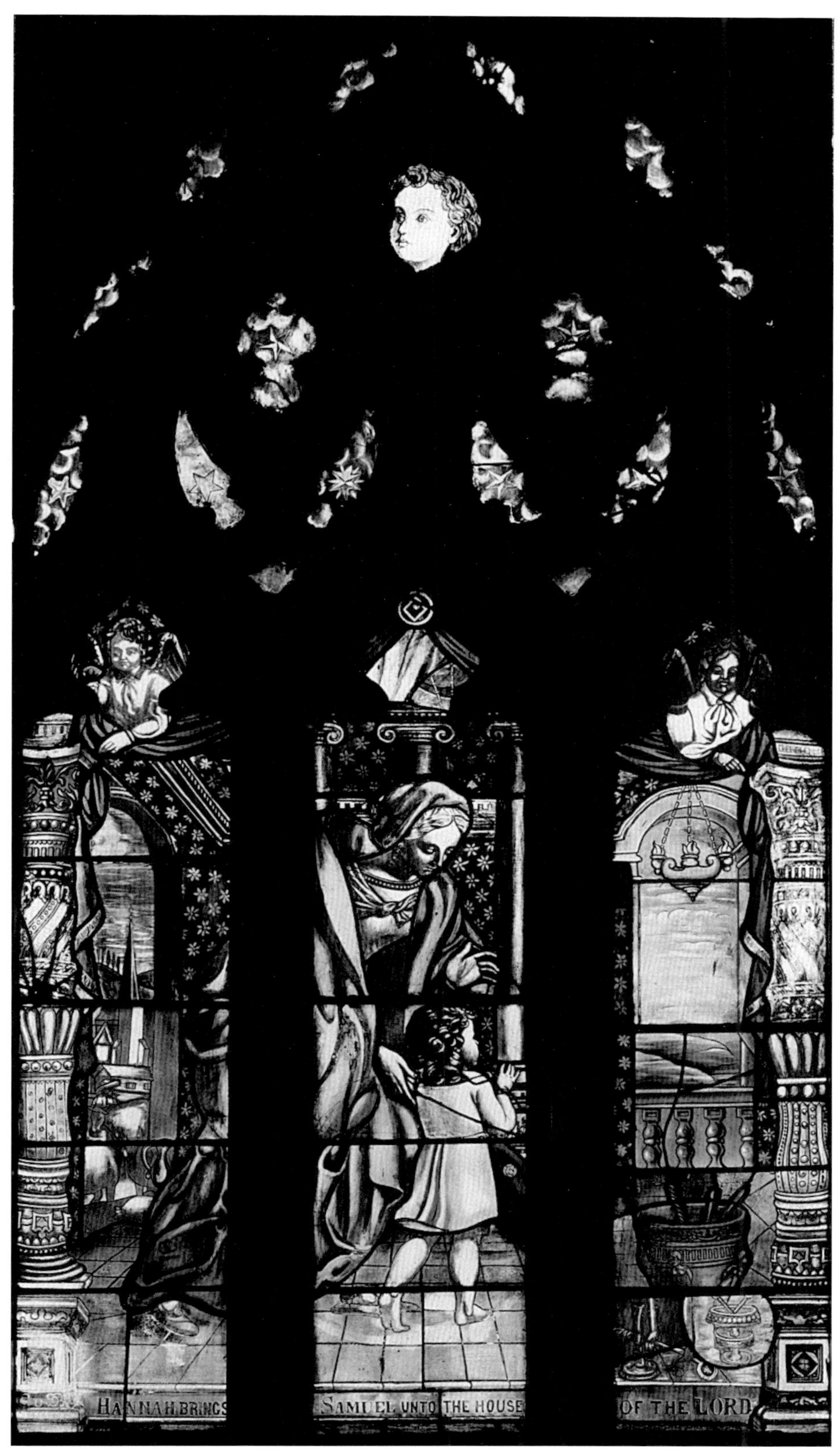

46. (St. Ann and) Holy Trinity, Brooklyn:
Hannah brings Samuel unto the house of the Lord   Cat. III:VI

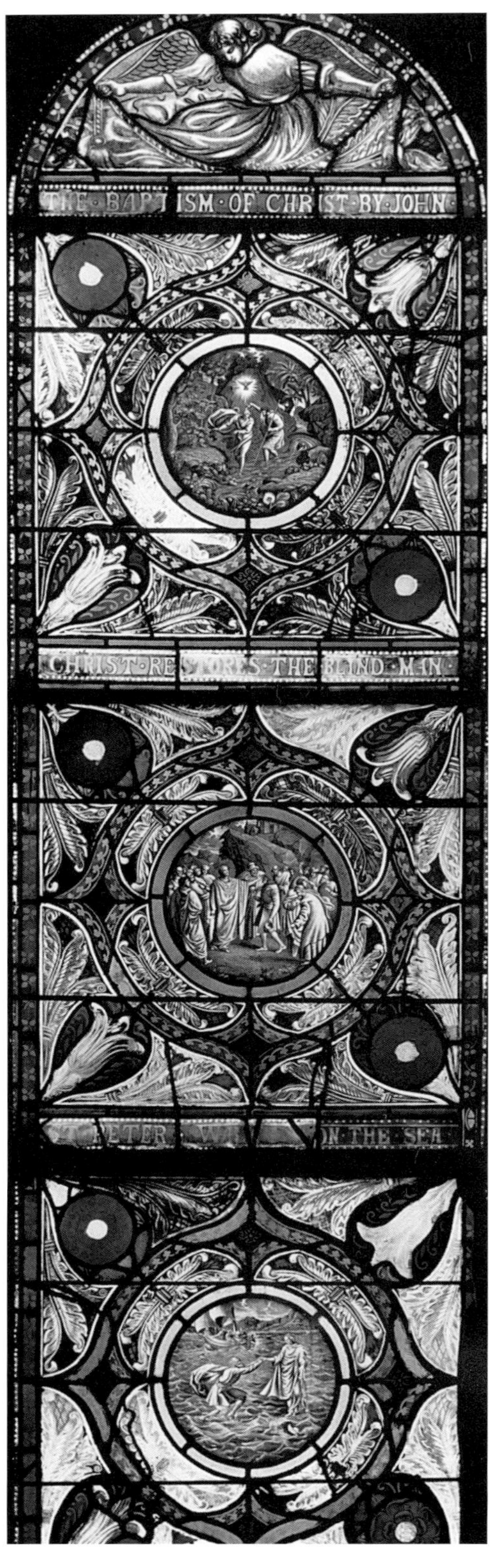
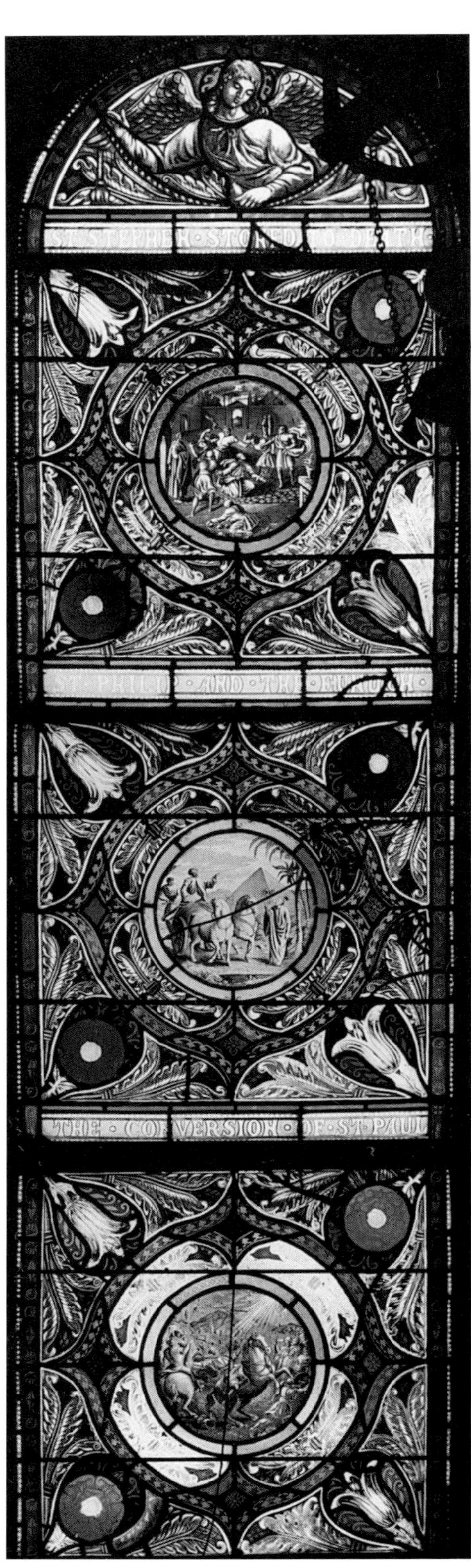

47. Holy Apostles, Manhattan: *The Baptism
of Christ by John, Christ Restores the Blind
Man, St. Peter Walks on the Sea*   Cat. IV:T8

48. Holy Apostles, Manhattan: *St. Stephen
Stoned, St. Philip and the Eunuch, The
Conversion of St. Paul*   Cat. IV:N2

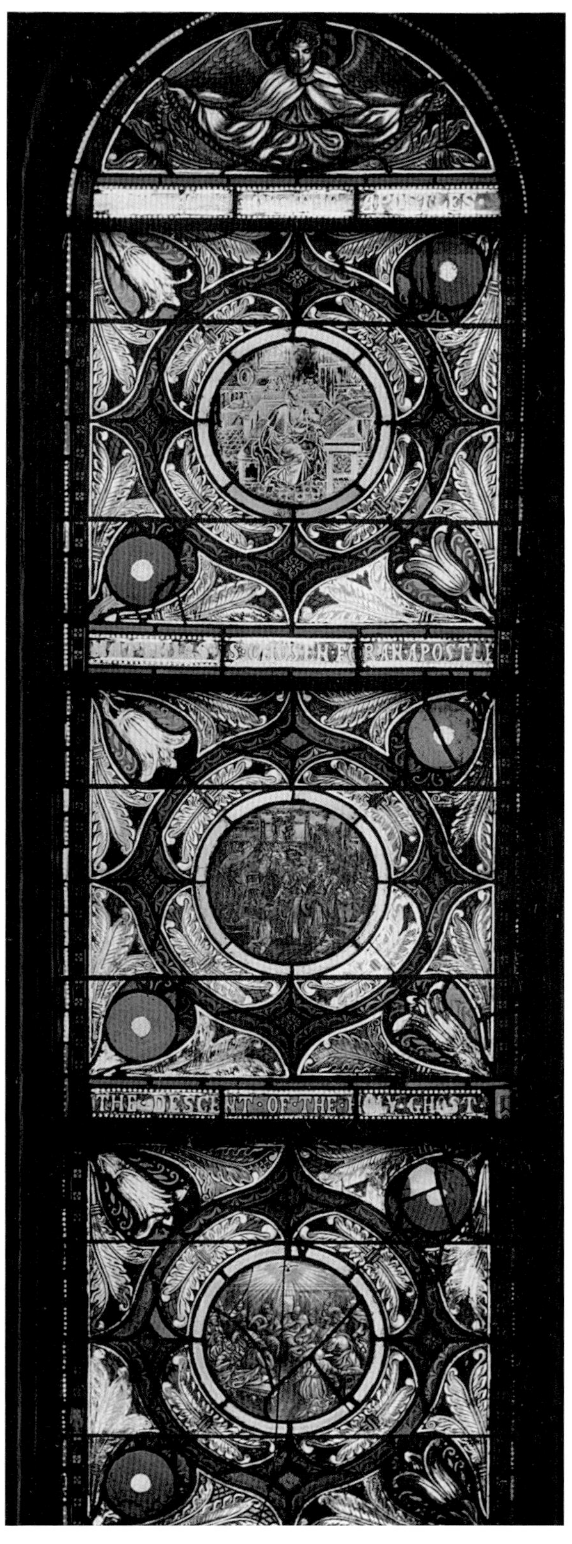

49. Holy Apostles, Manhattan: *The Acts of the Apostles, Mathias Chosen for an Apostle, The Descent of the Holy Ghost*   Cat. IV:N4

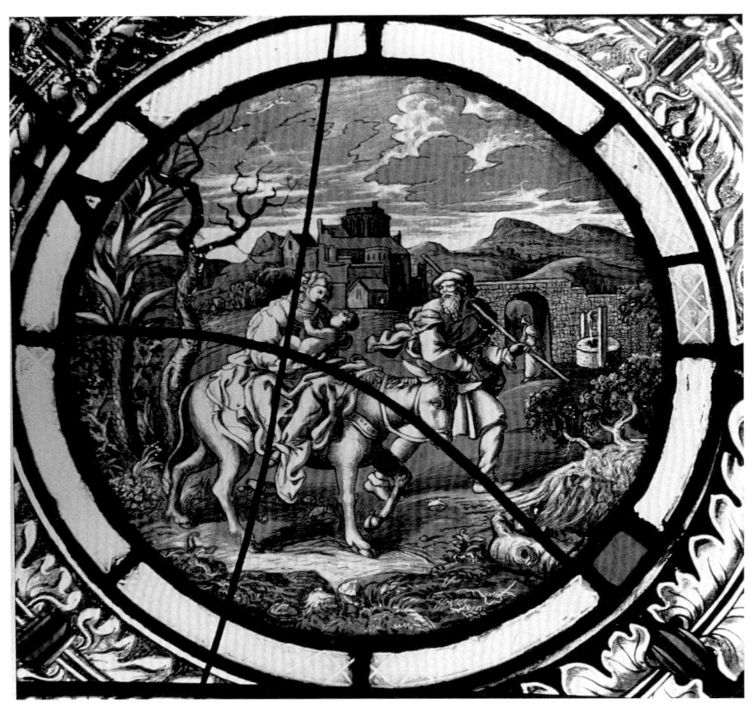

50a. Holy Apostles, Manhattan: *The Flight into Egypt,*
detail of Cat. IV:T1

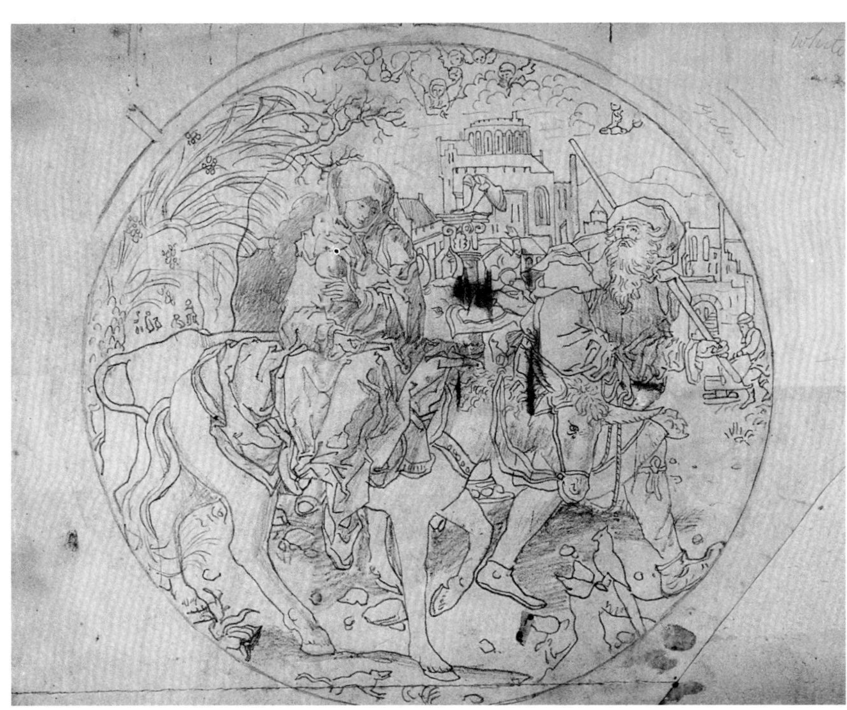

50b. Design attributed to Dirk Vellert, *The Flight into Egypt,* glass roundel,
Holy Trinity Church, Bradford-on-Avon, tracing by William Jay Bolton
(Long Island Diocese Archives, Garden City, N.Y.)   Cat. IX:12a

212

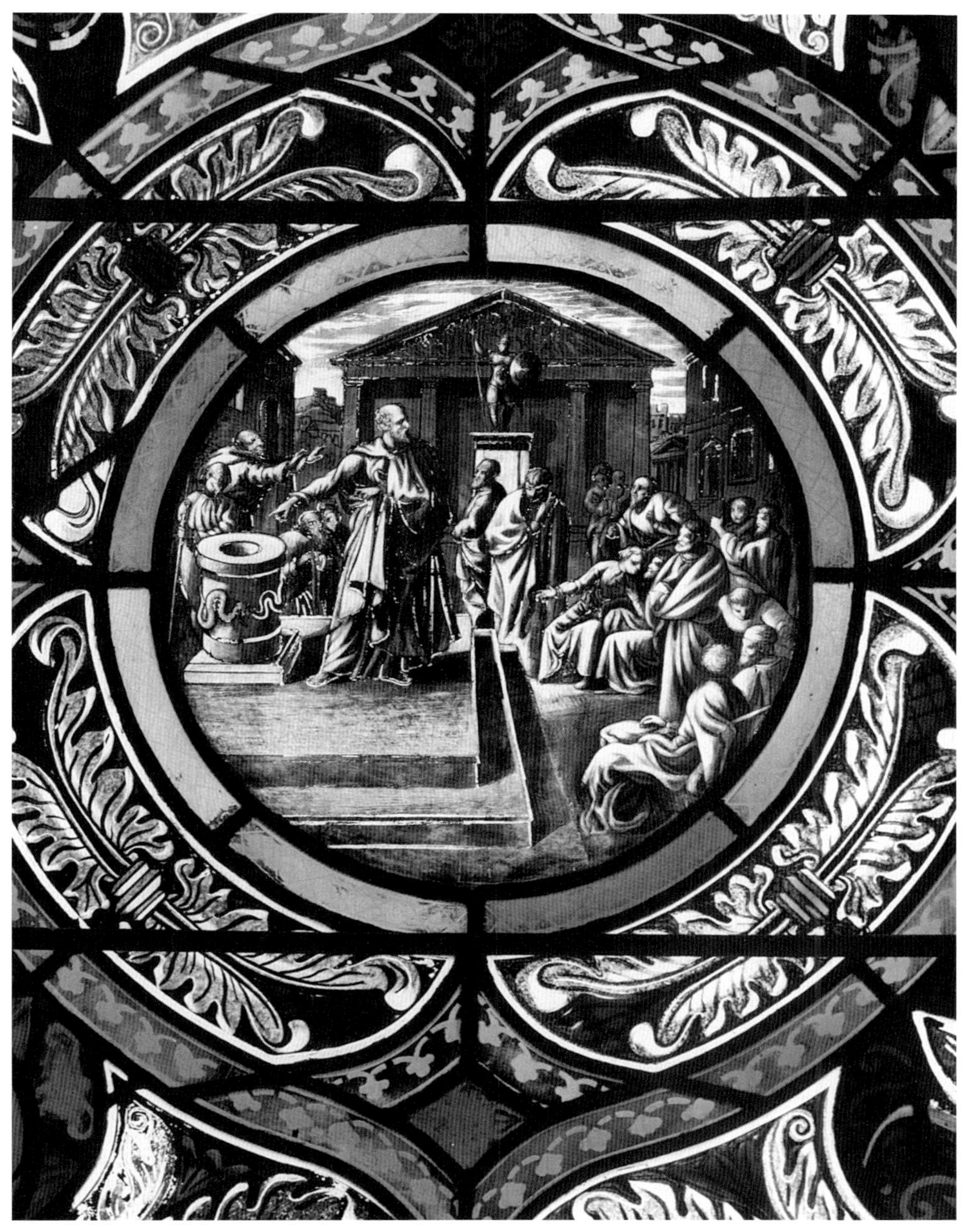

51. Holy Apostles, Manhattan: *St. Paul Preaching at Athens,* detail of Cat. IV:N6b

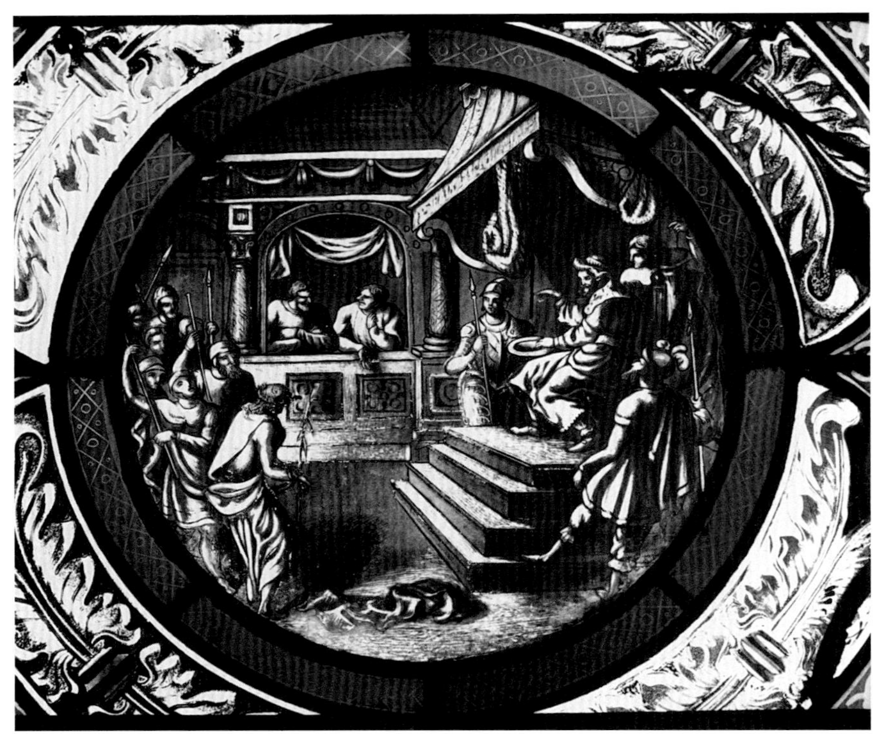

52. Holy Apostles, Manhattan: *Christ Tried before Pontius Pilate*, detail of Cat. IV:T2b

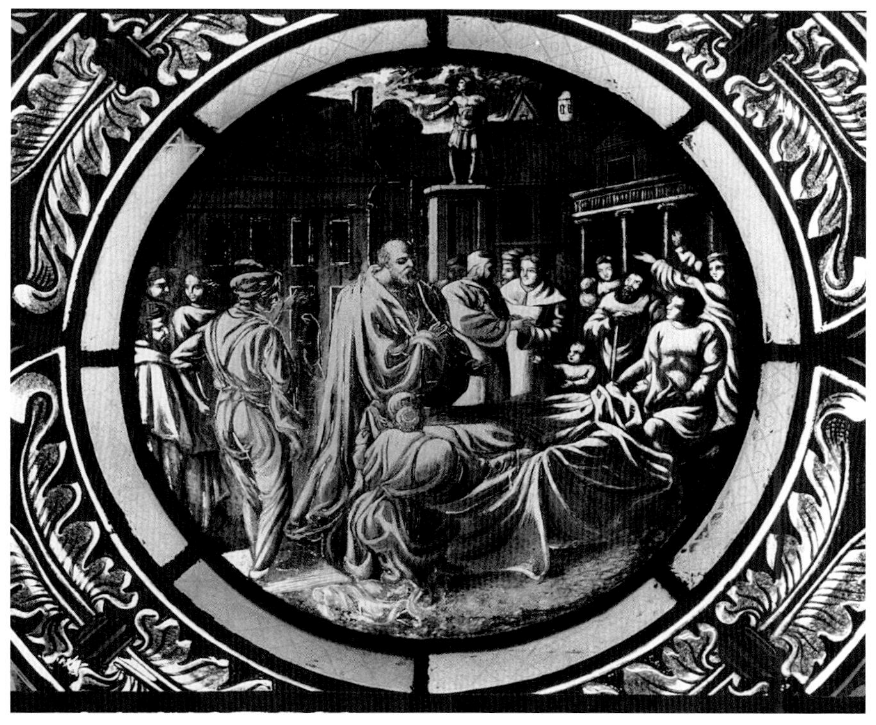

53. Holy Apostles, Manhattan: *St. Peter Healing the Sick,* detail of Cat. IV:N5b

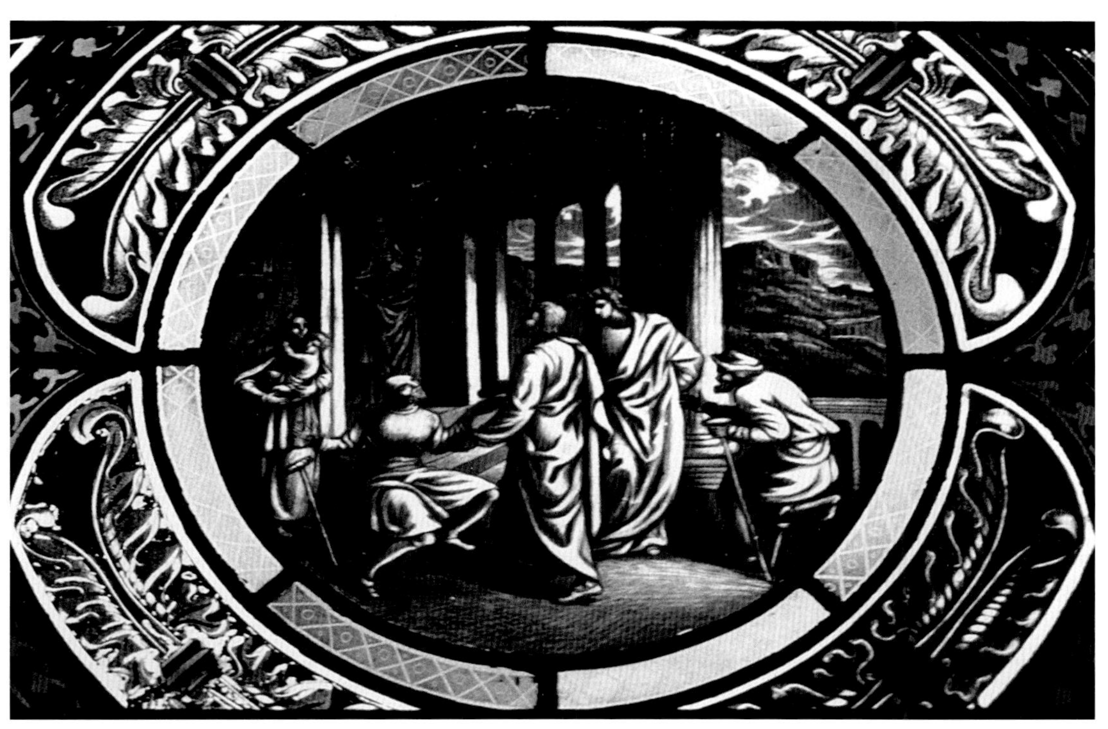

54. *St. Peter & St. John Heal the Lame,* detail of Cat. IV:N3a

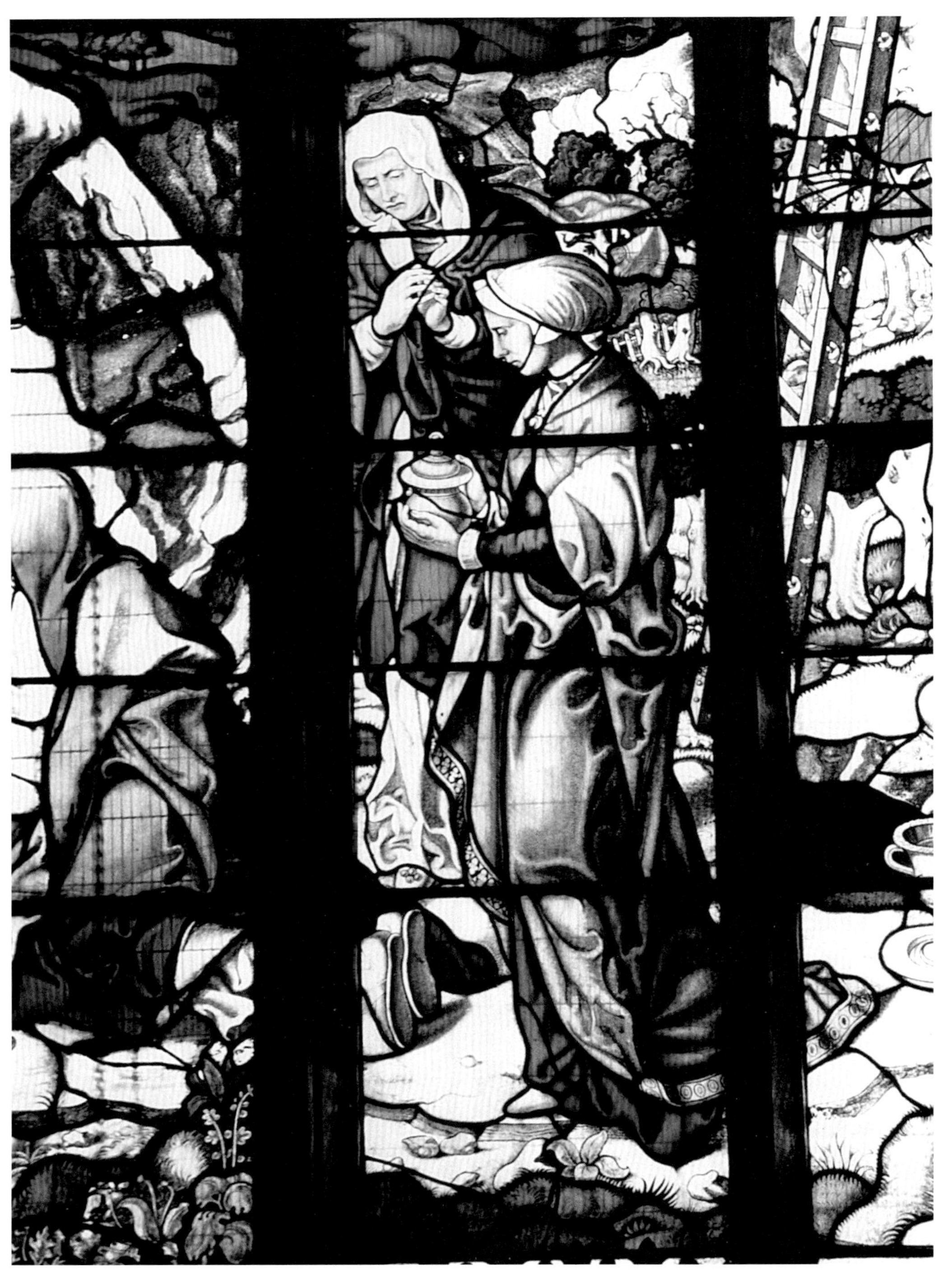

55. St. Peter's, West Lynn: *The Angel at the Tomb,* detail (Photo: W. B. Clark)

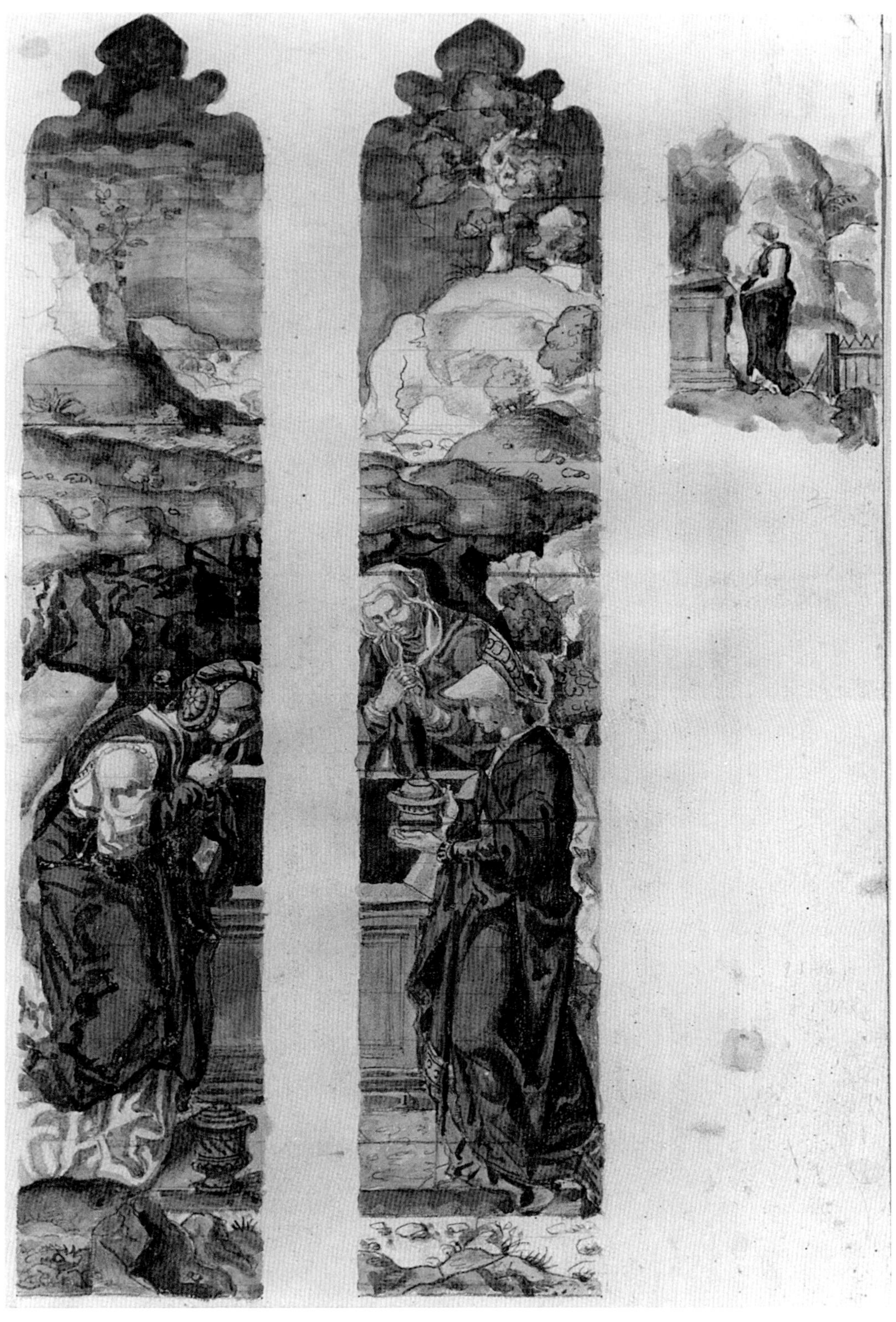

56. King's College Chapel, Cambridge: *The Three Women at the Tomb,*
window 17A, watercolor by William Jay Bolton
(Long Island Diocese Archives, Garden City, N.Y.)   Cat. IX:13i

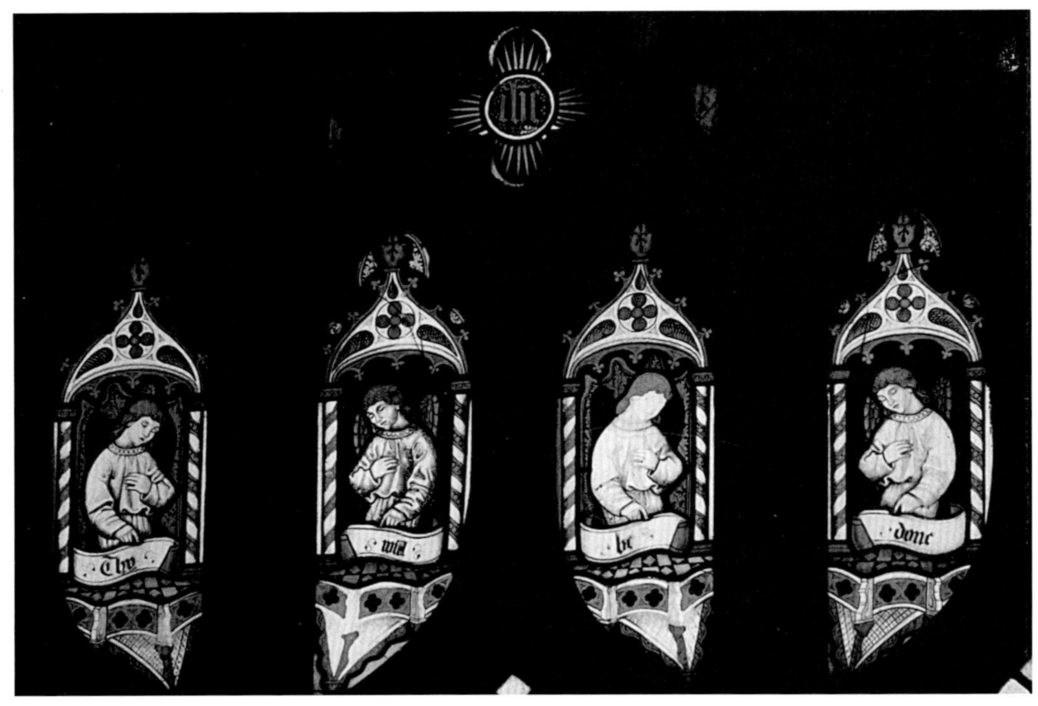

57. St. Peter's, West Lynn: Angels in nave window (Photo: Hilary Wayment)   Cat. V:N3

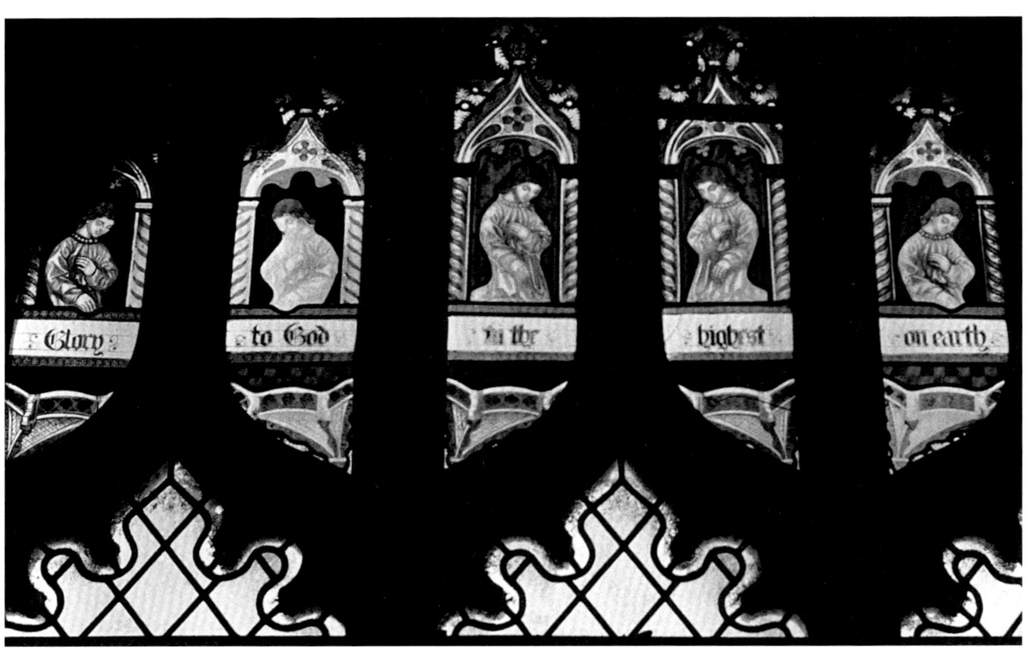

58. St. Andrew's, Cambridge: Angels in gallery window tracery
(Photo: W. B. Clark)   Cat. VI:G4

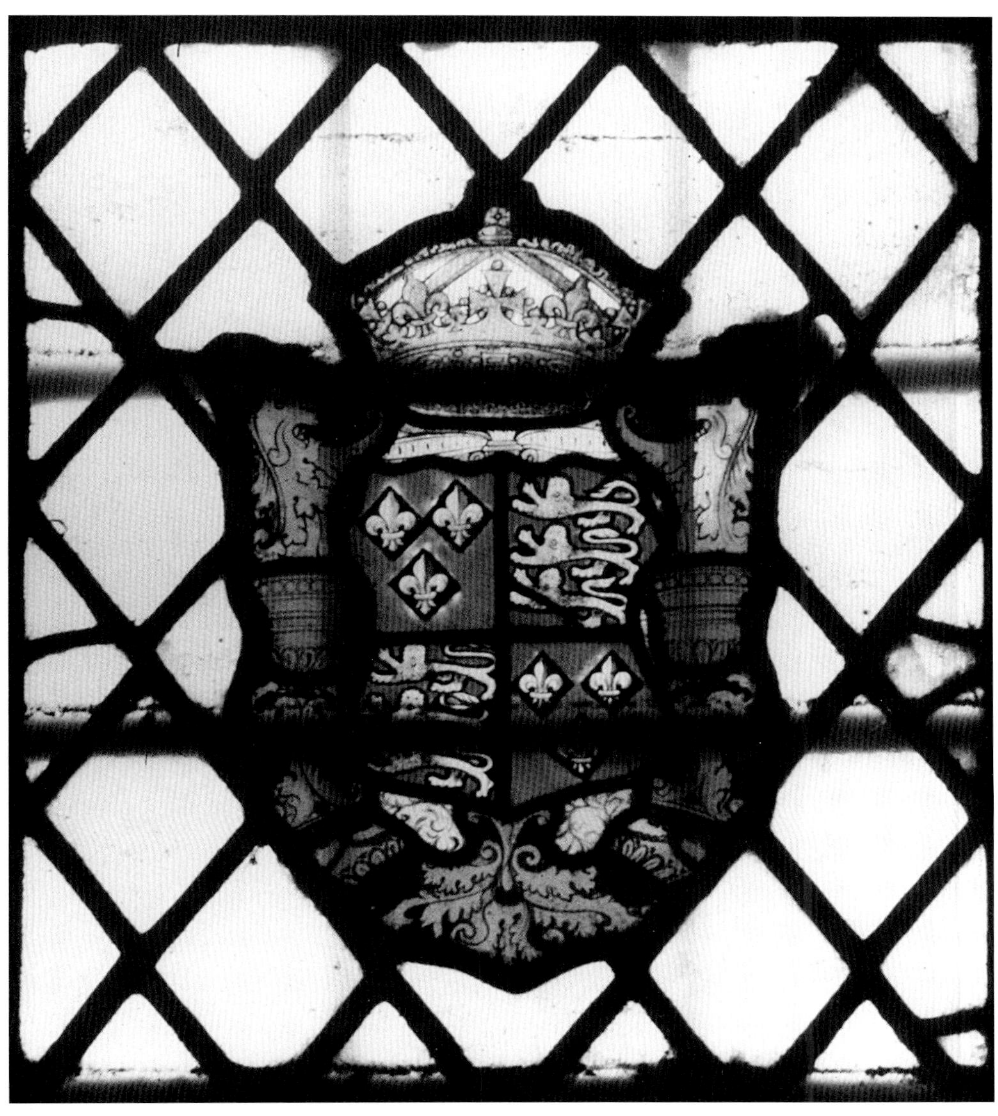

59. William Jay Bolton, armorial at King's College Chapel,
side chapel F, window 30   Cat. VII

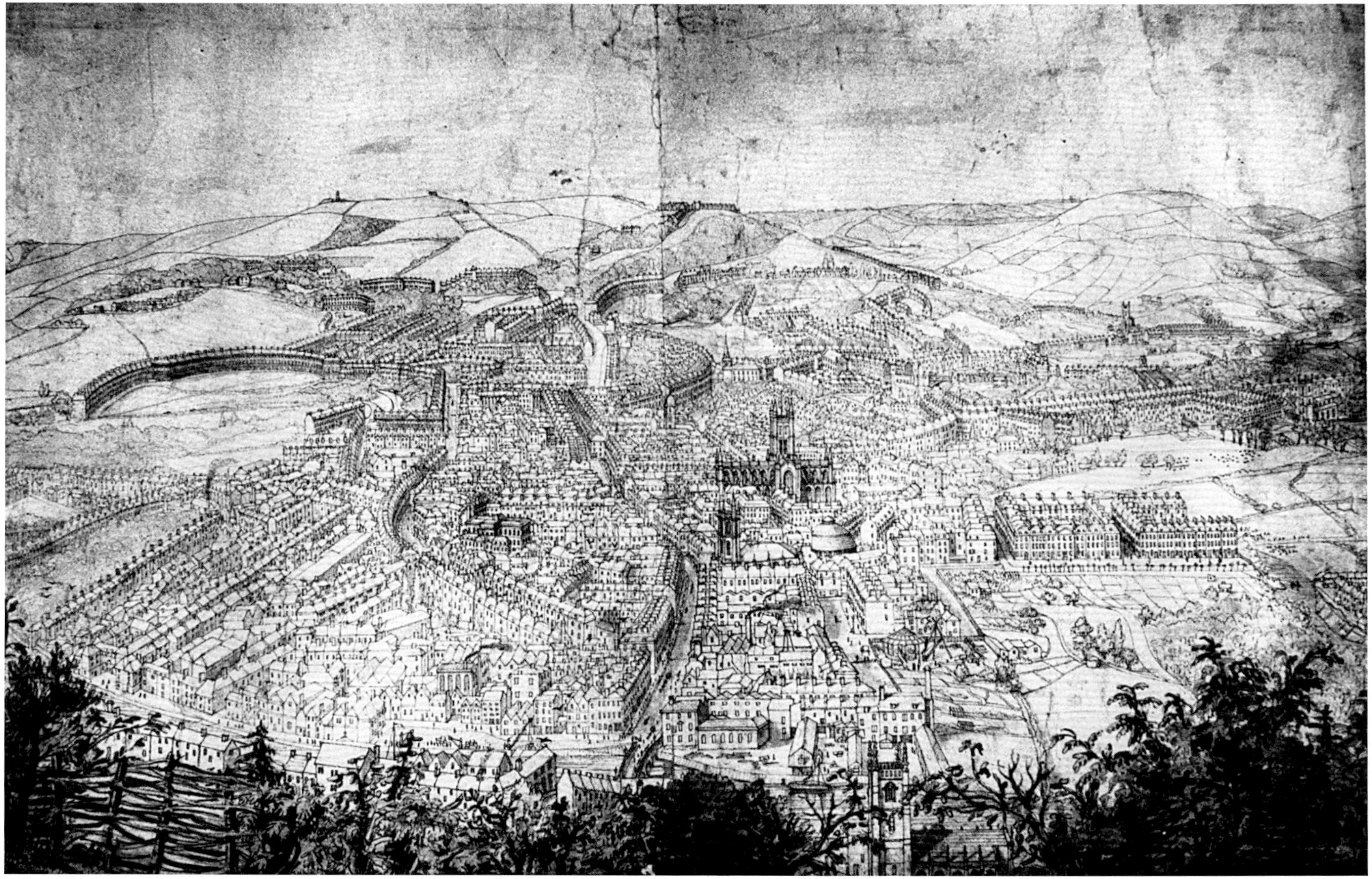

60. William Jay Bolton, *The City of Bath from Beechen Cliffs*, 1834 (Bath, Victoria Art Gallery; photo: the museum)   Cat. IX:5

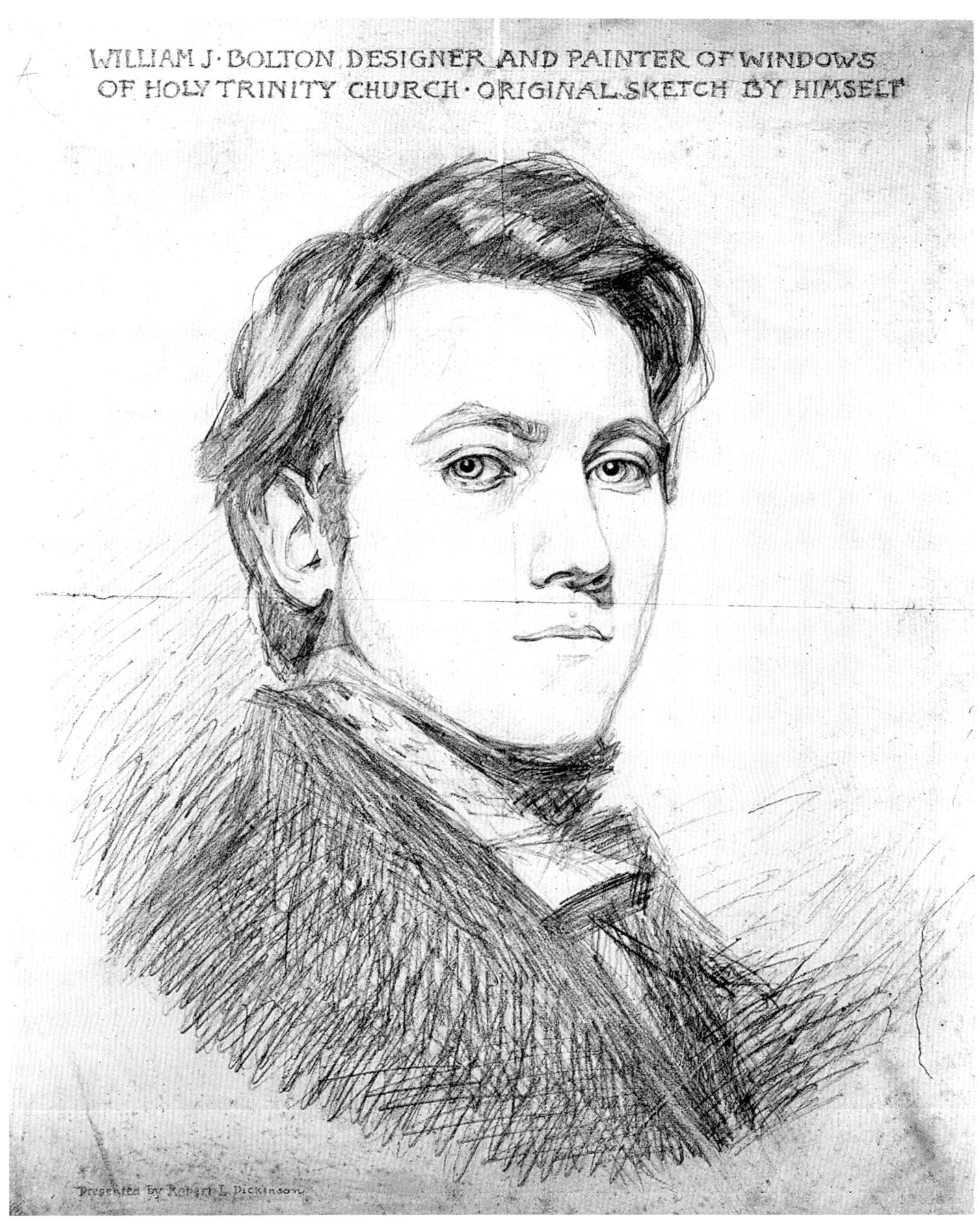

61. William Jay Bolton, self-portrait, pencil
(missing; formerly Church of St. Ann and Holy Trinity, Brooklyn)   Cat. IX:6

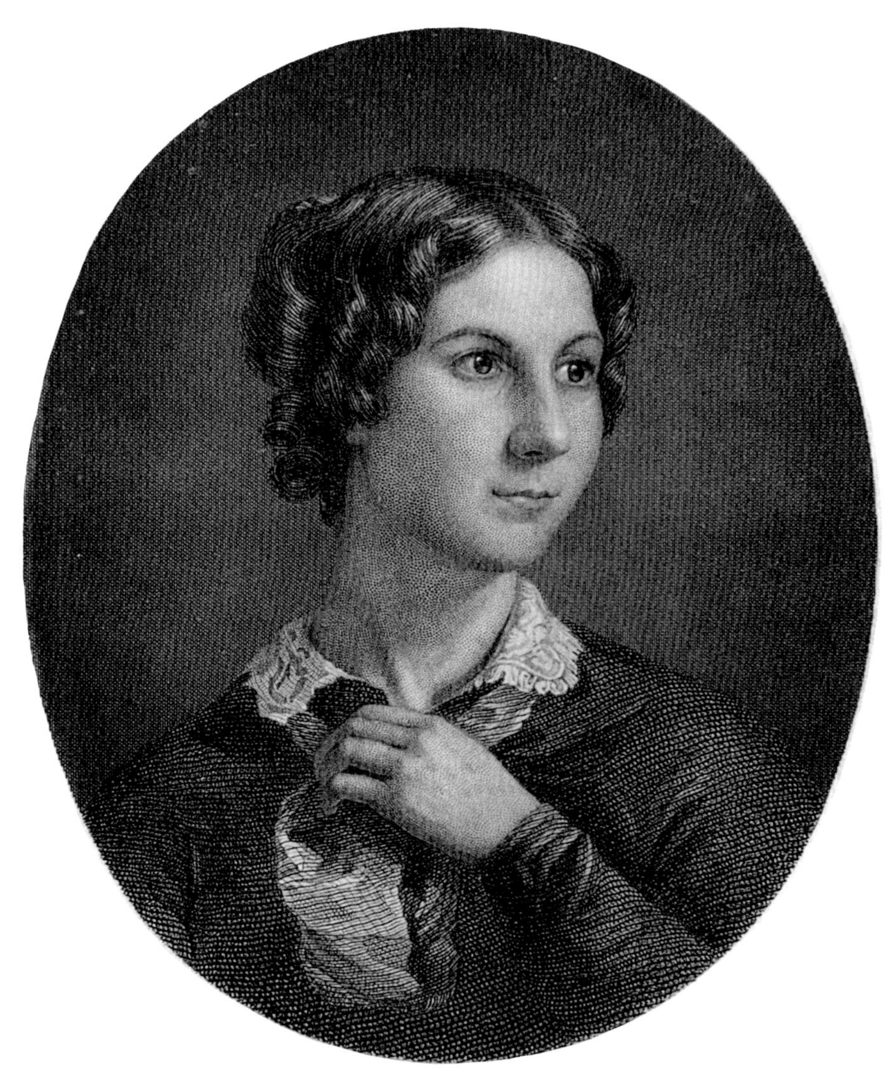

62. William Jay Bolton, engraving of portrait of Abby Bolton
(frontispiece, Rhoda Bolton, *The Lighted Valley*)
(Photo: Cambridge Univ. Library)   Cat. IX:4

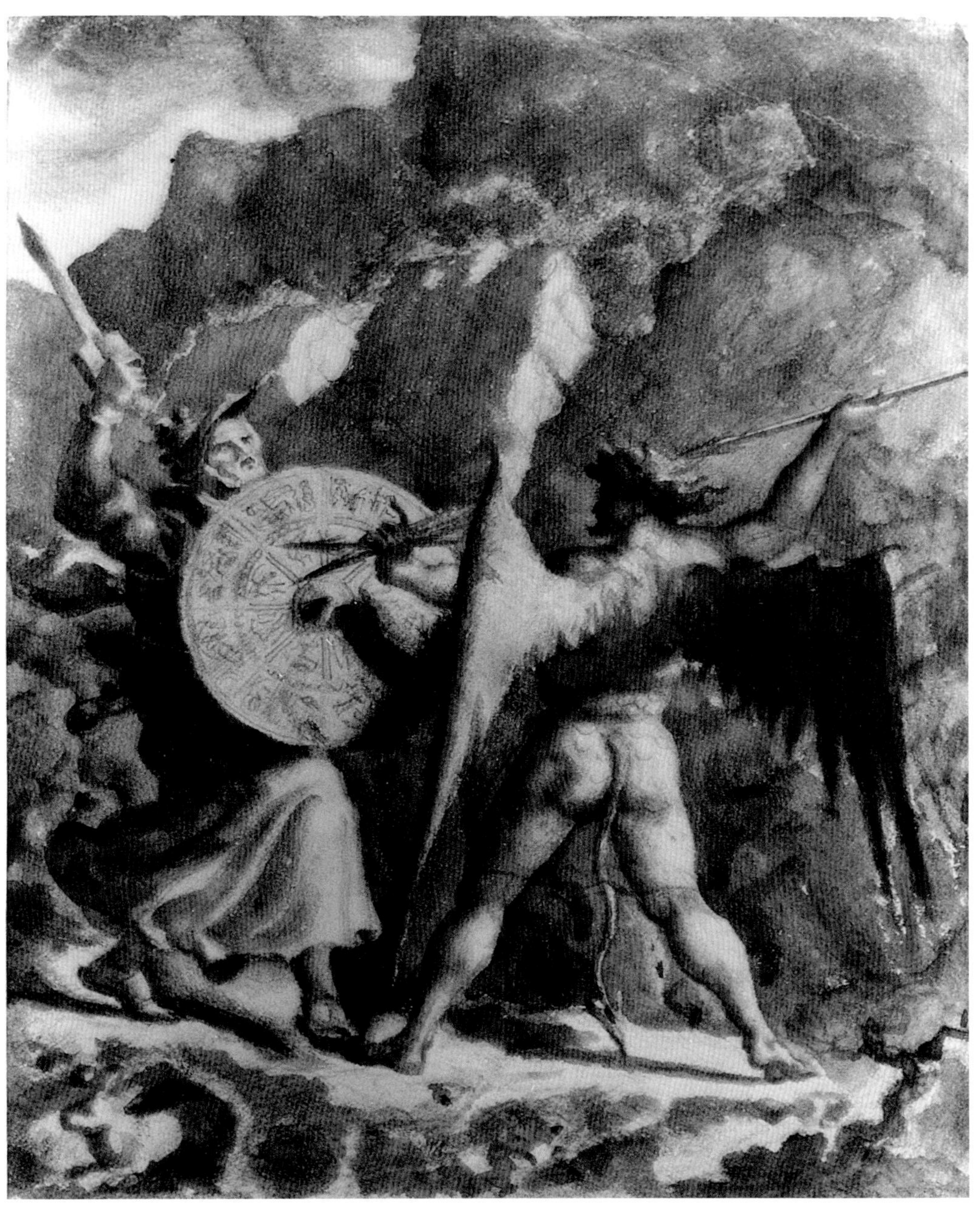

63. William Jay Bolton, *Man and devil fighting,* watercolor
(Long Island Diocese Archives, Garden City, N.Y.)   Cat. IX:9

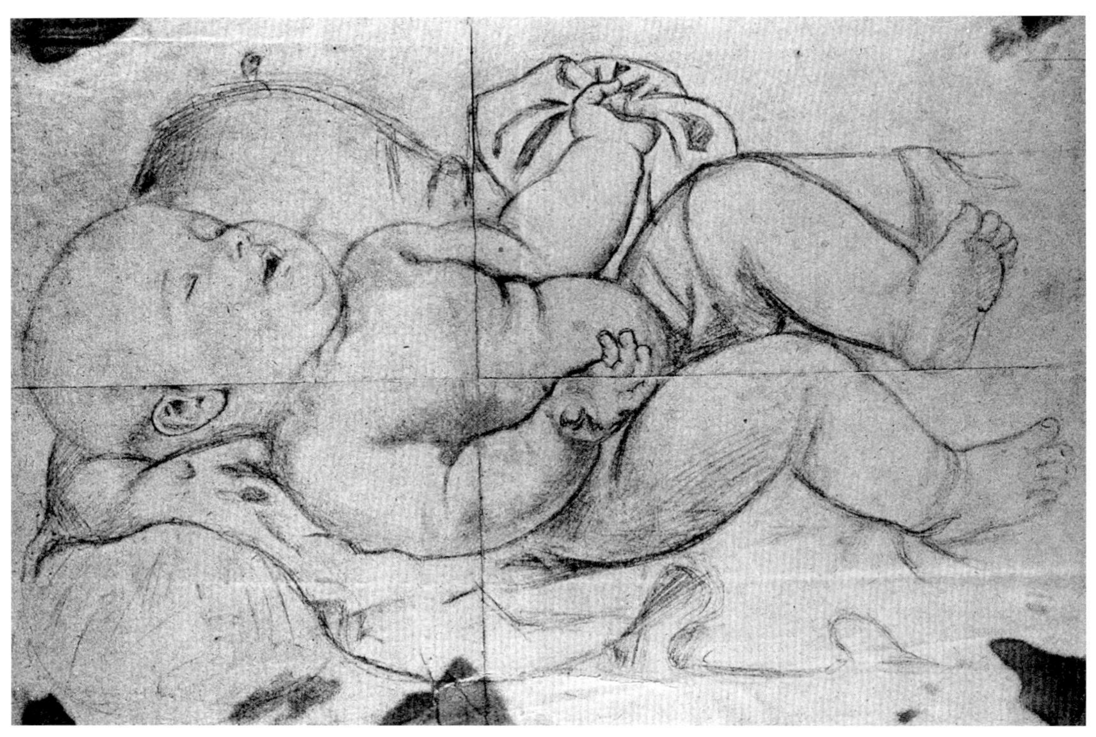

64. William Jay Bolton, cartoon for the Babe in *The Birth of Christ,*
(St. Ann and) Holy Trinity, Brooklyn, window G8
(missing; formerly St. Ann and Holy Trinity, Brooklyn)   Cat. IX:11k

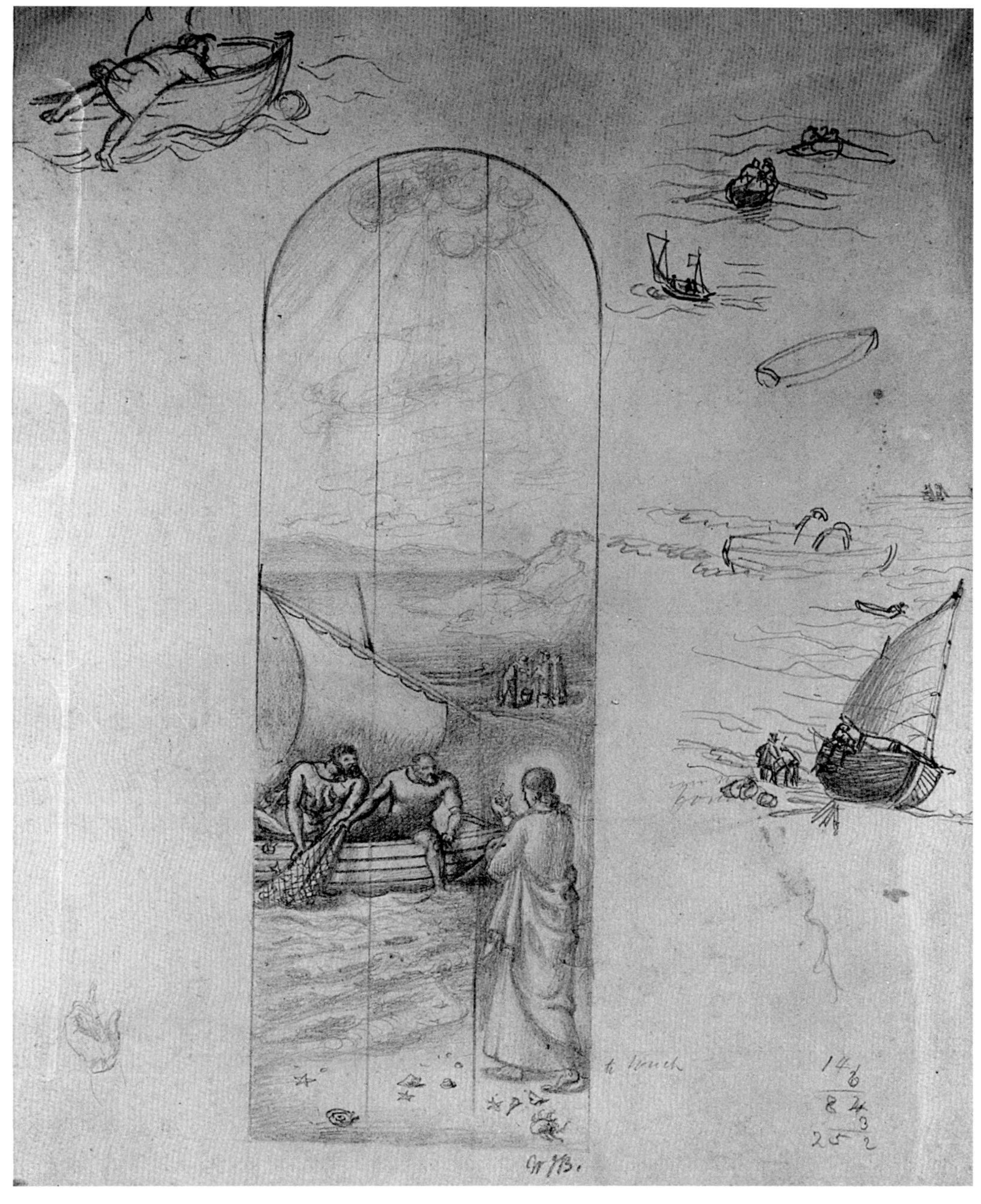

65. William Jay Bolton, *The Calling of Peter*, pencil
(Long Island Diocese Archives, Garden City, N.Y.)   Cat. IX:12c

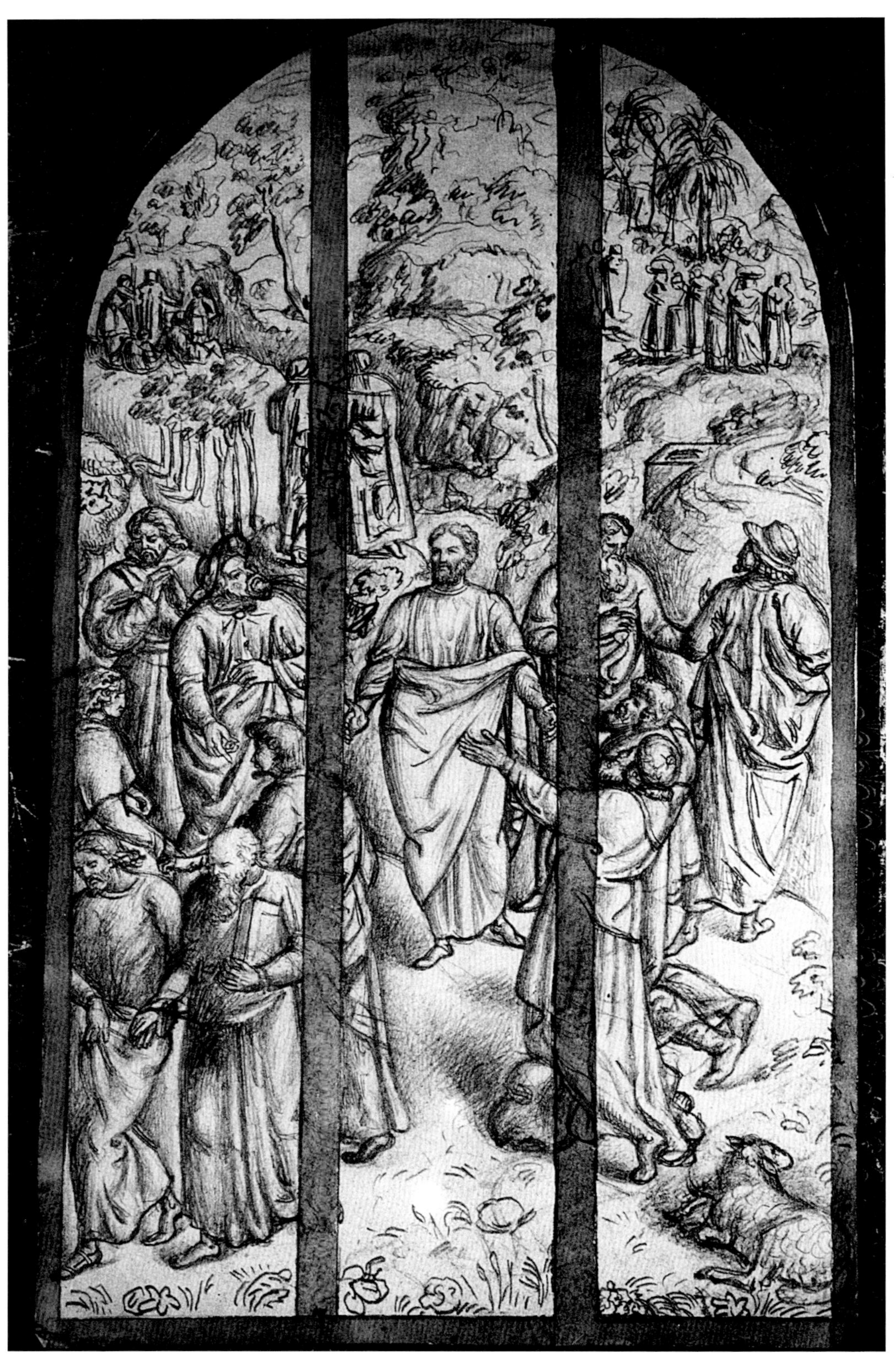

66. William Jay Bolton, *St. Peter Distributing Alms,* pencil
(Long Island Diocese Archives, Garden City, N.Y.)   Cat. IX:12d

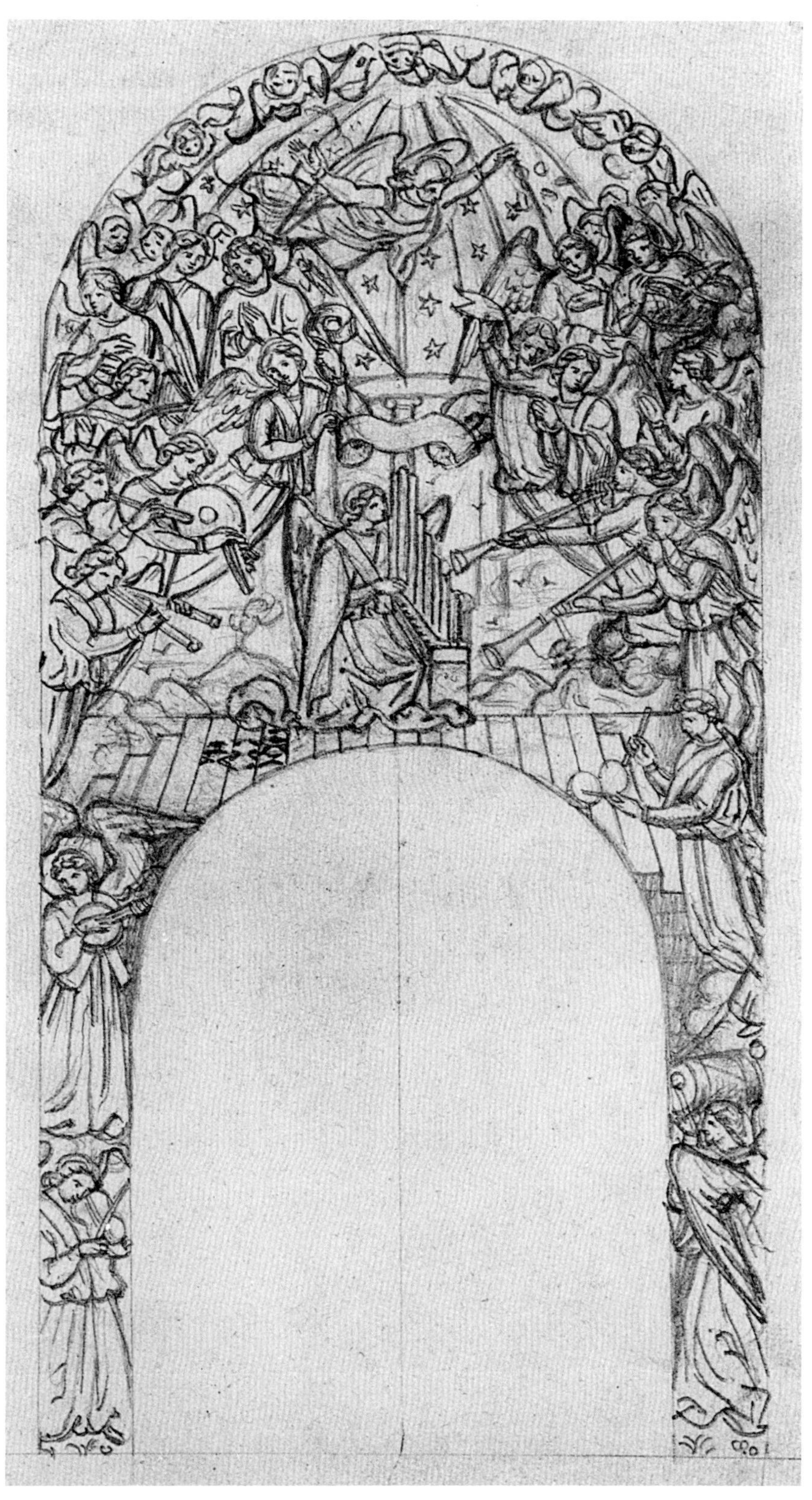

67. William Jay Bolton, Angelic musicians, pencil
(Long Island Diocese Archives, Garden City, N.Y.)   Cat. IX:12e

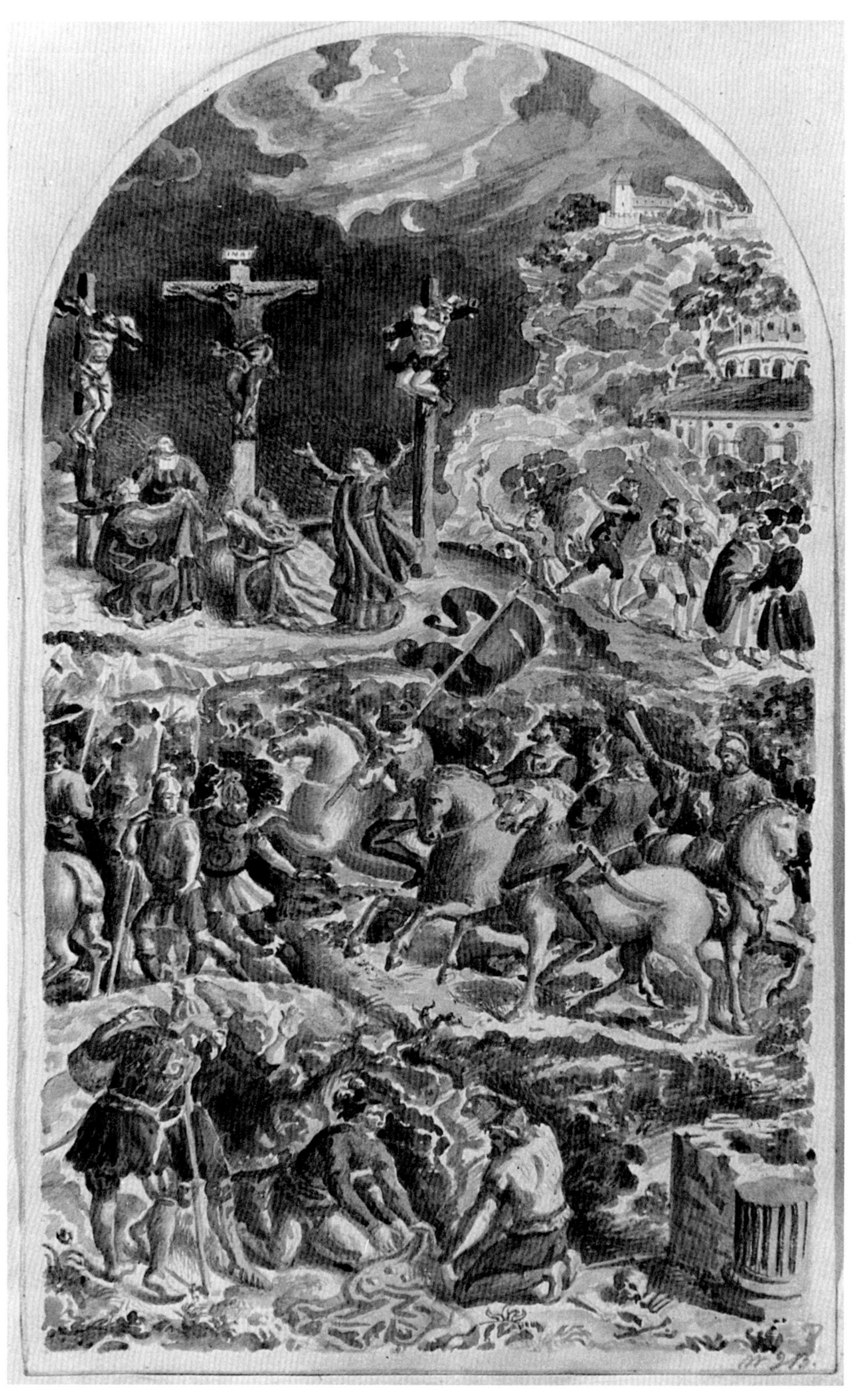

68. William Jay Bolton, *Crucifixion,* watercolor
(Long Island Diocese Archives, Garden City, N.Y.)   Cat. IX:13b

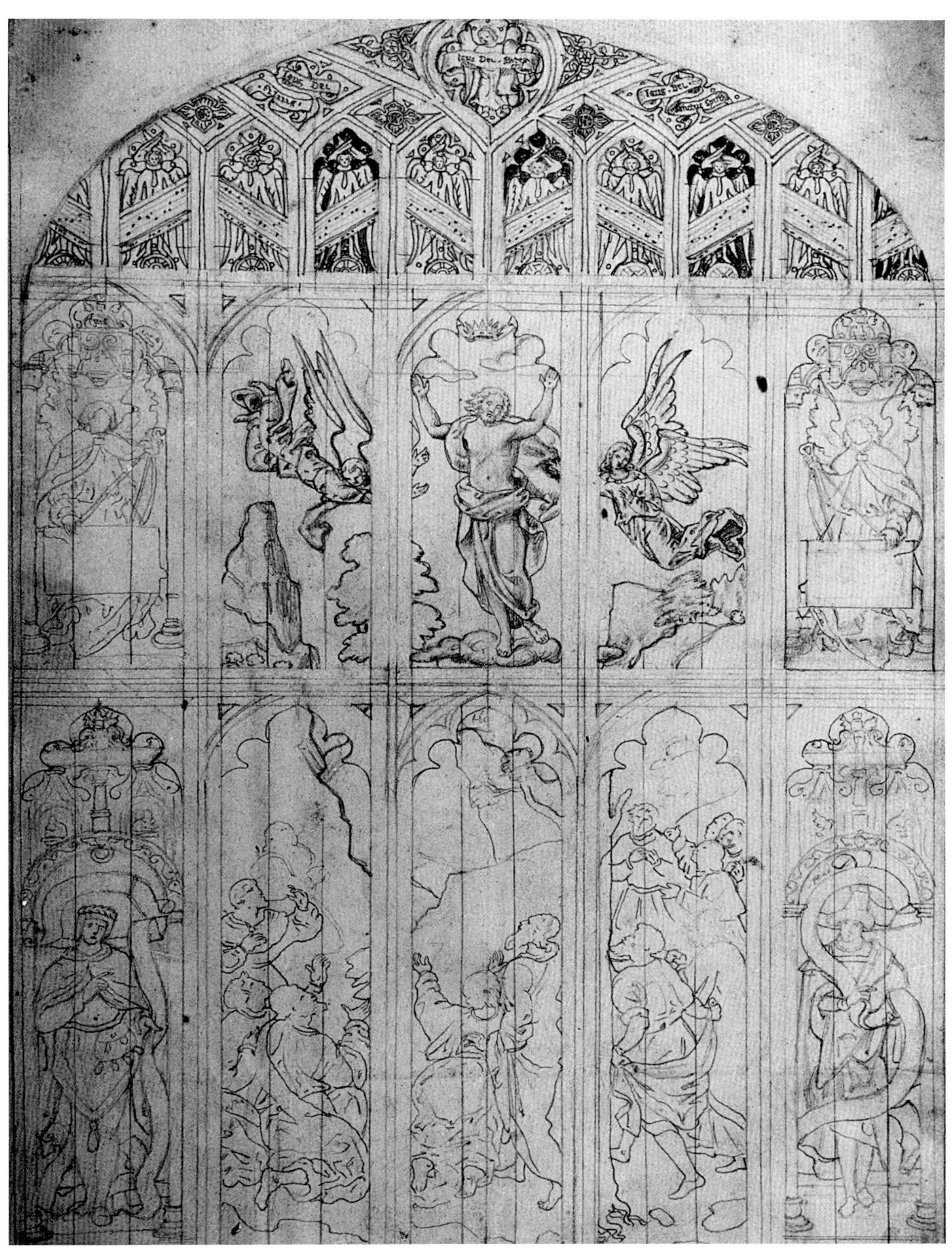

69. William Jay Bolton, *The Ascension of Christ,* pencil, pen and ink
(Long Island Diocese Archives, Garden City, N.Y.)   Cat. IX:13e

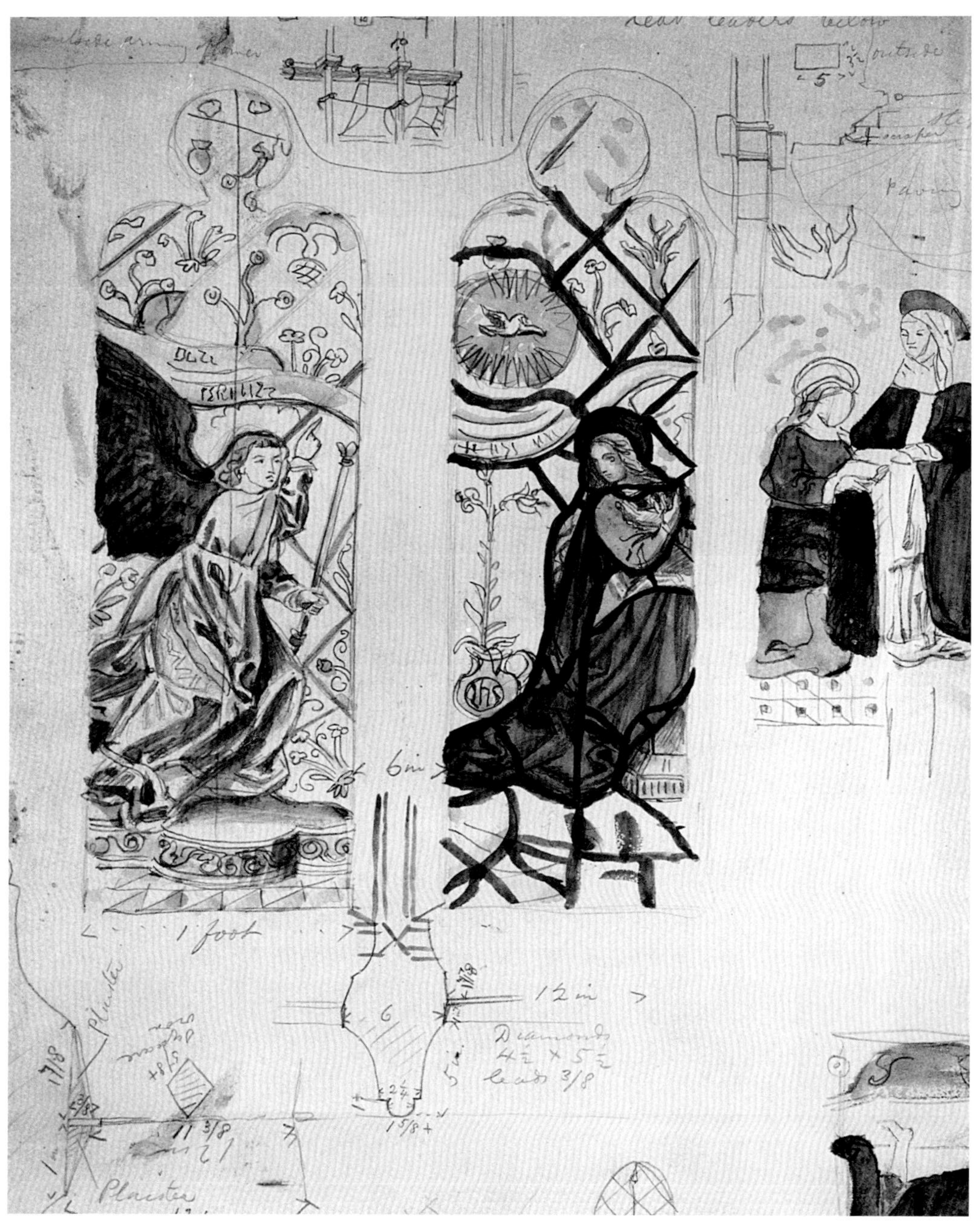

70. King's College Chapel, Cambridge: *Annunciation,* window 50, watercolor sketch by William Jay Bolton (Long Island Diocese Archives, Garden City, N.Y.)   Cat. IX:13i

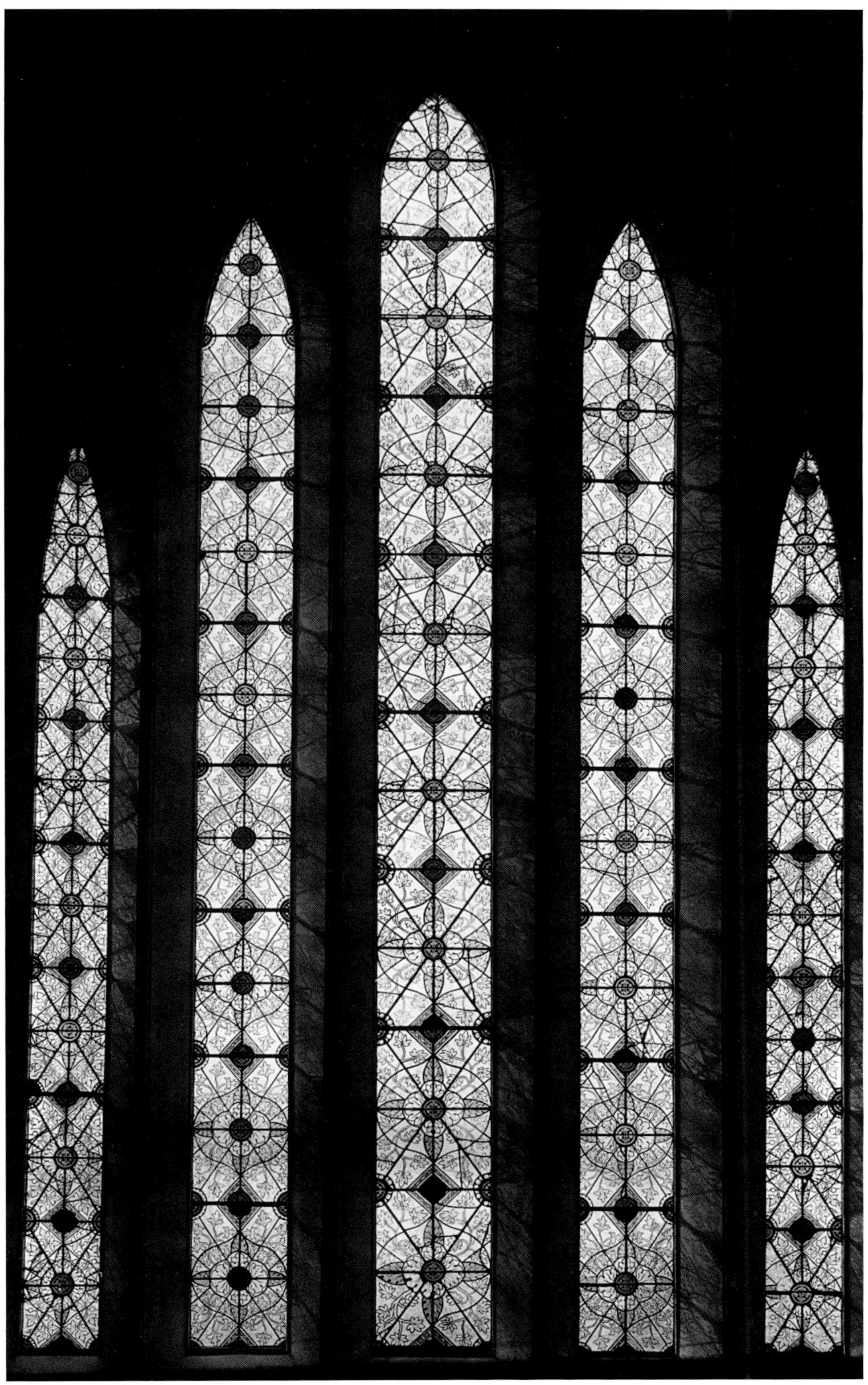

71. Church of St. Mary, Scarborough, N.Y.: Five west windows by John Bolton

231

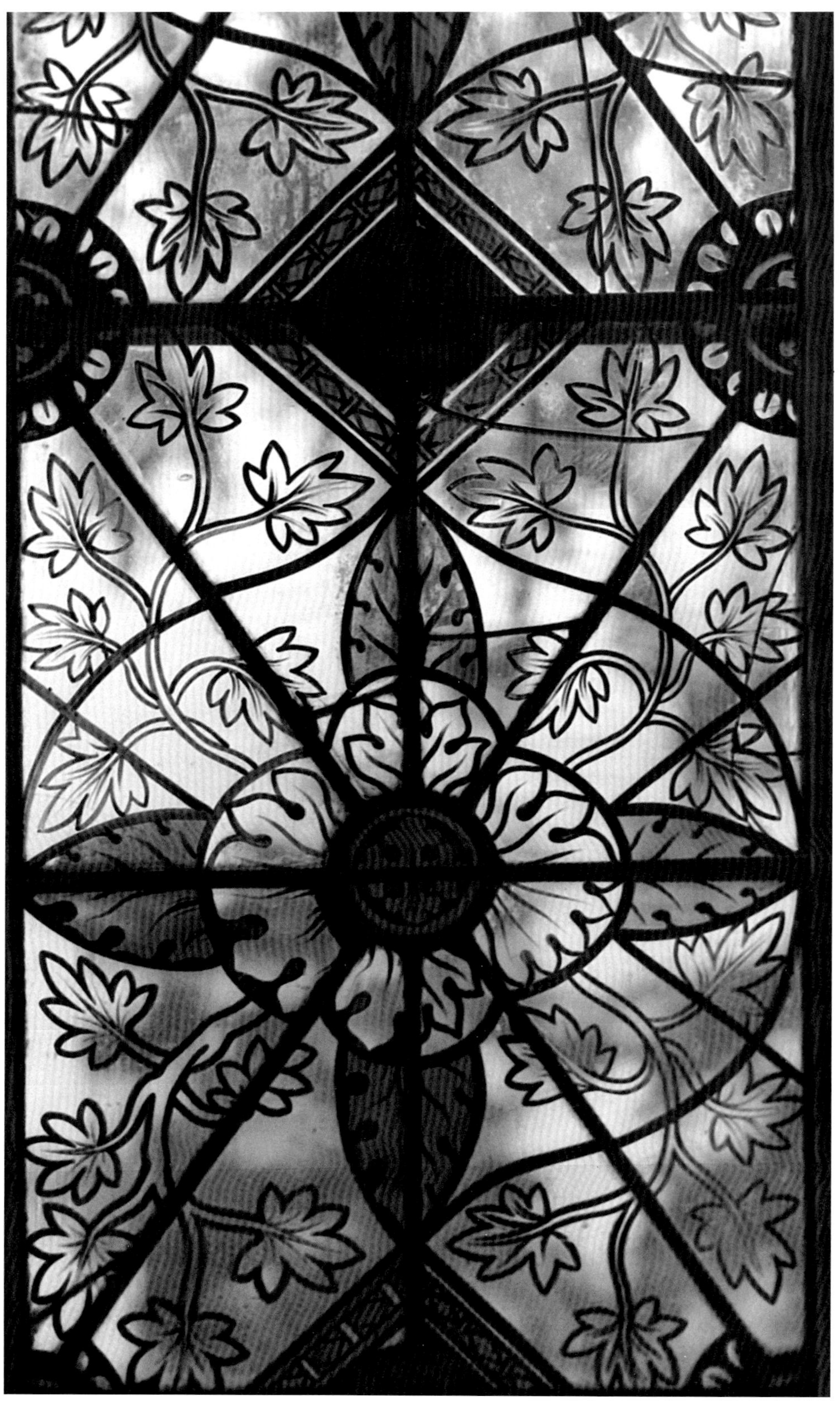

72. Church of St. Mary, Scarborough, N.Y.: Five west windows, detail

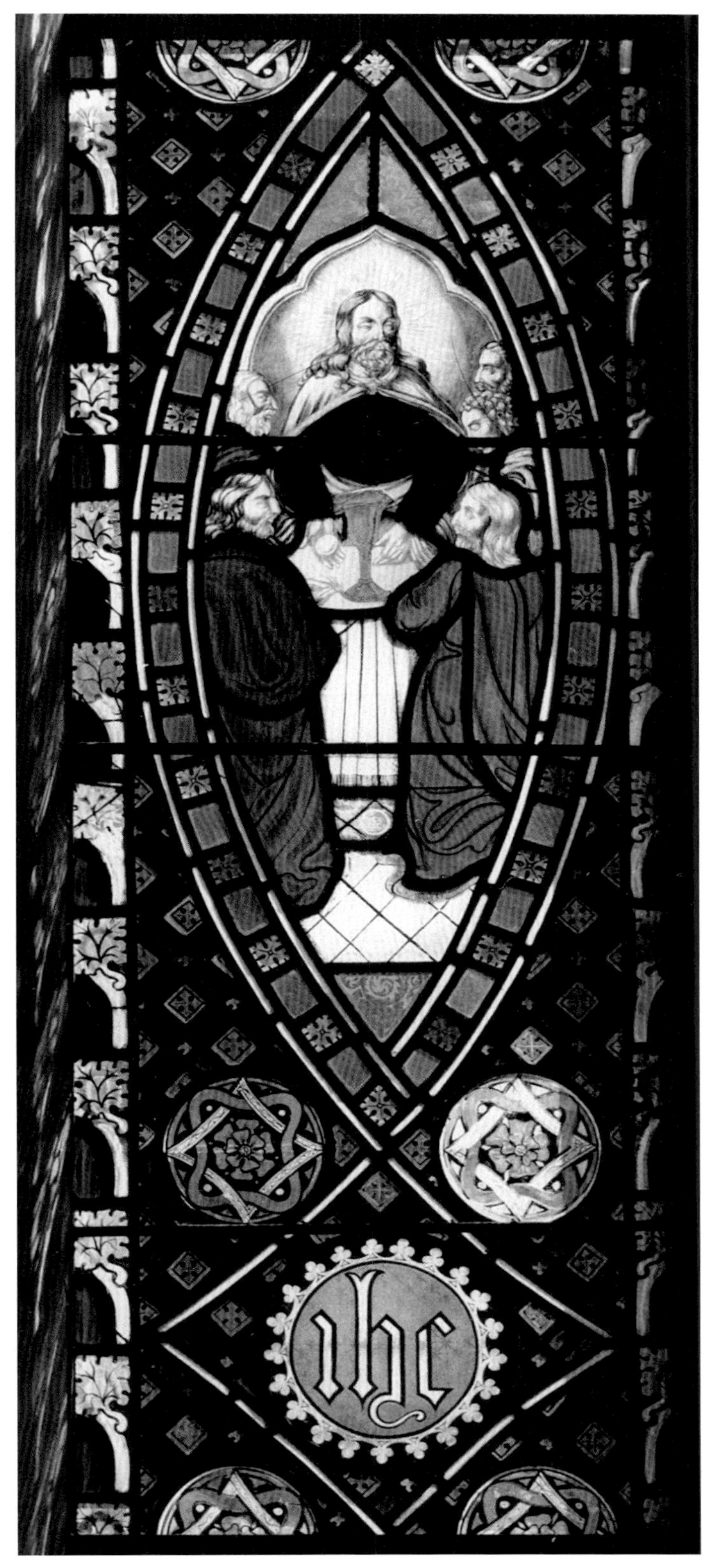

73. Church of St. Mary, Scarborough, N.Y.:
Altar window by John Bolton, detail

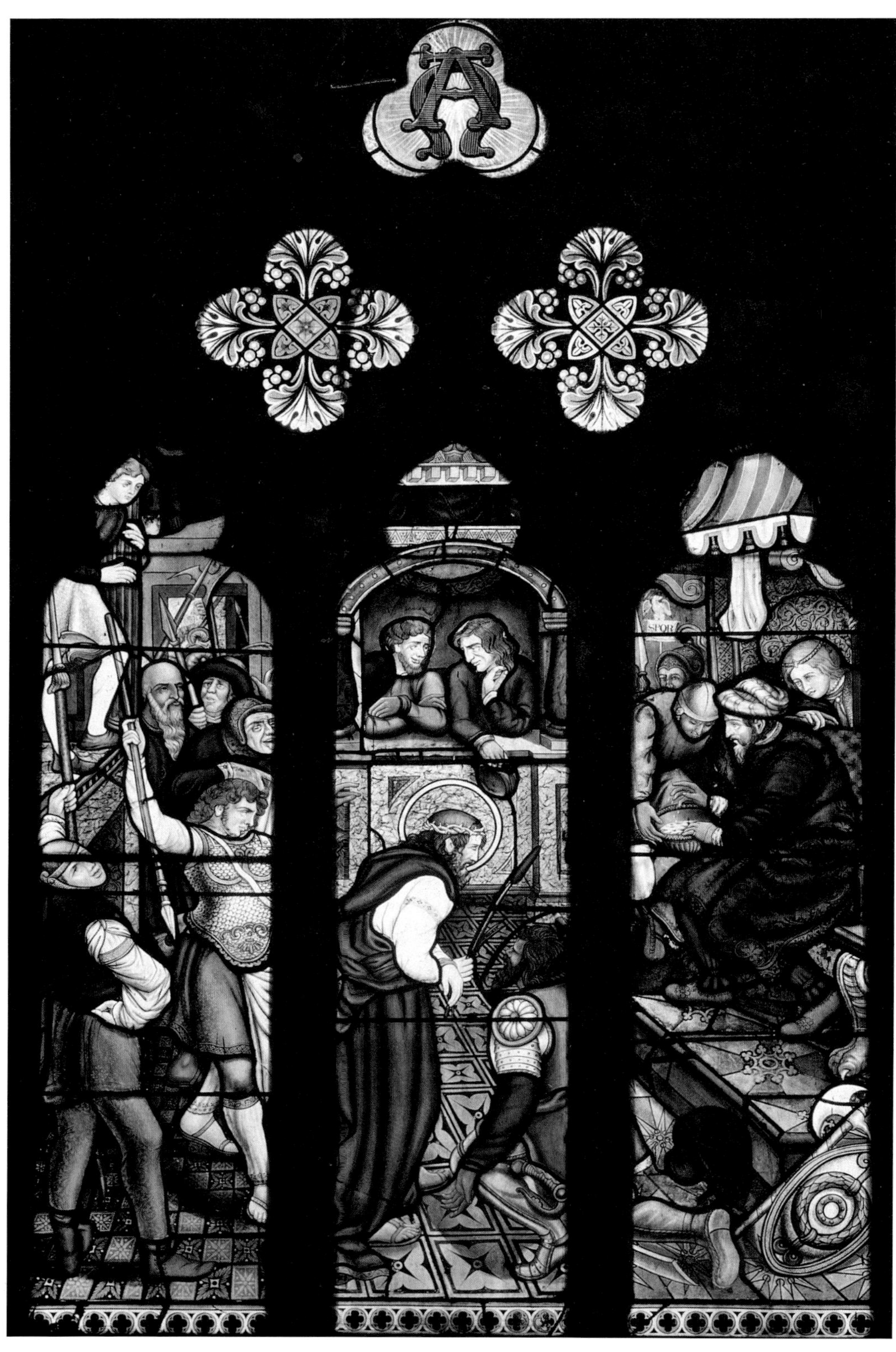

74. Grace Church, City Island, N.Y.: *The Trial of Christ,*
altar window by John Bolton on design by ?William Jay Bolton

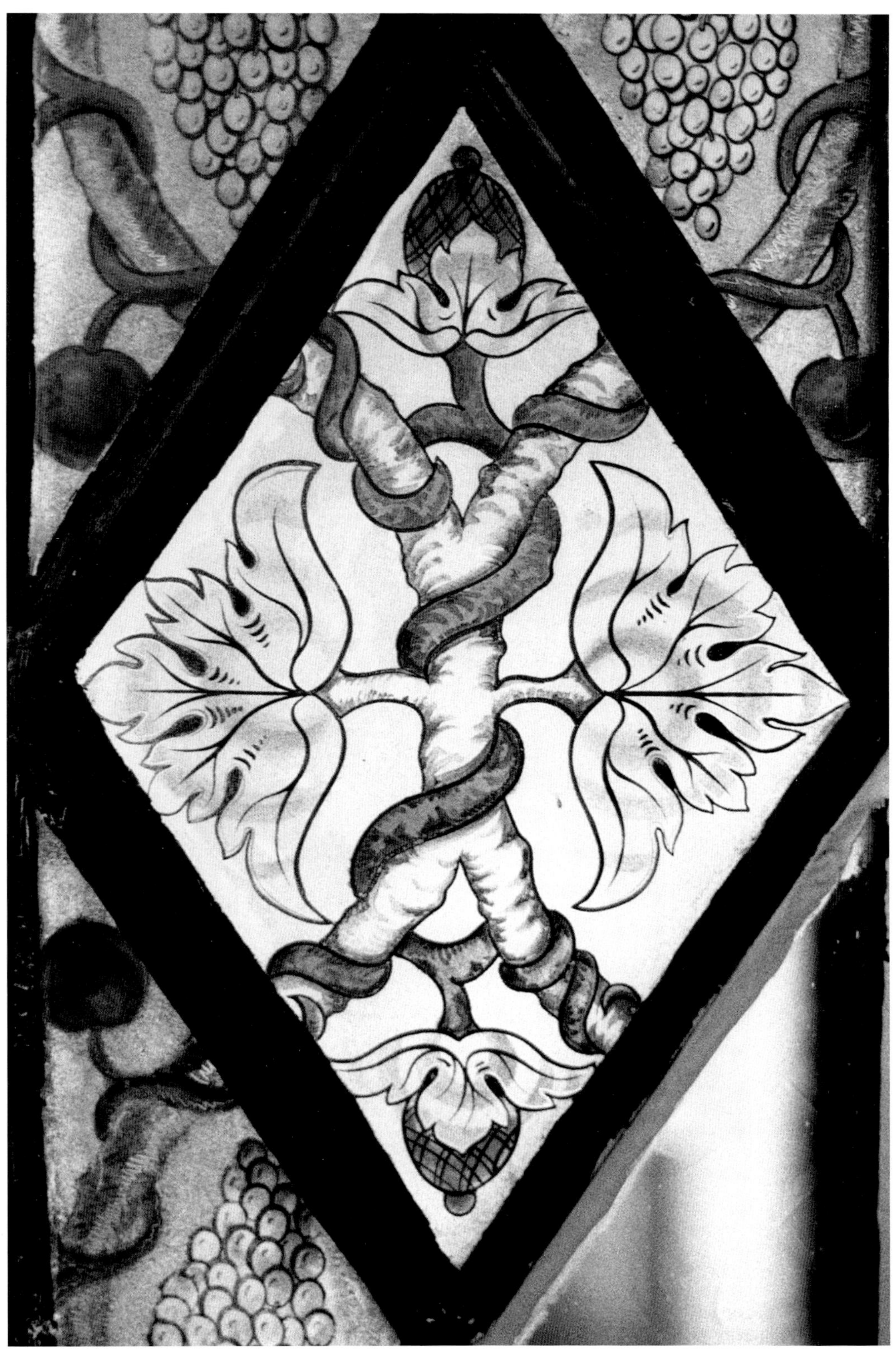

75. Quarry by John Bolton from the front door of the Francis Key
Hunt House, Lexington, Ky. (Photo courtesy Lexington Art League)

235

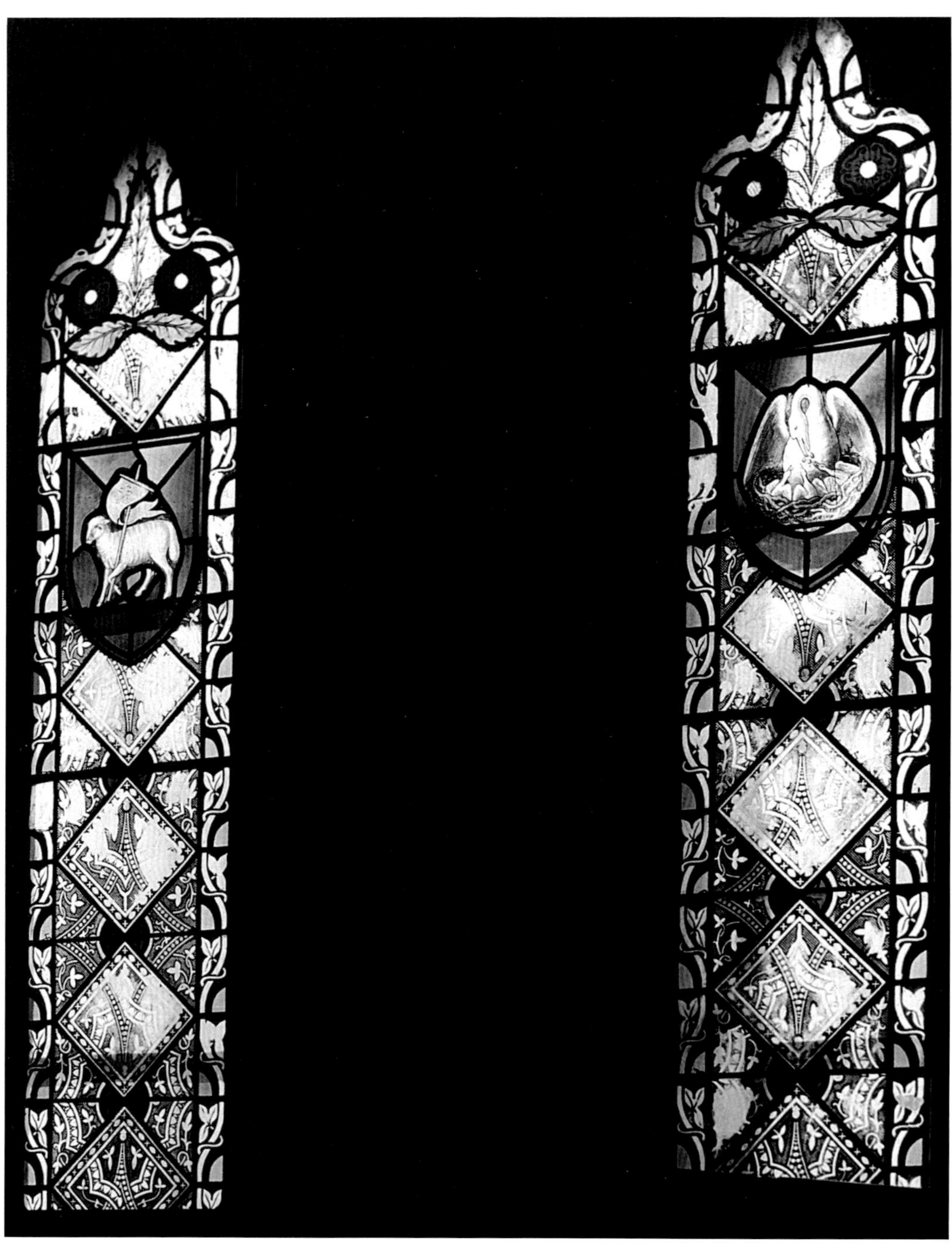

76. Church cf the Holy Trinity, West Chester, Pa.:
Windows in vestibule of the former rectory (301 South High Street)

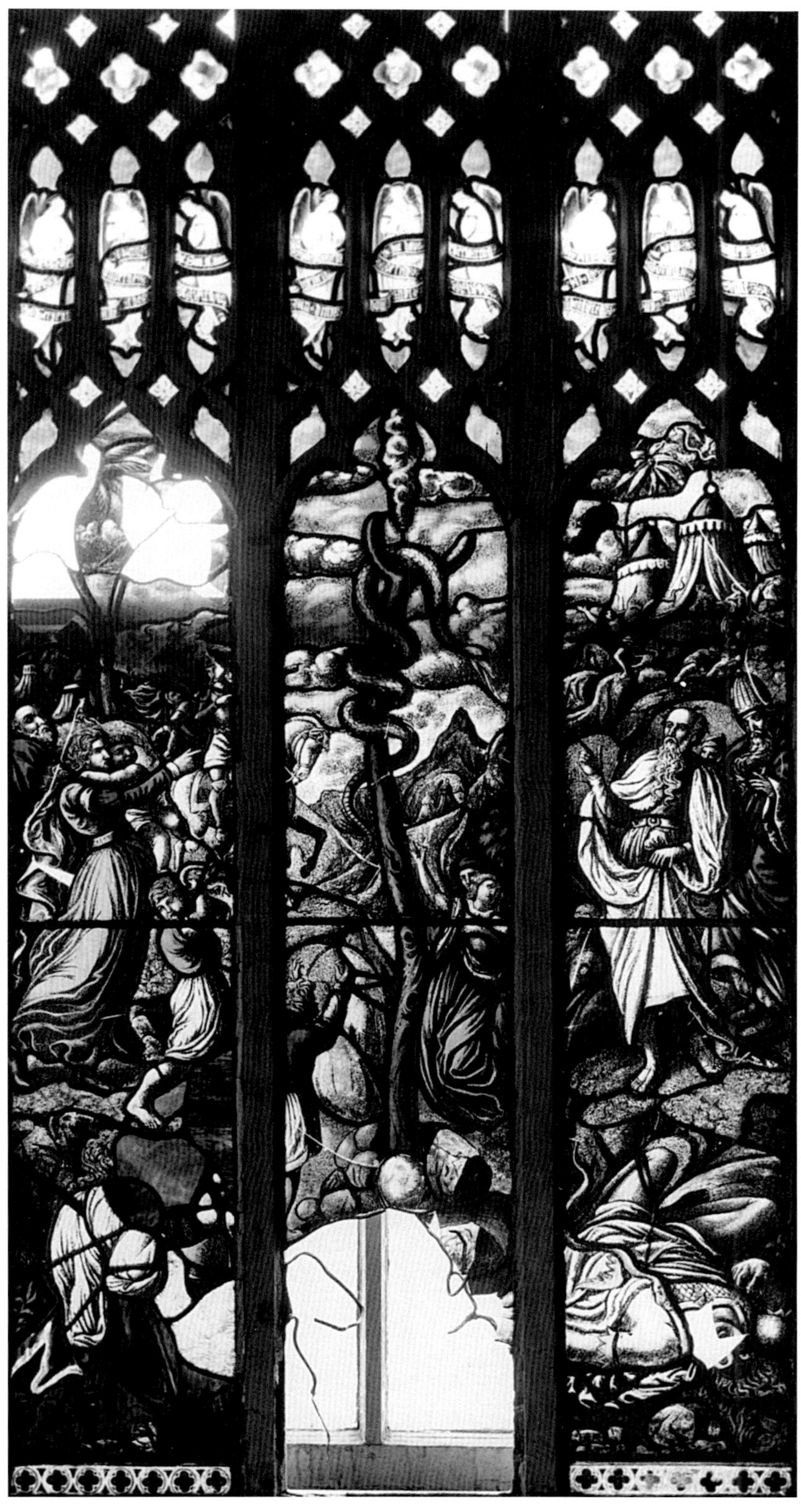

77. *The Brazen Serpent* by John Bolton, whereabouts unknown

237

Index

(Italicized numbers indicate illustrations.)

Armorial windows. *See* Bolton, William
Jay
Ashton, Mary Arabella Jay, 6, 7, 10, 16, 78,
125

Baldovinetti, Alesso, 117
Bartow, Edgar John, 20–22, 92
Bath, England, 3, 5, 7, 65
Beckford, William, 7
Bolton: family crafts, 10, 130 n.95; family
literary efforts, 10–11; family of, 4, 84,
124 n.12, Appendix C
Bolton, Abby, 26–27, 124
Bolton, Adele, 11, 27, 81
Bolton, Ann (Nanette), 11, 26–27
Bolton, Ann Jay, 5, 6, 15–16
Bolton, Arabella Jay, 10, 130 n.95
Bolton, Cornelius Winter, 6, 16, 52, 78,
80–81, 90–91
Bolton, James, 8, 11, 21, 27, 71; poetry of,
38
Bolton, John Jay, 6, 23, 69, 72, 120, Appen-
dix B; and Christ Church, 16–17, 130
n.95; and [St. Ann and] Holy Trinity, 56,
63, 92–93; style of, compared with Jay's,
58–59
—stained glass: grisaille and quarry win-
dows, 55–56, 80, Cat. II, *6, 71, 72, 75, 76;
Last Supper, 73; ?The Brazen Serpent, 56,
77; ?The Trial of Christ, 56, 74*
Bolton, Katherine Schuyler, 80, 120
Bolton, Margaretta Elizabeth Jones Wilkinson, 29
Bolton, Margaretta Grace, 7, 11, 13, 14, 28,
38
Bolton, Reginald Pelham, 12, 33
Bolton, Rev. Robert (of Pelham), 4–5,
15–16, 26
Bolton, Rev. Robert (Puritan ancestor),
4–10
Bolton, Rev. Robert, Jr. (of Pelham), 9, 14,
130 n.95
Bolton, Rhoda, 26
Bolton, Robert (of Philadelphia), 4
Bolton, Robert (of Savannah, cotton mer-
chant), 4

Bolton, Robert (of Savannah, postmaster), 4
Bolton, Susannah Welch, 27, 29, 136 n.178
Bolton, William Jay: academicism, classicism of, 49, 64, 67; art theory of, 22–24,
28, 39–41; birth of, 6; children of, 29;
color, use of, 22, 40, 43–44, 46, 55,
60–61, 63, 67–68; commissions to, 20,
23–25, 27; death of, 31–32; Gothic, definition of, 48–49; design sources of,
46–47, 53–54, 56–57, 59–60, 64, 65–68;
enamel paints, use of, 43–44, 55, 57, 89,
96, *see also* Cat. I–III for individual cases;
in Europe, 13–14; and fresco, 13; glass,
source of, 18; and iconography, 23–26,
36, 50, 62–63, 74; literary works of, 10,
11, 26, 27, 29, 34, 37–38; lost windows
by, Cat. VIII; matt and trace paint, use
of, 45–46; ministry of, 30–31; National
Academy, dispute with, 20; in period context, 68–69; stained glass, production
of, 17–19, 22, 42–47, 75, 138 n.48; style
of, compared with John's, 58–59; window installation by, 47. *See also* Cinque
Cento
—paintings, drawings, sketches by, 12, 13,
32, 43, 50, 54, 66, 68, Cat. IX, *27, 60,
63–70*
—portraits by, 49–50, 77, Cat. IX, *61, 62*
—stained glass by:
armorial windows, 32, 68, Cat. I, VII,
1c–d, 59
Christ Church, Pelham: Cat. II; *Adoration of the Magi,* 17, 19–20, 45, 52–54,
pl. I
grisaille windows, 55–56, 66–67, 91, 113,
Cat. II, *1d, 5, pl. II*
Holy Apostles, Manhattan: Cat. IV;
*47–49; Christ Tried before Pontius Pilate,
52; Deliverance of St. Peter & St. John,
67, pl. VIII; The Flight into Egypt, 66,
67, 50a; St. Paul Preaching at Athens, 51;
St. Peter & St. John Heal the Lame, 54;
St. Peter Distributing Alms, 66; St. Peter
Healing the Sick, 53*
St. Andrew's, Cambridge, England: Cat.
VI; angels, *58*
[St. Ann and] Holy Trinity, Brooklyn:

Index

Index

Index

The Stained Glass Art of William Jay Bolton
was composed in 10½ on 12 Bembo on Compugraphic 8600 digital
equipment by Connell-Zeko Type & Graphics Inc.; printed by sheet-
fed offset on 80-pound, acid-free Westvaco Sterling Satin by Southeastern Printing Company; and Smyth-sewn and bound over binder's
boards in ICG Arrestox B, with Rainbow Colonial endpapers by
Nicholstone Bindery; with dust jackets printed by Southeastern
Printing Company; design and production by Edward D. King,
Hillside Studio; and published by
Syracuse University Press, Syracuse, New York 13244-5160